Broken Badge

The Silencing of a
Federal Agent

NICK MANGIERI

Integrity Publishing, Inc.
Williamsburg, Virginia

Mangieri, Nick
    Broken badge : the silencing of a federal agent / Nick
Mangieri. Williamsburg, Va. ; Integrity Publishing, Inc.,
1998. 421 p.
Included index and appendices.
ISBN (paperback) 0-9665464-0-1
I. Mangieri, Nick   II. Title.

                                                98-07381·
                                                    CIP

The text of this book is composed in 11/12 Galliard,
with some display type in Helvetica.
Book editing and design by Karen T. Morgan.

Printed by Printwell Inc., Williamsburg, VA

To all who have ever carried a badge and have been frustrated in their attempts to do their job...and to current federal, state and local officers who will undoubtedly face those same obstacles and challenges during their career.

Acknowledgements

*T*his book has been a long time in coming – 16 years – but it is as fresh in my mind, today, as if were yesterday. For that very reason, my writing of it was deliberately put aside. No one wants to relive painful experiences or be reminded of unpleasant events. Many tried to persuade me to detail the obstruction of justice, with its ongoing cover-ups, that I was exposed to while I was a Special Agent in our nation's capital. Others, specifically family, tried to dissuade me. Eventually, however, it was something whose time had come and had to be told.

My initial thanks to my dedicated and frequently imposed-upon typist, Claire Campbell, who performed the herculean task of constantly accommodating my numerous rewrites and revisions. My special thanks to my literary agent, Maggie Allison, who although she recognized potential in my story and tried repeatedly to place it with a commercial publisher, was constantly thwarted because of its exposé quality.

When I finally decided to "bite the bullet" and self-publish in order to get it on the market, the support and advice that I received was phenomenal: Maurice Marsolais for his long-term interest, Mac Laird, Tom Trimble and Warren Kramer for enduring my daily problems associated with its writing and publicity, Ernie Panza for steering me in the right publishing direction, and Joe de Iulio for his inspiration of the book cover. In addition, VEW Arts for their creative implementation of the cover's design, Karen Morgan for her tedious copy editing and typesetting and, of course recognition to my printer, Printwell, Inc. for their technical expertise in accomplishing the final task.

The list is virtually endless as to those who contributed significantly in some form or another. My children, with my sister and my brother-in-law, especially suffered and endured with me. Last, but far from least, a special warm thank you to my wife, Jill, whose continuous patient understanding made this book possible.

About the Author

Nick Mangieri, a native-born New Yorker and Navy veteran was a Federal Agent with the Department of Labor attached to the Inspector General's Fraud Division. Prior to his retirement, he was assigned to South Florida and to Washington, D.C. His background and interests are equally wide and varied: Police Chief (Alaska), Deputy Sheriff (California), Private Detective (New York), Analyst (federal and state governments), University Instructor (criminal justice) and free lance writer (men's adventure magazines). As such, his self-imposed junkets took him into the interiors of Central and South America, where he diamond prospected in the jungles, hunted jaguar and mountain climbed. He graduated from the University of the Pacific and got his graduate degree from Virginia Commonwealth University. He's also attended law school and done post graduate work, including doctoral studies. He's an avid outdoorsman, jogs regularly and has even been a rodeo rider. Married and the father of four, he is a licensed Private Investigator.

... Table of Contents ...

... 1 ...

"Watch your back, Nick. Eder is out to get your ass."

He spoke slowly and carefully and stressed every word as he leaned forward in his chair across the desk from me.

I couldn't believe what I was hearing.

"What the hell are you talking about Dana?"

The speaker was Sgt. Dana Bedwell of the Organized Crime Bureau of the Florida Dade County Public Safety Department. The "Eder" he spoke of was Stuart Eder, my supervisor back at OSI headquarters in Washington, D.C.

My reaction of total disbelief must've registered in my face because Bedwell looked taken aback.

"You don't have to believe me," he persisted, "but just watch yourself."

His tone was low and firm, but he appeared sincere in what he said.

His comment, however, caught me completely off guard, and I was having a hard time trying to phrase an appropriate response.

"Is something going on behind my back that I'm not aware of Dana?"

He paused, not sure where to start.

"Yeah," he answered.

I waited for his reply.

"Well ... what?"

"Eder's been asking a *lot* of questions about you, like where you go, what you do, how long it takes you to do it — a lot of the same type of questions."

I looked at Bedwell quizzically, trying to fathom his response, and at the same time trying to rationalize Eder's questions to him. "Maybe he's just curious," I said half in jest. "He's just trying to justify his job."

"That's what I thought at first," he said, "but it's the same story *every time* he calls. He not only asks *what,* but he asks me *why.* It's like I told you Nick, I don't trust him. He's out to get you."

I liked Dana. He was quiet and clean-cut. He looked as if he had just gotten out of the academy, but at a sergeant's rank he must've had a few years under his belt. He also was on the small average side, and had a baby face that made him look even younger than his thirtyish age. Although he was easygoing, he was a little on the nervous side. I wasn't his subordinate, however, so his antics and tendency to be edgy didn't bother me. He was my main contact with OCB and he gave me all the administrative support that I needed on my detail to the Bureau. Undoubtedly, the fact that federal assistance, however meager, was provided them in their burgeoning caseload, contributed to my rapport with members of the OCB, and especially with Sgt. Dana Bedwell. His warning nevertheless stayed with me in spite of my sarcastic retort, and I began to wonder about Eder myself. Although his supervisory field trips to Florida were sporadic, there had been no complaints from him in the months I had been there. I felt we were compatible, although I was never crazy about his somber personality or his particular style of supervision. My six months in Florida had resulted in ten open cases, and that far exceeded the caseload that any other agent in the field carried.

Eder not only constantly commended me but also indicated that it made him look good. Further, the majority of my cases, if not all, were showing concrete results. My working relationships with the Public Safety Department and the U.S. Attorney's Office were excellent. Moreover, my witnesses and informants had been extremely cooperative and useful.

My federal agency, the U.S. Department of Labor, had assigned me to South Florida to investigate what was then known as "CETA fraud." CETA stood for the Comprehensive Employment Training Act. It was through this program that federal monies were being pumped into local communities to train and employ people in need. Unfortunately those federal funds were diverted into the wrong pockets. Across the nation, minor and major officials alike were taking the money for their own personal use. Daily headlines and detailed stories screamed these continuing abuses until Congress stepped into the act and pressured DOL to take remedial action. At that time, however, I was not on the federal rolls and not privy to the wondrous internal workings of government. I didn't know whether the chicken or the egg came first, whether Congress initiated reforms, or whether DOL, because of bad press, requested — and received — additional funding. All I knew then was that the Department of Labor was conducting a nationwide recruitment in mid-1978 to fill positions in its newly formed Office of Special Investigations. The purpose of this hastily created unit was to quickly combat the pervasive fraud that existed in the CETA program. The small unit, I later learned, was to be an initial federal shock force designed to immediately aid local law enforcement efforts in order to spearhead a greater federal effort planned for the near future. With my interest piqued for this challenging investigative program, I checked into the vacancy announcement and noted the qualifications for the new Special Investigator positions. I felt my prior investigative experience was what they were seeking, and I believed even more firmly that my type of aggressive delving was what they needed to uncover misuse of federal funds.

Although I, as a divorced parent, had three children, ages eight, twelve, and fourteen to raise on my own, and while I knew the job would create a conflict, I applied nevertheless. Having been without a job since I had relocated from Alaska months earlier, I didn't have the luxury of seeking the ideal job.

I wasn't alone in applying for what many considered a plum assignment. I soon learned that 200 other applicants also filed their SF-171s, their federal applications, for the vacancies. Whether my twenty years of prior federal and military service were considered or whether my proclivity toward persistent and forceful investigations was the determining factor in my selection, I never knew. It might have been something as simple as just being in the right place at the right time. Whatever the reason, on July 3, 1978, I was sworn in as a GS-12 Special Investigator in the new OSI office. My job was to enforce the federal laws under my jurisdiction and to uphold the Constitution. Four others were sworn in about the same time.

It was a proud moment. I couldn't know how the others felt, but for me it was a culmination of all my prior experience and — I thought — a harbinger of things to come. Little did I realize that the same oath of office that I and the others had taken so seriously would be held so lightly by others who followed. We five were the nucleus of a federal task force that would attempt to plug the dike to stem the ongoing flood of federal violations. Within the year, the new Inspector General concept would be used in most federal agencies, and with the sheer numbers that were promised, the turnabout of mushrooming fraud was to be all but assured. Yet, our oath of office was either ignored, or abuse of power was called into play to protect favored politicians being investigated. Local corruption, I was very familiar with. Corruption at the federal level, I was not.

At the onset of my appointment I was like a race horse anxious to break out of the gate and get into the field. I had just experienced some personal problems that I had no control over. My ex-wife had illegally taken my three children out of the state on their last day of school, and I had no idea where they were. Weeks went by before I had any word of their whereabouts. In the interim, I accepted the DOL offer and was eager to go to Florida as the solo agent from our department. The other four investigators fanned out like spokes of a wheel to various locales in the Northeast, Midwest and Mid-Atlantic states. Our field supervisor was Stuart Eder, or Stu as he liked to be called. He had never been a Criminal Investigator, nor had he ever been in police work. His background, I believe, was in some investigatory agency within the Department of Labor, and he managed to transfer in. His civil service job series was reflective of that experience in what is known as the "1810" series — that of Investigator. The five of us, although initially 1810s, were slated to become 1811s, Criminal Investigators, in the very near future. We all commented on Eder's limited background, but as a GS-13 he outranked us as our supervisor. He was slight-of-build, mousy-haired and thickly bespectacled. He looked to be more at home in a library doing research than in the field checking on our criminal cases. The other four Special Investigators were all different. First and foremost was Cameron Barron, a former agent with the Defense Investigative Service. Barron looked like the actor Danny Glover and at six-foot-four towered over the rest of us. I, a stocky five-foot-eight, fell somewhere in the middle. He also was a Reserve Navy Commander, and became a Captain shortly thereafter. We looked like Mutt and Jeff when we were together, but we soon became buddies. Our friendship lasted through the good times into the bad. It was that close association, that was to become tarnished as well when I became the target of future retaliation.

The second investigator was Charlie Richter, a former agent with the Naval Investigative Service. Small, wavy blond hair and quick, he was well-liked by all. He always had a smile and a ready response to any comment.

The third investigator was Eric Jann. He was young, slender, not as tall as Barron, but as sharp as Richter. I believe he was from New Jersey and transferred in from one of the DOL agencies.

The fourth man was Osvaldo "Pete" Castro. Hispanic by birth and a comedian by nature, he fit in well with the rest of us. A little on the chunky side, he could be volatile or happy-go-lucky, depending on his mood or the situation. He was from the New York area, and also formerly worked with one of the DOL agencies.

On our periodic trips back to headquarters for briefings and reports, we all met at the *bullpen,* our designation for the huge windowless office on the first floor of the U.S. Department of Labor. There, we compared notes on our travels and our cases, and not infrequently, socialized for lunch or a beer at the nearby D.C. Police Lodge down the block on Constitution Avenue.

There were two others who occupied the *bullpen,* although they weren't hired as Special Investigators. One was Tony Rossi, a short, balding, middle-aged administrative type who was always rushing around with a piece of paper in his hand. Then there was Cindy Rell, a well-built female, in her mid-thirties perhaps, with a shock of premature gray hair and pretty eyes. Unfortunately, she was married to some GS-15 somewhere in the great machinery above us.

Her prior experience also entailed some type of investigatory function within one of the other DOL agencies. Both she and Tony were at the GS-13 level. Although both were amiable enough, they weren't "one of us," and consequently there was a certain stand-offishness from our boisterous unit. Perhaps it was our gregariousness that turned them off, or perhaps it was just our cohesiveness, but there were times when they were working in their individual cubicles, that we were totally unaware of their presence.

When things began to turn sour for me within the DOL, it was Rossi — among others — who turned his back on me. Rell, on the other hand, still appeared to support me in her own quiet way. Surprisingly, it was one of our small group who later chickened out on me. Although we all jokingly called Castro, "Fidel," instead of his nickname, "Pete," I eventually came to call him by another name, "Judas," because I believed he was emasculating my future Washington-based investigations. At the time, I felt that he sold me out to my supervisors because he couldn't handle the political heat of our joint Washington cases. As time went on, however, after the ax had fallen on me and things had completely turned to shit, he redeemed himself. Unfortunately, no matter how well-meaning he was, and no matter how effective he could have been, his help came too late.

Although those future Washington cases were many months down the road, I was too involved with my Florida cases to see any handwriting on the wall — until Bedwell made his cautionary comment to me.

Within a week of being sworn in, I was en route to Miami and detailed to the Organized Crime Bureau. The fraud unit I worked with operated out of a two-story wooden building at the 36th Street airport There were six detectives in the unit including Sgt. Dana Bedwell and Lt. Ray Havens, the team leader. Dark, wavy-haired Havens looked like the star out of some Hollywood cop movie. The other four detectives looked the part of the typical briefcase-laden fraud investigator. They were all typically overworked. They were dedicated, and they were good. They welcomed me with open arms as they knew I would be assisting on their cases, or any new work thrown my way. However, because my investigative work included not only Dade County, but virtually all of South Florida, I was spread thin. In addition to assisting OCB locally, I learned when I got there that I had two fraud cases in Broward County, 25 miles north of Miami, and another two CETA cases in Monroe County, approximately 200 miles south of Miami. In the July 18, 1978, edition of the *Fort Lauderdale News and Sun-Sentinel*, the following headline appeared announcing federal government involvement in CETA fraud:

FEDERAL PROBE
OF LAKES BETA PROGRAM BEGINS

"Federal agents have begun a criminal investigation into the misuse of as much as $330,000 in federal employment funds by former Lauderdale Lakes officials and employees, Mayor Howard Craft has announced.

"Craft said the aim of the probe is to see if officials or employees benefitted from the improper use of federal unemployment funds from November, 1974, through September, 1976.

"The Broward Employment and Training Administration (BETA), administrators of the federal money told the city in May it must repay $137,257 of the funds because Lauderdale Lakes' hiring practices violated federal guidelines for the program.

"The city succeeded in shaving the amount to be repaid from $330,000.

"The current investigation, being conducted by the Office of Special Investigations of the U.S. Labor Department, is "criminal in nature," said Craft. ..."

It then mentioned that the target of the probe was the former city finance director, who had since been fired by the mayor after he took office in May 1976.

What amused me after the article came out was the opening reference to "federal agents" conducting the investigation. Inasmuch as I was the only task force member in that part of the state, or for that matter, in the entire state, I was impressed — if not surprised — by the impact already being made. My second case in Ft. Lauderdale produced the same result in the news media. However, my upcoming journeys into Monroe County, specifically Key West, were not to be of a solitary nature. Lt. Havens reminded me, "You've gotta be crazy to go into that part of the state alone, unless you want to wind up as food for the fishes."

Undoubtedly, his reference to my being fish bait was recently taken from "The Godfather" movie, but he made his point. Before I went afield on my Key West cases, Havens made sure I had a partner to accompany me. He was more my bodyguard than an investigator since we were not officially designated as Criminal Investigators at first. We were only Special Investigators and not entitled to carry weapons.

Havens was even more vocal in that regard, "You mean DOL doesn't allow you to carry weapons on the job?" he asked incredulously.

When I responded affirmatively that it was not yet policy to do so, he added, "Well, I'd rather be judged by twelve, than carried out by six."

The lieutenant wasn't the only one who voiced his surprise and feelings about our not being armed, especially in the Key West area. Other members of the unit spoke out as well.

"Don't those politicians in Washington have any idea what it's like down here? Don't they know what Key West is like? Haven't they been reading the papers? Everybody's involved in something down there."

The more they talked about it, the more I thought about it. It was comforting to know I had a partner to watch *my* back, but who was going to watch *his* back? Before I went into Key West, I decided to rectify a situation I considered asinine and potentially dangerous to both myself and the OCB detective with me.

It was a trip into Miami proper that led me to the course of action I would take in the immediate future.

About a week before I was scheduled to sojourn into Key West, Sgt. Bedwell asked if I would like to accompany him on a ride downtown to OCB's headquarters. Since I had not been into Miami for a while, having lived in Ft. Lauderdale in my bachelor days years earlier, I readily agreed.

Our unmarked white sedan pulled slowly out of the Dade County Public Safety Department parking lot as Bedwell made a right turn onto Airport Road. An Eastern Air Lines 747 had just jockeyed into position for a takeoff and its high pitched jet whine split the early morning summer air as it began its barreling liftoff down the runway. The deafening roar was increasing its vibrations as the silver aircraft lifted into the cloudless blue Miami skies, drowning out our conversation.

"How the hell do you guys hear yourselves think?" I yelled.

He smiled a pink-faced response, trying to be nonchalant about the noise.

"It doesn't bother us," he shouted back. "You'll get used to it."

The ride downtown was made pretty much in silence, except for sporadic comments about the changes to the city I observed in my 15-year absence from South Florida.

As we were driving over one of the raised causeways going into the downtown area, and adjacent to a large housing development, a loud, sharp crack suddenly broke the silence. Bedwell looked stunned as he grasped the wheel tightly in both hands and quickly glanced around the front of the car. Almost simultaneously his right hand dropped to his holster under his jacket as he jerked his head to look at me, his face full of concern.

His words were rapid-fire and his voice strained.

"Are you okay?"

"Yeah, I'm fine," I reassured him. "What the hell happened?"

"It felt like we were hit," he answered quickly, "but when I didn't see any damage, I thought for a moment that my gun had gone off. That's why I grabbed for it and asked if you were all right."

"Yeah, you're right. It did sound like a gunshot, and it did sound like it hit us but I don't know where." I turned around in my seat, checking the back for holes.

"We better pull over," he said as he swung the car to the right as far as he could without blocking traffic.

"I'll check my side, and you check yours, Nick."

He gazed at the length of the white car and then bent down to inspect the lower section.

I did the same on my side. There were no bullet holes anywhere that I could see. He stood up, shaking his head.

"I'll be a sonofabitch," he said, "I don't see anything."

"Me neither," I agreed.

"We're both not crazy," he continued. "We did hear something, and we did feel like something hit the car."

I shook my head in agreement, still looking while I felt along the molding at the top of the car.

Bedwell was doing the same on his side of the car when suddenly he stopped.

"Goddamn, look at this," and his finger traced a slight groove on the roof of the vehicle just above the driver's side."

I walked over to his side and fingered the same indentation. "Looks like somebody clobbered us with a metal rod," I said.

"Yeah," he agreed. "That wasn't there when I had it washed this morning."

"Well," I laughed. "We knew we both weren't crazy at the same time."

"Looks like someone took a pot shot at us from that housing development on our left, and just creased the top of the roof," he offered.

"There's hundreds of apartments not to mention rooftops," I noted. "How the hell would you ever find a shooter?"

"You wouldn't," he said, "and that's the problem. No one would know where to look."

"Right."

"Well," he continued still looking back at the congested area, "let's get down to headquarters, make a report and have them check it over."

"That's one hell of a reception Dana," I joked as I slid into the passenger's side again. "Does this happen often?"

"Not to me it doesn't," he replied tight-lipped.

Apparently, my humorous comment on the situation hadn't reached him yet.

At headquarters, he introduced me around, related our story, and requested that the groove on the roof be inspected. While he was writing out a report on the incident, a couple of the detectives in the area also found humor in the episode.

"You feds get in town and right away you're a target. The locals don't bother us."

"Anybody shot at you on that causeway lately?" the one asked the other.

"Not recently," he answered with a smile.

Bedwell, still not finding humor in the exchange, just shook his head and continued his writing. As soon as he finished, he handed it to one of his supervisors and advised me that he'd be right back.

Upon his return a few minutes later, he was his old smiling self. "I told you guys that we were hit."

"Yeah, we believed you Sergeant," they both chorused.

"Sure, you did," he added.

"Let's get back, Nick."

As we walked out, I asked him, "What did they find?"

"I don't know exactly," he said, "some form of residue in the paint confirming that it was undoubtedly a bullet that had caused it."

The thought had begun to sink in on me by now, and it was sobering.

Back at OCB, Bedwell had repeated the event to Lt. Havens.

"I don't know who they were after," he cracked, "one of our people or one of yours?"

"Probably one of us," I retorted. "We're new to the area, and they just want to get our attention."

"Now that we've got that resolved," Havens continued, "I've got you a partner for Key West. He's sitting at your desk now. Dana will introduce you."

"Thanks," I nodded.

Detective Bill Kennedy was waiting for me in the joint office I shared with the other detectives.

After Bedwell had gotten over the formal introduction, he said, "I'll leave you both together to work out your plans."

Kennedy, a ruddy-faced, red-haired individual, stuck out a beefy hand, and I responded with a firm handshake.

"I understand we're going to work together," he smiled. "Did they fill you in on me?"

I shook my head.

"Well," he continued, "I was in Vice, but because I'm due to retire in a few months the powers-that-be decided that I could put my remaining time with you."

It was a matter-of-fact statement, said evenly and almost pleasantly.

I liked him immediately. He was stocky, and his likeable demeanor detracted from his rugged appearance. He looked like the typical Irish cop, but more nattily dressed.

"I hear we're scheduled for Key West," he said.

"Yeah, so far I've got two cases down there. One's with the

local community college, and the other's with the city itself."

"What kind of cases?"

"Well, the first one, the one at college, concerns a supervisor who's accused of falsifying timesheets by stating that people who were supposed to be in training, were not."

"Where were they?" he asked.

"They were actually working somewhere in town holding down regular jobs, while they were supposed to be unemployed to qualify for the secretarial training."

"Nice work if you can get it," he smiled.

"Yeah, but Uncle Sam frowns on it," I replied.

"What about the other case?"

"That sounds a little more interesting," I said. "It concerns 'ghost employees'."

"Ghost employees?" his voice raised and his eyebrows went up. "What have you got, a supernatural investigation?" he asked, breaking into a wide grin.

I had to smile, too.

"Not quite, but it is about phony employees, and it does involve names from a cemetery project that the City of Key West got from CETA monies."

"Now you're cooking," he said. "Key West, the favorite place for the bad guys."

"So I've heard from everybody."

Have you ever been down there?" he asked in a more serious tone.

"Not in years," I said.

"Well, it's changed a lot since you've been there. Everybody's got their fingers in the pie."

"You mean drugs?" I asked.

"Drugs, guns — or anything else that involves money," he replied.

"Well, much as I'd like to get into everything down there, unfortunately my mission is only fraud investigation."

"I wish you luck in keeping it narrowed down, but — as you'll find out — the bad guys won't know that," he said in the same serious tone. "The same people are involved in everything. As far as they're concerned, you're *the man,* and that means you're investigating *everything* they're doing," he said.

"Yeah," I answered. "It oughta be fun."

"Well, it'll be interesting," he continued. "You're the boss, and I'm here to help you." He smiled as he said it.

"Glad to have you with me Bill," I said as I shook his hand.

"When do we head down the road," he asked eagerly.

"Probably in the next couple of days," I answered, "I've gotta wrap up some odds and ends here, and I've gotta let headquarters know what I'm doing."

"Yeah, the bureaucracy. I know what you mean. I've been through it too. Just let me know when you're ready," he added.

"You got it, Bill."

... 2 ...

Before we set off mid-morning on August 9, from OCB for Key West, Lt. Havens cautioned us again.

"Be careful down there," was his admonishment.

"You know me Lieutenant," Kennedy offered.

"Yeah, but you're still a long way from home. If anything happens to you guys, we can't get help to you."

"What about the local P.D. or the Sheriff's Department?" I asked.

"They won't be any help to you at all, so don't even try," Havens added.

Kennedy nodded his head in agreement.

"There is one Sergeant in the Monroe County Sheriff's Office though, who's a good man," Havens continued. "You can trust him. Just make contact with him as soon as you arrive, or if you ever want to get word out, he'll do it."

He gave us the name.

"Thanks, Ray."

As we turned to leave, Havens called out to Kennedy.

"After you're both settled in somewhere down there, give us a call and let us know where you are."

"Right, Lieutenant, and don't worry," he said as he patted me on the shoulder. "I'll take good care of *the man.*"

"You're all heart, Bill," I told him, "but I've never had a babysitter."

"Okay," he smiled. "Then you take care of me."

On the road out of town, we made small talk, with Bill telling me some of his Vice Squad tales while I added some of my own law enforcement war stories from California and Alaska.

"I hear you're not allowed to carry weapons yet," he interjected.

"Yeah, it's not authorized," I replied disgustedly. "Its supposed to be in the works but we hadn't heard when."

"You mean," he continued, "that if you see something going down in front of you, you can't take any action."

"I guess I could whack 'em with the briefcase," I said trying to make light of a situation that I didn't consider funny. Then, seeing Kennedy's wide smile, I added, "We're not real cops yet – maybe, one day."

He changed the subject.

"What's on our schedule first?" he asked.

"Well, after we get checked into a hotel or motel, we'll hit the Florida Keys Community College and look into their New Careers Program."

"Is that where somebody has been falsifying time sheets?"

I nodded in agreement.

"The amount of documentation available, and the extent of our interviews will determine how long we stay in Key West this time," I said.

"What about the city case?" he asked.

"You mean the 'ghost employees'?" I stressed.

"Yeah, that one appeals to me," he grinned.

"I'd like to make a brief visit there on this trip, too, just to get the lay of the land and see what we're faced with."

"Sounds good to me."

With the constant conversation and with the scenic view on both sides of the causeway going into the Keys, the three hour drive went quickly.

As we pulled into the city limits, Kennedy, who was driving the unmarked unit, asked me, "Do you have anything in mind?"

"No, I'll leave it up to you, Bill."

"All right. Let's see if we can find something on the beach road," he said as he swung off the main thoroughfare.

The car bounced down the road to a small motel that had a vacancy sign.

"What do you think?" he asked.

"It looks good to me," I said, eyeing the almost deserted stretch of beach that lay across the road from the motel. "Let's try to get an interior room," I added, "near the pool."

"Near the bar, too," he laughed.

After we checked into a single room and Kennedy called Miami, we set out to find the New Careers Program of the Community College, and found it down one of the side streets in town. The receptionist looked somewhat surprised when we showed her our credentials. She ushered us into one of the small offices to see the Director of the Women's Center, a Shirley H. A tall, attractive blonde introduced herself and told us that she was expecting us. When she saw my I.D. she nodded knowingly, but when she saw Kennedy's Dade County badge, she looked a little flustered.

"It's okay," I tried to reassure her. "It's a joint effort."

"Do you mind if I have the Project Director of the CETA Training Grant sit in with us?" she asked.

"Not at all, if she can be of some assistance in this inquiry," I replied.

"I'm sure she can," she said, and picked up her phone. "Can you come right in, please."

A minute later, a slim brunette, equally attractive, walked into the office. The blonde introduced us to Julie K., and Kennedy and I looked at each other knowing what the other was thinking. *This is my kind of duty,* I thought. *Key West isn't too bad yet.*

My momentary thoughts were interrupted when the brunette launched into a brief discussion of the complaint against one of her supervisors in the program, hence the reason for our investigative role. It seems that five ostensibly "unemployed" persons were attending classes in secretarial skills when they were in fact not in class but working in private businesses. The supervisor, a Brenda H., had falsified their timesheets. When the college detected her improprieties, she was fired. Early on in the case, I was to subsequently learn that each of the five participants in the program were paid $66 per week for several weeks while absent from the program. Their salaries, of course, came from CETA funds. The brunette then advised us that she would be glad to make the files available to us, as well as supply the address of the former supervisor.

"That's very efficient," Kennedy commented, and the blonde

director smiled in appreciation.

"You, of course, have the names and addresses of those five who never participated in the program?" I asked.

The blonde smiled again, "We have everything you need."

"I'm impressed," I added. "How early can we be here tomorrow to start in?"

She gave me the opening hours, and I looked at Kennedy.

"Any questions or comments before we leave?"

"Think you got it covered."

We thanked them for their cooperation and left. Outside we looked at each other and I commented, "This is going to be tough duty."

"While we're on a roll, are we gonna hit the city case today?" he asked.

"You bet, let's find City Hall."

We located it in the downtown section and asked to see the City Manager. Instead of being directed to his office, we were asked to wait in the lobby. We exchanged questioning glances.

A few moments later, out strode a dark-haired, fortyish man in shirt sleeves. We showed him our identification and told him the purpose of our visit, to inspect the CETA books. He checked our I.D.s carefully, and then slowly looked up at us.

"I don't care where you're from," he spat the words out. "This is my city, and I want you out of town."

"You *what?*" I said, although I heard him full well.

"I want you out of my city," he repeated again just as vehemently.

I could sense Kennedy tensing up as he stared hard at the man. I wasn't about to accept that kind of response.

"In case you don't know it, I'm a Federal Agent," and I stressed the title, "and I have every right to inspect your records, your books, and anything else that pertains to CETA monies, and how they've been spent."

Apparently the remark set him back, and he stood with his mouth open. Before he could say anything else, I continued.

"You just tell me where the records are, and who I see to make them available to me."

He looked back at Kennedy.

"He's not a Federal Agent, what's he doing here? He's from Dade County."

"He's with me," I said.

He looked back at me again, started to say something, but stopped. Then, in a staccato-like voice he shot out, "I'll send somebody out to you." He spun abruptly away and walked down a passageway.

Kennedy relaxed, nudged me and commented, "What were you saying about the duty here?"

"That son of a bitch," I said through clenched teeth. "Who the hell does he think he is?"

Kennedy replied unsmilingly, "We've got trouble partner."

A few moments later a woman emerged from one of the offices and introduced herself as the Assistant City Manager. I repeated our purpose for being there and added that it was only a preliminary visit. That was true, but hadn't told the City Manager because of his brusqueness. So, when she deferentially said that the city auditors were looking over the books and asked if we would mind returning in a day or two, I agreed. I realized that I might need more time to look into the background of the city project before I started pouring over the records.

Once outside of City Hall, I turned to Kennedy and said, "While we're downtown, let's touch base with that sergeant at the Sheriff's Office."

"I was just going to suggest that," Kennedy replied.

We found our man sitting in one of the back offices at the S.O. He was a mild-looking, middle-aged deputy, who didn't overreact at our low-key self-introductions, although he seemed somewhat surprised at our appearance there. Instead, he just blinked his eyes, looked around to see who else was within earshot, and then motioned us into a more secluded adjoining room. Once inside, we displayed our identification and explained our mission in Key West. He listened intently, and then said, "I'll be glad to be of whatever help I can. Obviously, you've been warned about the climate in Key West," and then motioning around the area, "even here."

We nodded our heads, and told him where we were staying.

"How long are you here for?" he asked.

"Just a few days this trip," I answered, "but we'll be in and out of here for weeks, or possibly months."

"If you need me, just call," he said, writing his home phone number down. He handed it to me.

"Any problems with us visiting you here today?" I asked.

"Naw, I'll just tell whoever asks that you were just inquiring about a prisoner."

"Yeah," Kennedy interjected, "we didn't broadcast at the front desk who we were, we just asked for you."

"Good," he answered. "When you leave, just use this rear entrance," and he gestured toward a door that exited at the back of the building.

"Thanks sarge."

We both shook his hand and left.

"He's going to be sticking his neck out for us," Kennedy said.

"Yeah, let's hope we don't have to use him," I answered.

"Where to next, boss?" Kennedy asked cheerfully.

"You're really getting into this stuff, Bill, aren't you?"

"Well," he said, "this work is a little different than Vice," and he smiled again. "It'll probably speed up the remaining time that I've got left in the department."

"How so?"

"Well, since I'm a short-timer, they pulled me inside to do paperwork," and he made a face. "That's not my thing."

"Let's check the town over," I said, "to see where everything is."

As we rode around the downtown area making mental notes of landmarks and places to eat, Kennedy suggested that we walk down the main street.

"Why not, it'll give us a chance to get some exercise."

He grunted in agreement, and we located a parking spot on one of the narrow streets. As we walked slowly down the main drag passing one bar after the other, Kennedy noted, "Goddamn, is that all these people do down here, is drink?"

As he said it, we were walking past another bar that had its wide doors thrown open to the outside.

I stopped and sniffed the air. "And that's not all. Smell that? That's pot."

He stopped and inhaled deeply outside the bar, taking in the sweet sickly smell of the marijuana that he hadn't noticed at first.

He began coughing, and grabbed his throat. "Goddamn," he said hoarsely, "you could get stoned just walking the streets."

"Yeah, let's get out of this area," I said, "and get a cup of coffee or something to eat."

We back-tracked to the car, and eventually found a small restaurant near the water.

"Smell that fresh air," I joked.

"Yeah, we need it," he agreed, as he mimicked another coughing attack.

We recapped the day's events and planned our schedule for the following day.

"What do you think of the City Manager?" Kennedy asked.

It was a question that I knew would arise, and I had been thinking about it since our encounter earlier in the afternoon.

"I think you're right, Bill, that sonofabitch is going to be trouble," I answered. "We're going to have to play it by ear."

He agreed.

"What had you heard about him before we came down?"

He thought about it a moment. "Not much, just the fact that most of the city and county officials down here are corrupt." He added, "Nothing specific tho', but," and he continued, "I really didn't get into it."

"Yeah, me either," and I hesitated, "but we're going to have to find out exactly who's who and who's doing what."

"Well," Kennedy interrupted, "we were warned."

We found our way back to the small motel, checked the still deserted road for any activity, had a quick dip in the pool and then a refreshing beer in a dimly lit room that served as the bar.

"Notice anything, or anybody unusual since we've been here?" I asked.

"No, you?"

"Uh uh," I responded.

"Let's just play it cagey tonight," I said. "I've been through this crap before elsewhere."

He nodded, "I agree."

Before we turned in for the night, we propped a chair under the doorknob of the door to the room, and Kennedy placed his nickel-plated .38 on the nightstand between the beds.

I looked at the butt of the revolver.

"What kind of a stock is that?" I asked.

"Oh, you mean the groove cut into the top of the stock," he

said, and flipped the right side of the gun up showing a deep ridge in its handle.

"I've never seen one like that before," I had to admit.

"You don't need a holster with it," he explained. "you just shove the gun inside your pants and the only thing that sticks out is part of the grip," and he demonstrated.

"What do you carry?" he asked.

"You mean *when* I carry," I answered him sarcastically. "My off duty was a 2" Chief's Special. I usually carried it in a pancake holster. They ride high. I liked it."

"Too bad," and he mocked a sigh. "Don't worry about it partner, I'm a light sleeper."

"Me too," and I rolled over.

Early the next morning we were back at the New Careers Program office.

The receptionist, this time, greeted us with a smile and told us to go right in.

"Coffee gentlemen?" the blonde asked.

"Sure," we both answered.

"Where do you want to start?" she asked.

"How about the time sheets for the period in question, and the folders on the non-attendees," I answered.

The brunette who had heard our voices when we entered, and our responses concerning the coffee, walked in carrying two containers.

"Now that's what I call service," Kennedy piped up. I had to agree.

Shirley, the blonde director, requested that since this was to be informal, that we call her by her first name. Julie, the brunette project director, requested the same. We readily agreed and also advised them to call us by our own first names. The session was loose and relaxed, and Julie supplied us with all the information that we needed. In addition, we were given the address of the former supervisor who allegedly had falsified the time sheets.

"Is there anything else we should know?" Kennedy asked.

"Only that she's making some kind of weird accusations," Julie responded.

"Do you know what it's all about?" I asked.

"We're not really sure," Shirley commented, "but I'm sure that she'll tell you when you see her."

Julie added, "Oh yeah!"

"Well, in that case, we're through here for now," and I rose taking the documentation with me.

"If you haven't already made copies, perhaps you should make some for your own records so we can have the originals."

"Gladly," Julie said, taking the folders with her.

When she returned with them a short time later, Shirley added a new dimension to the case that eventually would dwarf the initial investigation.

"I think you should probably stop in to see Dr. Smith, the college president."

We thanked her for their assistance and started to leave.

"We'll be in touch if we need any more information," I said.

"Any time," they both said pleasantly.

Outside, I again commented to Kennedy about how tough the duty would be.

"You single guys are all alike," he said with a straight face. "Let's hope the balance of the day is the same," undoubtedly remembering what had transpired at City Hall the prior day.

We located the Florida Keys Community College and had no trouble finding the Administration Building. Once inside we were directed to the college president's secretary who inquired our business with him. After we identified ourselves again, she excused herself and walked into an adjoining room. When she emerged a few moments later, she announced in a low tone, "Dr. Smith will see you now," and directed us to proceed into the office.

As we entered the room, I was amazed at its size and plushness. The head of the college sat behind a large walnut desk, that seemed oversized even for a large office. His high-backed, tufted leather chair seemed to engulf him. He was short, bald and rotund, and wore horn-rimmed glasses that gave him a grandfatherly look. On top of all that, he had a jovial manner.

He extended his hand, "How can I help you gentlemen?"

He seemed sincere enough, and when I explained that our mission was merely to look into the falsification at the Women's Center CETA program, he appeared concerned.

"I, myself, initiated the investigation when the discrepancy was discovered early in the summer."

We both nodded our heads in appreciation of his conduct.

"If there is anything that I or my staff can do to assist, please don't hesitate to ask," he continued.

It wasn't so much what he said, as the way he said it, and some additional repetitive remarks, that made me a little leery of his attempting to ingratiate himself to us.

"Anybody in particular I could talk to?" I asked.

For a moment, he hesitated. "Well, there's Mr. Ceeley, our Development Director, or Mr. Kinsey, our Business Manager, or ..." and he thought a moment, "you have permission to talk to my secretary, Mrs. Bazo."

Kennedy and I glanced at each other. I was wondering if he was getting the same vibes as I was.

We thanked him and proceeded to leave. He rose, but did not bother to shake our hands again. Although on the surface, he appeared to be pleasant enough, there also seemed to be a slight reticence in his manner.

"We'll be in the area," I advised him.

Once back in the lobby again, I turned to Kennedy.

"Let's go outside, Bill."

He nodded, glacing in the direction of the secretary, who was within earshot.

A hot blast of August air hit us in the face as we stepped out of the air-conditioned confines of the building.

"Damn, feel that," Kennedy said as we stared into bright sunshine.

"I've got a feeling, Bill. I can't put my finger on it, but ..." and I slowed down as I said it, "there's something about him that just doesn't feel right."

"Yeah, I think you're right. He's just run-on talk. I really don't think he really wants to help us."

"I think we should nose around first before we talk to anybody he suggested," I continued.

Kennedy thought a moment. "Wasn't it Shirley who put us on to him? Maybe she knows something."

"Good idea, and besides it gives us a good excuse to go back."

Kennedy smiled as he shook his head slowly, "You single guys never change do you?"

"Okay," I said. "I'll call first so I don't sound overeager."

"You feds are so cagey," he said mockingly.

I called first, as I said I would, and arranged to go back into their office later in the day.

"What do we do in the meantime?" Kennedy asked.

"Let's find a phone somewhere – not our motel phone – I've got some calls to make."

"Where?" he asked.

"Well, for one, the office to see if I had any messages, and two, I had spoken to the State Attorney's Office before we left."

"And?"

"I spoke to someone named Levenson who said he could probably get an IBM listing of apparent employees on the Municipal Cemetery Project."

"You sneaky bastard," he said admiringly.

"That's one of the reasons I didn't want to go back to City Hall yet," I said. "I want to know what we've got first."

"What are your other reasons?"

"The main reason is I want to find out as much as I can about our friend, the City Manager, and anybody else there."

"Sounds good to me," Kennedy said. "You're the boss, partner."

I found a nearby phone booth, called OCB for any messages and then placed a call to the State Attorney's Office, where I spoke to Steve Levenson and reminded him of our prior conversation. He recalled our discussion and said that he would be glad to help but that it might take several days or more.

"That's okay, I replied, "I've got to go back to Washington in a few days anyway. I'll contact you when I return."

"Fine."

I emerged from the booth, gave Kennedy the good news of the cooperation of the State Attorney's Office and then told him, "Let's see if we can find Brenda H."

"You mean the supervisor on the New Careers case?"

"Right."

Her address wasn't too far from where we were, but when I knocked on the apartment door there was no answer. Neighbors didn't seem to know where she was either, or for that matter anything else about her.

"Shit," I said aloud as the last neighbor closed the door on our inquiry.

"There are those kind of days," Kennedy philosophized.

"Let's get a cup of coffee," I said, "and then we'll head over to see the girls."

Kennedy ignored the last part of the remark, but made reference to the first part.

"Yeah, I can sure use one, all this heavy talk needs a caffeine fix."

"You missed your calling, Bill, I think you should have been a comedian instead of a cop."

"It's never too late you know," he said in mock seriousness, "there's always that second career after I retire."

After our second cup of coffee at a local restaurant, where we both probably stuck out like sore thumbs, we headed over to the Women's Center. The receptionist looked up at us again, checked her phone to see that there were no extensions lit up and said, "You can just go right in. She told me you'd be back."

Once inside her small office, I asked Shirley point blank, "What can you tell me about Dr. Smith?"

The question caught her by surprise, but when she answered there was a lilt to her voice.

"That depends on what you want to know?"

"Anything you want to tell us," I said.

Kennedy interjected, "Like ... is he hiding anything?"

She brightened up at the remark. "Well, I have heard some things."

"Like what?" we both asked.

"Well, like he's got a reputation around his female employees," she added.

Both our eyebrows must've raised at least an inch.

"What do you mean by a reputation?" Kennedy jumped in.

"Well," she continued, "there's been word that he propositions them."

"A college president?" I said incredulously. "That's not too cool."

"I don't have any details," she added. "Maybe Julie might have heard more." She buzzed her to come in.

"Hi, again," she said as she entered.

However, when Shirley asked her what, if anything, she could add to the rumor, she looked serious before she spoke.

"Yes, I've heard the same rumors before, but I can't give you any names. You probably could learn more over at the Administration Building. That's where these episodes were supposed to have occurred."

I'll be a son of a bitch, I thought. *No wonder he was babbling on to us, we were making him nervous just being there.*

Kennedy whistled softly to himself at the disclosure, and I looked at him and shook my head.

"This is getting deeper all the time," I said aloud.

"Now, I remember what else I heard," Shirley exclaimed. "I heard that there were some similar complaints a few years back, but I don't think anything came about because of them."

"Looks like we got some more digging to do," I said addressing Kennedy.

"Yeah, a lot more," he answered.

I changed the subject abruptly.

"We tried to find Brenda," I told them both, "but no luck. Would you know where else she's working?"

They both shook their heads.

"We're sorry we can't be of any more help," Shirley said.

"You've been of tremendous help," I said.

"Yeah," Kennedy added. "You're opening doors all the time."

They both smiled sweetly, but I wasn't thinking about either one. I was considering my next plan of action.

"Well, we gotta go again," I said, "but you know we'll be back."

"How long are you down here for?" Julie asked.

"Probably have to go back to Miami tomorrow, then to D.C., and then back again in a week or ten days," I answered.

"See you then," they responded.

We were unable to interview Brenda H. so we decided to cut short our stay in Key West.

"We're going to be busy next time down there," Kennedy noted.

"That's the understatement of the year, Bill. We came down on two cases, now it looks like we've got a third one with the college president."

"When you're hot, you're hot," Kennedy added.

The trip back to Miami was more pensive on both our parts, with both of us mulling over what had transpired and what would be done on our return.

"I think that the city might throw some stumbling blocks in our way – if not worse," Kennedy commented.

"I think you're right," I said. "I've been thinking about the same thing."

"I'll gather whatever intelligence I can on the players down there from our sources." Kennedy said.

"Good, we'll need it."

We pulled into OCB late that afternoon, saw Lt. Havens and brought him up to speed on the events of the past two days.

He nodded knowingly and turned to Kennedy.

"Next time you both go down, check out a shotgun."

Kennedy smiled, "Gladly, Chief."

I worked my way to my desk, completed some reports on the trip, and then called OSI headquarters in D.C. advising that I would be returning that weekend.

"When are you due back, partner?" Bill asked.

"Probably in a few days," I answered. "I've not only got a lot to do in Key West, but I've got the local cases as well."

"Wherever I can help," Kennedy offered.

"Thanks, Bill, I'm sure there'll be more than enough to go 'round."

The next morning I walked into the bullpen at OSI headquarters, and half of the investigative staff was already there. Barron, who was sitting at a nearby desk, was the first to greet me.

"How'd it go in Florida, paisan?"

"Nothing but palm trees and bathing beauties," I answered.

"Yeah, I had a ball in Detroit, too. Nothin' but dancin' girls waltzing all over town."

"I hear ya, Cam, now tell me the truth."

"Well, the truth is," he continued, "that I had some guy going back and forth over a bridge selling coupons that he shouldn't have."

"What kind of case is that?" I asked.

"It's a penny ante case, that's what it is," he retorted.

"Now tell me the truth about your bathin' beauties."

"Well," I went on, trying to prolong the suspense, "the real truth is that yes they're there, but they sure as hell weren't in any of my cases." and I hesitated. "There were two on one of the cases that weren't bad."

I then briefly hit the highlights on the four cases I initially was assigned, and the fifth case that was beginning to develop.

"Some people get all the breaks," he said.

Castro who had been listening to the exchange broke in, "Anytime you want to change locales, paisan, let me know."

"No," I replied, "I think I'll keep what I got, it's more challenging. Where you been, Pete?"

"Up in the cool north enjoying myself, but I'd much rather be down in the sweltering south."

"Tell Stu you want a change of scene and new cases. I'm sure he'll take it into consideration," I ribbed him.

"Yeah, I've got a big picture of that," he said making a face.

With that remark, Richter walked in.

"What am I missing?" he asked looking around.

"Nothing that transfers couldn't resolve," Cameron answered him.

Richter continued, "I've just come from upstairs. There's a meeting in about ten minutes, and we're all invited." He smiled as though pleased at what he had just said.

"Who's going to be there?" Castro asked.

"Rocky for one," he answered. "Then, there's going to be Dick Ross, Stu of course, and I think Paul Lehrman and Joe Gavalis."

Rocky was the nickname of Rocco DeMarco, our boss and the Director of the Office of Special Investigations. He had formerly been with Labor Racketeering in the Department of Labor and was selected to head up our unit.

Richard Ross, "Dick," was named as his assistant. Ross was a very likeable guy, half Italian on his mother's side, which contributed somewhat to our compatibility. Although he appeared to be easygoing, when he was stirred up, he went into orbit.

Stu Eder, our field supervisor, was nobody's favorite but he was the individual who we all reported to. Through him all our orders and assignments flowed. We all did our best in our relationship with him – at least in the early stages.

Lehrman and Gavalis were Special Assistants to Rocky, and their functions and tasks varied. Lehrman, a former military intelligence type liked to refer to himself as the "white fox," because of his premature white hair. Although our associations were sporadic, he was one of those responsible for my hire. Gavalis was the other one. As fleeting as my dealings were with Lehrman in the early phases of OSI, he was to become one of my staunchest supporters in my ongoing fight to expose corruption in D.C. – and even within DOL itself.

Gavalis, a former Department of Labor supervisor under DeMarco, I believe, was large and on the beefy side, but pleasant enough. Our dealings were few and far between, but because of his input into my selection, I liked him and we got along well.

Everyone attended the staff meeting, including Cindy Rell and Tony Rossi, our desk mates in the bullpen. It proceeded orderly with expectations from management and goals set forth for our unit. However, when the topic of weapons was brought up, everybody – especially the five of us – had some input. We all were eager to learn when the authorization would occur. We were advised that it was being discussed and worked on, but that there was no time frame for when it would happen.

The five of us looked at each other in disappointment. Barron, who already knew about the Key West warnings, glanced over at me with his eyebrows raised, his forehead furrowed.

With the meeting over, I lingered behind to talk to Eder about the Key West warnings I received at OCB, and about the hostile reception Kennedy and I received at City Hall from the City Manager.

"There's nothing I can do about it. You've got a partner to watch out for you." he said, as if unilateral aid was all that was needed in the field.

"Yeah," I said, "but who's going to watch out for him?"

"That's not your problem," he continued, "that's OCB's problem." "I'm sure that will make my partner feel better, when I tell him that."

"I'm sorry, but that's the way it is," he added abruptly.

When I returned to the bullpen, the others wanted to know what I had said to Eder, as apparently Barron had relayed some of my Key West information to them.

"What do you intend to do about it?" Barron asked.

"What can he do about it?" one of the others asked.

"I know what I'd do if I were put in that situation," someone added.

"I'll work the sonofabitch out," I said. "It's my problem."

There were more brief meetings and individual sessions about particular cases the balance of the week, and then on August 20, I was en route back to Miami.

I checked into the Marriott Hotel closest to the airport; it was to be my second home for the remainder of my time in Florida. I called OCB on my arrival, talked to Kennedy and told him that I would be in as soon as I had unpacked and rented a car.

When I walked into the office, Kennedy was sitting at my desk.

"How'd it go in the big city?" he asked.

"Looks like the bad guys are 6 and the good guys are 4," I answered comparing our efforts to a ball game.

"That ain't bad. I've seen worse scores."

"Yeah, me too," I said, trying to brighten up.

"What's our schedule now that you're back?"

"I want to check with Levenson over at the State Attorney's Office to see if those IBM listings came in," I replied. "Then I've got to call the U.S. Attorney's Office back. They said they wanted to see me when I returned."

"What about Key West?" Kennedy asked.

"Eager to go back, huh?"

"I wouldn't say that, but it might be interesting," he continued.

"A couple of days here, probably, and then we'll head down the road again," I said.

"Then," and I took a deep breath, "I've got a new Miami case."

"Sounds like business is booming," he smiled.

"Especially at this end of the country," I said. "The guys up north don't seem to have that many cases."

"Maybe they'll send you some help."

"I don't think so. There's not enough of us – at least not for a while."

With our preliminaries over, I called the State Attorney's Office and arranged to meet with Steve Levenson that afternoon. As Kennedy and I walked into his office, he handed us a sheaf of papers.

"That's the earnings of twenty-five employees on the Municipal Cemetery Project at Key West for 1977," he said.

"All I've gotta do is make sure that those people really exist,"

I said.

"That they're really not ghost employees," Kennedy added.

Levenson smiled at the remark.

"I've also requested identical information from Tallahassee for the years 1975 and 1976," he continued. "As soon as I get it, I'll give you a call."

We thanked him and left.

"Here's where our work really begins," Kennedy said as he leafed through the listings."

"That's what these investigations are all about," I said. "It's the nature of the beast."

Kennedy nodded.

Back at the office, I phoned the folks at the U.S. Attorney's Office to find out what it was they wanted. I spoke with a Jon Sale, the Chief Assistant U.S. Attorney, who suggested that we meet as soon as possible so that their staff could go over all my cases. I agreed and scheduled an appointment with him early the next morning.

Kennedy, who had been listening to the conversation, gave me a thumbs up. When I hung up the phone, he said, "You're getting into the big time now partner."

I had to agree with him.

"Sure sounds like it, Bill."

The next morning the both of us entered the Ainsley Building in downtown Miami, checked the directory and saw the name J.V. Eskenazi, United States Attorney, Room 300.

"That's ours," I said, and we rode up to the third floor.

At Suite 300, we paused and walked into a large office. After identifying ourselves, I mentioned that I had an appointment with Mr. Sale. The receptionist picked up the phone and announced our presence. Within a minute, a secretary emerged, escorted us through a large working area and then directed us to a large office in which five men sat around, apparently waiting for our arrival.

Jon Sale, who had been sitting behind his desk, rose, greeted us cordially and then introduced us to Pat Sullivan of the Criminal division and three of this staff members.

I knew that the purpose of the meeting was to discuss all of my cases in detail so I had reviewed them before I presented the file folders to him. The ongoing investigations encompassed the two cases from Broward County and two from Monroe County, as well as one from Dade County. The Broward County cases were one in Lauderdale Lakes involving the former city finance director, and one in Pembroke Pines in which nepotism and ineligibility were the prime focus. The Monroe County cases entailed the New Careers Program at the Community College and the Key West Municipal Cemetery Project. The Dade County case concerned a Farm Project program involving allegations of fraud as well. However, because the case had been investigated and developed before I arrived in Miami, I was not fully aware of its scope nor of the provable aspects against any of the participants. After a brief discussion among members of the U.S. Attorney's office, it was agreed that they would accept jurisdiction over all of the cases, with one qualification. Sale added that if there were no *kick-backs* to the former city finance director that could be shown, then their office was not interested in prosecuting the individual.

I nodded in agreement, with Kennedy observing quietly.

"Is there anything else you'd like to bring to the attention of this office?" Sale asked.

"Yes there is," I said, mentioning the allegations of sexual misconduct against the community college president.

"Now *that* I'm very interested in," Sale answered. "I believe there's a federal statue that cites improper inducement as a violation where CETA is concerned."

A couple of the staff members nodded their heads in agreement.

"I want you to look into those allegations," he continued, "and keep me posted."

"I'll be glad to," I said, glancing over at Kennedy, who smiled at the exchange.

In the hallway, outside the U.S. Attorney's Office, after we had both left, Kennedy gave me a thumbs up sign.

"Nice going, boss."

"We're off to a good start partner," I countered. "Now we've gotta work our ass off to produce."

"How 'bout I buy you a beer to celebrate?" he asked.

"Talked me into it," I said.

"Anyplace in particular?" he asked again.

"Well, the bar at the top of the Marriott is a classy place," I said. "Besides that, it's got a view."

We seated ourselves at the long cushioned bar and both took a swig on our cold draft beers.

"This is the kind of place I frequented when I had to work Vice," Kennedy said, as he waved his arm about.

"And you talked about my *tough duty* in Key West," I reminded him.

"Talk about Key West," he said, "do you know what I heard while you were in D.C.?"

I shook my head.

"There was an 'Operation Conch' a couple of years ago led by us and the state, and it netted some bigwigs in its net for drug smuggling."

He stopped to let it sink in. "On top of that, local police officers also were caught up in it."

"Terrific," I said. "That's why Havens told us to steer clear of the police and the sheriff's offices down there."

"Right," he said. "Our intelligence also tells me that anybody with a boat can pick up a quick 25 grand just to run offshore and bring drugs back in."

"What about the Coast Guard?" I asked.

"They can't cover the whole coastline, and these boats sneak in and out all the time."

I was dumfounded at the ease of the smuggling that was going on down there.

"There's not only drugs involved," he said, "but they're bringing in guns too."

"Now tell me they don't like outsiders sticking their noses into local business," I said.

"That's about the size of it," Kennedy answered, as he raised his glass to have another swig of the beer that had started to warm up in his grasp.

"And Havens said to check out *one* shotgun before we went down again," I said, trying to make a joke of it.

"Wish I could check out two," Kennedy answered in a more serious tone.

"Well," and I changed the subject. "We gotta go down tomorrow."

"What time?"

"Early."

"Do you want to pick me up at my house?" he asked. "You could drive your car over and park it there, and we'll take another unmarked unit down."

"Sounds good to me."

"How about 8?"

"You're on," he replied, "and I'll even supply the coffee."

At precisely 8 a.m. on August 22, I pulled into Kennedy's driveway as he was loading the shotgun into the trunk of the car.

He held up an extra container of coffee that I grabbed while I slid into the front seat beside him. As I turned in my seat to throw my jacket in the back, he glanced at my right side.

"What's that?" he asked in mock surprise.

"Oh, that's just my Chief's Special," I said nonchalantly, as I patted the pancake holster reassuringly.

... 3 ...

There was no other reference to my .38 on the trip down, but Kennedy did mention the other Special Investigators and wondered if they were doing the same thing.

"I don't know if they're packin'," I replied, "but then I don't know their situations either. Then I recalled our conversations in the bullpen. "At least one of them said that he'd know exactly what to do if he were faced with the same situation."

"It's like Havens said," Kennedy continued, "it's better to be judged by twelve jurors, than carried out by six pallbearers."

That comment partially capsulized my feelings on the subject. However, I had an additional obligation – I had a partner. He deserved no less of my consideration or attention than of the assistance and protection that he was giving me.

The trip down was interspersed with sporadic showers that are usually prevalent that time of year in South Florida, especially in the Keys.

Upon our arrival in the city, Kennedy made a good suggestion. "Let's try someplace else," he said.

"Makes sense to me."

He found a similar motel in the same general area, and we checked in. After we had unloaded our personal gear, Kennedy asked, "What's our first stop this time?"

"Since Sale indicated his interest in the college president, we'll try there first," I said, "and then we'll try to locate that female supervisor again."

"What about the city case?" Kennedy asked.

"We'll alert them in advance that we'll be enroute sometime this afternoon so we don't waste any time after we get there."

"Right," he concurred, "and undoubtedly we'll stop back over at the Women's Center."

"Undoubtedly," I stressed. "If not today, then certainly tomorrow."

As we pulled up in front of the community college, Kennedy wanted to know who our primary interviewee was going to be.

"Well, Smith says we have his permission to see his secretary, so that's a good start."

"That was nice of him," Kennedy remarked sarcastically.

We found her sitting at her desk, and when we told her that she was the purpose of our visit, she seemed surprised if not flustered. Our questions were in a general vein, initially, and then we zeroed in on her boss. Our specific questions concerned allegations we had heard about him. We asked if she could confirm or deny them. Her answers were either vague or evasive. We knew – or rather we felt – that we were on the right track because of her type of replies. When her responses dried up, we asked where we could find William Ceeley, the Development Director that Dr. Smith had previously mentioned. His answers were basically in the same mode, although we were able to extract the names of former students from him, a Judy B., a Jeanne G. and an Orelia R. In addition, he supplied us with the name of a Kathy M. in the payroll section. The payroll clerk was at the college, and the former students fortuitously nearby. However, none of the information gleaned from them was enough to use against the college president.

Continued investigative leads did, however, produce the name of a former college secretary. I subsequently located her mid-state Florida and had her testify in a Grand Jury as to Smith's sexual improprieties with her. Ceeley, the Development Director, because of his knowledge, also was required to testify before that Grand Jury.

The trip into the Keys on August 22 proved to be rewarding, not only from the information gained from the newly opened college president's case, but from the New Careers Program over at the Women's Center.

Midway into the afternoon of the 22nd Kennedy said, "Why don't we try Brenda H. again since we're near her address."

The second time was a charm. She was at home.

The former female supervisor, who had allegedly falsified time sheets of five "students" in the college's secretarial training program, was very personable when she invited us in. She was a comely slender type, who appeared to be in her mid-twenties. There was no nervousness about her when we identified ourselves. On the contrary, true to what Shirley and Julie had indicated, she did want to talk. Her very convincing denials of the falsification episodes were punctuated with her own allegations of sexual improprieties made against her by her own male supervisors. The more she spoke, the more impressed we were with her performance. Finally, when I could interject myself, I asked her, "Do you mind giving a written statement to that effect?"

She readily agreed, and I set a time the next day for her to meet us at the Women's Center. She again agreed.

After we left her apartment, Kennedy asked, "Do you believe her?"

"I don't know, but she sure sounds convincing."

Kennedy nodded his head. "I'm not sure, either, whether she's lying or not."

"If she's that persuasive in person," I said, "giving us a written statement won't phase her a bit."

"Maybe we can talk her into a polygraph test," Kennedy offered.

I was impressed by the suggestion, "Can you set it up, Bill?"

"I think so," he answered. "All I've gotta do is get the Lieutenant's permission."

"When?"

"We didn't check in with him earlier, so when I call him I'll put it to him," he said.

Kennedy made the call, gave Havens our new motel location and then told him of our contact with the former female supervisor, and her believable – but questionable – allegations.

"Can we put her on *the box?*" he asked.

Apparently the reply was an affirmative one because Kennedy smiled.

"We'll let you know Lieutenant."

"So far so good, partner," he said.

He hung up the phone and turned to me.

"All we need is her permission," I said.

"Yeah, and even if it doesn't stand up in court, we can use it to help us. Either it will support her or discredit her, and we can go either way with it," he said.

"I'm gonna miss you when you retire, Bill."

"It is starting to get interesting," he said.

The last stop during our busy afternoon was at City Hall again. This time we didn't ask to see the City Manager. Instead, we asked to see Lucy Hicks, the Assistant City Manager who had met us in the lobby on our last trip. I subsequently learned that she also was the Finance Director for the City of Key West. Although she didn't look pleased to see us, she was not as openly antagonistic toward us as her boss, the City Manager, had been. When I asked to see the books on the Municipal Cemetery Project, she led us into a cluttered office past stacks of files to a woman sitting behind a desk.

"This is Gloria Smith, the supervisor in this section. She'll give you whatever assistance you need," she said before she left.

After I explained to the woman that we were interested in looking at the Cemetery Project, she produced sheaves of listings, some bound and others still loose.

Kennedy and I looked at each other and shook our heads. We were directed to two partially cleared spaces in the crowded office for our use. We delved through endless listings, making periodic notes of time periods and employees involved, and then left after an hour's inspection.

"We'll be back," I said to the woman, "but we'll need more backup on some of these people."

"Just let us know what you need, and we'll try to help you," she countered.

"Sure they will," was Kennedy's caustic remark as we stepped into the hallway.

"Where to next, boss?" he inquired lightly.

I checked my watch.

"Let's try 'the girls' again before they leave the office and tell them we're bringing in Brenda tomorrow morning."

"I bet they'll love that," Kennedy responded.

"When I confirm what they already told us, they'll probably get a kick out of it."

"Hadn't thought about it that way," he said. "You're probably right."

I placed the call and luckily caught Shirley before she left the office. When I told her what our plans were for the next morning, she said, "sure," without hesitation and asked the time.

I cradled the phone and turned to Kennedy, "I told you so."

"That's because women are basically curious," he commented.

After our return to the motel, and our customary beer in another dimly lit bar, we had dinner nearby.

"Notice anything out of the ordinary?" he asked at the table.

I looked around the small restaurant again, and then outside, and shook my head.

"Maybe we'll luck out this trip," he said. "Not enough people know we're in town – or where we are."

"Or maybe not enough of the wrong people," I added. "In any case, the time to watch is after dark."

The balance of the evening was uneventful, and after we retired for the night, Kennedy brought the shotgun in from the car. He placed his nickel-plated .38 on the nightstand closest to him, and I placed my blued .38 closest to me.

"Loaded for bear," he quipped as he turned out the light.

The next morning at the Women's Center we were cordially received by Shirley and Julie with a welcoming container of coffee. Shortly afterward, the former supervisor arrived and greeted her former bosses as if they were old friends. The two of them, not to be outdone by her mannerisms, greeted her in the same way. I had to inwardly smile at the reception extended by all parties in view of their last association. Kennedy was to wonder also at their seeming friendliness toward each other. When we questioned the girls about it later, they remarked that she was likeable and that they had all gotten along well when she had worked there. "Of course," they added, "she's a great actress."

Her written statement didn't waiver from her oral statement of the day before, and when I reviewed it, I asked her in a matter-of-fact fashion, "You wouldn't mind taking a polygraph test about this would you?"

If she was surprised, or even concerned, she exhibited no such tendencies because when she answered, it was in an unhesitating even tone.

"No, of course not," was her reply.

Kennedy and I both looked at each other, each undoubtedly questioning ourselves, but we made no supportive comments to her at that time.

I addressed her as I gestured toward him.

"He'll have to set it up," I said. "It's with his office."

"Just let me know when," she said, and then added before she got up to leave, "I have to be in Miami some time next week, maybe it can be then."

"I'll see what we can arrange," Kennedy answered. "We'll be in touch."

After she left, Julie said, "We told you so."

"I've gotta admit, she's cool," I said.

"We'll see how good she is when we get her on the box," Kennedy added.

As it turned out, as *cool* as she appeared, she still flunked the polygraph. When we questioned her about it shortly thereafter, her unabashed response was, "I thought I could beat it." Her admission of deception, however, simplified our subsequent investigation of her allegations, inasmuch as we did not have to pursue her concocted story.

Although I was somewhat surprised, it was not so much that she had not passed the polygraph examination, but that she had the audacity to challenge it. I should have realized at the time that there are individuals who think they can beat the test. Undoubtedly there are a few who can. I had the same experience when I was the Chief of Police in a small town in Alaska. One of my officers swore up and down that he was not screwing a local female in one of the patrol cars while on duty. To support his adamant contention, he even *volunteered* to take a polygraph. He flunked, as well.

There were two more forays into the Key West area during the month of September, with Kennedy as my sidekick. With each trip, our presence became more known and our inquiries more extensive.

On one of our debriefings, at OCB, Lt. Havens told us, "You've both been lucky. Just continue watching it."

Headquarters at OSI in Washington had heard reports of corrupt Key West officials – and even more specific information. They also heard I was expanding my investigations. I was pursuing every imaginable lead possible to prove city official involvement in fraud activities. Eder's comment to me on one particular trip north was to the effect that "You're going far beyond the scope of your mission there."

My reply at the time was that it was impossible to segregate my investigations. I had to be aware of the extent of various target involvement in any other illegal activity. I could not go into any investigation blindfolded, not being conscious of individuals' participation in other crimes. I knew I was sticking my neck out, but I also knew that the individuals I was investigating didn't know there was an imaginary line I was not supposed to cross. To them, I was *the man,* and *the man* was asking too many questions. I also was mindful that my delving could just as easily have uncovered drug or gun smuggling, as it did fraud. However, I also reminded Eder that I was gathering useful and productive information on my cases and that the U.S. Attorney's Office in Miami was satisfied with my efforts in the Keys. I further advised him that there was an upcoming federal Grand Jury panel scheduled for late October in Key West and that I 'was directly involved.' That information seemed to quiet him, at least temporarily. On my October 18 trip into the Keys, which also was to be Kennedy's last one with me because of his retirement, our movements were tracked as soon as we hit the city limits. We were alerted to this fact as soon as we walked into City Hall, and we were told, "We heard you were back in town."

It had been our first stop as soon as we entered Key West. Apparently, their intelligence had been working effectively because although we had changed vehicles again, as we had constantly done on each trip into the area, we were still spotted.

"Watch your step partner," was Kennedy's solemn comment. "They know as soon as we arrive in their fair city."

I nodded my head.

"I noticed, too."

"Who's going to look after you when I'm gone?" he said in a half serious tone.

"I'm sure OCB will take care of it," I said.

"I hope so," he remarked, "because we know that DOL won't."

"Cheer up, buddy. Just remember, you're going to be a happy citizen soon, and you won't have to worry about crap like this anymore."

"Yeah, you're right. I've put my time in."

"Have you finally decided where you're heading to?" I asked.

"Yeah," he replied. "My wife and I have decided to open a restaurant in North Carolina. If you ever get up that way, the coffee's on me."

"That sounds exciting," I said almost sarcastically.

"That's one thing I've had my share of," he said as he gave a quick smile, "and, besides ..." he continued, "you've done your damnedest to contribute to more of the same."

"Nobody's perfect," I joked.

"I've also noticed in the past couple of months," he went on, "that you have trouble keeping your nose clean down here."

"That reminds me," I said. "Remember the last time we were down and I was putting feelers out for information?"

"And?" he asked cautiously.

"Well," I continued, "I'd gotten word before we came down that someone wants to give us some."

"Who?" he asked.

I gave him a name, but he shook his head.

"He was the result of our knocking on doors last time," I said. "One of the people we spoke to told him that we were looking into everything."

Although that comment was a slight exaggeration, Kennedy knew what I meant as to piecing together information.

"I figured that we'd contact him later, after I've made my federal services."

"Who do you have to serve today?" he asked.

"I've got two this trip," I answered. "One for Ceeley, the Development Director at the college, and ..."

"The other?" he asked.

"One of our more pleasant targets," I said, "Brenda, our talkative former supervisor."

"The Grand Jury ought to have a ball with them," Kennedy quipped.

"I'll have more to serve after you're gone," I said, "and at Grand Jury time I'll really be in good company."

"How's that?" he asked.

"One of the Assistant U.S. Attorneys will be flying down with me."

"Talk about class," Kennedy said mockingly.

"If you call flying down in one of those bucket of bolts, those DC-3s or 4s — or whatever the hell they are — 'class' then you're overdue for retirement."

"Yeah, you're right," he continued in the same mode. "I don't think they reach much altitude either." He demonstrated using his hand in simulated flight over a nearby flattened surface.

I thought he was exaggerating until I took that flight down on the Air Sunshine airline less than a week later. The aircraft appeared to skim the waves although we were 100-200 feet above the ocean. The flight pattern never varied until we landed at the Key West airport.

The day after I served the federal subpoenas, I was knocking on a door in the downtown section.

A.G. answered the door, and although apparently eager to see us, looked up and down the street furtively. He was a fountain of information having been a Key West resident for some time.

He wanted to know why it was necessary to tear up Green Street, downtown, at a federally funded cost of $175,000 and why two years had passed and the job was not yet finished?

I naturally shook my head but nevertheless made a note of it to present to who-knows-who upon my return to Miami.

He continued.

"Why," he again wanted to know, "was the Mayor receiving an additional $2,400 a year in federal funds when he wasn't fulfilling the terms of the grant?" Again, I shook my head, but continued to take notes of the session. I was aware that information received is not always relevant, but made a mental note to check his allegations.

When he launched into his latest piece of information, I was not sure if it was particularly helpful. He first mentioned that the City Manager had a dual title. When Kennedy asked what that was, he replied that he was also the Public Safety Director. Although his filling a dual role was not that unusual, it was not the norm in most cities. However, when our informant turned his attention to the Police Chief, we were definitely interested. He said the Chief once was fired as a Corporal and then fired again while a Lieutenant. How was it possible for him to become the Police Chief?

Kennedy and I both glanced at each other quizzically, wondering the same thing.

After we thanked him for his information and took our leave, Kennedy made his typical comment, "Nice town you're working in. I'm really gonna miss it."

"I'll bet you are," I stressed.

"Remember," Kennedy said in a concerned voice, "if you want to collect on that free coffee, you gotta stay healthy."

October 19 was the last time we worked together, and shortly after our return to Miami he retired and then departed the area. Although he had only been my partner for a couple of months, we worked well together, and I missed him. I didn't give much thought as to who would be my next OCB-assigned partner because my days were overloaded with work and travel.

After I returned from the mid-October trip to Key West, I had multiple sessions lined up in Miami. There was the appointment with Michael Griffey, the CETA Director at the South Dade Consortium. They were the prime sponsors of CETA contracts in the South Florida area, so he wanted to know how my cases were progressing. Although I couldn't go into detail with him about the specifics on each case, not wanting to expose my hand and endanger any upcoming indictments, I did give him the highlights. He was, of course, interested in the Key West cases, as was everyone else who heard about them. His concern not only included existing cases, but new cases he wanted to see resolved. In that context, I received another case to work on, still as the solo Investigator in Florida. It was referred to as the "Dance Foundation" case. Although I didn't carry it through to its final resolution, I did open it and work on it in conjunction with my other cases.

In addition to the Griffey contacts concerning my cases, I spoke to Levenson at the State Attorney General's Office regarding the Key West Municipal Cemetery Project. One of the items discussed was a $40 difference for a Lisa W., a former project employee whose earnings for the first quarter of 1977 on the IBM listing was less than what appeared on her W-2. I tried to track her down at a cafe she once worked at in Key West, to no avail. Although the amount was, on its surface, insignificant, there were twenty-five other employees, and there were multiple pay periods involved. The possibility of numerous frauds existed, but as I explained, it would entail in-depth paper investigation coupled with indepth interviews

— and hopefully Grand Jury interest.

On October 24, I flew back to Key West on the 7 a.m. Air Sunshine flight with the Assistant U.S. Attorney who was to appear before our first federal Grand Jury. It proved to be an all-day affair in the old courthouse, with multiple witnesses being called, as well as myself.

By late afternoon, we caught a flight back to Miami, and by 11 p.m. I was en route back to National Airport, at Washington, D.C., via Eastern Airlines. It was 1 a.m. before I arrived bleary-eyed at my apartment in suburban Maryland. By 8 a.m. I was back in the bullpen at DOL.

Barron, who already was at his desk, greeted me effusively as usual. "Nickolai," he shouted, a term that he used interchangeably with *paisan*.

"You must live here, Cam," I said tiredly. "Every time I walk in you're already here."

"That's because you high-class types have to live in the suburbs," he cracked.

"Yeah, yeah," I said. "You're jealous."

"Want some good news, paisan?" he asked.

"I could sure use some," I answered.

"Check your in-basket," he continued. "We've got our new 50s."

He was referring to our SF-50s, the government designation for Standard Form 50s, which was used whenever there was a change in the personnel aspect of our federal records.

I flipped through the basket and found the paperwork. Sure enough, our classifications had been changed from 1810s —Investigators — to 1811s — Criminal Investigators.

"It's about time," I said.

By then, the others had joined the discussion of our new designations and what it would mean to us.

One of the groups mentioned that perhaps, "we finally would be allowed to carry weapons." Another said, "Not yet, but I hear that it's getting a lot closer."

Barron spoke up again.

"We get our new credentials this trip too, miniature gold badges in a fancy carrying case, and all ..."

"Just like real cops this time," I said sarcastically.

It was a comment I initially had made to Kennedy on our first trip to the Keys, but it was appropriate this time as well.

"More like G-Men," Castro interjected. "Our new title is now Special Agent."

Richter added, "How's that for class?"

The balance of the week was taken up with reports, briefings, meetings, and the shifting of locales and cases for the men, but I still retained my Florida assignments. To add to the hubbub of activity at the office, Congress was acting on the new Inspector General Act. We were becoming the Office of the Inspector General – as were several of the other agencies. Our former Office of Special Investigations was officially eliminated. Rocky DeMarco, our former director, was now the Acting Inspector General, and Dick Ross was his Acting deputy, pending Senate confirmations of new Inspector Generals for all the agencies involved. I was glad I was away from the confusion and politics at headquarters, now known as the "National Office." The word was out, too, that "hundreds" of agents would be hired nationwide and offices opened coast to coast.

At the local D.C. Police Lodge late one afternoon, where Barron and I were relaxing having a beer after a hectic day, he asked me about my Key West work. I told him I had jumped the gun, and was carrying my own weapon while I was in the field.

"He replied, "I don't blame you buddy, you've got to look out for No. 1."

"Not only No. 1," I repeated, "but your partner too."

He raised his glass to that.

On October 31, I left Washington bound for Miami again. Upon my arrival, I saw a rather lengthy article in the *Miami Herald* that immediately caught my attention:

CETA PROBE YIELDS NO INDICTMENTS

"A federal Grand Jury in Key West probing alleged misuse of funds in a federally funded job-training program has adjourned for several weeks without returning any indictments.

"Assistant U.S. Attorney John Sale refused to say Monday whether the jurors will resume their investigation of alleged fraud in a career training program run by Florida Keys Community College when they meet again. ..."

It closed out by referring to the college president, although he was not cited by name.

> "Grand Jurors also returned no indictment after hearing testimony alleging sources said, that a high official at the Keys Community College had solicited sexual favors from women college employees.
> "No evidence was given that the official was successful in his alleged endeavors, sources added. The allegations surfaced as a result of the investigation into the college's CETA program, but the official was not connected with alleged misuse of CETA funds, sources said."

The "allegations" heard by this Grand Jury were but the opening salvo in the continuing investigation against that official. Although it was stated that there was "no evidence" given to show that he was successful, subsequent Grand Juries would hear otherwise.

That article and subsequent ones about our investigative efforts in the Keys would be in the public eye for months to come. However, it didn't lessen my ongoing workload in the Miami area.

Shortly after my arrival on the 31st, I had several witnesses to interview in my Miami cases. One of those interviews also entailed picking up seven boxes of material to be analyzed. By November 3, I was headed back to Washington. I spent a brief two days in our newly designated *National Office,* and then boarded an Eastern Airlines jet to Miami, once more. It seemed as if I spent as much time in the air as I did on the ground.

Upon walking into the OCB office, there was a note from a Bob Richardson, who I learned was to be my new partner. I called him so that we could meet and discuss our schedules and my cases.

Within the hour, he walked into the office and introduced himself. He was in his early forties, dark-haired and solidly built. He also was close to retirement. Although he wasn't as effusive as Kennedy could be, he was equally easy-going and personable. Like Kennedy, he was thoroughly professional, and for the next several weeks we worked together harmoniously. After his departure he accepted a job as a Chief of Police in a small town in Georgia, much like my former position in Alaska. So, our interests were similar.

The day after our initial meeting, we were driving down to Key West for a continuation of my investigations. Richardson had heard about all of the adverse aspects of Key West and knew what might lay in store for us, so he was as cautious as Kennedy.

We noted after our arrival that the local paper, the *Key West Citizen,* was not to be outdone by its bigger brother, the *Miami Herald.* Their longer headline proclaimed:

FUNDING MISUSE ALLEGATIONS ARE PROBED AT JUNIOR COLLEGE TRAINING PROGRAM

Although the article, consistent with its headline, led by stating that a federal grand jury and investigators from the U.S. Department of Labor were looking into "allegations of federal funds" at the local college, it went a step further. Under a sub-head of "Sex Favors Alleged," it quoted a statement by Michael Moore, the assistant U.S. Attorney heading the investigation. It wrote that he, "also declined to comment on reliable reports that a high-level official at the college is under investigation for allegedly attempting to obtain sexual favors from female employees under threat of their losing their jobs or being denied pay raises or promotions."

The paper noted that:

> "*The Citizen* has confirmed, however, that the Labor Department investigators were seeking evidence of past allegations of sex-related illegalities on the part of at least one official ..."

The three days following our investigations in the Keys appeared to be routine, but were actually much more productive. The information I was constantly gathering was becoming extremely useful to other law enforcement agencies. I had heard that the Florida Department of Law Enforcement was starting to conduct its own investigations into the area. Unfortunately, our paths didn't cross. If they had, it would have been mutually advantageous. After we returned to Miami, I met some FDLE agents at OCB who said they would like to work with me as well. That comment was the same type of remark I received from the local FBI agent in Key

West on our trip there. I had looked up Russ Sullivan, the resident agent-in-charge of that office, and when I told him what I was uncovering, he was eager to get into the act.

These supportive statements, and the distinct possibility of joint cooperative efforts with both the FDLE and the Bureau, excited me. However, Eder didn't view it that way. When I told him what I considered great potential in not only enhancing and resolving my own cases, but in assisting others as well, he repeated what he had told me previously.

"You're going beyond your mission there."

Perhaps I was. Perhaps I was overzealous in the performance of my duties, but I knew we were all working the same gigantic crime puzzle. Whatever pieces I came across, I was more than willing to contribute to the big picture. These feelings were shared by the FDLE and the FBI, but it did not appear to be DOL philosophy. It certainly wasn't Eder's.

From that point on, events moved rapidly, not only in my work environment but my personal life as well.

When I returned to Washington for the Armistice Day holiday, I unexpectedly learned that my three children, who had been abducted by my ex-wife, had been living in Misssissippi for the past six months. Having been awarded full custody of them in Alaska, I had to formulate immediate plans to get them back. I also had to make living arrangements once they had been recovered by me. Fortunately, my sister who lived nearby, advertised for a live-in housekeeper. She screened prospective applicants, and I then selected who I considered a suitable woman for their care. Upon my next return north, the children, then ages 15, 13 and 9, were returned, enrolled in schools, and life moved forward once more.

As inconvenient as the situation was with my Florida assignments, it was my job, and I did have a caring, reliable housekeeper. On weekends, I usually managed to fly home to be with them. However, within three months, that planned arrangement was to change abruptly with my reassignment back to Washington. It was a move that I tried unsuccessfully to block by seeking a permanent transfer to South Florida. It also was an action that the U.S. Attorney's Office in Miami tried vainly to forestall.

By the end of November, I felt compelled to write a letter of commendation for Kennedy for his assistance. It was initialled off as approved by Eder, and by Ross, as his immediate supervisor. It was directed to E. Wilson Purdy, Director of the Dade County Public Safety Department in Miami.

The letter stated:

> "This office wishes to officially express its deep appreciation for the cooperation between your Bureau and our Department — especially the efforts expended by Detective William L. Kennedy of your office.
>
> "Detective Kennedy was assigned to assist Special Agent Nick J. Mangieri from August 9, 1978, to October 19, 1978, in two CETA fraud investigations in Key West, Florida. In spite of the fact that the Key West area has traditionally been a hotbed of corruption and criminal activity and, notwithstanding the potential for violence and danger that are ever present for "outside" law enforcement officers, Detective Kennedy was not intimidated and conducted his investigations in an aggressive manner.
>
> "His perseverance, his adherence to detail and his expertise in the field have all significantly contributed to the success of both cases under investigation by this office. In addition, other leads and sources of information personally developed by him will be pursued to determine other possible violations.
>
> "Detective Kennedy's efficiency and dedication in the performance of his supportive duties are commendable, not only for the professionalism that he exhibited, but are indicative of the same type of professional behavior demonstrated by members of your staff on other joint investigations."

It was signed, of course, by DeMarco, as Inspector General - Acting.

Shortly thereafter, a response was sent to DeMarco from Director Purdy:

"Thank you for your letter of November 20, 1978, in which you commend Officer William L. Kennedy of our Organized Crime Bureau.

"It is pleasing to know that a member of our department has been of assistance to the United States Department of Labor in the CETA fraud investigations.

"In October, 1978, Officer Kennedy retired from our department. A copy of your letter of appreciation will be forwarded to him.

"We thank you for taking time to write to us in this regard and assure you of our continued cooperation in all matters of mutual interest."

I was given a copy of the letter for my files. There was no particular comment from Eder, however, when he handed me my copy.

Barron, who had been aware of the correspondence, made one of his typical remarks.

"Nice going, paisan. You've got the big boys giving us recognition now."

Lt. Havens, who also had been told of the DOL letter to Kennedy, pulled me aside one day as I walked into the OCB office.

"We appreciate what you're doing," he said sincerely.

"It's been a two-way street, Ray, for what you've done for me," I answered just as sincerely.

My workload continued with my new partner, Bob Richardson, giving me all the assistance I needed, both locally and in Key West. I was spending a great deal of time in the CETA Consortium office discussing my cases. I also picked up two additional cases, the Miami Sanitation case, and the Culmer Program case. In the course of these investigations, Richardson and I spent countless tedious hours analyzing reimbursement vouchers and payroll registers. There was another trip to the Keys in late November and two more in December. During the course of these "hit and run" excursions, more and more information was given to me as a result of my probing. In addition, the evidence against the college president was becoming stronger. I even located and interviewed a former college secretary living in central Florida. who stated that Dr. Smith had not only made explicit sexual remarks to her but also "grabbed at one of my breasts."

That information in conjunction with other incriminating statements from former female employees pleased the U.S. Attorney's Office, and plans were made to have another Grand Jury session in early January 1979.

Just prior to the Christmas holidays, I was back in the National Office again filling out the usual reports when Barron said something that caught my attention.

"What was that again, Cam?" I asked him. "I caught something about being deputized as a U.S. Marshal."

"You heard right, Nickolai," he continued. "There's some kind of provision that we could apply to be deputized as Special U.S. Marshals, if the situation warrants it."

"Well, what the hell do they call my situation," I exclaimed.

"I was thinking of you, paisan, when I heard it," he said quietly, trying to calm me down.

"What are we supposed to do?" I asked.

"I guess just a letter to Rocky, through Stu, stating your reasons."

"Goddamn they want reasons, I got reasons," I said emphatically.

"I know you do buddy," he said reassuringly.

"I even qualified at Dade County's range earlier this month," I informed him, "anticipating our being given permission to carry."

"We've all been expecting it," he answered, "but ..." and he continued, "... we're still waiting for the word *when.*"

"Well, Cam, your info gives me the ammo to officially request it, and at the same time, put all my reasons down in writing."

"Yeah," Barron added, "who knows what Stu ever passed on to the front office."

That afternoon, I composed a detailed two-page memo to DeMarco, that again had to go through Eder as the Supervisory Special Agent. The subject was "SPECIAL U.S. DEPUTY MARSHAL," and it covered all the points I heard in Miami, or had uncovered in Key West itself:

> "This is a request to be deputized as a Special
> U.S. Deputy Marshal because my caseload involves
> extensive investigations in Key West, Florida, an

area that is heavy in drug trafficking, gun smuggling and political corruption.

"One of my cases involves the President of the Community College, an influential figure in the community, who not only has acted with impunity in all his actions but has bragged that he is untouchable.

"My other case is with the City of Key West in which the Public Works Director and the City Manager appear to be implicated. The City Manager has not hidden the fact that he is openly antagonistic to my presence in City Hall and my investigations into the CETA grant.

"In addition, other complaints have been brought to my attention involving a grant with Monroe County (the area encompassing all of the Florida Keys). Further, informants have sought me out citing irregularities and corruption in other federal monies in Key West and the area.

"Corruption and violence in Key West have long been known to lawmen in South Florida, outside of the Key West area. "Operation Conch" two years ago by the Florida Department of Law Enforcement (FDLE) and the Organized Crime Bureau (OCB) netted the Fire Chief, the City Attorney and other lesser officers in drug trafficking. The former Police Chief, along with a former City Councilman, have been indicted for murder. Four Key West police officers were recently indicted for drug smuggling (one of whom was a Lieutenant). Four other police officers, according to my source at FDLE, are to be indicted shortly before a grand jury for smuggling, as well. The present Police Chief, now reported to be a figurehead to the City Manager, who actually runs the Police Department, was suspended and fired several times for illegal activities during his police career. The examples are endless!

"The OCB of the Dade County Public Safety

Department has voluntarily assigned a detective to act as my bodyguard in Key West because of their knowledge of the lawlessness that exists there. FDLE has stated that other law enforcement officers have been "set up" on solitary investigations in the past and stress that I do not go into the area alone.

"My numerous trips into the area have verified all of the above and future trips will uncover even more. My next excursion will take me back into City Hall with a federal subpoena for their records. Future witnesses include the Police Chief, and his stepson (who is Key West's leading criminal defense attorney and was formerly the above-mentioned City Attorney who was indicted for drug trafficking in "Operation Conch").

"As the FDLE Special Agent-in-Charge aptly phrased it, "Everything is related in Key West." Not only are my investigations uncovering other violations, but those that are involved in any illegal activities are becoming very paranoid that I might uncover these activities or others accidentally.

"The Chief Assistant U.S. Attorney in Miami is cognizant of the Key West lawless climate and is impressed with our incursion into the area."

I felt sure that there would be little doubt that my request would be acceded to, but I heard nothing before I again departed for Miami and Key West.

I told Havens about my written request, and all he could do was shake his head.

He confirmed what I had known all along.

"You've got to look out for yourself," he added.

Richardson was in the process of leaving to accept the Chief's position in Georgia, and I was left without a partner. Havens apologized but said there was nobody who could be spared. I knew I had a job to do and continued my solo ventures into the Keys mindful of the growing warnings from the law enforcement community. Because I still had heard nothing about my written request, on my next trip north, I renewed it.

On January 12, I amplified my original memo by couching it in more specific terms. My subject matter now read:

POTENTIALLY HAZARDOUS DUTY/REQUEST FOR SPECIAL DEPUTY MARSHAL STATUS, WEEK OF 1/15/79

"As pointed out in my memorandum of December 21, 1978, a need exists for my being accorded Special Deputy Marshal status in the Key West, Florida area because of the personal danger involved.

"As a result of my fraud investigations:

"(1) The President of the Community College, an influential politician, is being forced to resign his position.

"(2) The City Manager, City Mayor and other officials are apparently implicated in my CETA fraud cases.

"(3) My name and face are known in the Key West area.

"On my last trip to that area, I was advised by an informant that the City Manager, City Mayor and at least one or two City Councilmen are involved in drug trafficking and in "boleta" gambling. I was also advised to "be careful" who I spoke to because I was now tying in these officials in new investigations against them. They were described as "powerful and vicious."

"The Miami FDLE (Florida Department of Law Enforcement) agent in charge warned me to "watch my step." He advised me that four more City of Key West Police Officers were recently indicted for drug trafficking. I also learned that there was a very recent allegedly drug related murder in Key West.

"I recently served two federal subpoenas for records on both the Community College and the City of Key West, to be returnable on January 17, 1979, at a Grand Jury in Key West. These records, especially those from City Hall could very well implicate City officials in further indepth investigations.

"Since I must appear before the Grand Jury to retrieve these records, I renew my request for status as a Special Deputy Marshal for the week of January 15, 1979, because of the potentiality of personal hazards."

The reference in my memo to the President of the Community College "being forced to resign" was rumor that I had heard before I left Miami.

Little did I realize that those words would take effect as quickly as they would because of the intense publicity that would accompany the final incident. For that matter, I was equally unaware that in spite of my intensive investigation into Key West politics, I would not see the fruition of my work – nor would there be any resolution of it after I left.

... 4 ...

On my return to Miami on Sunday, January 14, I was greeted by a full-page spread in the "KEYS AREA NEWS" section of the *Miami Herald*. Emblazoned across the top of the page was the headline:

ALLEGATIONS AGAINST COLLEGE CHIEF PROBED, with the sub-heading, "3 Former Employees accuse Smith of Sexual Misconduct."

The actual article noted that:

> "A federal grand jury is investigating allegations by three former employees of Florida Keys Community College that college President John Sylvester Smith threatened to fire them unless they engaged in sexual conduct with him, The Herald has learned.
>
> "Sources familiar with the investigation said the grand jury heard allegations by two former female employees in October.
>
> "A third woman, a former secretary at the college, told The Herald she was fired in 1975 after Smith ordered her to have sex with him. Her allegations, the sources said likely will be presented to the grand jury at its next session beginning Wednesday in Key West.
>
> "The two other women, one a program supervisor and the other 'in a staff position' at the college,

testified at the October grand jury session about more recent incidents, the sources said. They also claimed Smith threatened to fire them if they did not submit to his sexual demands, sources said.

"The 64-year-old Smith, president of the college for almost a decade and an ordained Presbyterian minister, refused to comment on the allegations made by two of the employees. He flatly denied those made by the secretary interviewed by The Herald.

"Smith termed a reporter's questions about the matter 'a fishing expedition ... a witch hunt.'

"The former college secretary, who no longer lives in the Keys but did not want to be identified because she said she is afraid of Smith, said he told her 'that I had to do certain sexual acts with him ... if I valued my job.'

"She said he called her into his office where he 'grabbed my arm ... and took my hand and pulled my face toward him.' 'This will only take three to five minutes of your time,' he said. 'Nobody will find out.'

"Then, she said, 'He pulled his zipper down and grabbed my breasts ... I started to get up and walk away. He grabbed my breast ... and turned me around, turned my face toward him.'

"The secretary said she broke away from him and left the office. 'I had bruises on my arm and face,' she said.

The next day, she said she was fired. She did not complain to college or police authorities, she said, because she was frightened`..."

    Although the story quoted Smith as saying, "it didn't happen," and that he didn't want to comment on the other allegations, "sources," according to the reporter, "said the allegations, if true, could constitute 'sexual extortion.'

        " 'We think of extortion as dealing with money,

but it's making someone do something he doesn't want to do in the broad sense,' said Assistant State Attorney General Ray Marky. 'Someone could say, 'You will be fired if you do not submit (sexually). That's a form of extortion in one ...sense of the word.' ..."

The article also went on to say that trustees of the public college had heard "whispers" about Smith, and had also received unsigned letters regarding him, but that no one had publicly accused Smith of misconduct.

The story further noted that Smith had also been an ordained Presbyterian minister for 18 years and still preached at the local Keys church. It then stated:

> "Sources in the church said affidavits from nine persons, most of them college employees, were gathered and sent to the church's South Florida headquarters in 1973 by some church members attempting to have Smith replaced. The affidavits included allegations that Smith 'made repeated embarrassing and suggestive remarks' to a college employee at a party and roughly pulled her toward him by the neck, leaving red marks. The sources said they had no knowledge of any action taken by church officials."

The lengthy article then concluded by mentioning what I had also written in my memo to DOL that, "the jury will also investigate a CETA tombstone cataloguing program run last year by Key West."

After I had read the detailed account, I was elated at the results of the many months and countless hours that went into the investigation. There was, however, no Kennedy to celebrate with, and even Richardson was gone. I figured that Bedwell and Havens had seen the story, as well as other members of the OCB unit, but for the moment I was in a hotel room, alone, at the Marriott congratulating myself on a job well done.

I had that beer at the bar upstairs and silently toasted my former partners.

The next morning at the OCB office, not only were there congratulatory comments, but as expected there were sex-related remarks concerning the college president's totally unacceptable behavior. I placed a call to the U.S. Attorney's Office to see if there would be any changes in the Grand Jury session on Wednesday. I was advised that the hearing would go forward as planned with testimony scheduled for those who were subpoenaed to appear before the panel.

On Tuesday, January 16, I received an early morning call at the office from one of my sources in Key West.

Had I seen the *Key West Citizen?* the local paper, I was asked.

When I indicated that I had not, the headlines were read to me over the phone:

SMITH QUITS COLLEGE

I was then read the opening paragraph to what was fast becoming a rapid series of events:

> "Florida Keys Community College President
> Dr. John Sylvester Smith announced his resigna-
> tion at last night's regular meeting of the FKCC
> Board of Trustees following published reports that
> he is under investigation by a federal grand jury for
> allegations of sexual misconduct."

According to the article, he cited "the pressures" of his position on his health when he gave his resignation statement to the board.

When I inquired as to what the balance of the account read, I was caustically told that in spite of the mounting allegations against him, board members were unanimous in their praise for him. The caller quickly scanned the after reports of his resignation and said that Dr. Smith was called "a Godsend," and that there were "sobbing colleagues," and still an even more unbelievable comment by one of the professors. He wished that Smith would stay "to contest the vicious attack on the part of the Fourth Estate."

Evidently, the good professor was not privy to the good president's actions.

Half in disgust, at the obvious bias of a local paper's coverage, I thanked the caller and hung up.

The day of the Key West Grand Jury, I was in town with the Assistant U.S. Attorney and the witnesses I subpoenaed. The former secretary from the central part of the state, who I had previously interviewed and taken a statement from, also was there. Her testimony, I knew, would be particularly damaging to the college president — in spite of the board's apparent disbelief of the allegations against him.

The morning of the Grand Jury, the *Miami Herald* had already hit the newsstands in the city. I turned to the Keys Area News section and saw splashed across its face, the bold headlines of the resignation. The smaller sub-heading paraphrased Smith, "Says sex probe played no part in decision."

I was thankful that at least the Miami paper was more objective in its reporting than the *Key West Citizen* was in its slanted presentation. Although the *Herald* reported that his resignation was "because of health reasons," the paper also noted that his action fell on the heels of their disclosure of the federal Grand Jury investigation of allegations of sexual misconduct, just three days prior. The paper also covered the fact that Dr. Smith's resignation would not become effective until February 15, and that he, "would stay on at the college as a consultant until August 18, his birthday, trustees decided unanimously." The article closed out its story by again mentioning that two former employees had accused Smith of dismissing them unless they engaged in sexual conduct with him. Both, had previously testified before the October Grand Jury. There also was reference made to the third employee, with similar allegations, who was scheduled to testify that day.

As successful as that investigation proved to be in South Florida, raising that same specter of sexual blackmail in our nation's capital months later would turn out far differently for me.

At the conclusion of our Grand Jury session in Key West, the Assistant U.S. Attorney and I flew back to Miami.

"How do you think it went?" I asked him on the short return flight.

"I think it went well, extremely well," he said.

The next morning, however, I received what I considered a disturbing phone call. Eder confirmed the rumors that I had already heard whenever I visited the National Office. He told me I would be pulled out of South Florida in the near future, and in the interim would be temporarily assigned to the newly established Atlanta office. When I asked what that meant, he replied that all my cases would be transferred to that office to monitor. I was thoroughly immersed in my Key West investigation of City Hall and was scheduled to appear before further Grand Juries, but when I questioned the new policy, he cut me off.

"It's not your decision," he announced curtly.

I knew that any further explanation of the practical necessity of my remaining in South Florida was useless. As we spoke, I continued getting negative vibes from him. I began to realize even more fully that what Bedwell had told me several weeks prior, "watch your back," was on target. Over the past month, I had thought about all of Eder's words and actions, something that I never felt the need to do before.

I decided to initiate a plan of action I thought would help me accomplish my objective of remaining in Florida until my cases were successfully concluded. It was more than just a personal thing to stay with them until the end, it was a strong belief that my cases wouldn't be handled right. I had put in too much time and effort to see all that work go down the tube. I knew my informants and my sources of information personally, and I didn't think that anyone coming in behind me could, or would, maintain the same working relationships. The citizens of Key West who wanted to see justice done were distrustful of anyone they didn't know or hadn't dealt with before. Accordingly, I called Jon Sale at the U.S. Attorney's Office and asked to see him as soon as possible. An appointment was scheduled for that afternoon.

When I walked into his office, he greeted me cordially and also congratulated me on the work that had been done, and especially on the Key West Grand Juries.

When I informed him what I had just heard about my upcoming transfer out of the area, he looked concerned.

"I don't think that's a good move on their part," he said. "Not at this stage of the game."

I agreed with him thoroughly and then added, "Besides I don't want to leave yet either."

He brightened up at my disclosure and asked, "What can I do

to help you?"

"I was thinking that maybe a letter to DeMarco might help," I said.

"That's a good idea," he replied, "and easy enough to accomplish right now," and he called in his secretary.

I also mentioned that although his letter should be effective as a stopgap measure, that I also was going to request a permanent transfer to DOL's local OCP office. It was an acronym for a newly established Organized Crime Program.

"Who's heading that office up?" he asked.

"Hugo Menendez is going to be the Special Agent-in-Charge of the Miami office."

Sale indicated that he also knew Menendez and would send him a copy of the letter as well.

Although I had met Menendez at his office near the OCB office, I knew him only slightly. We appeared to get along well, and I thought that it was a good suggestion.

Dictation was taken and it produced the following letter:

> Dear Mr. DeMarco:
>
> I understand that your office has determined that investigations in Florida will be handled out of your Atlanta office and that Mr. Mangieri will no longer have responsibility in Florida. I would like to suggest that you consider permitting Mr. Mangieri to continue his investigative efforts in Monroe County. As you undoubtedly know there are special problems inherent to an investigation in Key West. In my judgment Mr. Mangieri has tackled those problems very effectively. I would, therefore, recommend that you consider permitting Mr. Mangieri to continue with investigative responsibilities in Monroe County.
>
> I look forward to working with you in the future.
>
> > Sincerely,
> > J.V. ESKENAZI
> > UNITED STATE ATTORNEY
> > By

JON A. SALE
FIRST ASSISTANT U.S. ATTORNEY
cc: Hugo Menendez,
Special Agent in Charge, Miami, Florida

I was impressed not only with the tone of the letter, but with his willingness to write it and his immediate action on it. I felt that if anything would do the trick, it was that letter from the U.S. Attorney's Office. I was, however, wrong. Nothing ever came of it. If, there was a written response to Sale's letter, I never heard. I heard that budgetary problems played a part in my being moved out of Florida. I also heard that transfers couldn't be affected between divisions, inasmuch as I had been assigned to the Fraud Division, and Menendez was in the Organized Crime Division. However, the logic in that escaped me. Criminal Investigators in either division had the same requirements and basically the same duties. Any specialized work required of any individual in the *1811* series could be accomplished with a minimum of cross training. Again, either that was never considered, or — which was even more likely — in-house politics played a major part. Although DeMarco was the director, he was unfortunately only an acting director until a permanent Inspector General was appointed. Below DeMarco were his subordinates who undoubtedly played important roles in everyday decisions.

Several days after my meeting with Sale while awaiting what I still expected to be a favorable response, I sent a memo to DeMarco who was still in his acting director capacity. It was to be, regrettably, one of the last pieces of direct communication that I was to have with him. Future correspondence was to be directed to Richard Ross, as the Deputy Inspector General - Acting.

The memorandum that I sent to DeMarco dealt with the status of the Smith case. In my report, I officially advised him of the date of the college president's resignation, and of his retention as a consultant until the end of the summer. I also informed DeMarco of the specific provisions on his retention:

"He will not, however, have any part in the hiring or firing of personnel, nor will he have any responsibility in the receipt or application of CETA funds."

I knew the terms of that agreement had been worked out

between Smith's attorney and Sale, as the chief ASSISTANT U.S. ATTORNEY. I also felt that my memo kept DeMarco personally up-to-date on that particular case which had generated a lot of outside interest.

In closing out the memo, I made reference to a nagging concern that I felt wouldn't be followed up on, in the event of my departure:

> "As reported in my confidential memorandum to you of December 27, 1978, a condition precedent to the cessation of federal investigation — or of referral to state authorities — is not only his resignation but also his agreement to undergo psychiatric examination. His adherence to this latter condition is yet to be seen."

My *concern* of his psychiatric exams proved to be a valid one. Had I remained in the area, I would have monitored the terms of the agreement, having been intimately involved with all the details and facets of the investigation. My replacements, however, were not as caught up in the case so as to follow all the movements, nor the provisions in the agreement.

In spite of all my efforts to be transferred to Miami, I received a copy of a memo from Ross on February 1 officially assigning me to Atlanta "for case supervision."

Cameron Barron I learned was assigned to Philadelphia, Pete Castro to New York City, and a new agent, Peter Ives, to Boston.

The memorandum to the various new Supervisory Special Agents in those cities advised them that "case assignment, direction and review" would be their responsibility. It further advised them that any decisions on case presentation to the U.S. Attorney would be under their supervision.

Although the notification didn't sit particularly well with me, having been my own boss in the field for almost eight months, there was little I could do. I don't believe Barron or Castro were enthralled with the idea either, but they knew that it was only temporary. It didn't change our permanent assignments as we still reported to the National Office, and we all still lived in the Washington, D.C., area. Other than the change of case supervision the only other noticeable change was the necessity of additional review in our new offices. In my case, that meant Atlanta visits as well as the Washington trips.

Fortunately for me, the monitoring never came about because of an innocuous incident that occurred in Key West in early February. That incident was blown entirely out of proportion by someone in the National Office. I would learn who on my next trip north.

Shortly after receiving Ross' February 1 memo, I was back in Miami and headed toward Key West in an ever-growing probe of City Hall activities.

The *Miami Herald* in its Keys Area News section on February 9, accurately reflected what was happening:

U.S. PROBE INTO CETA IS EXPANDED

The story stated that a U.S. Department of Labor investigation into alleged fraud in federal job-training money had widened to several city departments "including the police department," in its use of CETA funds for personnel and materials. In addition, the article noted that allegations were also received on the misuse of federal funds on the college's construction program.

Upon being approached by the reporter, and in appropriate law enforcement jargon, I was quoted as saying that I, "would neither confirm nor deny reports of new charges against the community college and the police department," because of the confidentiality of my ongoing inquiries.

The article in true investigative reporting fashion also covered the fact that in addition to myself, investigators from the IRS were conducting probes for possible income tax fraud by suspected drug smugglers, and also that investigators from the FDLE were engaging in their own independent inquiries.

On Monday, February 12, I reported into the National Office, as usual. Barron, who was busy on the phone, waved at me as I sat at my desk and started going through my in-basket. At the top of the stack of paperwork was a short memo from Ross *reassigning* me to the Philadelphia office, effective immediately. At the bottom of the notification was a scribbled handwritten message, "See me! — Stu."

I looked at it for a moment letting it sink in, and as I was doing so, Barron had just hung up his phone. He must've seen me staring at the piece of paper in my hand.

"What's going on buddy?" he asked.

"What the hell is this?" I yelled out as I thrust the memo into his hand.

He read it, and then shrugged his shoulders.

"You got me," he answered. "I thought you were assigned to Atlanta."

"I thought so too," I said.

It's not that I minded so much the switch from Atlanta to Philadelphia, as it was closer to home and my kids, but it was *the way* that it was done. Also, I didn't know what that meant to my South Florida cases, whether I was off them immediately or whether it was still to be a temporary phase-out until my permanent reassignment back to Washington. I voiced both my displeasure and my concern to Barron.

"What happened this weekend down there?" he asked.

I quickly related a brief episode in Miami where I met the supervisory special agent of the Atlanta office, and then my inability to make contact with him when I went to Key West.

"So," was his comment, "is that it?"

"That's it," I said emphatically. "Further, I don't know where the problem is, at that end or at this end."

"When are you going to see Stu?" Barron asked.

"Right now," and I picked up the memo from my desk.

I found Eder, on an upper floor, sitting behind his desk. He glanced up with a complacent look squinting behind horn-rimmed glasses. Before he had a chance to say anything, I pushed the memorandum in front of him.

"What's this mean?" I said.

"Exactly what it says," he replied. "You're reassigned."

"Why?" I asked.

"Apparently you ignored Mitchell's orders," he said looking down at the piece of paper in front of him rather than meeting my gaze.

"Is that what Mitchell said?" I demanded.

"More or less," he answered. "If not in those exact words, then pretty close to it."

"That's bullshit. Do you believe him?"

"It's not for me to believe him or you, it's Ross' decision," he said, "not mine."

I didn't believe him for one moment. Although I knew Ross as the Acting Deputy was the last word, I also knew that Eder had input into any decision involving field agents.

"What about my Florida cases?" I asked.

"Bring them all up-to-date and then submit them to me for review. I'll see that Atlanta gets them."

"What about the U.S. Attorney's Office?" I wanted to know.

"That will be Al Davis' concern, he'll be taking over that part of Florida out of the Atlanta office."

He's not going to be able to handle it," I said.

"That's not your problem anymore," he added. "Besides he's a *12* just like you and should be able to pick up where you left off."

The more I looked at him perched behind his desk, the more he reminded me of a weasel, and I turned to leave.

The weasel spoke.

"Ross says that he wants a report of the Florida incident on his desk as soon as possible."

I grunted acknowledgement.

"One more thing," he said.

"Yeah."

"Why did you come back this weekend?"

I looked at him quizzically.

"Why?" and I raised my voice in response to what I considered a stupid question.

"Because Ross gave me permission before I left last week, that's why."

He seemed nonplussed at my answer and looked up at me blankly. I waited for a comment, but there was none so I left.

Back at the bullpen, Barron glanced up as I strode into the room.

"Well?" he asked.

I shook my head disgustedly, and I tossed the reassignment memo back on my desk.

"I'll tell you about it later," I said, as I grabbed a yellow pad to write my requested response to Ross.

My initial subject matter was, "Incompatibility with Atlanta Fraud Office," but after thinking it over decided that it was not an objective subject heading so I changed it to:

MIAMI/KEY WEST TRIP (FEB. 5-10, 1979)

The detailed explanation was as follows:

"In accordance with a recent 'detail' to the Atlanta Fraud Office, I met with Michael Mitchell, Supervising Special Agent of that office, on Tuesday morning, February 6. At that meeting I was advised that Al Davis of the Atlanta Office was 'lead' Agent in Florida and I was to report to him on all my cases. Inasmuch as I have worked all my cases solo for the past seven months in Florida with conclusive results (see attached newspaper articles), I was somewhat surprised at this order. As a Journeyman Investigator, I felt that by placing me under the direction of an equal investigator indicated a lack of trust in my abilities and further denoted a desire to monitor my movements. However, I accepted this provision to preclude any disagreement at our initial meeting. If there was to be a monitoring concept, Mr. Mitchell as the area Supervisor should have been my control official, not an equal rank investigator. I was further advised that when I arrived at Key West, Florida I was to call Miami at 10 p.m. and notify Mr. Mitchell. However, when I arrived in Key West I encountered problems in obtaining a room because the area was at the peak of its tourist season and a rain storm was building. By the time I managed to locate lodging it was between 10:30 p.m. - 11 p.m. and pouring rain. The following morning I placed a number of phone calls to Mr. Mitchell to establish my presence in the Key West area:

"(1) Person-to-person to his hotel room;

"(2) The Organized Crime Bureau of the Dade County Sheriff's Office;

"(3) our own OCP office in Miami. I left messages with the Dade County Sheriff's Office and our own OCP office that I was settled and was attempting to reach Mr. Mitchell. I also advised them that if I failed to make contact I would attempt to contact him upon my return Friday, February 9.

"Upon my return to Miami Friday night, about 10 p.m., I again attempted to reach Mr. Mitchell, who I learned was out of town. I then spoke to Al Davis and related the situation I encountered upon my arrival in Key West. During our conversation Agent Davis indicated no problems, nor were there any messages from Mr. Mitchell. I concluded business and returned to Washington on Saturday, February 10. In addition to the failure to contact Mr. Mitchell, I also was questioned by Stu Eder and Paul Lehrman as to why I had returned to Washington. I advised them that I had discussed my return on weekends with you since I have the additional sole responsibility of caring for three children. You had concurred and given me permission. Therefore, my immediate reassignment from Florida to the Philadelphia Office was to say the least, a complete surprise and can be attributed only to the Atlanta Office. It is unfortunate that the set of circumstances described above triggered the extreme reactions encountered by myself. However clarification could have resolved what appears to be misinterpretation and subsequent misinformation. It is a matter of record that I have had more cases than any other Agent and that I have spent more time in the Field than any other Agent. I have never been challenged before nor has my judgment been questioned. I have thoroughly immersed myself in my assignments in Florida and enjoyed my work. In addition, I have established an excellent rapport with the U.S. Attorney and other Federal State and Local law enforcement agencies in that area. In view of all of the above, plus the fact that I must be both father and mother to my three school-aged chil-

dren, I request that I either be granted a transfer
to the OCP office in Miami or that I be transferred
to Miami to handle all fraud investigations in the
South Florida area."

The reference made to Paul Lehrman in my memo to Ross was
a brief encounter with him after my session with Eder. He, too,
wanted to know why I was back in the National Office. Either the
left hand was not telling the right hand what was going on, or there
was a concerted effort, by Eder, to undermine me as Bedwell had
previously warned. In either case, I never received a written reply
— nor an oral reaction from anyone at National.

Because of the hastiness of my reassignment, I had to make a
final return trip to Miami to clear my desk at OCB. Lt. Havens,
Sgt. Bedwell and the other staff bade me farewell and wished me well
in Washington. I thanked them and regrettably packed my gear
and boxed my paperwork.

My last phone call was from Susan Sachs, the *Miami Herald*
reporter in Key West, who had handled the last article in the Keys
Area News on my last trip there. When I told her I was being reassigned, she seemed genuinely surprised that I would be pulled out
of the Keys when the investigations seemed to be progressing.

"That's show biz," I said halfheartedly, but she could sense my
disappointment in leaving. Her perceptive comprehensive and very
lengthy article on February 18 not only reflected my views but
those of the National Office and the Atlanta Office, as well:

FINANCES SEND KEYS CETA INVESTIGATOR PACKING

She noted in her article after talking to Lehrman on the phone
that I had "been taken off the assignment to save money, leaving
only three investigators to cover an eight-state Southeastern region."
In response to her pointed questioning as to *why*, she was advised,
"From a management and cost point of view, it's not practical to send
him down there. We can't afford to support an investigation in Key
West from Washington, D.C."

In her call to the Atlanta office, she was advised by Al Davis
that, "We'll be in and out of there." He also told her that he and
two other investigators had to respond to other complaints about

"programs such as workmen's compensation and employee integrity, for all eight states," and that they had "a lot to cover."

I knew what they were faced with. I also knew that my Key West investigations would suffer — and they did.

The reporter in her final interview with me closed out her article concerning my effectiveness, with some off-the-record comments: "Now people are coming forward, where they didn't before, because they know me."

A couple of days after my return to the National Office, Acting Inspector General DeMarco was sent a congratulatory letter from the head of the OCB in Miami for my detail to that office.

> Dear Mr. DeMarco:
> In July 1978, Special Agent Nicholas Mangieri, of the Office of Special Investigation, was assigned to assist the Dade County Public Safety Department, Organized Crime Bureau, in an investigation of CETA fraud in South Florida. Since his assignment, Agent Mangieri has exhibited the qualities of a professional and dedicated investigator. The assistance he rendered contributed significantly to the overall success of the CETA investigations in the South Florida area. Additionally, the cooperation provided by Agent Mangieri has provided an excellent basis for future joint investigative efforts between the U.S. Department of Labor and the Public Safety Department. Please extend our congratulations to Agent Mangieri for a job well done and be assured of our continued cooperation in all matters of mutual concern.
>
> Sincerely,
> Steven A. Bertucelli, Commander
> Organized Crime Bureau

It was subsequently handed off to me by Ross, as the Deputy, without any fanfare or comment, but it was something that I cherished regardless of the lack of recognition by my own department.

... 5 ...

As disappointed as I was in having to leave South Florida, the pluses of the sudden transfer soon began to outweigh the negative aspects of the various incidents that surrounded it. First of all, I was with my three kids on a full-time basis, and could enjoy their company once again after being deprived of them for that six-month period. Secondly, my subsequent assignment to the Philadelphia office for their "case supervision," also did not materialize. The change in the Philadelphia assignment came as a result of the establishment of a Washington Field Office. I, and two other agents were permanently assigned to that post, which was physically located in Arlington, Virginia. It was the convenient proximity of that new work station to my own home in suburban Maryland that was definitely the third major plus in my having to work in the Washington metropolitan area.

That office, however, would turn out far differently than I had initially anticipated. It would also prove to be more damaging to my cases, and more threatening to me, than any potential danger that I faced in Key West.

The other two agents were: Pete Castro who was reassigned from the New York Office, and Peter Ives, who was reassigned from the Boston office. Then there was our new supervisor, who was scheduled to be the Agent-in-Charge of the Arlington Office, Arnold Juliano. He had been a former IRS agent somewhere along the line, and more recently had done a short stint as the Agent-in-Charge of our New York Fraud Office. In addition, we were fortunate to have a very pleasant, very comely and very efficient sec-retary, Charmayne Parks. This apparently compatible group com-prised our small staff. Within a short time, my buddy, Cameron Barron, and a new agent, Norman Romney, a retired New York City police officer, would also join us. There was one other agent, Lafayette Vance, who was with us for a brief period and then returned to the National Office on Constitution Avenue in downtown D.C.

There was one minor drawback to our rosy beginnings, and that was the reputation of our new supervisor. Before I ever met Juliano, I heard derogatory reports from several people at the National Office. I was told that he had an abrasive manner in deal-ing with some of his former employees and even with some of his associates.

"Watch him," I was warned.

I laughed off their admonitions and told them that I could han-dle Juliano. Even Castro, who was normally laid-back, was con-cerned about working for him again. He previously had been detailed to the New York Office for a short period of time, while Juliano was still there. Although he never said what had occurred between them in New York, there had been, according to Castro, some type of confrontation. Castro, therefore, was not overly thrilled about renewing his relationship with him. However, when we discussed our new office, compared to where we could have been, we agreed that in spite of the apparent handicap that we were getting in our new supervisor, we would try to make the best of the situation.

In addition to our own personal state of affairs, a general cloud hovered over the 200-odd agents dispersed throughout the coun-try. All, to a man, were virtually dubious about the new *Inspector General concept* that resulted from the Inspector General Act passed by Congress in October 1978. None of us had much — if any — experience with the I.G. way of doing business, or in our case, of conducting criminal investigations. The general consensus among all the agents was that we would take a "wait and see" attitude. This view was especially pronounced because our new political nominee head was said to be female. It wasn't so much her gender that concerned me — and others — as a female Attila the Hun would have been totally acceptable. It was more her politically ori-ented background and her perceived aversion to traditional police methods — and certainly to any hard-core investigatory techniques

— that made her an unlikely candidate to head up a new investigative agency. We felt, validly, that she would never whole heartedly pursue any type of politically sensitive investigation.

How true that conviction would turn out to be.

In the interim, our former OSI Director, "Rocky" DeMarco, was named the Acting Inspector General. The expressed opinion, shared by many, was that the administration within the Department of Labor had given Rocky the shaft by not supporting him as the nominee for the Inspector General position. We all believed he was worthy of that position because of his prior efforts in attempting to gain recognition of the Department of Labor for its aggressiveness in law enforcement.

In early January, probability replaced possibility. Marjorie Fine Knowles was nominated to be the first Inspector General for the Department of Labor. She was not, however, to assume her post until several months later.

Although all this political intrigue and maneuverings were occurring while I was still in Florida, I would receive periodic updates on my return trips to Washington. By the time I was pulled back into the National Office and reassigned to Arlington in March of '79, DOL was still deeply mired in the throes of change and indecision concerning the new I.G. appointment. Rocky had been given a position as the Deputy Assistant Undersecretary of Labor. Dick Ross was running the shop as the Acting I.G., and Stuart Eder wrangled the slot of Acting Chief of Investigations.

For me, however, there had been no new changes, nor had there been to the other agents in the new office during the entire month of March. We were all becoming acclimated to our new surroundings and to each other. We were all, of course, anticipating receiving interesting cases rather than the sporadic mundane workmen's compensation cases that had been doled out to us.

That anticipation was to become realized sooner — and more dramatically — than I had expected. The evening of April 4, 1979, while having a second cup of coffee after dinner, I noticed an article in the now-defunct *Washington Star* that caught my eye:

GRAND JURY VOTES TO INDICT
DISTRICT PERSONNEL DIRECTOR

The front-page story gave the lurid details of the assault by

George Harrod, the Personnel Director for the District of Columbia, on one of his former female staff employees because she attempted to end their sexual relationship. In reading further, I noticed the woman originally had been hired under the federal Comprehensive Employment Training Act (CETA), and more importantly (at least to me) — had submitted to his sexual demands under coercion of threats to terminate her employment.

I zeroed in on the magical acronym "CETA" to make sure that what I had seen actually applied to the victim described. Sure enough, she had been employed under the CETA program. I read the article again more carefully to make sure I hadn't overlooked the specific criminal charge I considered pertinent to the indictment. My second reading confirmed it. There was no indictment based upon *sexual coercion* but only upon the simple assault charge. Having just worked a sexual coercion charge against the college president in Key West less that three months prior, I was very familiar with its application and effectiveness. Elated at my discovery, I clipped the article to take to the office the next day.

As I swung into my office on the morning of April 5, politics was the furthest thing from my mind. All I could think of was the potential of a new case, one that was very similar to the one in South Florida.

Juliano greeted me warmly as he had since our first meeting almost a month ago.

"Hey, paisan, I like your suit."

It was a typical salutation since he was somewhat of a fastidious dresser and appreciated it in others.

We made small talk concerning our wardrobes, and I started to enter my own small room off the large hallway entrance.

"When you've got a minute, Arnie, I've got something to show you that might interest you," I said before I broke off our minor discussion of wearing apparel.

"I'm free now," he responded. "As soon as you're settled step into my office."

I dropped my briefcase on my desk and took out the newspaper clip. I then walked into his corner room and gave it to him. He read it very slowly, placed it back on his desk, squinted at me through his glasses, adjusted them and said, "So what? What does this mean to us?"

Half expecting his perplexed and almost disinterested response, because of his lack of familiarity with the federal statute, I very carefully and methodically explained to him DOL jurisdiction and showed him the specific criminal code citation that applied.

"Where did you get your information?" he asked.

"As you can see," I continued, "under 18 USC 665(b), *Improper Inducement,* it is a crime for anyone to induce any CETA employee to give up 'something of value.'"

He still looked unconvinced.

I read it aloud this time, verbatim, to him:

"Whoever, by threat of procuring dismissal of any person from employment or of refusal to employ or refusal to renew a contract of employment in connection with a grant or contract of assistance under the Comprehensive Employment and Training Act of 1975, *induces,*" and I stressed the word *induces:* "any person to give up any money or thing of value to any person (including such grantee agency) shall be fined not more than $1,000, or imprisoned not more than one year, or both."

Before he had a chance to voice any more objections, I continued.

"Case law has it, that a 'woman's body' has been found to be a 'thing of value.' Therefore, anybody who forces a woman to submit to him sexually under threat of dismissal violates 18 USC 665(b) and can be fined, or can go to jail."

He looked impressed this time, and I breathed a little easier.

"When I worked Florida," I went on, "Jon Sale in the U.S. Attorney's Office in Miami and I used this statute very successfully against the head of a small college in Key West."

Those were the magic words that he wanted to hear, that someone had used this particular statute before. The fact that it was a U.S. Attorney unquestionably sealed his decision.

His look of initial perplexity was gone after my summary explanation.

"Write a memo to the file," he said, "and start a folder on this."

"With your permission," I said, "I'd like to contact the U.S. Attorney's Office in the District to see if they're interested."

"Just make sure to keep memos of everything you do."

I nodded and returned to my own office. Several phone calls later, I had made direct contact with Earl Silbert, the U.S. Attorney for the District of Columbia. I briefly explained what I had just explained in more detail to Juliano. He was interested, he said, but suggested that I contact Jim Owens, one of his assistants, who had personally handled the Harrod indictment. A short while later I was speaking to Owens, the Chief of the Misdemeanor Section. He was an individual with a booming resonant voice who exhibited not only sincere interest in what I told him but questioned me in-depth about the statute and my experience with it in Florida. He promised to relay the information back to Silbert and suggested I call him back in about a week to see if the new charge would be pursued.

The week dragged by slowly because I was anxious to get into gear on a case that showed potential. I wasn't that interested in pursuing a sexual inducement charge against a solitary individual. I was interested in numbers and was hearing that the Harrod case was just the "tip of the iceberg."

I called Owens again about April 13 to find out what decision had been reached. Silbert, he said, was interested but concerned about the possibility of double jeopardy. Owens, himself, did not think the concept applied in the situation with Harrod and the alleged victim of his assault. Would I mind calling him back in a couple of weeks, he asked. In that period, he said, he would monitor the situation. He added that if I uncovered any new information to keep him posted. A little disappointed in the delay to move forward, I nevertheless agreed to do as he requested.

The *Washington Star,* however, resolved both our problems and our questions. On April 27, bold headlines covered the front page:

SEX COERCION BY D.C. OFFICIALS PROBED

The words were like manna from heaven; it was the break I was looking for. As I quickly scanned the joint article by reporters

Kenneth Walker and Michael Kiernan, I found what I wanted. According to the story, sources within city government told the *Star* there had been a "vast conspiracy" by several District officials involving the sexual harassment of many females initially employed in temporary positions, including those hired under the federally funded *Comprehensive Employment Training Act*. The article further stated that these officials, or as one of the sources had described, a "clique of cronies," had in effect "traded" women from one agency to another in a longstanding practice of exchanging jobs, promotions and other privileges for sexual favors from these female employees.

I called Owens as soon as I finished reading the article.

"I've been expecting your call Agent Mangieri," he boomed.

"How soon can we have a meeting about this new development?" I asked.

"How about Monday, the 30th," he responded.

"Fine, what time?"

"How does 3 p.m. sound?"

"Perfect, I'll see you then." I hung up.

I located Juliano, showed him the new article, discussed it briefly with him and told him of my Monday meeting with Owens.

"Just make sure you keep a record of all your conversations," was his immediate comment, and then added, "and don't forget to put that new clipping in the file."

I assured him I would and had.

Before I turned to leave his office, he asked whether I wanted him to accompany me to the Owens meeting on Monday. I stifled a smile and assured him I could handle it alone.

That type of lingering concern over the most trivial item was a harbinger of what I was to experience from him. It never varied; it never lessened. It had to be some form of paranoia.

When I mentioned his behavior to Castro, following that Friday afternoon session with Juliano, his only comment was, "I could've told you so."

At 3 p.m. on April 30, I walked into Assistant U.S. Attorney Jim Owens' office in the District Court Building and was impressed with what I saw. A large man who matched the deep voice rose from behind a huge desk that complemented him. His appearance and his demeanor reminded me of the actor James Earl Jones. His

desk was stacked with files, folders and various legal memoranda
that inevitably ended up there because of his position. He was gra-
cious and friendly as he grasped my hand and motioned for me to
sit.

"Tell me about your experience with the statute you mentioned
that deals with sexual coercion."

"18 USC 665(b)," I responded.

I handed him a copy of the statute and told him about the coercion case I worked in the South Florida area with Jon Sale, Deputy
U.S. Attorney in the Miami Office.

"I'm sure Mr. Silbert will want to check with him. He's very
thorough," Owens added.

"Sure, we got along very well."

The conversation then turned to the recent article in the *Star*
and the scope of involvement by some of the District officials.

"It appears to be pervasive," he said. "Apparently Walker and
Kiernan, the *Star's* investigative reporters, have been working on this
a long time and have uncovered a lot of information."

"I didn't realize this kind of thing went on in the nation's capital," I said. "I expected corruption in Alaska, where I was the Chief
of Police in a small town, and I expected it in Key West and in
Miami where I worked on CETA fraud, but not here."

He smiled.

"Washington is no different from any place else."

I asked him what the procedure was for me to initiate the CETA
investigation. He said he would advise Silbert of DOL interest and
jurisdiction in the CETA cases. He told me to proceed and keep him
apprised of my progress. We shook hands firmly, and I left.

Juliano was waiting for me when I returned to the office.

"Tell me about your meeting with Owens," he demanded.

"Before or after my memo?"

"Before, and then write it up when we're through."

I nodded, stepped into his room and gave him a short briefing
on the salient aspects of our meeting. He interrupted me several
times to ask what I considered were picayunish questions. Whether
there was anyone else present during our session? Whether he had
given me a letter of authorization to proceed with the investigation? Even whether Owens wanted to personally meet with him
before I began the investigation into the allegations raised by the

latest newspaper article? It was becoming obvious that Juliano was extremely concerned over the potential immensity of the investigation since it allegedly involved several District officials.

"Keep me informed on what you do," he stressed. "I've got to keep the National Office advised."

I nodded again in affirmation but wondered why we had to keep them posted almost daily as we were supposedly an autonomous Field Office. I didn't question him on it, although it became increasingly clear to our small Arlington staff and to the secretarial staff at the National Office in D.C., that Juliano was constantly on the phone to Stu Eder, his new superior.

"I'll be commencing my investigation tomorrow," I told him. "I'll probably be starting with the city's Office of Human Rights."

"Why there?" he wanted to know in a strained voice.

"According to the article, that office 'actively discouraged' female employees from filing complaints on sexual harassment," I continued in a low voice. "I want to check their records and interview some of the women and the EEO Investigators who took their complaints."

He surprisingly acknowledged the merit of that decision, and I quickly returned to my own office to commit to memo form what had already begun to shape up as an unending battle of paperwork.

I was unaware at that time that what I considered to be typical bureaucratic bumbling and ineptness on Juliano's part, would, in reality, be to my advantage. The endless memos I was forced to write would actually be the ammo that I needed to enhance my own position in the ensuing months.

... 6 ...

Early Tuesday morning, May 1, I received a call while I was still in the office.

"Is this Agent Mangieri?".

"Yes, how can I help you?"

"I can probably help you," the voice continued. "I'm Ken Walker from the *Washington Star*."

I recognized the name as the reporter who had written the sex coercion articles, but I was taken by surprise by a call that I didn't expect, and my hesitation showed.

"Hello," he repeated.

"I'm sorry," I said.

"I understand that you're investigating sexual harassment of the CETA females in the District government," he said.

"Word sure gets around. How did you know?"

"I make it my business to know," he said. "Are you interested?"

"Sure I'm interested, but I can't make any deals or commitments with you."

"I understand," he said, "but I'm not asking or expecting. You can have what I'm finished with."

"When?" I asked.

"I'll be in touch," he answered. "I'm working on another headline that should break soon."

"Fine, whenever you're ready."

We both hung up. I pondered a minute about the conversation and then wrote a detailed memo covering exactly what was said because I knew Juliano would question me on it. As soon as I had completed it, I took it into Juliano's office and showed it to him. As he read it, he raised his eyebrows, adjusted his glasses, fidgeted in his chair a little and began his questioning:

"Why did he call you? What did you tell him? Did you make any deals with him? What's he going to give you? When?"

The questions were all in the same vein, and those that didn't receive a quick negative response from me were pointed out as, "It's all in the memo, Arnie."

I assured him I wouldn't meet with Walker without advising him in advance, and that seemed to satisfy him, at least for the moment.

As soon as I was able to clear the office, I was in Washington visiting several of the District of Columbia offices to learn of the procedures that employees had to go through to file complaints. The information eventually led me to the Office of Human Rights. There, I spoke to a couple of the investigators who handled Equal Employment Opportunity (EEO) complaints, where the sexual harassment complaints were filed. When questioned, their recollections were poor as to specific names and they were of little help in identifying female complainants who had raised the sexual issues as forms of discrimination. Immediately upon learning of my presence in the office, the Associate Director of OHR took the responsibility of answering my questions himself in lieu of my questioning his investigators. In response to my query of specific names, again, he replied that he "believed there were only three." However, he was unable to give them to me. When I pressed him for an answer, he telephoned the Acting Director of OHR, who saw to it that some of the names and folders were made available to me. There were, according to the Director, six female complainants of which four folders were in that office and two were elsewhere. I was welcome, he said, to inspect them although I would not be allowed to remove any part of them from their office. I made necessary notations of the four folders that I had inspected. They tended to indicate that the allegations of sexual harassment reported in the *Star* were true. I then left at the end of the day and went home without making any additional stops or calls.

The morning of May 2, 1979, dawned like any other bright spring day. It was sunny and mild, and the weather report called for high temperatures to reach the low 70s. The radio, like the newspapers, said it would be a "gem of a day," with the same forecast for the following day.

Unfortunately, that forecast *only* pertained to the weather.

It was a day I wouldn't soon forget, and I'm sure it had become a day others wished had never begun. En route to work that morning, I had to stop at the National Office before I headed to Arlington. As I passed a local newsstand the large headline on *The Washington Star* edition jumped out at me:

U.S. PROBES SEX CHARGES IN D.C.

"Damn," I muttered, as much in surprise as in a sense of excitement.

I pulled over to the curb to get a newspaper and noted the byline was by Kenneth R. Walker, my recent phone contact.

At a red light, I managed to read the first paragraph:

> "A special U.S. Labor Department strike force has begun an investigation to determine whether District officials used a federal jobs program to extort sexual favors from young women, *The Washington Star* has learned."

I smiled to myself and the news description of the "special strike force," since — again — I, alone, was that special strike force. The first time a paper referred to me in the plural was in the Ft. Lauderdale newspaper account of my investigation into the Lauderdale Lakes case the prior summer.

Anxiously, I tried to read more of the article that covered the entire top of the first page, but traffic forced me to move on. Finally, I pulled into a parking lot a few blocks from the Department of Labor, and read on:

> "The investigation is centering on allegations that female city government workers hired under the Comprehensive Employment Training Act, were coerced to provide sexual favors in exchange for permanent jobs, promotions, and other privileges,

federal government sources said.

The Labor Department began its investigation following last week's disclosure of the alleged practices in *The Star.*"

I was impressed with Walker's coverage, but by the time I reached the third paragraph, I wondered where he got his additional information since I never mentioned any specific coercion incidents when we spoke:

"The strike force has conducted investigations of sexual coercion of CETA employees across the nation. The investigators most recently conducted a probe of similar allegations in Florida that led to the resignation of one official as part of a plea-bargaining arrangement, sources said."

The balance of the article recapped past allegations and then accurately touched on my visits to "several District agencies," including the City's Office of Human Rights. The story further noted that the OHR "also actively discouraged' females from filing complaints of sexual coercion."

As soon as the initial shock of the headlines wore off, I tried to assess the situation. I knew Walker must've had sources within city government who alerted him when I visited several District offices. Once knowing that, it didn't take him long to bang out a story that made headlines. I also knew that what I read in the complaint folders at the Office of Human Rights on the previous day indicated there was sexual harassment by several officials in at least three different agencies within District government. My gut reaction then was that publicizing the investigation was a good thing. I hoped it would give those women who were sexually abused the courage to step forward.

What I didn't know, however, was the Department of Labor's reaction to the news. I knew, or thought I knew, that the present policy within the Office of the Inspector General was not one of aggressive law enforcement. However, I sensed that any displeasure emanating from our new nominee I.G. would be mellowed by the Secretary of Labor. If anything, I believed our office would be commended by Secretary Marshal for uncovering CETA fraud, no matter where it was found. I especially felt that with all the pressure being exerted for women's rights, our investigation into protecting female workers would be applauded.

It was with this pro and con type of outlook that I walked into our National Office to pick up something I had left in my old office. Fran, one of the older and more outspoken secretaries who was in the process of retiring, stopped me.

"Hey Nick, I see your sex case made the headlines."

Surprised somewhat, but no longer shocked, I tried to appear nonchalant as I replied, "Yeah, I know it. I just read it."

"Well you better call Arnie, he's been busting a gut to find you."

I dialed the Arlington Office and spoke to Juliano. He was just as hyper and agitated as I expected he would be. I mockingly held the receiver away from my ear, as Fran winked at me with an appropriate derogatory response about my supervisor.

"Yeah Arnie, I'm en route," and I hung up.

"Good luck, tiger," she waved good-bye before she resumed her typing. "Sure glad I'm leaving," she muttered.

As I walked into our Field Office, Castro met me at the entrance.

"Hey hot shot, your sex case is all over the front page."

"Do *you* want it?" I asked him.

"You couldn't pay me to take that case," he said.

"How's our boy doing?"

I motioned toward Juliano's room at the end of the long office.

"You'll find out," and he turned and walked into his own room.

Juliano had overheard our voices and called out to me.

"Be right there," I yelled back to him.

I checked my box for mail or messages and walked to his room. He was nervously fidgeting in his chair and had the newspaper spread out on the desk in front of him.

"How could something like this happen?" he demanded.

I tried to calm him down with a simple explanation as I saw it, but it didn't slow his pace.

"How could Walker have known about your Florida case?"

"I don't know, maybe Owens told him. What difference does it make? That case was closed out six months ago."

"I'll tell you what difference it makes," and his voice started to rise. "I've been getting calls all morning since this came out," and his hand slammed down on the paper. "They say you've been talking to the papers."

"Wait a minute," I interrupted him, "I have no control over the *Star.* I haven't seen or spoken to Walker since I gave you that memo about Walker. That information about my investigation into the District could have come from anywhere. I was all over the city yesterday."

That seemed to quiet him down a little, but he continued.

"Knowles is concerned about this publicity. It could hurt her chances now that she's up for Senate confirmation."

I could see that he was deadly serious, but I thought that the "concern" was ridiculous.

"How could this possibly hurt her chances for confirmation as the Inspector General?" I queried. "This publicity should help her," and I stressed everything I said.

He didn't respond to my specific question, nor to my response about the publicity.

"Stu wants a full report on everything you did and said yesterday, and he wants it before you leave the office today."

I acknowledged that I would.

"Anything else?" It was hard to contain my annoyance with his abusive line of questioning and his absurd comments.

"Just make sure it's complete," he said. "As soon as Stu can get together with Ross, there'll be a meeting at National this week, and you and I will be there."

The implication was ominous, but I nodded and left to do the report. I wondered why Dick Ross was suddenly in the picture, but figured that as the Acting Deputy I.G., he, too, was caught in the politics of this whole thing. I had always liked Ross, not only because he had been part of our original OSI office, but because he had always been an aggressive investigator. However, if reports we all had heard were accurate, Ross was on tenuous ground with Knowles. Therefore, I could only surmise that he was pressured by her to lean on me. Contrary to Ross' seeming loss of favor with Knowles, Eder appeared to be rising in her estimation according to other accounts.

In either case, I still didn't understand the faulty logic behind such paranoid concern that my investigation would threaten her confirmation.

Faced with the implications of what lay in store for me from this new rising "star," I completed my report in detail and left the office to resume my investigation in the field. Unsubstantiated allegations from witnesses that afternoon indicated that two named officials within the D.C. Department of Labor also were involved in the "sexual coercion" of female employees. According to their statements, they were happy to see that the U.S. Department of Labor had finally taken an interest in an ongoing situation that should have been rectified long ago.

The following day, Thursday, May 3, I learned from Castro that Juliano had received a call from a minor official within the D.C. Department of Labor who wished to remain anonymous. The caller, also heartened by the headlines of the previous day, felt secure in relaying additional information about various improprieties within D.C. Labor, including that of the oft-quoted "sexual coercion" charge against specific officials. The same names of the two officials I was given the prior afternoon surfaced again. Although I hadn't spoken to the caller myself, I was sure Juliano should have passed the information on to me to assist me on my case. However, because I didn't want to let Juliano know I was aware of the subject of the call, I nonchalantly asked him about it.

"Was it of any value in my own investigation?" I asked.

He assured me that if coercion were indeed the topic of the phone call I would not only receive the information but also get permission to meet with the caller to conduct my own investigation. I felt certain he was deceiving me. The next day, May 4, my suspicions were confirmed.

In reviewing our open cases, a normal daily occurrence in an office as small as ours, I noted that Juliano had, on the previous day, opened two new cases as a direct result of the phone call he had received. Each case involved the two same-named officials uncovered on May 2. However, the cases were not assigned to me, as was the usual practice when an agent became initially involved in a case, but were assigned to Agent Castro. When I asked Juliano about it, I pointed out the similarities in the three cases and the fact that I had already started an investigation into the allegations. I also told him that I had already interviewed witnesses in the two "new" cases, and advised him of the potentiality of unnecessary duplicate work by Castro and myself. Juliano, however, was adamant about the assignments and said that there would be "no change."

The meeting with Eder and Ross was scheduled early in the afternoon of Friday, the 4th, and Juliano accompanied me to the meeting. They were both waiting for us. Ross looked preoccupied and wasn't in his usual happy, wise-cracking mood. Eder was somber as if the weight of the world rested on his narrow shoulders. There were few, if any, amenities and the session got under way quickly.

"We've read your report," Eder began. "Is there anything else you'd like to add?"

He looked at me intently as if it were obvious that I was lying and this was his method of intimidating me with a baleful stare.

However, his eyeballing me was far from daunting, if that was his intent. I couldn't imagine it ever working on anybody.

I looked back at him, casually sitting on a couch beside a window with the impressiveness of the Capitol in the background. If there ever was an incongruous scene, that was it. Not only was the setting completely out of context with the triviality of the episode enfolding within the room, but Eder compounded it. Here was an Acting Chief of Investigations trying to act like a *real* Investigator, but his demeanor didn't generate respect. Besides that, with a slight-of-build body, and thick glasses he always did remind me of a weasel.

I finally answered his question.

"That's it," I said, glancing over at Ross sitting behind his desk.

"Arnie tells me that you're concerned over Castro being assigned two new cases," Ross said.

I agreed that I was and briefly gave him my reasons. I decided not to mention the deception I experienced with Juliano.

Ross nodded, but continued, as if what I said wasn't important.

"For now, I want you both to coordinate your efforts."

His abrupt statement left no room for questioning, and I saw no point, at that particular time, in commenting further about my feelings on the case.

Eder started again. "How long is this case going to take you?"

I gave him a perplexed look, and he asked me again.

"Don't you have any idea how long it will take you?"

The question was a ludicrous one, inasmuch as I had just started my investigation and really had no idea where it would lead me.

To my recollection, it was the first time I had ever been asked that type of question in the early stages of an investigation. Anybody would — or should — realize there was no possible way of knowing the duration of any case while it was still in the developing stage. I answered him accordingly, adding, "It's growing all the time."

Either he didn't hear me, which I found hard to believe, or he ignored what I said, because his response was not consistent with my remarks.

"Let's wrap up your case as soon as possible."

What, initially began only with my questioning Juliano's abilities as a supervisor, now was developing into something much more. I was beginning to get an uneasy feeling about the Department's reaction to the case, and to my superiors' conduct toward it — and me.

I reiterated what I had said concerning the growth of my case but added, "I'll try."

To that final comment from me, Ross interjected that I should be prepared to give Knowles a briefing on my case.

"I'll be glad to, any time," I said.

Juliano, who had been sitting quietly most of the time, apparently felt compelled to say something, "I've already told Nick to prepare a chart on his case."

Ignoring his self-serving statement, I directed my answer to Ross, "I'll have one whenever you're ready for Knowles."

We left and returned to the Arlington office.

Later that afternoon, I received a call from Walker asking me if I was interested in receiving additional information that he had uncovered in his investigative reporting and no longer needed. I indicated that I was. We set a Monday morning appointment to meet in his office in the D.C. Superior Court building. I wrote a short memo for the record and gave it to Juliano. He had no noteworthy comments to make, although he did close the door to his room after I left his office. I knew he was on his private line because I could hear a muffled conversation from within, and I was fully aware that he was alone. I also noticed that none of our other lines were lit. However, my speculation as to whom he was speaking, and what about, was mere conjecture as I left for the day.

His habit of using his private line, with his door shut, would increase with frequency and duration as my cases progressed.

Monday, May 7, exactly one week after I officially was given the jurisdictional green light to proceed on the CETA investigations by Assistant U.S. Attorney Jim Owens, I was scheduled to brief him on the events of the previous week. As I was getting ready to leave the office, Juliano advised me that he would accompany me. I shouldn't really have been surprised that I was being *baby-sat* but, nevertheless, I was. It just wasn't normal operating procedure for a supervisor to accompany an agent to the U.S. Attorney's Office on a routine briefing. However, after the recent actions of my superiors, nothing really surprised me.

The meeting with Owens was early because of the later morning meeting with Walker. Because he had previously requested it of me, Juliano knew my itinerary. As we were ushered into Owens' office and I completed my intro of Juliano to him, I immediately launched into the recital of my investigation of the prior week. It was, as I described it to Owens, "mushrooming." I mentioned the names of the officials who were allegedly involved in sexual coercion of CETA females, and also other information that I had uncovered which, if proven, would involve them in other, more serious, violations of the U.S. Code. I further pointed out that I had run across certain stumbling blocks imposed by reluctant District of Columbia officials to release information pertinent to the investigation. Owens replied that he would see to it that the information I requested would be provided. Juliano, throughout my briefing, remained quiet and unobtrusive. However, at a lull in the conversation, he queried Owens as to the propriety of my meeting with a *Washington Star* reporter since, as he put it, "The Department of Labor was concerned about it."

I interrupted Juliano, at this point, because I didn't want the information to slip through our fingers. As diplomatically as possible, I suggested to him that if he was "concerned about the meeting," then perhaps he should also be at that same meeting with Walker. I emphasized, as much for Owens' sake as for Juliano's, that Walker's evidence was important to the case and that he was willing to turn it over to me. Juliano, however, was firm in his decision for me not to meet with the reporter and asked Owens if he would call Walker cancelling my appointment that was set for later that morning. Owens looked at me quizzically but agreed to do so. He then placed the call to Walker cancelling our meeting and requested that the newsman bring the evidence and whatever information he had to Owens' office. Walker agreed. After Owens hung up, he voluntarily offered to pass on to me what he received. Juliano agreed to the arrangement and pressed Owens still further. Would he mind when he obtained any future information or evidence that Walker might have to deal with him directly instead of the reporter contacting me personally. Once more, Owens looked at me curiously about my supervisor's behavior, but again he agreed to be the intermediary.

Just prior to our departure, Juliano brought up once again the subject of publicity about the CETA case and stressed, to Owens, that the Department of Labor was "concerned" about such publicity. It was a word that was rapidly being overused and I was tired of hearing it. Apparently Owens' response that the media, in some instances, can be a useful investigative tool did not satisfy Juliano, because after we left, he mentioned it to me as well. I told him I not only agreed with Owens but thought that in our particular case it was making our office and the Department of Labor "look good." He didn't like my answer, nor did he like it when I repeated what I told him previously, that I didn't think there was any way pursuing the case at that time would adversely affect Marjorie Fine Knowles' impending confirmation by the Senate as the Inspector General for DOL.

I returned to Owens' office, unescorted, later in the day to pick up the material Walker dropped off for me. Owens was amused by the earlier incident with Juliano. We commented on it briefly, with appropriate disparaging remarks about his nervousness before we turned to the Walker information.

"Have you read any of it yet?" I asked him.

"I just glanced through it, but it looks like you've got your work cut out for you," he replied.

I took out some of the sheets enclosed in the thick manila envelope and flipped through them — names, places, allegations, copies of letters and related info. It was quite a compilation.

I shook my head at what I saw and wondered how I could possibly "wrap this case up as soon as possible" as Eder had instructed. I hadn't voiced my own unease about the case with Owens, nor the direction I was receiving from Eder, for a couple of reasons. First, I didn't know Owens well enough to talk about my apprehension about my superiors, nor how that information would affect an active investigation. Second, I didn't want to promote the feeling of disharmony and non-professionalism within our agency, although it was becoming uncomfortably obvious after Juliano's visit..

Owens interrupted my musings.

"I want you to keep me posted on this, Nick. It has far-reaching implications into City Government."

From what I had seen, I was aware that what I had begun to explore was just the tip of the iceberg and I told him so.

"Good luck," he said, pumping my hand firmly. "If there's anything you need, let me know."

His confidence and cooperation were inspiring. I thanked him and left. I didn't return to the office because I had some field work to do. Also, based on the new allegations I had, my case had suddenly expanded. I needed time to organize my thoughts and analyze the new scope of the investigation. It was becoming very clear that I was going to need help on the case. I knew Castro hadn't started work on the names given to him, and I made a mental note to contact him first thing the next morning.

Tuesday, May 8, arrived and it, too, proved to be a memorable one in the unusual chain of events that had accompanied my case since it began. My first priority that morning was to alert Castro that his "coordination" started that day with me.

"If it's okay with Arnie, it's okay with me," he said.

I didn't go into detail about what I would need because I wasn't really sure how far I could trust him. We had always gotten along well before, but things seemed to be different with the new "sex case," as Castro constantly referred to it. Previously, he told me he didn't want any part of my case or the two "new" offshoot cases given to him.

"We'll work 'em just the way you want Nick. Don't fight them on my two cases, it's not worth it. You tell me what you want done and I'll do it. I write my reports and you get what you want accomplished. That way everybody's happy."

It was a simplistic approach and all things being equal, it probably would've worked out. However, there were "flies in the ointment" I was unaware of that would further complicate and hinder my investigation.

The next order of business on that Tuesday morning was to see Juliano, brief him on my second meeting with Owens and show him Walker's material. *Surprise* would not be an apt term to label his reaction to the voluminous information. *Unhappy* would probably be closer to describing it. Although he could have read the allegations and documentation as easily as I had on the previous night when I thoroughly digested the contents of the envelope, I nevertheless took the time to point out salient bits of information to him. I expected him to gloss over it or minimize its content. He did neither. He sat quietly watching me.

There were names of high officials in the District Government who had allegedly coerced females for sexual favors. There were places allegedly used as trysts for these sessions. There were even names of some of the women, and also witnesses who were both cooperative and non-cooperative. The allegations didn't just include sexual improprieties with the CETA females, but also indicated fraud in the alleged misuse of CETA funds. In addition, there were copies of letters to and from certain high officials further implicating them in fraudulent practices. Walker had done his job well. When I made an off-handed reference to the state of Walker's art and his efficiency in the compilation of the information, Juliano was not amused.

I returned to my own office to continue my analysis and develop a projected plan for proceeding with the investigation, leaving Juliano to his own devices. His door again closed in a now-familiar routine that would occur whenever there was a new development in my case — or with my own actions. There was the usual muffled voice, undoubtedly talking to someone at National, and of course, none of the regular lines were in use.

Mid-morning it began! I received a call from Jim Owens telling me that Walker had just called him, to advise me to contact a Denise R., an alleged victim and a potential witness against one of the high District of Columbia officials. His message was to do it as soon as possible because outside pressures were making her reluctant to talk. I immediately contacted her at work, identified myself, and asked if she would cooperate in giving me a statement about her specific allegations of sexual coercion. She agreed, and a time was set to meet that evening at her home. I hung up the phone, satisfied that I had my first cooperative witness. Ten minutes later she called me back to verify that I was who I represented myself to be. I assured her that I was and hung up again. Twenty minutes later she called again and said she felt uncomfortable about being interviewed at home. She asked if she could be interviewed in the office. I naturally agreed, and we reset the appointment for late that afternoon. I hung up a third time feeling increasingly uneasy about her nervousness and the extent to which she would now cooperate. A short while later she called once more, our fourth telephone conversation within an hour. This time, however, she phoned to apologize for her prior actions, that of double-checking on me and also of changing her mind about the place of the interview. I tried to calm her down to make sure she would show. She promised she would meet with me but said she had become "paranoid" over her situation after having read the recent newspaper headlines dealing with coercion in D.C. Government. She knew that it was just a matter of time before she would be contacted and interviewed.

Just before noon I walked back into Juliano's room for a second time that morning to inform him of what should have been a routine bit of information, that an alleged victim — a Denise R. — was coming into the office to be interviewed.

Instead of normal acquiescence, as I had expected, he suddenly blew his top, ranting and raving that I had "no right" to bring her into the office without first contacting him and getting his permission.

I looked at him like he was crazy but tried to maintain some semblance of order and balance in response to his totally unexpected outburst. I explained to him, as quietly as I could under the bizarre circumstances, that it was Assistant U.S. Attorney Jim Owens who had contacted me. I also told him that Owens had considered it a good lead because of Walker's prior solid investigative reporting. I even described the woman's extreme nervousness and reticence in being interviewed at all. However, none of what I was saying appeared to sink in. It seemed as if I were talking to some erratic individual who didn't know what the hell was happening around him. In exasperation I also told him that I saw "nothing improper" in my standard procedure of bringing in cooperative witnesses for interviews without getting his permission in advance. I emphasized that I had never seen any investigator being subjected to this type of tight control and that it was hampering my investigation. He looked at me blankly, as if not fully comprehending what I was saying.

"You lack courtesy," was his vehement response.

I was dumfounded by his reply.

"You lack courtesy. You lack courtesy."

It was a shrill repetitive cry that he kept saying over and over again. I couldn't believe what I was hearing.

When I finally managed to question him as to his choice of the term and what it meant to our discussion, he loudly exclaimed in a tone that was filled with annoyance over my apparent inability to grasp what he was saying:

"You lack an understanding of courtesy."

It became painfully obvious from his irrational responses that we were not communicating at all. Charmayne, his secretary, who had long since closed the door to his office in apparent embarrassment, left for lunch. Juliano's behavior instead of subsiding after his emotional outbursts, continued his boisterous tirade toward me. I had never in all the years that I worked for any governmental entity experienced that type of excessive over-reaction from a supervisor. I had to remind him on several occasions to control himself and lower his voice.

Those cautions, however, only inflamed him further and the session degenerated into a personal attack on me.

"You're nothing but a 'hot dog,'" his words were icy and derisive.

"A what?" I asked.

I had heard him clearly but the tone of his voice was insulting, and instead of replying to him immediately, I just stared at him. I wanted to see if he'd be foolish enough to repeat it a second time.

He didn't disappoint me.

"You heard me, a 'hot dog,'" he stressed the words.

He didn't stop, but continued his harangue.

"You've got a reputation as being difficult to control."

I still couldn't believe the situation. Here was a supervisor who was completely out-of-control and saying whatever popped into his head. Although I was tempted to blow my own top in response to Juliano's asinine behavior, I thought about it a moment.

"Where did you get that information from?" I demanded.

He didn't respond, and I pressed him for a direct answer. "From

Stu Eder?"

"It's none of your business, I don't have to account to you," was his reply.

From his actions that morning there appeared to be little doubt that not only was my case in jeopardy but I was as well. I could see the handwriting on the wall. There unquestionably was a plan to dump me from the case. I didn't know where that plan came from, but I felt it was higher than Juliano. He was being used but was a willing tool from my observation.

Not to let his antics go unnoticed, I continued in the same vein that he had started. I reminded him that both Castro and I knew of his poor reputation as a supervisor in the New York office. Taken by surprise by that remark, he, too, wanted to know where I had gotten that information from. I then told him of a report written about him and of the numerous complaints about him in New York and at the National Office. In spite of that disclosure he didn't appear to be fazed at all.

In a last ditch effort to keep our personalities out of our confrontation so that I could be allowed to concentrate on my work, I tried a personal low key approach. I told him that prior to his Washington assignment, Castro and I had both decided to help him and make the office "look good." From his expression, I could tell that even that remark had fallen on deaf ears. His only reply was, "I don't need your help."

With the finality of that curt comment there was little else that could be said.

For the next couple of hours, in an attempt as the government expression goes, "to CYA" — *cover your ass* — I wrote three memos. All three were directed to Eder. As the Acting Chief of Investigations he was Juliano's immediate superior and I wanted it on record to him so that he could not, at a future date, disclaim any knowledge of events that had transpired within the past two days.

The first memo, subject matter:

GEORGE HARROD INVESTIGATION

CASE #01-9-0012-9-01 reiterated all of the occurrences of the previous day — our meeting with Owens, the entire conversations between Juliano and Owens, between Juliano and myself, the cancellation of my appointment with Walker, the reasons for it, and then the subsequent actions that ultimately involved Owens again as an intermediary. In addition, and probably the most important bit of information that I included, was the notation that I had constantly been reminded of Knowles' "concern" over the publicity given my "sex case" at a time that she was due for Senate confirmation. I not only wanted Eder *on notice* but, knowing that he would report to her directly, I wanted her *on notice*, as well, in the event that my case would not be pursued for some perceived political ramification. I knew it was a dangerous game I was playing — that of bringing her name out into the open — and the stakes were my head. However, from the rapid chain of events that had occurred, ever since I opened the case, there was little doubt in my mind that my assumptions were correct. Somebody was trying to bury my case — if not me. I felt my only means of survival was extensive documentation to use whenever it might become necessary or appropriate to do so.

My second memo was also sent to Eder. It dealt with everything that had occurred that day from the moment I was contacted by the U.S. Attorney's Office to telephone a nervous witness to the bizarre episode that had just transpired in the meeting with Juliano. It even named the alleged sexual *coercion* defendant, a term I always preferred to use in lieu of the more innocuous sexual *harassment* phrase. The individual identified by the alleged victim was at present the Chairman of the District of Columbia City Council.

My third, and final one, was a brief and hard-hitting MEMORANDUM FOR THE RECORD, addressed to Eder. It was simply and appropriately titled:

UNDUE INTERFERENCE WITH OFFICIAL INVESTIGATION

The memo read in full:
"Arnold M. Juliano, Supervising Special Agent for the Washington Field Office of the Inspector General's Office is unnecessarily interfering with my official investigation of the George Harrod Case, thereby, impeding the performance of my duties and the expeditious resolution of the case.

"His timidity in "moving" without first consulting the National Office on every issue, no matter how inconsequential, his total paranoia about a case of this magnitude, his reluctance and delay in making any "on the spot" decisions without first checking with his supervisors in the National Office, his inability to adapt to the spontaneity of Field investigations and his total lack of control in dealing with subordinates all contribute to bogging down the investigation and unless he is prevented from further unnecessary unreasonable interference, the final outcome of its success will be in danger.

"His short-lived reputation as a Field Supervisor in the New York Fraud Office has preceded him and his inability to cope with stress, frustration and his employees are common knowledge throughout the Inspector General's Office, especially at the National Office level.

"For the good of the office and for the good of the Department his picayunish antics should be stopped so that I can continue my investigation in accordance with the wishes and direction of the U.S. Attorney's Office."

Although my memos, especially the last one, were strategically devised to single out Juliano as my antagonist, my purpose went far deeper. It was to alert Eder and his superiors to my lack of hesitation at officially complaining to the U.S. Attorney's Office about any attempts to sandbag my investigation of the District Government. Even though I felt Juliano was being used by those superiors to stop me from conducting an unfettered, meaningful investigation, I had no sympathy toward him as an individual because of his abnormal actions toward me. In addition to his personal proclivities, he was perverting his position of authority and compromising his integrity.

I never received a response to these memos, nor an acknowledgement that they were received. As the months wore on, the policy of refusing to respond to my memos and the ignoring of specific allegations raised therein, was the tone set by the new Inspector General and by the staff within her "Immediate Office," as it came to be known.

Even my threat of U.S. Attorney involvement was neutralized — at first subtlety, and then dramatically.

It was late in the afternoon of May 8 when Miss "R," my reluctant witness, arrived. She was a slender, well-groomed, exotic-looking black female who still exhibited traces of nervousness. I called Castro into my office, introduced him and briefly informed her of the reason for our investigation into D.C. Government. She agreed to cooperate voluntarily and had no objection to the use of a tape recorder. The name and position of the official was well known to us both, but not in the context of previous allegations against him. She proceeded to give us a long narrative discourse, which was allowed primarily to relax her. When it became obvious that it was becoming overly long, questions were interspersed to bring her on target. She then told of his persistent unsuccessful attempts to interview her at her apartment before her employment.

Before and after being hired as a CETA employee, she described various episodes. The first noteworthy event occurred before she was employed, when the official made a written request for her services, stating that she had qualifications she did not possess. Her other accounts mentioned various forms of sexual harassment she was constantly subjected to by the official. After several months of successfully warding off his advances, she claimed his ardor toward her began to cool and she was asked to resign.

Her statement was credible. In addition, she offered the names of witnesses and other alleged victims, who not only experienced sexual harassment but who allegedly succumbed to coercive methods. She was thanked for her cooperation and advised that she would be recontacted if there were any further questions. Also, because it was on tape, she was told that it would have to be reduced to hard copy and from that a sworn statement extracted for her signature. She understood and agreed to sign the statement. I looked over at Castro to inquire if there was anything he wanted to add. His eyebrows raised in a typical gesture I had grown to understand meant a multitude of things to him — wonderment, concern, a problem area.

"Nothing else," he said. "We'll be in touch with you."

She thanked us and left. It was after 6 p.m. Charmayne, the secretary had gone, as had the other agent, Peter Ives, and even

Juliano. I cautioned Castro not to discuss the contents of the interview until we had time to analyze it. He said he wouldn't, and we locked up for the night.

The next day the atmosphere in the office was strained, especially whenever Juliano came in sight. However, he didn't mention the incident of the prior day, and I didn't either. I did request, of him, that I be allowed to use Peter Ives to assist me in interviews of several females I had lined up because I learned that Castro was still involved with some other work. I half expected another argument but surprisingly, there was none.

I walked into Ives' office.

"Okay Clark Kent, you're up for today."

A younger agent, he was the spitting image of the mild-mannered reporter who kept sneaking into phone booths only to jump out wearing a tight blue suit with an "S" emblazoned on his chest. He liked the comparison and even wore the brim of his hat turned up to further heighten the effect. After the first Superman movie came out, he was continually being stopped and greeted with the same remark that I had made.

"You mean I gotta work that sex case with you," he said feigning disappointment.

"Don't be so unhappy, it's only temporary. Pete is finishing up another case he's on."

In an office our size we had the unusual, if not confusing, distinction of having two "Petes" out of the three agents assigned there. Ives, however, used the more formalized name of "Peter," while Castro answered to "Pete."

As we left the office I briefly went over my immediate plan of operations and stressed the need for his assistance. I further explained that the D.C. Department of Labor had agreed to ostensibly help us by making available their office space so that we could interview specifically identified female employees. Other employees had complained about them receiving "special favors" because of their alleged "cooperation" with certain officials within that department. Their new Acting Director, Matthew Shannon, stated to me in an interview that he was eager to lift the taint of impropriety or favoritism from their city agency, which recently had been subjected to adverse publicity in the media. I hesitantly accepted the use of one of their vacant offices for interviews. Although I would have preferred to have seen them away from the intimidating influence of their own management staff, I nevertheless decided in favor of the idea because of the convenience and practicality of the situation. All of the females worked in that particular District building in downtown Washington, while our office was located across the river in Arlington, Virginia.

During the next few days we interviewed approximately eight to ten females, the majority of whom were, or had been, CETA hires at one time or another. Virtually all denied anything improper in their conduct or in the manner in which they had received promotions and extra overtime pay. They also denied being sexually coerced by anybody, especially the officials against whom allegations had been made. There was one exception, however. One of the interviewees admitted that another high official in one of the other District agencies had attempted to take her out socially. He made it clear, she said, that a refusal to accept his invitation would cause him to blackball her for any permanent position within city government. Although her statement was on tape, she made it equally clear that she would not file any type of complaint against the individual. Her refusal to do so, although disappointing, was predictable in light of the publicity that would inevitably accompany a charge of that nature. However, her information was helpful. It indicated that where there was smoke there was fire.

On May 13, another article appeared in *The Washington Star.* This piece, by Michael Kiernan and staff writer, Laura Murray, dealt with another aspect of the sexual problems. The story, titled "D.C. Labor Chief Suspects Sex Used For Advancement," dwelt on the observations and experiences of the Acting Director of D.C. Labor, the director I interviewed several days before. Matthew Shannon, that director, was quoted as saying that the problem within the D.C. Department of Labor was not the much-heralded cry of *sexual harassment* but rather that of *sexual favoritism.*

Whether that statement was his personal opinion or the official party line to throw us off the scent was not discernible at that time.

Shannon was quoted as saying that "some of these women were unqualified for their jobs, receiving salaries beyond their skills." He added that some had received "preferential treatment based on sexual favors and other non-objective criteria." Although he acknowledged that the practice "probably was pervasive" in the department's previous administration, an administration that changed in the mayoral election of 1978, the article noted that this unique practice was contra to other city agencies where women had lodged complaints against their superiors for sexual harassment. According to Shannon, Mayor Marion Barry, Jr. was "already on record" as saying that he would neither tolerate sexual harassment nor favoritism in the city government.

It was a statement that was as far removed from the truth, as were the denials of sexual harassment, sexual coercion, or even the allegations of sexual favoritism in city government.

The newspaper coverage of this element of the story called attention to the fact that many of these young female employees had apparently gained higher graded positions, GS-12s, 13s and 14s "with inequitable speed." The names given these women, who occupied "the penthouse," the upper two floors of the department's Employment Security Building, were: the "dancing girls," the "harem," the "sunshine girls," and the "dancing dolls."

After reading the *Star's* account of a slightly different version of sexual conduct in that particular agency, I decided to amend my questioning accordingly.

The next day I was back in D.C. Labor with Ives, interviewing the females alluded to in an effort to gain additional information on my case. The interviews stretched out for a couple of days. Their response, however, differed little from those of the prior week. Those interviewed did confirm a component undeniably common to all, that of youth and beauty.

In the midst of one of my final interviews for the week, I was interrupted by Shannon and his Acting Deputy Director, Mattie Taylor, to meet a well-dressed individual who stood outside the office I was using. The introduction was hurried and brief with no title used, and it took me a moment to realize that I was talking to the Mayor. There was little, if any, small talk that passed and once the formal amenities of exchange of names and handshake occurred, the Mayor came right to the point.

"When do I get to see your report?" he asked.

I was taken by surprise, not only by the directness of the question but by the fact that it was asked at all. I explained to His Honor in as diplomatic a manner as I could, that inasmuch as a criminal investigation was being conducted, it was not policy to issue reports to the entities being investigated. Apparently my response elicited as much of a surprise to him as his question did to me, because his air of confidence seemed momentarily shaken and his brief queries to me, lacked his initial directness. I explained further, that only my immediate superiors within the Inspector General's Office and the Secretary of Labor would be entitled to see my completed report. It was obvious that he didn't like my reply nor my non-acquiescence to his request, and his final remark to me was to the effect that he would take the matter up beyond my authority. I conceded that he could, and our very brief meeting terminated.

Once back in the room with Ives, I noticed a forced smile on his face. Undoubtedly, he had seen the Mayor when I opened the door and stepped into the hallway. The female who was being interviewed, also, must have seen him because she suddenly had nothing else to say.

I decided that it served no future purpose to continue my interviews, and I wrapped-up the session quickly.

En route, I told Ives about the meeting with the Mayor and our conversation — his request, and my denial.

"You like to live dangerously, don't you?" he asked in mock seriousness.

"Sure do, Peter," I answered in the same tone.

However, the more I thought about it on the drive back to the office, the more I began to realize the investigation, because of its ever-increasing implications and complications, was rapidly becoming a nightmare.

Juliano was briefed on my unexpected episode with the Mayor after I had written him a memo detailing the discussion between us. His over-reaction to the mere mention of the Mayor's name was expected, although I repeated exactly what had occurred — neither adding nor deleting anything. I could tell that in his eyes the case had grown to vast new proportions because of the Mayor's emergence on the scene. I couldn't predict the effect it would have on the National Office, but I soon learned. Based on all that had befallen me in the two short weeks since I had opened the case, I could only surmise the frenzied activity that would occur from that point onward.

The next day I received a strange call from Barron, who was

still assigned to the National Office. His voice was hushed and his tone was not as animated as it usually was whenever we spoke:

"Cam, what's up?"

"Just thought I'd let you know, buddy, that there's some funny stuff going on here that just doesn't quite look right," he said, his voice lowering as he spoke.

I asked what he meant.

"I know the trouble you've been having with Eder, and I know what's going on in your case."

It was true. Cam knew exactly what had been happening with me since we started together, and I periodically brought him up-to-date whenever we ran across each other.

"Well," he went on, "Eder has been up here a lot seeing Art Braver and whenever he does, he shuts the door while they're talking."

I still didn't see what he was driving at.

"What does that mean to me?" I asked.

"I've got a feeling that they're talking about you or they wouldn't shut the door when they know I can hear. Besides, in case you don't know," and he stopped momentarily to lower his voice still further before he spoke again, "Art is head of our new Internal Affairs Unit."

... *7* ...

The significance of May 18 was reflected coincidentally in various ways. The most obvious one, of course, was the fact that Marjorie Fine Knowles, our new Inspector General, began her duties on the same date that some type of investigation was being prepared against me. It also was the date of another major potential DOL problem, one that would involve the audit division and would be an additional source of embarrassment to the Department of Labor.

A two-page memorandum written to Knowles from Gerald W. Peterson, the Acting Chief of the Audit Division, stated that, "We are in the process of developing a guide to be used in examining CETA sponsor operations for fraud and/or fraudulent conducive situations."

The memo then went on to say that this "guide" would "encompass the original FAPS concept of internal control review."

The "FAPS" designation referred to was a Fraud, Abuse, and Prevention Survey developed by Peterson and his audit division.

The memo then proposed to initiate a test of a Washington, D.C., CETA subgrant "the first part of June."

That laudatory proposal would, however, in the near future cause Peterson to receive some flak because it would involve City Hall and the Mayor. When I learned that Peterson had received such undeserved heat over a worthwhile in-depth probe to discover fraudulent conditions in the city, it caused me to question the new I.G.'s motives — and delve even further in my investigations.

Juliano, apparently not being aware of a new can of worms that

I was ready to open, proceeded with his harassment of my cases —
only more subtly.

On May 24, I received a short memo from him requesting status reports on the four cases I now had. He also wanted my "estimated work in hours necessary in the next 30 days."

His concern was no doubt triggered by another disturbing front
page headline that appeared on the previous day's edition of *The
Washington Star:*

PROBE OF SEXUAL COERCION
IN D.C. GOVERNMENT EXTENDED TO CITY COUNCIL

The lengthy newspaper article by reporters, Walker and Kiernan
opened their investigative piece with:

> "A U.S. Labor Department investigation into
> charges that some District officials used a federal
> jobs program to extort sexual favors from young
> women has been expanded to include allegations
> against members of the D.C. City Council."

While I was reading the first paragraph of the story on the day
before, I could visualize Juliano's reaction to the news about *City
Council members.* However, not being in the office, when the paper's
"Home Final" hit the streets, I fortunately was spared his histri-
onics. It was the balance of the article that I was sure not only agitated him, but shook up the people in the National Office, as well.

> "Since uncovering the evidence, federal inves-
> tigators have taken statements from several former
> and present council employees, including some who
> were hired under the federally funded Compre-
> hensive Employment Training Act."

The article then brought out specific events that Walker, himself, had uncovered. Although the information had been passed
on to me via Owens, I was sure it caused Juliano, and those above,
to be apoplectic.

"In addition to charges of sexual coercion of female CETA workers, the Labor Department strike force is also investigating whether the councilmen made false statements on governmental forms requesting CETA positions for the women."

The rest of the story gave a fascinating account of how the practice of hiring was conducted within the city council:

"One woman, formerly a CETA employee for a councilman still in office, gave a statement to federal investigators after being interviewed by The Star.

"The woman said she was referred to the councilman after seeking a job with a special interest group, headquartered in downtown Washington.

"An official of the organization interviewed the woman and told her the group's budget wouldn't permit any new hires, she told *The Star.* 'Let me keep your resume,' she quoted the man as saying. 'I have friends all over town.'

"The next Friday, the woman said, the man called to ask whether she would be interested in working for 'a relative of mine on the city council.'

"Even though I lived in his ward, I'd never heard of him, but I said, 'of course.' Ten minutes after he hung up (the councilman) called and said he had heard about my great qualifications, said the woman, then an attractive 24 year-old with a high school diploma. He asked if he could come over to my apartment to talk about the job.

"I asked him if there was some reason we couldn't talk in his office, she said. He told me that after hearing about my great qualifications that he wanted to come over to talk about the job before anybody else snatched me up.

" 'I still thought that was a little odd so I said I was on the way out, but that he could come by the next afternoon,' she said. The more I thought about it, the stranger it seemed. So when the time neared for him to arrive, I got dressed like I was going somewhere and went down to the lobby.

"When he arrived I said an emergency had come up. I gave him a copy of my resume and asked him to call me Monday so I could come into his office for an interview. Then I rushed out of the building leaving him standing there.

"During the interview, the woman said she voiced doubts about her qualifications to become the councilman's administrative assistant. But he kept insisting I was perfect for the job. He asked what my sign was and whether I had a boyfriend, and whether I lived alone.

"The woman said after the councilman persuaded her to take the job, he then prepared CETA documents stating she had worked for 12 months as a staff volunteer. Included in the documents, the woman said, 'were qualifications I didn't have and had told (the councilman) I didn't have.'

"Among the duties the councilman listed on the documents which were obtained by *The Star*, was 'legwork for the committee.'

"Shortly after starting the job, the woman said '(the councilman) started making passes at me.'

" 'The first time,' the woman said, 'he asked me when I was going to invite him up to my apartment to see my PlayPen sofa.' Then he winked. He made several suggestions like that after the first time. I always played them off.

"It was by then that I learned the women in (the councilman's) office all had reputations in the District Building as 'sex-retaries,' she said.

"Then one day, at around 5 p.m., he buzzed my phone and asked if I needed a ride home, she said. I did and agreed to accept the offer.

"During the trip, the woman said (the councilman) asked if he could come up to my apartment so he could unwind. 'You know what I mean,' the woman quoted the man as saying. 'No, I don't know. Why don't you tell me,' she said she responded.

" 'Well,' the woman said the man told her, 'all work and no play makes (me) a dull council member.'

"I put him off again and he didn't say anything the rest of the trip, she said. That was when the relationship turned sour, she said. He began piling work on me that I told him from the start I didn't know how to do ..."

The article then stated that:

"Shortly thereafter, the woman contacted two local reporters, both of whom urged her to quit her job. Both reporters recently confirmed they were contacted by the woman."

The story noted that the city councilman asked the woman to resign a few days later.

The young female described in the headline-grabbing edition sounded exactly like the very nervous woman I interviewed several days before.

There was an immediate reaction to that bomb-shell article. The newspaper story appeared on a Wednesday morning and Juliano's brief memo to me came first thing Thursday morning, the balance of the week was unusually quiet in the office — at least on Juliano's part.

An editorial in the Sunday paper on May 27, titled SEXUAL COERCION IN CITY GOVERNMENT should have brought out an immediate tirade from Juliano on that Monday morning, especially when it stated, "Federal investigators, according to *The Star's* Kenneth Walker and Michael Kiernan, have been compiling a record of pervasive sexual coercion in some areas of the city government."

An even more sweeping and damaging statement followed.

"The federal inquiry has extended into the District's executive and legislative branches, and includes allegations against a former and two sitting members of the City Council."

I was even more sure that its specific content would elicit a heated response from Juliano.

However, *nothing* was said. In fact, the remainder of the entire week was to be even more strangely quiet, especially in light of the mounting publicity given not only the sexual coercion allegations, but more importantly, the constant references to "federal investigators."

Even Castro, who never wanted to have any part of the "sex investigations," was quick to comment on the lack of apparent interest on Juliano's part.

"Maybe," he said with a half smile trying to convince both of us, "he's gotten used to the idea."

I looked back at Castro, without a smile, and then shook my head slowly.

"I doubt it, Pete."

I knew, especially after Barron's call, that something was going on behind my back at the National Office.

I also felt that our supervisor was just a puppet in our office, dancing to Eder's tune.

Because I was still unsure exactly what was happening in the cases I shared with Castro, I sent Juliano a memo on Monday, April 4. The subject matter was:

"Clarification of Workload on Case Numbers: 01-9-0012-9-01, 01-9-0018-01 & 01-9-0018-02."

The first case number was the George Harrod case, that was assigned to me shortly after I contacted Assistant U.S. Attorney Jim Owens.

The other two cases were those that Juliano had assigned directly to Castro on the basis of an informant's call from the D.C. Department of Labor. It was one of the departments I had visited in early May. Initially Juliano emphatically stated that neither of the two individuals named were involved in sexual coercion, however, subsequent inspection of the cases showed they were indeed.

In my memo to him, I reiterated my concerns about the duplication of work done by both Castro and myself. I also mentioned that Agent Ives, a GS-9, was "pulled off" my cases involving the interviewing of females, and in his place Agent Castro, a GS-12, was substituted.

I questioned his procedure when I pointed out that, "Inasmuch as the majority of my interviews are being conducted in the U.S. Attorney's Office, and inasmuch as all of these sessions are taped, it is my suggestion that it is unnecessary and wasteful of investigative man-hours to utilize the services of two GS-12 investigators for these interviews."

I requested a written reply. But none was forthcoming.

On that same day I was instructed to submit status reports and total time on my four active cases. Undoubtedly, that demand fell on the heels of my impertinent request of workload clarification.

In response to that direction, I submitted a capsulized report of those cases, to him:

> "Case No. 01-9-0012-9-01, the Harrod case that I wrote about in my previous memo, was again summarized. In addition, I reported that I had located and interviewed another "victim" of the D.C. Personnel Director.
>
> "Case No. 01-9-0012-9-02, the second case that I had opened, dealt with the Chairman of the D.C. City Council and repeated the allegations of sexual harassment against him. It also noted that not only was I interviewing additional females in that same regard, but that I opened up another avenue of investigation. I stated that "evidence had been uncovered" indicating that he had "name requested" certain females and had falsified their background.
>
> "Case No. 01-9-0012-9-03 concerned the former Secretary of the D.C. City Council, who via letters to the D.C. Department of Labor had also "name requested" specific females. I further wrote that he, too, had falsified their experience. In my closing comment on the case I noted that I was pursuing his alleged conspiratorial role with the subject of case No. 4.
>
> "My last open case, No. 01-9-0012-9-04, involved a Director of Operations who had allegedly conspired with the former Secretary in Case No.

3 to hire ineligible CETA participants. To expand on this final case, I also reported that the Director had allegedly refused to refund a CETA contract on a local bail bond company because the female Deputy Director had refused to submit to him sexually.

In closing out my fairly detailed memo, I added a comment that I was sure neither he nor Eder wanted to hear:

"The estimated work for the next 30 days is difficult to estimate as the cases are expanding to encompass new witnesses and subjects."

However, because I was pressed by Juliano to be specific as to total time anticipated — an admonishment I thought was unrealistic — I nevertheless complied.

"The number of hours expended by myself would be from 40-50 hours per week for the next month at least. Undoubtedly, the work undertaken by Agent Castro would be the same. Should Agent Ives be involved on a lesser scale to assist both Castro and myself, it is conservative to state that at least 20 hours of his time per week for the next month could be expended on this workload."

For the moment, the three of us, Castro, Ives, and myself, were on the same wavelength. Although Castro was always reluctant to work the cases assigned to him, he nevertheless did so without any prolonged complaining. Ives, the young and eager agent was always compliant throughout all of the work involved.

The three of us not only collaborated on a short memorandum to Juliano on the morning of June 5, but the memo specifically noted that it was from the three of us. That suggestion came from Castro. It discussed our joint concern over amendments to instructions for coding the case tracking forms that Castro had accidentally discovered in the filing cabinet.

It stated in part:

"We will be unable to correctly and in a timely manner complete said forms without such instructions being communicated to us.

Please ensure that subsequent memorandums and other pertinent materials are distributed to the Special Agents. Only in this manner can we do the conscientious job you expect of us and we expect of ourselves."

That jokingly constructed and happily executed memo was to be the last cooperative effort among the three of us.

It also was the last time Castro and I would ever be on friendly terms again.

During the afternoon of that same day, I had been going over the numerous interviews I had previously taped in the U.S. Attorney's Office. In one of them, the name of the Mayor popped up as being possibly involved in the sexual coercion of a specific CETA female. I backed up the tape and replayed it to make sure I had heard correctly. As I was doing so, Castro, who was nearby, stopped in to hear the remarks. His eyes widened as he heard the familiar name again.

"Damn, Nick," he exclaimed. "Did you hear that?"

"Yeah, Pete," I agreed loudly, "but I don't think it refers to the present."

I was stalling. I knew it didn't make any difference whether the allegations were past or present, assuming they were valid, and of course, providing they fell within the Statute of Limitations.

"I think these allegations refer back to when the Mayor was still a City Councilman," I told him. "Besides, I've got to check further before I even think of putting him down as a suspect."

Castro was looking at me intently as I said it.

"Not the Mayor?" he questioned, as his voice rose.

I looked back up at him casually, "Why not, if he's guilty, he's guilty."

Castro shook his head, "He's the Mayor, man."

"So what," I said. "Mayors come and go. *If* he's guilty," and I stressed the *if*, "then he's no different than anybody else."

"Yeah, but ..." and his voice trailed off.

"It's my case, Pete, and I'll work it the same as I do the others."

Castro was still holding his ground, not quite believing I would proceed with *business as usual* if the Mayor were involved.

"We've got a directive here somewhere," he said as he rushed into his office.

When he returned, he flipped through paperwork we had recently received from the National Office.

"It says here that we're supposed to notify the National Office with incidents like this."

I was getting tired of being pressed by him.

"I don't know *anything* for sure yet, Pete," I said, exasperated. "I told you, I've gotta check it out first."

"It's your neck, man," he said in a low voice as he shuffled back to his own room.

Ives was out of the office and Charmayne, who had just returned from lunch, advised me that Juliano would be in the National Office the rest of the day.

"Good," I replied enthusiastically to her wide smile.

"I'm gonna grab a quick bite somewhere, and I'll be back," I said as I headed out the door.

"Castro's still here," I yelled back.

She nodded and waved me off.

When I returned I asked her if there were any messages and she shook her head.

"Castro's out of the office," she said, and returned to her typing.

I walked back into my own room to resume listening to my tapes. I saw a handwritten memo in large scrawl in the center of my desk. I picked it up. It had my name scribbled at the top with Pete's name scratched almost illegibly across the bottom. *What the hell is this?* I said to myself.

The verbatim note read:

"In view of the directive #11, which I gave you, I thought it best to advise Stu and Arnie of Mayor Barry's implication in the sex case. I told Arnie you had it on tape but that in view of the delays in typing we thought we should make them aware." I read it again.

"What is this bullshit?" I said through my teeth.

Charmayne heard me and called back to me.

"You okay?"

"When's Castro due back?" I wanted to know.

"Soon," she answered.

Not soon enough, I said to myself.

I read the note again, not understanding why the hell he had called them behind my back.

While I was still mulling the situation over and gritting my teeth even more, Castro came back into the office.

He had no sooner entered his own room when I strode in and held his handwritten memo up in front of him.

"What the fuck is this?" I demanded to know.

He looked flustered.

"It's the directive," he said nervously. "We have to do it."

"What the fuck do you mean we have to do it," I roared. "Since when do you speak for me? It's my case and my decision when to go forward," I reminded him. "They're only allegations, and I need more evidence. When I had more proof, I was going to tell National. I'm the lead agent, not you," I stressed.

He stood there with his mouth open.

"Don't you see ..." he said feebly, trying to defend his actions. "He's the Mayor, and we got the directive to tell National."

"Bullshit," I said, cutting him off. "You said it was *my* neck, so why the hell are you getting involved?"

"Yeah, but ..." he started to repeat himself.

I was getting tired of listening to the same excuses.

"You're nothin' but a fuckin' Judas trying to get on their good side, and for what?"

I glared at him waiting for an answer, but there was none. I abruptly turned on my heel, walked out of his office and into my own.

The next morning as I reported to work as usual, I saw the reason for the abnormal quiet in the office of the past week and for Juliano's prolonged absence on the 5th.

Lying in the middle of my desk, again, was a more conspicuous piece of mail. It was a large official manila envelope with the Office of Inspector General imprinted in the corner.

What do we have this time? I asked myself.

I opened it quickly and removed several sheets of a typed letter addressed to me and dated the prior day. I flipped through the sheaf — five pages — and started to read. The opening sentence caught me completely by surprise:

"This is to notify you that, in order to promote the efficiency of the service, I propose to suspend you from duty and pay for three (3) days from your position of Criminal Investigator GS-1811-12 in the Office of the Inspector General for the following reasons and specifications:"

Before I read any further, I threw the letter down on my desk and was set to confront Juliano, but I stopped myself.

That son of a bitch, I said in a low tone. *That little son of a bitch.*

I picked the five-page letter up again and started reading where I had left off.

"Reason #1," under his proposal to suspend me, listed a single "Specification." Reason #2, cited four Specifications. Then, Reason #3, listed two more Specifications.

Under Reason #1, he had "Misuse of Office Personnel and Equipment."

What the fuck is this?

Under his Specification, he stated that he, "observed the Office Secretary, Charmayne Parks, typing a legal deposition for you in connection with a lawsuit in which you are a party as a private individual and which is being heard in the United States District Court of Alaska. The lawsuit is not related to your work with the Department of Labor.

The Secretary spent the entire afternoon (approximately four (4) hours) doing this personal work for you."

That lousy son of a bitch, was all I could think of.

Charmayne in an extensive affidavit that she would give in May 1981 not only refuted his charge, but noted that he was "a very high strung individual."

In my own retort to his proposed letter of adverse action, I would send Eder a detailed answer on June 22. Eder, according to the Juliano letter was the proper person to reply to "regarding the reasons and specifications contained herein."

So much for the confirmation of collusion between Juliano and Eder, I thought.

In my official written reply to his Reason #1 and his Specification #1, I stated:

> "*RESPONSE:* I requested the secretary, Charmayne Parks, to do personal typing for me during her lunch period and not during business hours. She agreed. She told me later that Mr. Juliano had told her that she had worked all afternoon on it. She told him that she had not and that he appeared to agree with her. She further related to me that she had frequently worked through her lunch hour on our heavy typing and deliberately did so for the next three days to more than compensate for the 1 1/2

to 2 hours that she did the typing for me (which she stated also included numerous interruptions)."

After that particular RESPONSE, I also added an additional pertinent comment:

"Note: It was observed that during the early days of Mrs. Knowles' visits as Acting Inspector General, several of the head office staff had their 171's typed by office secretaries on government time. I also personally observed Stuart Eder's being typed. It is further noted that this practice is prohibited in all other Federal agencies."

His Reason #2, "Failure to obey instructions from your supervisor," was even more outlandish.

It gave five detailed Specifications, with numerous dates beginning from May 7, 1979, to May 29, 1979, alleging that I had repeatedly "failed" to do as I was constantly reminded by him to do.

It was again obvious that his *documentation* to build a case against me began immediately after my meeting with Eder and Ross. It was at that Friday meeting on May 4, that Eder instructed me to "wrap up your case as soon as possible."

What appeared to be even more of a causal relationship between his letter and certain events were the dates themselves. In his letter, he cited the specific date of May 7, as the *beginning* of my "failure" to obey my supervisor. It was that same date that Juliano had attended a meeting with Jim Owens and myself. It was also at that session that Juliano reminded Owens that the "Department of Labor was concerned" about my case — especially as it related to my meeting with, and receiving information from, an investigative reporter.

My specific responses to his ludicrous specifications, numbered 1-3, answered each one in detail, and then added various appropriate phrases:

"The successive mentioning of dates is a self-serving statement that is without merit," was my extended reply to a written report that he already had seen but conveniently forgot.

"Mr. Juliano is aware that these sheets are not officially approved by the Department of Labor and are an additional unnecessary time-consuming workload upon the Agent who has already prepared memos to the file, reports of investigation, and reports of interview on the same information."

This comment covered his instructing me "to bring the case history sheet up to date immediately."

My final written remark about his Specification #3 was in the same vein as the first two, since it ostensibly dealt with my not "keeping all material pertinent to investigations in the case files at all times."

Once more, I wrote:

"Mr. Juliano's allegations are again self-serving statements that are best known only to his recollections."

It was, however, his Specification #4, under Reason #2, that I really took exception to as I had to straighten out his absurd accusations as quickly as possible.

In that particular Specification, Juliano in tiresome reference to a "missing" FBI report, alluded to the fact that I was remiss in not having it in the file. To prove his assertion, he referred to eight individual dates, again from May 7 to May 29, in which he had personally checked the files to find "the FBI report."

My reply to what I'll call the "Doris Walters" case is as follows:

> *Specification 4*
> "RESPONSE: Mr. Juliano's ponderous reference to the 'Doris Walters' case is not only largely fabrication on his part, but his repeated reference to it being an 'FBI Report' is a cry wolf attempt to point attention to what would appear to be a blatant compromise by myself of an 'FBI Report' that he is attempting to equate with some breech of National Security. Mr. Juliano is well aware that the Walters 'case' was only a 'monitoring' case. We only received a tissue copy for our file for informational purposes only. Mr. Juliano is further aware that I called the U.S. Attorney who handled the case and was advised that it was an FBI case and that we were to do nothing. Further, Mr. Juliano's continued quotes of my replies to him throughout the regurgitation of the Walters 'case', are figments of his very fertile imagination."

Juliano's third, and final, Reason why I was to be suspended from duty for three days was:

"Non-compliance with OIG Policy Directive Number 2 (Operations) by discussing investigations with the media."

In his Specification #1, he cited the May 2, 1979, article in *The Washington Star* "U.S. Probes CETA Sex Charges in D.C.," and stated that I was responsible for the article.

However, as soon as that event had occurred, I immediately had disclaimed any association with it, knowing the paranoia that Juliano harbored. I reminded him, at that time that I had never met nor spoken to the reporter who did the article. That information was gleaned directly from my investigation at D.C. government offices, a fact that I could hardly hide.

Juliano also made a point of stating that Ross and Eder had cautioned me "on numerous occasions" about making statements to the news media.

In my written answer to Juliano's charges, I again had to set the record straight:

> "*RESPONSE:* My reply noted a May 2, 1979, and May 3, 1979 memo to Mr. Eder which stated that I did not 'leak' any information to the newspaper. Mr. Juliano's recollection of our meeting of April 20, 1979, is again incomplete and taken out of context. Further, in our meeting of May 7, 1979, with Assistant U.S. Attorney Owens, he informed Mr. Juliano that using the press was an investigative tool and he condoned it. Therefore, Mr. Juliano's continued reference to my being cautioned 'on numerous occasions' by Mr. Ross and Mr. Eder is used for the purpose of engendering sympathy for what has already been characterized as a fabrication."

In Juliano's last *Specification* in his final *Reason,* he dredged up an episode while I was still in Florida, which would have been before I was ever reassigned to Washington. In his Reason, he stated that the *Miami Herald* article, "U.S. Probe into CETA is Expanded," was indicative of my talking to the media.

My final disgusted reply appeared in a form that I couldn't resist:

> "*RESPONSE:* This final allegation is consistent with Mr. Juliano's confused, illogical and vindictive state of mind in a last ditch attempt to 'get me.' As Mr. Juliano is aware, the article spoken of in the *Miami Herald* was written in *February* 1979. Mr. Juliano was not my supervisor until *April* 1979. Therefore, this last specification is totally without any merit or relevancy and its conclusion only substantiates my contentions about Mr. Juliano."

I also added a final comment, "It should be further noted that the only way for this information to come to Mr. Juliano's attention was via my supervisor at that time, Stuart Eder."

Between the time that I had read Juliano's letter on June 5 and my upcoming reply via Eder on June 22, much had transpired — too much.

My first inclination upon reading that proposed letter to suspend me was to march into Juliano's office and drag the little bastard screaming across his desk. However, I didn't think it would look too professional, and besides, I didn't want to upset Charmayne. Fortunately, he was out of the office most of the day, and then I had to go into the field as my investigations were still continuing.

Before I left the office that day to head into the District, there was a phone call from Eder with more unexpected news.

"You're being *detailed* to the National Office," he said in his typical low monotone.

After Juliano's letter, nothing really surprised me.

"Do you mind me asking why?" I inquired as evenly as I could under the circumstances.

"Your work is too important to be in the field office," he said.

It was a phony line. I knew it, and he knew it, but I also was aware that there wasn't a thing I could do about it.

When I didn't respond to his transparent comment, he continued.

"You'll report to Paul Lehrman on the 11th. He'll supervise your work."

I grunted an acknowledgement, wondering what was going to happen to my cases.

"Any questions?" he asked in as an authoritarian manner as he could muster.

"Yeah. For how long?" I wanted to know.

"Probably 60 days, maybe longer," was his low response.

Just what I need, I told myself.

Charmayne, who already had heard about the detail, came into my room.

"I'm sorry Nick. We're going to miss you here," she said.

"You and who?" I asked with a slight smile.

"Me and Peter of course," was her reply.

Ives who had just entered the hallway heard his name mentioned.

"Somebody paging me?" he said in his usual upbeat manner.

After Charmayne explained what was happening, he became concerned.

"Hey, man, I'm sorry," he said sincerely. "Is there anything I can do?"

I thanked him, and replied. "It's only temporary."

"Does Pete know?" Ives inquired of Castro.

I didn't answer, as I headed toward the door.

"I've got some work to do in D.C.," I said.

The morning of the 7th, I was back at my desk in Arlington looking over my cases, when Juliano came to my doorway.

"You're being *transferred* to National," he announced almost gleefully.

I looked at the little son of a bitch.

"You mean *detailed* don't you," I corrected him.

He pretended he hadn't heard what I had said and continued speaking from the doorway.

"I want you to clear everything out of your office and turn in your keys to the front door and to your locked file cabinet," he said pompously.

"You want me to do what?" I asked, my voice rising.

He repeated himself.

"For your information," I said firmly, getting up from behind my desk, "Eder said that I was permitted to leave my personal effects in my office."

He acted a little bewildered.

"Further," I added, "he said that I was only to take my case material regarding my City Government investigation to National."

He looked at me again, not quite as assured as he was a few minutes earlier.

"We'll see," he said and walked away with his brisk little steps.

After he left, I wrote up another memo for him covering the subject matter of our brief meeting, so that neither of us would forget what had transpired between us. Also, because I was getting fed up with his nervous little old lady antics, I closed the short memo out with:

"I can unequivocally state that I have never been anywhere in Federal Service where a "detailee" would completely relinquish his office and turn in all keys to that office, especially if that detailee has been granted permission to keep his personal effects in his office. Therefore, I can only attribute your ultimatum to turn in my keys as another example of your continuing petty vindictiveness, an attribute that is unworthy of a supervisor."

I was no doubt getting under his skin with my memo of the 7th, concerning the office keys because he responded with one of his own on the 8th.

He began his memo by reminding me that my "six cases involving sexual harassment of CETA participants by certain D.C. public officials are being transferred effective June 11 to the National Office." He also repeated what I had already known, that I was to be detailed there "for 60 days to work those cases." He then added the obvious, that I was to take to National *all* investigative material pertaining to those cases with me. His memo, however, did not end with the recitation of facts already discussed concerning the detail. He undoubtedly felt compelled to add to the letter comments about my *personal effects:*

"With regard to your personal effects, which you insist on leaving behind hanging on your wall, they consist of two photographs of yourself in police uniform, a police shoulder patch, several advertisements of bargain travel trips, a circus poster of a tiger, a circus sign over the inside entrance of your office reading 'Greatest Show On Earth,' and a cartoon drawing of yourself labeled 'What a Kook.'

It would be absurd for me to allow you to retain office keys on the basis of your leaving the above described personal effects behind.

That is your choice, not mine."

His selective reference to specific personal effects in my office was doubtless done to minimize their importance. In addition, unquestionably, some of these personal items were offensive, or impertinent, to him because of his overly sedate makeup. It was a typically old-ladyish demeanor, and it was one that we all recognized and spoke about. I did not appreciate his comments as it was my personal office to do with as I saw fit so long as it was not in bad taste. The question had never arisen before, nor had there ever been any remarks about how or what should be hung in any of the other agents' rooms. Inasmuch as I had received his memo late in the afternoon on Friday, June 8, I made a point to answer that memo when I was in National on Monday.

... **8** ...

I reported to Paul Lehrman early Monday morning with all the investigative material on my six cases. He was seated, not in some individual room of his own, but in the middle of a crowded, clustered arrangement of desks and file cabinets in a wide-open section on the fifth floor that was devoted to part of the I.G.'s office.

He saw me looking around at the compressed jumble of items squeezed together in some crazy quilt-work pattern of wood and metal objects.

"What is this shit?" I exclaimed, not taking into consideration that I was reporting to a new supervisor, albeit a temporary one.

He took no offense at my first comment on our initial contact and waved his arm about him.

"We'll do our best to make it workable," he said. "We can move some of those partitions around us," and he gestured to some that were propped against the wall.

I nodded silently, but he could still tell that I was not happy about the arrangement.

"Just remember," he said sincerely. "I'm on your side."

He had a low voice and a slower mode of talking when he wanted to emphasize something.

I gave him a forced smile.

"That's good to know," I said, as I shook his hand.

However, to myself I said, I hope so.

I was leery, not only of the abrupt detail to the National Office, but also of Lehrman, himself. Although I had always liked him, and had always gotten along well with him in the past, I was unsure of his new role at headquarters. I didn't know where he stood with the new Inspector General or how close he was to Eder. I, especially, didn't know if it was by design that he was put over me as my supervisor to monitor my movements and to block my investigations. For that matter, I didn't even know how he felt about "sex investigations," or even if he was gun-shy about any type of political investigations.

In time, I was to learn that my concerns were groundless.

At that moment, however, looking around at my cramped surroundings, and getting lip service from a new supervisor, didn't sit well with me.

"Where am I supposed to put all my stuff?" I asked Lehrman, patting the bulky case material that I brought with me.

"This will be your desk," he said, pointing to a large vacant metal desk a few feet from his own, "and we can use this file cabinet," and he said, motioning to a nearby upright one that looked weather-beaten.

"Does it lock?" I asked him.

"There's a long bar that we can use to secure it," he answered.

"Great." I tried to keep the sarcasm out of my voice. As Lehrman saw me unpacking the material and arranging it on my desk methodically, he commented in a low key.

"Whenever you're ready to discuss your cases, just let me know." He turned his attention to some work in front of him.

"Sure."

I then focused my attention on what I had spread out before me. However, every few moments, someone was either passing by our desks or a nearby phone was ringing and being answered loudly by someone in our immediate vicinity.

Lehrman could sense my annoyance with the situation, and finally asked me, "What's up, buddy?"

His voice was reassuring, with a touch of a familiar northern accent, but I was not in a frame of mind to be soothed.

"You don't mind if I drop Eder a memo, do you?" I asked.

He didn't hesitate as he responded. "Just run it by me first, so I can look it over," he answered pleasantly enough.

I knew the hierarchical procedure, and also took no offense at his answer. "Of course," I said matter-of-factly.

The subject matter of the short Eder memorandum was:

"Privacy to Conduct Investigation on Case No. 01-9-0012-9-01, et al."

It was factual and to the point:

> "In view of my 'detail' on June 11, 1979, to work under the supervision of Paul Lehrman, in lieu of my present supervisor, Arnold M. Juliano, I request a certain modicum of security to continue my investigation of subject cases. Since you stated to me in a telephone conversation of June 6, 1979, that the reason for my 'detail' was the extreme sensitivity of subject cases, my request is consistent with your stated purpose.
>
> Such 'privacy is necessary to ensure the confidentiality of incoming and outgoing phone calls, the playing of taped interviews and other related aspects of the case that require a certain amount of secrecy, e.g. the 'spreading out,' of various types of work sheets to facilitate my extensive and voluminous investigation. Therefore, my work area should not be subjected to the constant traffic of the area proposed for my new desk space. As you know, many of the subjects in my investigation are 'highly placed' individuals in City Government and any exposure of my notes, memos and the like will compromise that investigation and the damage done could be irreversible."

Lehrman looked it over, and smiled.

"Tell you what," he said. "If I initial this, it means I approve of your memo," and he thought a moment. "Eder will probably question why I let you write it ..."

I waited for the rest of his analysis.

"If we let this go, as is, without my initials, it might be more effective for you," and he stopped to let the words sink in.

"Yeah," I agreed, "I've got more documentation to back me up, should I ever need it."

He smiled, "You got it," and then he continued, "besides, I can claim ignorance of what you were doing."

His expression changed momentarily to a more serious one as he added, "I don't think it'll fly, buddy."

I didn't particularly like the response, but nevertheless, I was beginning to trust Lehrman.

The balance of the day, I briefed him on my cases and showed him whatever documentation I had gathered.

He took a deep breath, and breathed out noisily.

"No wonder they want you over here," he said softly.

"There's more," I said confidently. "And it keeps building."

Although I had a good feeling about him, I still didn't know how far I could trust him, or what he'd carry to Knowles' "Immediate Office."

"We'll have to keep this locked up most of the time," he observed.

"That's my contention," I said, looking around the open office.

"Those partitions around us will help," he said, "but I'll see what, if anything, else can be done."

I didn't hold out much hope for his apparent optimism, being more aware than he was of the circumstances that preceded my detail there.

The next morning while I was reviewing my own notes, and while Lehrman was going over my cases, I noticed a memo on his desk. It had just been typed up and was addressed to Knowles. It was from him and Gerald Peterson, of the Audit Division with the same subject matter that I had seen a few weeks earlier, "FAPS."

Lehrman saw me looking at it.

"You interested in the prevention survey program, too?" he asked.

"Sort of," I answered. "I read the Peterson memo to Knowles last month. It said that he wanted to hit a D.C. CETA subgrant this month."

Lehrman smiled and nodded his head.

"I see you've been doing your homework well," he replied. "You can read it, if you want. It might help you."

I noticed at the top of the brief memorandum that it originated from a "W. Rhea." I soon learned that it referred to a Wendy Rhea who worked in the Audit Division. Apparently she had prepared it with copies sent to both Lehrman and Peterson for their concurrence, and then it was forwarded to Knowles herself.

The memo stated that a draft had been completed of the revised FAPS guide, and that the approach was somewhat different from the previous one. It went on the say that it "focuses more on detection of fraud and abuse." The following paragraph then noted that:

"We have chosen Youth Pride, Inc., a subgrantee of the District of Columbia ..."

Although I had never heard the designation "Youth Pride" before, it was to become a focal point of my investigation in the near future and would make more headlines.

The balance of the memorandum routinely cited training that would be given the investigators and the auditors, and then gave the numbers of personnel that would be used. It was in the closing of the message that Knowles was to take adamant exception to:

"We will contact Mayor Barry's Office and the D.C. Department of Manpower and brief their representatives about the pending FAPS on 6/29/79."

I never knew how Knowles reacted to the memo. Peterson, was the Acting Chief of the Audit Division, and I was an agent in the Investigations Division. Generally, we would have had no connection in our working relationship, as the chains of command were different. However, as things frequently happen in any investigation, a chance occurrence can suddenly develop out of the blue to make things fall into place.

That is what happened in my growing investigation. It pointed out even further the extent of cover-up by our new Inspector General and confirmed what we had all originally believed about her lack of responsiveness to any political investigation.

One day in late November 1979, I heard an offhand remark by someone who initially was involved in the request for the Youth Pride Audit. They were told that it was permanently *out of bounds* for any audit. Although the scope of my investigative efforts lay in other areas, the manner in which that information was given intrigued me. When I inquired as to what was meant by that comment, the only reply was, "Why don't you ask Jerry Peterson?"

Peterson originated the FAPS audit several months before, but I never heard any more about it. I was too involved with my own work to follow up on the two memos I saw addressed to Knowles early in the summer. However, when I heard Peterson's name again concerning that D.C. audit, it jogged my memory. I also heard that Peterson left DOL some time during the summer, but didn't know the reason why, nor did I pursue it having had no cause to do so.

When I asked where I could find him, I was told he was now the Assistant Inspector General for Audit for the U.S. Department of Agriculture.

With that new lead, I immediately contacted him and set up an early appointment. If he was surprised at my wanting to see him, he didn't indicate it on the phone. When I arrived in his office in downtown Washington he rose to greet me. He was a large man, who by all accounts was good at his job and was well-liked by present, and past subordinates. I also heard he was respected by his new superior at DOA.

"I've been expecting you, sooner or later," was his first remark as we shook hands.

I didn't waste any time in my approach.

"What can you tell me about the Youth Pride audit?" I asked him.

He went into all of the aspects of the request for an audit of Youth Pride at the city and why it was turned down.

I studied him for a minute, digesting all I heard. I can't say I was surprised because nothing concerning politics surprised me any more. Certainly nothing concerning DOL's aversion to conducting *any* meaningful investigation into D.C. government shocked me any longer.

"Would you mind giving me an affidavit to that effect?" I asked him.

"I'll be glad to," he said firmly. "If you'd like, I can even include how it was a waste of time and money when we didn't go forward with it," he added.

"Whatever you think is appropriate to your affidavit," I answered, "just put it in."

While I waited, he wrote out a detailed affidavit that he handed to me to review before he had it typed. I couldn't help smiling to myself as I read the final product again:

"Prior to my present position, I was the Chief

of the Audit Division with the Office of the Inspector General for the U.S. Department of Labor.

"On or about June 15, 1979, in response to a memorandum sent to MARJORIE FINE KNOWLES, the Inspector General, Department of Labor, I was called into her office to discuss the subject of that memo, FAPS (Fraud Abuse and Prevention Survey). In attendance at that meeting, to the best of my recollection were: MRS. KNOWLES, myself, and GUY ZIMMERMAN, the Chief of Program and Resource Planning and Evaluation, Office of the Inspector General, Department of Labor. SHELLY REPP, her Special Assistant, may also have been there.

"One of her first remarks to me were that: 'This is not too smart,' referring to the memorandum of June 11, 1979, to her, from both myself and PAUL LEHRMAN, concerning the proposed FAPS audit of YOUTH PRIDE within the District of Columbia.

"When I questioned her as to what she meant, she replied: 'Don't you know that the MAYOR'S (MARION BARRY) Inauguration Parade, started at PRIDE?'

"When I expressed ignorance to the fact that it did and if so, what possible effect it could have on the MAYOR, she advised me that: 'We're not going to do it!'

"I responded to the effect that we were only going to audit within the last year or two, and that it should have no effect on MAYOR BARRY.

"She then stated that: 'He's still closely related to it. (PRIDE),' and then advised me that we would 'have to come up with something else.'

"I told her that it would be 'a real problem' coming up with another target that met the criteria for the audit but she left no doubt in my mind that it was a closed issue and that YOUTH PRIDE was not to be audited.

"It took an additional two weeks or so before it was determined that Milwaukee, Wisconsin, would be the site of the new FAPS audit. However, the team wasn't on site for three or four weeks.

"In the interim, a training group for the D.C. Audit had to be rescheduled, and the decision by MRS. KNOWLES caused resultant delays in training and in implementation of the FAPS plan.

"Two of the primary reasons for the selection of YOUTH PRIDE in the District were:

"(1) it met the annual funding criteria of between $500,000 and $1 million decided upon previously among Audit Division, Program Division and Investigation Division.

"(2) it was 'close to home' and was easily monitored by us.

"In addition, budgetary restrictions were also a consideration for a close-to-home survey. The Milwaukee audit lasted for three and one half months and in my opinion that was untimely excessive expenditure, that could have been put to better usage in the immediate area.

"Throughout our discussion, MRS. KNOWLES was adamant about not letting us proceed into the FAPS audit YOUTH PRIDE and gave no other reasons than those I've offered above. The words used, to the best of my recollection, are those used by MRS. KNOWLES, and indicated that YOUTH PRIDE was off-limits to our audit."

Peterson, then signed it, and I had it subscribed and sworn to before me in my official capacity as Special Agent.

As I casually read that June 11 memorandum from Lehrman and Peterson to Knowles, I had no indication what would develop in the months ahead. At that moment I was still concerned about my detail to National and to answering Juliano's latest asinine memo about the "office keys."

I fired off a response to his June 8 memo informing him that he had "incorrectly summarized" my personal effects suggesting that he had done so for the "purpose of engendering support" for barring me from my office. I then completely listed more serious and important "personal effects": a University of the Pacific diploma, a DOL training certificate, a certificate of completion from both the Anchorage Police Department and another for "Intermediate Police Officer Training" from California, as well as a Certificate of Appointment as an Administrative Officer for the Alaska Public Defender's Office. In addition, I also referred to other personal work-related literature.

I closed out my memo by advising him that his choice of the word "absurd" in allowing me to retain my office keys was "undoubtedly geared to prejudice a reader other than myself."

On that same date, I called Eder to request an extension to Juliano's letter of June 5 proposing to suspend me for the three-day period. That letter noted that I had ten calendar days to respond, and that if I needed extra time to answer, that Eder was the official to contact.

Eder agreed and granted me a week's extension to reply to Juliano's proposal of adverse action.

Lehrman, who had already heard of that proposal, only shook his head when I let him read the letter.

"Just do what you got to do," he said. "The cases aren't going anywhere."

Barron, who was working in an adjoining office, stopped by my desk early in the week. He, too, had heard of Juliano's letter.

"This wouldn't have happened under Rocky," he said sadly, referring to the close-knit family relationship that we enjoyed under DeMarco's leadership.

On June 22, I composed the comprehensive four-page rebuttal to Juliano's charges, addressing each of his *Reasons* and his *Specifications* in detail.

After I opened my letter in the usual routine manner of referring to the letter of the 5th, I launched into a hard-hitting condemnation of the episode, and especially of Juliano, himself:

> "Mr. Juliano, in a unique display of unbridled juvenile behavior, has wasted a great deal of everybody's precious time and of Government money in attempting to exact undeserved homage for his

strange proclivities. His reputation as a chronic complaining Supervisor in the New York Fraud Office preceded him before his assignment to this area. His abrasiveness drew the wrath and dismay of contemporary officials in the New York area. His nonresponsiveness to his New York employees hampered their effectiveness. His condescending attitude toward the clerical staff in the National Office alienated him long before his arrival. In short, Mr. Juliano has earned his dubious reputation as being 'paranoid' and 'ridiculous.' Now, he has attempted to perpetuate his incompetence in a new 'plum' improperly handed him — the Washington Field Office. He has further attempted to undermine the morale and effectiveness of the Washington Field Office, and more importantly, has by subterfuge and fabrication — has attempted to victimize me."

The main body of my letter contained my specific answers, but when I reached the final paragraph, I couldn't hold back my contempt of Eder any longer.

"It would appear from the above and from other information received concerning your direct involvement and collusion with Mr. Juliano that you are not an unbiased decision-maker and, therefore, should voluntarily disqualify yourself from rendering a decision. For you to remain in this adverse action process would be a serious breech of your responsibilities as a supervisor because of ignoring ethical procedures and acting in a manner devoid of fairness and objectivity. You would undoubtedly compromise your 'standing' in the Department if I am forced to carry this to its highest resolution. I truly hope that it will not be necessary to do so. I have been forced to digress from my cases and respond to allegations that are not only frivolous but should have been stopped by yourself long before this. The effort expended by all parties is extremely wasteful and should be resolved immediately."

As soon as I had completed my official response, and had it typed up, I showed it to Lehrman, who I was beginning to feel more comfortable with.

He read it over slowly and glanced up at me with a quick smile. "You don't mince words do you buddy?" he quipped.

"Nope," I stressed, and then added, "especially when I'm right."

"I knew I had a good feeling about you when I recommended you to Rocky," he said.

"I'll bet that Eder and Juliano wished you hadn't," I said, and couldn't help but smile myself. I hand-carried the letter to Eder, who accepted it unsmilingly without comment. When I returned to my own desk, Ives was waiting for me.

"Hey, Nick, how you doing?" he inquired sincerely.

"Hey, Clark Kent," I replied jokingly. "How are you doing?"

"Good, man," he answered. "I had to come to National today, so I thought I'd look you up."

"Glad you did Peter," I said, then asked, "How's Charmayne doing with our boy?"

"Same as ever, man," he said. "You know he's never going to change." He then added in a more serious tone, "I wish I was out of there too."

I sympathized with him, and when he asked, I brought him up-to-date on my response to Juliano's charges. When I referred to Juliano's Reason #3, concerning his allegation of my *Non Compliance with OIG Policy Directive Number 2 (Operations) by Discussing Investigations with the Media,* Ives brightened.

"That's a load of crap," he said, "I was at that May 7 meeting with you and Owens, and I know what was said."

"That's right, you were," I said loudly, recalling the incident.

"Do you mind giving me a statement on that Peter, I can have it added to my original letter."

"Hell, no," he answered. "Just give me a pad."

I readily complied, and after he had thought about it a moment, he wrote:

STATEMENT OF PETER N. IVES
"On or about 5/24/79, the writer attended a

meeting during which Assistant United States Attorney James Owens was briefed by Special Agent Nicholas Mangieri and the writer as to the status of the then Washington, D.C., Fraud Office, Office of Inspector General, U.S. Department of Labor Case number 01-9-0012-01. At this meeting, the following newspaper article attached as Exhibit 1 from *The Washington Star,* Home Final Edition, for Washington, D.C., dated Wednesday, May 23, 1979, was discussed. The discussion of the article, to the best of the writer's recollection, was initiated by Owens with a remark to the effect that he wondered if he should call Arnold Juliano as Owens did not want Juliano to think that Mangieri had talked to the newspaper what with all the references to the U.S. Department of Labor. Owens went on to explain that he hoped that by his talking to the newspaper and generating publicity in the case a special grand jury might be convened on the matter, as the case was not strong enough to go to that point of itself at that time. It is the writer's belief that Owens wished to build pressure and public concern regarding the matter by utilizing the newspapers. As further evidence of this, the newspaper article attached as Exhibit 2 appeared in the Editorial Section of *The Washington Star,* Sunday, May 27, 1979."

I looked it over, and said, "Great, Peter. this will give them sonsabitches something to think about."

"Any time," he answered animatedly.

I had it typed, and Ives signed and dated his statement. I then added a cover letter as Addendum #1, attached the statement to it and wrote:

"Agent Ives will substantiate my response to *Specification 1 of (Reason) #3* — and will further refute the allegations raised by Supervisor Arnold Juliano in his subject action."

I, again, hand-carried the addendum to a still unsmiling Eder.

Although my investigations, and even the ability to follow

through on them at the office, had slowed down considerably, I did my best.

On one particular trip to see Jim Owens at the U.S. Attorney's Office, he remarked that he hadn't seen or heard from me in several days. I had passed the phase of being overly concerned about what he thought of DOL, and I recapped the events of all that had befallen me lately.

He looked pensive as he hunched quietly in his chair.

"I'll send your new I.G. a letter of commendation about you," he suddenly volunteered. "Perhaps then she'll not only take your investigative efforts seriously, but ..." and he hesitated, "... maybe she'll realize that this office is deeply interested in the results."

I liked the approach and told him so. He rose from behind his desk and held out a large hand.

"Let's hope this works," he said. "You're a good man, and I don't want to lose you."

I grinned and grabbed his outstretched hand.

"Thanks."

"I'll dictate this to my secretary," he continued. "Just stop by to see her at the end of the day and she'll give you your copy."

After talking to Owens, I began to feel better about the situation. I firmly believed that with him in my corner and with the might of the U.S. Attorney's Office behind him, all my troubles with my superiors would eventually disappear.

Unfortunately, that's not the way the scenario would play out. There were actors in the wings who would change the entire picture.

At the end of the day as Owens had promised, a copy of the letter to our female Inspector General was waiting for me.

Being eager to see its contents, I read it as soon as she handed it to me. Dated that afternoon, June 26, 1979, it read:

> "Dear Ms. Knowles:
>
> "As you are undoubtedly aware, Special Agent Nick Mangieri of your office has been working under the direction of this office on CETA Fraud cases in the District of Columbia Government.
>
> "I have closely observed Agent Mangieri in the performance of his duties pursuant to the investi-

gation of these cases. He has periodically kept me
apprised of the results and the scope of his efforts,
and I am impressed with his initiative and dedication
to these exceedingly complex cases.

"In my opinion, Agent Mangieri has not only
effectively demonstrated a wide understanding of
the issues involved but has applied that knowledge
to the proficient handling of day-to-day investigations. His professionalism is to be commended and
is a tribute to your office and to the Department
of Labor.

Sincerely yours,
By:
JAMES N. OWENS, Chief
Misdemeanor Trial Section

His secretary, who had been sitting nearby, gave me a wide
smile as she commented about it pleasantly, "Good luck, agent."

Undoubtedly, she could tell by the expression on my face that
I was obviously pleased with its contents.

"Thanks, again," and I returned her smile with one of my own,
equally as wide. I returned to the Department of Labor, which was
only a block away, and then to my own office. Lehrman, who was
waiting for me, asked how I fared with Owens and I showed him
a copy of the letter.

"Not bad," he said, as if he were somewhat amazed. "This
might make some difference."

I acknowledged that I thought it would.

The next day I decided to send Eder another addendum in reference to Juliano's letter of adverse action. I didn't want to leave any
stone unturned, and I wanted to have a continuing chain of documentation to support my position.

Accordingly, in what I identified in my letter as Addendum #2,
I wrote and sent the following:

"The following attached letters are indicative
of my work performance in the Field and of the
reputation that I have enjoyed as a result thereof:
"(1) Letter from 1st Assistant U.S. Attorney in

Miami, Florida, dated January 18, 1979.

"(2) Letter from Commander, Organized Crime Bureau, Dade County Public Safety Department in Miami, Florida, dated February 20, 1979.

"(3) Letter from Chief, Misdemeanor Trial Section in U.S. Attorney's Office, Washington, D.C., dated June 26, 1979.

"You are also aware that you yourself signed:

"(1) a six-month Supervisor's Report on Employee After Placement, dated December 4, 1978, which stated that my performance 'has been entirely satisfactory.'

"(2) a U.S. Department of Labor Adjective Performance Rating, dated March 8, 1979 — and approved by Richard J. Ross, Acting Deputy Inspector General on March 12, 1979 — that my performance was satisfactory.

"In view of the above and more, best known to my fellow workers and others I have worked with in the Field, it is suggested that this farcical adverse action:

"(1) be terminated immediately

"(2) cause my supervisor, Arnold Juliano to be disciplined

"(3) that I receive a letter of apology and — last but not least —

"(4) that I receive a long-overdue letter of recognition for my performance in the Field, a performance that is continually cited by those who are able to observe the results of my investigative work."

Lehrman, who was becoming even more interested in what seemed to be a daily battle with my supervisors, felt compelled to remark after he read it, "You don't give up, do you buddy?"

"Did you think I would, Paul?"

"Can't say I blame you," he said. "I'd probably do the exact same thing as you if I were in your boots."

It was nice to know that at least I had additional support from an unexpected quarter.

The next morning, on the 28th, Barron excitedly stopped by my desk with a grin that was a mile wide.

"What's up, Cam?" I asked in surprise.

"You seen today's *Star*?" and he threw a section of the paper down in front of me.

"Uh uh," I answered.

"Look at the section I've marked," he responded gleefully.

He pointed out a gossip column called, "The Ear," and then tapped his finger on a portion he had circled in red.

"Read this bad momma," he said, in the same excited tone.

I read where he had indicated, and couldn't help feeling the same sense of excitement.

". . . And all are atwitter at the Labor Department. The new Inspector General, Marjorie Fine Knowles, is having her Ceremonial Bathroom custom installed smack next door to her office as befits a Presidential Appointee. Several Investigators who've been swept out of their office to clear the way for the john, or joan, are behaving disgracefully. Some refer to the Necessity as 'The Appointment,' others as 'The Throne Room.' Ear is absolutely appalled."

"I love it. I love it," I said, as I finished reading it, and then handed it to Lehrman. "This is the kind of boss we got. More interested in luxuries than in getting the job done," he said contemptuously.

"I knew you'd love it, paisan," Barron said.

Lehrman who had read it, threw the article across the desk, and said disgustedly, "This is what happens when you bring in political appointees ... female appointees, at that."

I was to read again, that the price tag was about $20,000 for the work. That was one hell of an expensive potty for the time.

Later on in the afternoon of that same day I received a memo from Eder relative to the proposed three-day suspension. It was his first written communication to me. In it, he asked for additional information in connection with Reason No. 2, *Failure to Obey Instructions From Your Supervisor.*

"This asshole's gotta be kidding," I said half to myself and loud enough for Lehrman to hear.

"What's the problem now, buddy?" he asked.

"Eder not only wants me to provide him with the case files on my investigations of allegations of sexual coercion by D.C. public officials, but a string of other stuff," I said in exasperation.

"What else?" Lehrman asked wearily.

"He also wants the name of each individual interviewed, the date of the interview, the date the interview was dictated or written, the date the report of interview was typed, who typed the report of interview, and whether the interview was taped."

I tried to mimic Eder's voice in a falsetto-type whine to minimize our frustration.

"You've got to be kidding?" Lehrman said.

"Here you read the sonovabitch," and I pushed it across to him.

"We're both wasting our time on this fuckin' work," he said as he slammed the brief memo down on his desk.

It was the first time that I had seen him lose his cool in the two weeks I had been there.

"Now you've got a rough idea of what I've been facing ever since I took the lead on these cases," I added.

"Yeah," he said morosely.

"Both he and Juliano have sandbagged me every step of the way, and I'm getting tired of all this bullshit."

"What do you plan to do now?" Lehrman asked in a low voice.

"Two can play this game," I answered.

"I'm gonna get this asshole's attention," I stressed the words as I said them.

"How?" he asked.

"Just watch me," and I grabbed a pad to write on.

I began the subject matter with:

"Proposal To Initiate Charges Of Incompetence/Harassment/Conduct Unbecoming A Supervisor."

I then opened my letter with:

> "It is apparent from your actions, both expressed and implied, that you do not intend to disqualify yourself from rendering a decision on the proposed adverse action against me, dated June 5, 1979."

I continued by citing my years of working in the criminal justice system, and "that I have encountered very few, such as yourself, who when faced with allegations of bias that I have offered, together with the proof that I have submitted, would blatantly ignore ethics and would openly flaunt the law."

I then advised him in no uncertain terms that I would expose him to his contemporaries and to his superiors and would start grievance procedures in the Department of Labor and with the Merit System Protection Board.

If that wasn't enough to get his full attention, I also included a list of 24 detailed questions hoping to extract from him whatever information I could. I knew that the likelihood of him responding to those questions was remote, but I wanted to put him on notice that I was aware of his personal involvement with Juliano in the proposal to suspend me from duty.

I led off the questions by asking him:

> "• Whose initial idea was it to frame an adverse action letter about me?
> "• Who wrote the initial draft?
> "• Did you discuss the letter with Juliano and what was said?
> "• On what dates did these meetings occur?"

I handled the content of the letter as if I were submitting legal "Interrogatories" or conducting a "Deposition" with him.

I had used that tactic effectively in the past when I had been in Alaska.

Throughout much of the letter, I interspersed questions specifically about Juliano himself, such as:

> "• Was former Agent John Hurley of the New York Fraud Office ever contacted by yourself to ascertain his reasons for quitting while under the then supervisor Arnold Juliano?
> "• Was Sam Duke, the present Acting Supervisor of the New York Fraud Office ever questioned about Juliano?
> "• What is the content of Agent Tony Rossi's report of the New York Office?"

These questions were designed to let Eder know that I was

aware of Juliano's unusual proclivities and his abnormal antics.

I then threw in additional pointed questions about Eder, himself:

>"• What action did you take when I advised you that Juliano's behavior in the Arlington Office was becoming a problem with the other two agents as well? Specify.
>
>"• Why did you fail to respond to my two memos to you, dated May 8, 1979, pointing out:
>
>"a) Juliano's inability to handle my growing sensitive case into D.C. City Government?
>
>"b) Juliano's 'lack of control' and 'paranoid behavior.'
>
>"• What action did you take?
>
>"• If none, why not?"

I even put in a few questions about my Florida work, such as:

>"• Why was I immediately pulled out of my Key West case, contrary to the U.S. Attorney's wishes?
>
>"• Were you aware that just prior to my 'pull-out' that the Acting Deputy Inspector General advised the U.S. Attorney in Miami that I would finish my Key West assignments?"

I reread my hastily drawn up draft and was satisfied that I had covered everything. I let Lehrman review it for his reaction.

His prematurely gray eyebrows went up after he had looked it over.

"You're either going to shut him up," he exclaimed, "or he's going to come after you with both barrels blazing."

"We'll see," I said.

Apparently, my desired intent as to the former contingency worked. He never pressed me for the response sought in his latest memo. As to the latter contingency, it did happen later, but at the level above him.

On the same day I had hand-carried my caustic, informative

letter to him, he wrote his second memorandum to me. Although it was not in direct reply to my own memo of the previous day, it did attempt indirectly to get back at me.

The subject matter of his memo was, "Acceptable Level of Competence."

In it, he noted that although I was eligible for a within grade increase on July 1, 1979, he had given "serious consideration to denying (my) step increase," because of "deficiencies in the quality of (my) job performance." Then, in a typical wishy-washy about-face, he stated:

"However, given the changes in supervisory personnel and the lack of consistent direction and management control, I have concluded that there are circumstances which possibly mitigate your deficiencies. Therefore, I am granting the within grade increase, but I take this opportunity to put you on notice that your performance must improve."

Bullshit, I said to myself.

Lehrman looked over as I was drumming my fingers on the top of the deck.

"Anything important?" he asked.

"Naw," I said, "just the weasel trying to sound like a boss."

He smiled at the comparison.

The balance of his memo then repeated the same worn-out line that Juliano had used: that my interviews must be typed within 48 hours. I had repeatedly told Juliano that it was the typist's function — not mine — and that they were all on tape, anyway. I'm sure that Eder was aware what I had written to Juliano, since it was Juliano's nature either to pick up the phone to whine, or to run over to National to complain every chance he got.

The weekend came and went, with me mulling over the memos and letters that had passed between Eder and myself. On Monday, July 2, I decided to cover my bases even further, and visited our Personnel Department. I spoke to an individual who I thought was knowledgeable about adverse personnel actions and could advise me accordingly. I specifically asked him if once an adverse action had been put in print, whether additional complaints — or expanded charges could be initiated — especially if they were done by the originator's supervisor. Absolutely not, was his reply.

Armed with that clarifying information, from a personnel source who should have known, I wrote Eder another letter on July 3. In it, I noted that:

> "You are, of course, aware that your fishing expedition approach is not only highly improper but prohibited by Federal Personnel Rules and Regulations."

I then added:

> "As the 'Acting Chief' of Investigations, you are permitted to view my case file. However, because I cannot compromise the content of that file due to its political sensitivity and because I am in the process of preparing for an imminent Grand Jury, it is strongly suggested that you view the case file at my desk. Further, inasmuch as I am actively involved in the investigation of this case, I need all the material at my fingertips and not somewhere else to further hamper and delay my investigation."

Confident that I had gotten the message across to him that I was personally aware of his improper behavior, I closed out the letter by referring to my source:

"I have been advised by Mr. Raphael of personnel that he has admonished you on your written request to me. This action was in response to my query of him regarding the ethics of your letter to me."

Lehrman, who by now had become deeply entrenched in my continuing battle, read the letter.

"I'll bet he's really beginning to hate your guts," was his smiling comment.

"Good," I said. "I'm not letting that puny bastard get by with anything."

"So, I notice," Lehrman said.

"If I let him get by with any of his crap, he'll shut me down. That's been his intent all along. All this other shit that he and Juliano have ginned up, is all smoke screen. They don't want me investigating City Hall. PERIOD."

I looked back at Lehrman after I caught my breath.

"I can't argue with anything you've said," he observed seriously. "Everything you've told me seems to bear out."

"I don't open my mouth unless I've got something to back me up," I reminded him.

"You might be right as hell," Lehrman warned me, "but I just can't wonder what that little vindictive bastard will pull next." I was to find out soon enough.

On Friday, July 6, I received what I thought was an unusual call from Jim Owens.

"If you get a chance, Nick, why don't you stop by my office. I think you'll find what I have to say interesting."

It was an intriguing call. I thought that it dealt with some aspect of my cases that he didn't want to discuss over the phone.

"Sure, Jim," I said quickly. "How about an hour?"

"Fine, see you then."

With our close association over the past few months, titles or formalities had long since disappeared between us. We were both on a first-name basis.

After I had walked into his office, he, too, had a serious look.

"What's up, Jim?"

He then proceeded to tell me that two officials from the Department of Labor had visited him and had questioned him, in detail, about my relationship with the reporter from *The Washington Star*.

I was dumb-founded at his disclosure.

"Who?" I demanded.

"Stuart Eder," he replied, "and somebody named Schatz."

"That's some other flunky over there with Eder," I enlightened Owens.

"What's going on over there?" he wanted to know.

I briefed him on the more recent events and communications between me and my higher superiors.

"I won't let them shut your cases down," he promised.

The more that I thought about what they had done behind my back the more worked up I became.

"Them sonsabitches," I said. "Them goddamn sonsabitches."

"I know," he said. "Just watch yourself and keep me abreast of what's happening over there."

I thanked him and returned to my own office. Once there, I

recapped the conversation with Lehrman.

"I just knew he'd pull something like this," he spat the words out. "What are you going to do about it now?"

I thought about it a moment. "Just what I've been doing all along."

"What's that?"

"Another memo," I said. "Only this time, over Eder's head."

"You mean to Marjorie?" he said, referring to her by her first name. We didn't have enough respect for her to use her last name, nor even her official title.

I nodded, enjoying the idea of it.

"I gotta see this one," Lehrman beamed.

"You will."

I drafted the official letter to her as the Inspector General, and identified the subject matter as: "Unprofessional Conduct Of Acting Chief Of Investigations, Stuart Eder."

I wrote:

"Dear Mrs. Knowles:

"Mr. Eder in a continuing personal vendetta has gone beyond the bounds of propriety and objectivity in pursuing totally frivolous allegations raised by my former incompetent supervisor, Arnold Juliano, against me.

"Mr. Eder has attempted to enlist the aid of another Federal Agency, the U.S. Attorney's Office in an attempt to justify his untenable position of investigating Mr. Juliano's ludicrous allegations.

"On July 5, 1979, Mr. Eder in the accompaniment of another GS-14, Graham Schatz, visited the Office of James Owens, the Chief of the Misdemeanor Section of the U.S. Attorney's Office and questioned him extensively about my 'leaking' information to *The Washington Star.* These questions were resolved — or should have been resolved — by:

"1. My May 2, 1979, memo to Stuart Eder (thru Arnold Juliano) describing, in detail, all events and discussions regarding the George Harrod Investigations, from April 5, 1979 - May 2, 1979.

"2. My May 8, 1979, memo to Stuart Eder regarding my May 7 meeting with Assistant U.S. Attorney James Owens, in the accompaniment of Arnold Juliano.

"3. My June 22, 1979, response to Stuart Eder regarding Arnold Juliano's 'Proposed Letter of Adverse Action, dated June 5, 1979.

"4. My Addendum #1, dated June 22, 1979, to my 'Response' which contained Special Agent Peter Ives' statement regarding the alleged 'leak' to *The Washington Star.*

"Mr. Eder continues 'to beat a dead horse' and is literally costing the Government thousands of dollars by perpetuating his selfish proclivities. He has succeeded in alienating the support of the U.S. Attorney's Office by his harassment of me that is completely without merit. He has demonstrated poor judgement by such unprofessional conduct and has held the Office of the Inspector General and the Department of Labor to ridicule by his amateurish behavior.

"I am concerned for the uncalled for and unnecessary questioning of my credibility to a senior official in another agency for whom I am performing noteworthy investigations and want his actions terminated before he brings complete discredit to our office and our efforts. His actions — or lack of action when he was in an affirmative position to do so — while he was my supervisor in Florida resulted in my being pulled out of a Grand Jury in Key West, an action that left a poor image of our effectiveness to the U.S. Attorney's Office in Florida. (See Addendum #2, dated June 22, 1979).

"It is hoped that this letter will bring your timely intervention and re-establish our credibility with allied agencies before it is too late.

Sincerely,
Nicholas J. Mangieri
Special Agent

I read it over again to satisfy myself that I left nothing out for Knowles to consider and then handed it to Lehrman.

He reviewed it slowly, gave me a quick tight smile and then slid it across his desk to me.

"Well, you've officially got her in the loop now," was his comment.

"It's about time," I said.

"I just hope this works out for your sake," he added.

"What else could I have done, Paul?" I asked exasperated.

"I guess you're right," he continued. "They did have your back against the wall."

"Yeah, nothing ventured, nothing gained."

It was a philosophy I had always followed and this time was no exception.

Because it was late Friday afternoon, however, I decided to wait until Monday morning to get it typed up. I had been using one of the local secretaries on the floor, who I had become acquainted with and felt I could trust. After it was done early that afternoon, I hand-carried it to the first floor where the new I.G. occupied a full suite, with her various assistants branching off into adjacent rooms. Her private secretary accepted it from me and date-stamped it in.

It was to be the first of many in the ensuing months that I would personally deliver to her "Immediate Office."

Over the next few days I heard from no one and was not being hassled by Eder. I commented to Barron at one of our trips to the nearby D.C. Police Lodge how quiet it was.

"I haven't heard a thing either, Nikolai," another one of his favorite names for me. "And I've kept my ear to the ground, too."

"I've got a feeling that something's gonna break soon," I said, "especially after my last letter to Marjorie."

Sure enough, on July 12, exactly three days after my letter to Knowles, I received a response from her. It was addressed to me by name only, not with my official title of *Special Agent*. She would naturally always include her own, as *Inspector General*. It was an omission that I did not particularly notice at the time, but it was a slip that was to be pointed out to me later.

"It's her way of not acknowledging who you are," I was told.

I came to realize the validity of that off-handed incisive remark before too long. However, when I received that official memorandum from her, I was momentarily pleased at its content.

> "After reviewing Arnold Juliano's June 5, 1979, letter proposing to suspend you for three days, Stuart Eder concluded that he should not participate in the decision in this matter because Reason 2, Specification 2 and Reason 3, Specification 2 in that letter concern incidents in which he was personally involved. Accordingly, he has asked me to designate someone else to render a decision.
>
> "Consequently, I am designating the Deputy Inspector General, Ronald Goldstock, as the deciding official in this matter. Mr. Eder will forward all the pertinent documents, including your written replies, to Mr. Goldstock. Mr. Goldstock begins duty as Deputy Inspector General on July 16 and will render a decision after carefully reviewing the relevant material.
>
> "Since you did not previously know that Mr. Goldstock would be making the decision in this matter, you are being given an opportunity to consider whether you wish to make an oral reply to Mr. Goldstock or file an additional written response. If you do, please advise me in writing before the close of business July 13, 1979, and inform me how much additional time you need."

I showed Lehrman her reply and had to remark, "So far, so good."

"Let's hope it continues," he said.

"Who is this guy, Goldstock?" I wanted to know. "Where did he come from?"

Lehrman shrugged his shoulders, "I think he's some kind of professor," he said. "Just remember, Marjorie hired him, so I wouldn't get your hopes up too much."

"Thanks, buddy, I needed that," I replied sarcastically.

Because I didn't want to have any loose ends or unanswered questions, especially where they involved Eder, I sent the following memorandum to Knowles on the 13th and requested an extension as per her suggestion:

> "I am happy to see that the new Deputy Inspector, Ronald Goldstock will be the deciding official in subject matter.
>
> "I note from your July 12, 1979, memo that Stuart Eder has only now after five weeks from Arnold Juliano's letter of June 5, 1979, concluded that he should not render a decision because he was 'personally involved.' Mr. Eder has known from the inception that he was personally involved and should have declined participation at the very onset because of that reason. Yet, Mr. Eder has personally involved himself in all of the interviews in an unsuccessful attempt to substantiate the malicious false allegations raised in the June 5 letter.
>
> "I suggest therefore that perhaps Mr. Eder is trying to extricate himself gracefully from a contrived situation that could prove very embarrassing to him and to others involved. Accordingly, it is my intention to file additional written responses directly to Mr. Goldstock and request that I be granted a five-day extension, until the close of business on July 18, 1979, to prepare those replies."

Because I had requested that five-day extension to the 18th, and because I wanted *all* documentation to be in Goldstock's hands by that date, I wrote another memo to Eder. It was a three-page piece summarizing my prior correspondence with him and reminding him of my prior experience in the criminal justice field, where it had always been necessary for me to write comprehensive detailed reports and summaries. I, then, recapped that experience in my memo — specifically for Goldstock's knowledge — since he was apparently unaware of my background. I also did so, because Eder attempted to denigrate my failure to accomplish *written* reports with his incessant repetitious reference to a "48-hour" period. I noted, in that memo, again for Goldstock's benefit, that:

"(1) this 'issue' has not been raised to the detriment of other investigators.

"(2) this 'issue' is not in fact followed consistently by other investigators.

"(3) there has never been a definition of, nor clear understanding, what constitutes a 'writing' ..."

In completing that final memo to Eder, and in sending a copy of it to Goldstock, I hoped to accomplish a dual purpose. First, to alert Eder that the additional derogatory information was going over his head to his new superior. Second, I felt that the in-depth information that I offered Goldstock would be of some assistance to him in his decision process.

Only time would tell the results.

In the interim I wasn't going to let that little son of a bitch, Juliano, slide on any of my actions. I wanted him to be fully apprised of what I knew about him. I had a plan\. In short, I wanted him to sweat. I also sent him a detailed three-page letter, titled the same as the one I directed to Eder at the end of June:

"Proposal to Initiate Charges of Incompetence/Harassment/Conduct Unbecoming a Supervisor."

In the letter I indicated I was aware there was a conspiracy hatched between him and Eder. To further confound Juliano, I asked him basically the same questions I had asked Eder in his letter: whose idea was it to initiate an adverse action, who wrote the initial draft, etc. . ., etc.

. I then asked specific questions about his former employees in New York and his relationships with them, and even queried about the derogatory Tony Rossi report about him. I followed up that line of questioning with precise inquiries about my Washington cases: Why did he assign a new sexual harassment case to Agent Castro when I was already pursuing similar allegations against the same subjects? Why did he never prepare a Report of Interview of his phone conversation with a confidential interview, as required? Did he ever advise anyone in the National Office that I had written six memoranda of my D.C. cases dating back to April 19?

I closed out my rather lengthy letter on a more personal note, since he never had any qualms about raising personal issues with me. Moreover, his personal comments never had any bearing on anything relevant. I thought I'd follow suit. The final paragraph read:

"Further, inasmuch as I am in possession of certain information and details regarding your *'compassionate'* transfer to the Washington Field Office from New York, kindly advise, If the home you had up for sale in Virginia prior to your accepting the supervisor's job in the New York Office was over-priced?"

I had heard that he had used that as leverage to return to Virginia.

I'm sure that a soon as he received my comprehensive letter, he was shitting little bricks. That was my intention.

I decided it wasn't necessary to send a copy of the Juliano letter to Goldstock as it would undoubtedly muddy the water. However, I did decide to forward to Goldstock on the 19th, a "Supplemental Memoranda" with the following notation:

> "Attached find six additional memoranda, which I have good reason to believe, were not given you by Stuart Eder and which would constitute a "complete" background of my allegations against both Eder and Juliano.
> "• May 8, 1979, memo to Stuart Eder
> Subject: George Harrod Case
> "• May 8, 1979, memo to Stuart Eder (not a duplicate)
> Subject: George Harrod Case
> "• June 4, 1979, memo to Arnold Juliano
> Subject: Clarification of Workload
> "• June 7, 1979, memo to Arnold Juliano
> Subject: Office Keys
> "• June 12, 1979, memo to Arnold Juliano
> Subject: Office Keys
> "• Undated memo to Stuart Eder
> Subject: Privacy to Conduct Investigation"

Knowing Eder as well as I knew Juliano, I didn't want the deck stacked against me in front of what I believed to be an unbiased official. I was sure that whatever Goldstock received would have been a partial file, and then only what was favorable to both Eder and Juliano.

The balance of July and into August I surprisingly was allowed to continue my investigations into City Hall unfettered. The targets on my cases expanded, as did the in-depth info that I received on them.

"How lucky can I get?" I commented to Lehrman one day.

Ever the cautious type, he remarked, "Don't count your chickens yet, buddy."

"Don't be so pessimistic, Paul. Things are going well, and nobody's blocking me," I reminded him.

"Yeah, but they haven't resolved your three-day suspension yet, have they?" he countered.

"True, but it's been about six weeks, and I'm still on the job."

"Maybe you're right," he conceded graciously, "but I still don't trust them — any of them."

"Well," I said, "I'll worry about that when I get back. I've got 11 days at the Federal Training Center at Glynco for 'White Collar Crime,' and then I'm taking some annual."

"I'll bet they're sorry they're sending you," Lehrman quipped.

"Yeah," I agreed, "but I also bet they're not counting the days 'til I get back."

... 9 ...

Upon my return from leave at the end of August I was ready to get back in the saddle again. I was surprised, however, that there were no memos or messages from anyone above me requesting, or demanding, anything. I called this lack of communication to the attention of both Lehrman and Barron.

"Consider yourself lucky, buddy," was Lehrman's typical wary response.

Barron, on the other hand, was more upbeat. "Maybe you've got them licked, paisan," was his comment.

As much as I liked Barron's reply, I had an uncomfortable feeling that Lehrman was right.

When I checked in with Owens, he also gave me something to think about.

Once we had gotten over the amenities in greeting each other, he announced in his deep voice.

"Nick, I've some good news and bad news for you. Which would you like first?"

"I always like to start out with the good news first, Jim."

"Well, the good news is ..." and he hesitated briefly.

"Yeah."

"The good news is ..." and he continued, "that your cases are being upgraded to felonies."

"I knew it!" I said confidently, but then cut myself short in my jubilant reply, "and the bad news?" I questioned him slowly.

"The bad news, my friend," he said quickly, "is that you're

being removed from my jurisdiction in the misdemeanor section and being transferred to the felony section."

His words sunk in, and I took a deep breath. "Goddamn it," I said in a low voice almost under my breath, but he heard my disappointed remark.

"I'm sorry, Nick," he continued, "but that's what happens when you do your job too well."

"I guess I should be thankful, Jim, that the U.S. Attorney's Office recognizes my work, but ..." and I thought about it a moment before I finished the reply, "I wonder what that will mean to my cases?"

He understood my unstated concern, especially as it pertained to my superiors. I had briefed him fairly regularly concerning the ways I thought they were blocking my efforts.

"You mean their obstructing your investigations?" was his perceptive comment. "I'll brief the felony people on what you've told me," he said. "I don't think your superiors would be stupid enough to try to pull anything."

"I hope not," I said forlornly, but with Owens out of the picture I wasn't optimistic in having to deal with somebody new. I didn't know how they would react to my disclosures about my superiors at DOL. It would not only be time-consuming having to piece together all their actions against me, but it would be hard for them to believe these same superiors would be conspiring to obstruct my investigations. After all, they didn't know me from Adam, whereas Jim Owens had been in with me on the ground floor ever since this whole sexual investigation had started.

Owens saw the concern in my face and added, "Don't worry, Nick. There are some good people over there. I'm sure they'll be on top of it."

I still wasn't convinced, but tried to mask my disappointment.

"Thanks, Jim. It was good working with you."

"It's been my pleasure," he said, as he extended his hand.

I gripped it firmly and then rose and turned to go. As I was exiting his office, he called out, "Whenever you're in the building, just stop by any time."

I smiled and nodded.

Little did I realize that his casual comment would develop into a far longer-lasting relationship than our short five-month association had been.

As I took my leave of him and headed back toward my own office, my immediate concern was my next plan of action. Lehrman, too, after being told of the latest results was as pessimistic as I was about the proposed switch. If, the transfer to the felony section was to be forthcoming, neither I nor Lehrman were to hear about it for a week or so. In the meantime, I would continue with my work, interviewing and continually expanding on the cases. With each new bit of information, Lehrman would comment on the depth of the cases and the extent at which they were growing.

"Yeah, we'll have plenty of ammo in the felony area," I agreed.

"It's looking good, partner," he remarked one day after reviewing additional data I had gathered. "The sooner we get over to the U.S. Attorney's Office, the better."

"You mean before we get shot down by the front office?" I noted.

He shook his head in agreement.

Although events were already being planned in that regard, I was not made aware, nor had Lehrman heard anything to that effect. If anything, my hopes were raised by an unexpected call from "the hill" one morning in early September.

"This is Rosemary Storey," the caller announced.

"Who?" I asked, not having heard the name before in connection with any of my cases.

"I'm with the Subcommittee on Investigations in the House of Representatives," she announced.

Taken by surprise at the call, I asked her to repeat herself. When she did, and I echoed her response for Lehrman's benefit, who was sitting nearby, she added, "It's with the Committee on Post Office and Civil Service."

I was impressed.

"What can I do for you?" I tried to sound nonchalant.

She then told me she had heard about my investigations into *sexual harassment* in government and would like to meet with me. I didn't want to correct her usage of the innocuous term sexual *harassment,* since I was delving into what I considered was even more insidious, that of sexual *coercion.* So, for the moment, I agreed with her. When could we meet, she wanted to know. I was tempted to jump at the opportunity and tell her right now, but I didn't.

Instead, I advised her I would have to notify our "head office" for approval. As eager as I was, I knew I had to follow procedure.

As soon as I hung up the phone, I told Lehrman of the conversation.

"You better get on the horn right now," he said, "and tell downstairs what's going on."

"I can't wait," I said.

"I'll bet they shit when they hear *The Hill* is interested," he said expressively.

I called Shelley Repp, Special Assistant to Knowles, who was the point of contact for matters such as these. If he was shocked, surprised, or even the least bit interested he didn't indicate it. His reply was just a matter-of-fact response that he would, of course, relay it to the Inspector General and then would be in touch with me. Although I didn't expect any enthusiasm from anyone in the I.G.'s office, I did expect some sort of reaction, even if it was lukewarm.

Repp, as I was aware, was one of Knowles personal hires, and, in my opinion, was no different than anyone else in that *Immediate Office*. He soon grew to be one of my least favorites, as well. He was an anemic-looking young attorney who was forever scurrying around like a rat in a cage. I was not to be favorably surprised by a prompt answer, even though I did anticipate a fairly quick turn-around to a congressional request.

It took several days for the *head office,* a more easily used term to describe the honchos below, to decide that it was necessary for the subcommittee to formally request, in writing, my presence before that group. When I called Storey back and relayed the information to her, she said it would be done right away.

On September 12, James M. Hanley, Chairman of the Committee on Post Office and Civil Service, sent Ronald Goldstock, as Deputy Inspector General, a letter stating that "it would be beneficial for my subcommittee staff to meet with Special Agent Nicholas Mangieri, of your office ..." and then apprised him that Rosemary Storey could be contacted directly. However, instead of an immediate DOL answer to Representative Hanley's letter or of an instruction to me to call Ms. Storey, as per the letter's request, *nothing* was done. Finally a full two weeks later, on or about September 27, Storey managed to reach Special Assistant Shelley Repp. I was subsequently notified by Ms. Storey that she had placed three of four calls to his office in vain. They, not surprisingly, went unanswered and also failed to be returned. When she ultimately was able to make contact with him, she was advised that before I would be permitted to speak to the subcommittee, there would have to be "ground rules" established. She was somewhat aghast at the Department of Labor's stonewalling my efforts to meet with that group, but stated she would relay DOL's new position on the matter to Chairman Hanley.

The committee staff then somehow decided that since the scope of my investigation dealt with sexual harassment within the *District of Columbia,* it did not encompass sexual harassment within the *federal government.* The fine-line distinction was more than I or Lehrman could comprehend.

On the basis of their decision, they, therefore, reversed themselves and told the staff member who had initially approached me that they were not, now, interested in meeting with me.

As soon as she was informed of their change of heart, she called to tell me the unfavorable determination. Again, I was amazed by their about-face, although by this time nothing should have confounded me.

Lehrman saw the agitated expression on my face and from the conversation could sense the news. I hung up the phone, and held my displeasure down to a muffled reaction, because of our open area, "What the fuck is going on?" I asked in an agitated voice.

It wasn't really a question that could have been answered, but more an observation of what was going on around us. Lehrman, however, responded wearily, "It's politics, buddy, pure and simple politics."

"Politics hell, it's cover-up."

"Welcome to the wonderful world of Washington," he sarcastically exclaimed.

I was in no mood for sarcasm, even though he was on my side and I knew he was right. It was just the way it was done that bothered me. I still couldn't fathom why after all their expressed interest in my investigations, and in the subcommittee's continued attempts to meet with me, there was a complete reversal in their position.

I was to learn many months later, that the DOL officials had been proficient in their condemnation of me to staffers on the hill.

I was labeled a "hot dog" agent, who went off on tangents; a "supercop" who thought that everything was illegal; even a racist, because I was investigating Mayor Barry and City Hall. In that final smear, nobody bothered to mention that my buddy, Cameron Barron, was black. In fact, he was one of the few, who would stick by me no matter what was going down against me. It eventually caused his own early retirement.

While the hubbub was going on in the bowels of the Immediate Office concerning Congressional interest in my investigations, other traumatic events were shaping up.

On September 10, Lehrman and I accompanied by the new Acting Assistant Inspector General for Investigations, Gerald Gotsch, met with elements of the fraud division in the U.S. Attorney's Office. My cases were discussed with them, and I was given new direction to concentrate on "three or four good defendants," in lieu of the many that I had been investigating. I agreed, and Lehrman also nodded his head in agreement. Gotsch, who had been an observer apparently for Knowles and her Deputy, Goldstock, said very little as he was new to the whole investigation and evidently knew nothing about the details being discussed. After the meeting terminated and Lehrman and I returned to our own office, we began to zero in on our files for the best defendants. Gotsch stopped by later in the day to view our work. He said nothing, in particular, but noticed our prospective layout of what we considered good potentials. When he left, I asked Lehrman, "Do you trust him?"

"Not really," he said slowly.

"Me neither."

Over the next two or three days, Gotsch repeated his process. On about the third day, he made his announcement.

"I want you to concentrate on *one* defendant only," he said.

I looked at Lehrman in amazement when he said it, and then back to Gotsch again.

"The U.S. Attorney's Office wants us to concentrate on *three or four*," I said firmly, and I stressed the numbers.

"I don't care," he said. "I just want you to do one."

Lehrman stared at him quizzically for a moment, "and who did you have in mind?" he asked.

"Harrod, the Personnel Officer," he answered quickly.

"Then what?" Lehrman asked him facetiously.

"Then," he continued, as if he were talking to sixth-graders, "I want you to pick another defendant."

I couldn't keep quiet any longer.

"That's not what we were told," I reminded him. "If we did what you want," I continued, "we'd not only alienate the fraud division, but we'd be here all year."

"That's what I want, and that's what you'll do," he insisted and walked off.

"Goddamn it, Paul," I muttered in disgust after he had left, "what next?"

He took a deep breath before he spoke.

"They don't want these cases to go anywhere, partner."

"They?" I repeated the word, but I knew what he meant.

"You don't think that Gotsch came up with that decision by himself, do you?" he asked.

"Hell, no," I said. "It had to come from above."

In response, he gave me a quick smile and then nodded his head rapidly up and down, "and there's only two above him," he noted.

"Yeah, I know, it's either Knowles or Goldstock," and then added, "or both."

"It's your cases, buddy, you're the man," he said looking at me intently. "What are you going to do now?"

"I've got to mull this one over, Paul," I answered. "I want to keep all my ducks in order."

He smiled.

"You know I'm behind you," he said. "But just let me know what you're going to do."

I thought about it awhile and suddenly realized I had never received a retraction from Juliano on the three-day suspension. I had been assured by Goldstock when he came aboard in mid-July that he would see to it that Juliano would retract his letter of June 5 to me. I decided that before I started rocking the boat I would get that matter resolved, or at least, under way.

I then wrote a short memo to Goldstock on September 13 repeating his promise of July 13 to me. I also reminded him that upon my return from leave in late August, I had called to advise him that I had not received a letter from Juliano. I closed out the memo by stating:

"As of this date, I have not received a formal letter of retraction nor has a timely formal decision in writing been rendered on my case in accordance with the provisions of FPM Ch. 752."

As I was in the habit of doing for all memos going downstairs, I hand-carried this below *before* I initiated any further action regarding the Gotsch situation. Either my stars were in the right place in the heavens, or I caught Goldstock unaware, because he must've called Juliano immediately. In the mail delivery of the following morning, I received a brief five-line letter from Juliano to me. In it, he wrote:

"Pursuant to Deputy Inspector General Goldstock's instructions, this is to notify you that I am rescinding my June 5, 1979, proposal to suspend you from duty and pay for three days from your position of Criminal Investigator GS 1811-12 in the Office of the Inspector General."

I read it quickly and excitedly called over to Lehrman, "I told you the little sonuvabitch would change his mind."

He read it, and gave me a thumbs up.

"What had you decided on the Gotsch thing?" he asked.

I showed him a draft of a memorandum that I had composed the day before and had addressed to Knowles. I had labeled it "Confidential" at the top, as I wanted to make sure that she took it seriously. I also explained to him that I wanted the Juliano notification to come first and was pleasantly surprised that it happened so fast.

"Maybe they just want to throw you off track," Lehrman suggested.

"It didn't work did it?" I said proudly, as I shoved the memorandum in front of him.

"Where's the final draft?" he asked.

"It's being typed now," I said. "In the meantime, read this."

He glanced over it quickly, and whistled to himself softly. "I've got to read this slowly," he exclaimed, as he noticed certain words and phrases. The subject heading caught his attention, as I'm sure that it did when Marjorie Fine Knowles saw it:

INTERFERENCE WITH OFFICIAL INVESTIGATION

The informative, but accusatory, memo stated:

"I am concerned that my three-month investigation into sexual coercion within the District of Columbia Government is being emasculated because that investigation involves highly placed individuals not only within D.C. Government but in City Hall itself.

"At a September 10, 1979, meeting with the Deputy Chief of the Fraud Division, U.S. Attorney's Office and with one of his Assistants, the scope of my cases was discussed and a new direction given. It was agreed that rather than proceed in the manner I had been pursuing — that of establishing probable cause of violations within several agencies in D.C. Government for the specific purpose of convening a Special Grand Jury — that I should now concentrate my efforts on 'three or four good defendants' and the U.S. Attorney's Office would go for direct indictments in lieu of the investigatory Grand Jury approach.

"(*Note*: Prior to the meeting my 'authority' in the initial investigation, was at the direction of the Chief of the Misdemeanor Section, U.S. Attorney's Office. However, a recent decision by the U.S. Attorney was to transfer my investigation to the Felony Section dealing with major crimes and corruption in government and that I was now to report directly to that Section. Hence, the reason for the meeting described above.)

"Subsequent to this September 10 meeting, I began to proceed in accordance with the instructions given by the Assistant U.S. Attorney — that of working up cases on 'three or four good defendants.' However, within the next day or two, one of the attendees at that session, a highly placed U.S. DOL/OIG official advised me *not* to concentrate on the three or four defendants as I was specifically instructed to do but to concentrate solely on *one* defendant only, namely GEORGE HARROD, the former D.C. Personnel Officer. Then, when that case was resolved to go on to the next defendant and so on. Inasmuch as I presently have at least ten possible defendants, of which four are good defendants and inasmuch as some of their actions are intertwined, I questioned this new direction which was now at odds with that which had been previously agreed upon in the U.S. Attorney's Office. I advised him that his instructions were directly contra to those given me by the Deputy Chief of the U.S. Attorney's Office and concurred in by his Assistant, under whom I would be working for directly. Further, I advised him that I had equally good cases against other D.C. Government officials including City Councilmen. I stated that they could and should be pursued at this time. However, he was adamant in his decision in not allowing me to continue with my investigation in those areas.

"I am left with but one conclusion; that is, there is reason to impede my investigation at this point. Further, I am of the opinion that this reason is predicated upon the political ramifications of my investigation. An investigation that could shake the City Administration. I cannot in good conscience stand by silently, oblivious to a situation that has all the earmarks of a subtle 'cover-up.'

"I truthfully find it hard to believe that the individual who so advised me did so on his own. However, I also find it equally hard to believe that he was given the approval by 'higher authority.' An authority that should be cognizant of all of the ramifications that such a course of conduct could produce."

In my last paragraph, when I mentioned that I found it "hard to believe that he (Gotsch) was given the approval by 'higher authority' ... I did so to put Knowles on record that I was aware of her involvement in obstructing my investigations.

After Lehrman had read and analyzed the entire memo, he mockingly wiped his brow.

"You're not subtle are you?" he asked half in jest. Then he added seriously, "You're really gonna piss them off this time, Nick."

"Wrong is wrong, and right is right," I answered. "They swore the same oath as I did."

"I doubt it," Lehrman said caustically.

A full three weeks would elapse before I was to receive any type of response to my highly incriminating *confidential* memo to Knowles. Neither I, nor Lehrman, could believe that the Immediate Office would ignore potentially dangerous accusations. Even Barron, who by now was clued in to exactly what was going on commented, "They must be crazy not to defend themselves some way."

Lehrman who had been silent while the three of us were discussing the situation added, "They've got something up their sleeve. You can't turn your back on them. They're not just gonna fold."

He was right.

On October 1, I received a half-page memorandum from Ronald C. Goldstock, Deputy Inspector General, again with my title not being used. Oversights abounded when they had to address me in their official correspondence. To acknowledge my official investigative capacity would digress from their mission of evasion.

His subject merely referred to, "Your Memorandum of September 13, 1979."

In the reply, which apparently Knowles decided to have him handle, he submitted a lame response and an even more phony resolution:

> "I have read a copy of your memorandum to Marjorie Knowles regarding 'Interference with Official Investigation' that you have sent to me. The charges and allegations made by you in that memorandum regarding what you consider 'a situation that has all the earmarks of a subtle cover-up' are obviously extremely serious. In order for me to evaluate those charges and allegations, I am requesting that you submit to me, as soon as possible, your investigative plan in the underlying matter. The investigative plan should consist of a list of potential targets and/or goals of the investigation, a synopsis of the investigative predicate, and an analysis

of the alternative means by which this investigation
may be conducted. You also ought to note the
problems or potential problems associated with each
of the alternative means of investigation.

In drafting the investigative plan, if you have
not already done so, please detail the evidence that
is currently in your possession regarding 'D.C. Government Officials, including City Councilmen.' It
would also aid me in evaluating your charges in
being supplied with any additional information
which leads you to believe that your superiors are
'emasculating' your investigation for political reasons."

I read the response, shook my head and then flicked it across
Lehrman's desk for him to look at.

He snickered as he threw it down on his desk.

"They must be confused down there," he said. "You never
sent your memo to him, you sent it to Knowles directly."

"They're all chasing their ass down there." I said, "They don't
know what the hell they're doing."

"I'm afraid they're cagier than we're giving them credit for,"
Lehrman interjected. "Now they're throwing up a new smoke
screen."

"You mean his *investigative plan* and all the bullshit that goes
with it," I answered.

"That's it," he said. "Do you realize how much extra effort
that's going to entail?"

Before I had a chance to respond to his theoretical question, he
continued.

"They're bogging you down, buddy," he grimaced. "You're
never going to get your cases over to the U.S. Attorney's Office."

As much as I hated to admit it, it looked like he had the situation pegged.

I didn't answer him, but instead turned my thoughts to the
recent fiasco concerning the sudden lack of congressional interest
in my investigations.

As had been my habit of filling in all the holes with documentation, I decided to write up a *Memorandum for the Record* to

describe the bizarre events that occurred relative to the first contact by Rosemary Storey. As a further reminder to myself, at some future date, of exactly what had transpired, I entered at the base of the memo:

"*Note:*

(1) The scope of my investigative efforts was briefly discussed with the staff member who called me and even the fact that allegations were raised that went beyond the D.C. Government came out (i. e. within HUD).

(2) Ms. Storey, the staff member, was evidently dismayed and impatient with the lack of timely attention to the Committee letter and to her several phone calls."

For the next two weeks, following Goldstock's last memo to me, which effectively derailed me from my investigations, I prepared what I thought was a thoroughly comprehensive *investigative plan*. It was submitted to him on October 15, and was again titled, "Interference with Official Investigation." I retained that subject matter because that was the initial topic that was raised, and discussed, in my September 13 confidential memo to Knowles, which, in turn, prompted Goldstock's response to me on October 1.

What was different about this reply was the addition of his requested *investigative plan,* a *plan* that covered eight pages. However, because I knew that I was dealing with our own *City Hall* and had to be circumspect in my own response, I laced it with phrases that would support my contentions, if ever they were to be analyzed: "I have prepared the specific information requested therein. However, I am in all truth, faced with ambivalent feelings concerning that reply."

I then noted for his benefit that:

"On the positive side, your query does present the opportunity to show the importance and the extent of the investigation into City Government."

However, I also felt compelled to note:

"From a negative view point, however, your query is of considerable concern to me because it is an additional impediment to my investigation. It not only further dilutes my solitary efforts on the case by diverting my energies from being 'in the field,' but it prematurely exposes a wide-ranging confidential case to certain administrative — and possible political — scrutiny."

For his specific attention, and for that of the head of our agency, the Inspector General herself, who at the very least would be facing adverse publicity, I followed up with:

"The purpose of this memorandum is neither to accuse nor to intimate improprieties beyond those mentioned herein. The following incidents indicate a pattern that appear to be by design. I am sure you would want these brought to your attention to preclude allegations of obstruction of justice being raised."

I then cited the various memoranda that I had sent to both Juliano and Eder, commencing with May 2 and ending with June 11. I also included the reference to the September 13 memorandum to Knowles in which I reiterated Gotsch's apparent interference with my investigations.

Before I launched into Goldstock's requested extensive investigative plan, I closed out the opening phase of my memo with:

"From viewing the aforementioned events, it is obvious that my investigation has never been encouraged and has become increasingly shackled to the point where my efforts and the momentum necessary to carry it forward have been, as I have stated in my September 13 memorandum, 'emasculated.' The reasons are best known to my superiors. However, in light of the extensive publicity given this case (See Exhibit 'E,F and G') in the press and in light of the information that I have uncovered to support those allegations — plus, the events cited above — it would be reasonable, if not overwhelming to believe, that politics is, and has been, involved." The bulk of my memorandum then listed five major areas: *Potential Targets, Potential Criminal Charges, Potential Charges on Individual Targets, Synopsis of Investigative Efforts, Action Taken, and Scope of Future Investigation.*

Under the first category of *Potential Targets*, I gave the names of 22 individuals, including the name of the Mayor, three sitting City Councilmen, and one former City Councilman. There also was the name of a former Secretary to the City Council. The dizzying roll of targets with the District of Columbia government then included: the former personnel officer, five former directors, a former administrator, and employed assistant director, a division chief, a superintendent, two supervisors, a clerk, a former interviewer, and finally two former officials at the Federal City College.

Under my second category, of *Potential Criminal Charges,* I listed 11 criminal violations of the U.S . Code that would, in its totality, apply to those potential targets:

"• 18 USC 665 (a) — Embezzlement (CETA Funds)
"• 18 USC 665 (b) — Improper Inducement
"• 18 USC 1001 — False Statements
"• 18 USC 1341 — Mail Fraud
"• 18 USC 1510(a) — Obstruction of Criminal Investigation
"• 18 USC 641 — Public Money, Property or Records
"• 18 USC 286 — Conspiracy to Defraud Government with respect to claims
"• 18 USC 287 — False, Fictitious or Fraudulent claims
"• 18 USC 600 — Promise of Employment or other benefit for political contribution
"• 18 USC 207 — Disqualification of Former Officers and employees in matters connected with former duties or official responsibilities
"• 18 USC 371 — Conspiracy"

In addition to the 11 federal violations, I also called attention to my entry of a criminal violation under the D.C. Code, 22 DC 2306 - Intent to Commit Extortion by Communication of Illegal Threats and Demands.

I made a brief notation following that citation, "it is a potentiality that will have to be pursued more fully to establish validity of the elements of the crime."

Under my third category *Potential Charges on Individual Targets,* I zeroed in on the targets mentioned and cited, beside each name, the particular charge I was investigating. Those potential charges had developed from interviews, leads and other documentation that I had gathered in the course of my work.

Nine of my targets had one potential charge opposite their names, five of my targets had two potential charges, six of them had three charges and there were two individuals who had four and five potential charges, respectively.

Although my initial investigations began with the George Harrod case and my suggestion to the U.S. Attorney's Office to consider other violations of 18 USC 665(b), the *Improper Inducement* of CETA females, it soon mushroomed. I was pursuing as many felony allegations as I was misdemeanors. While half of my targets, ten in all, had allegedly engaged in sexually coercing females, many of those same targets had become involved in multiple potential felonies as well.

The greatest number of potential felony violations, a total of eight, not surprisingly lay in 18 USC 1001 — *False Statements*. The next sizable number of probable charges was in the violation of USC 371 — *Conspiracy*. Other potential felonies were interspersed among the various targets that I had listed in my memorandum to Goldstock.

By the time I reached my fourth category in my lengthy memo, that of *Synopsis of Investigative Efforts,* I wrote what I considered to be a brief summary of what I had done: allegations by specific sources, and the actions that I had taken in regard to interviews, documentation and field investigation.

In my final category, *Scope of Future Investigation,* I also included, not only what I thought was expected of my future work, but also information that I believed Goldstock might have sought in his memorandum of October 1: locating witnesses, interviewing, obtaining documentation, the preparation of charts and the request for additional manpower to accomplish all these objectives.

At the bottom of that memorandum, I added a final notation giving the number of "potential targets" and "potential criminal charges" that I had delineated above, and then stated:

"... these numbers are based upon present allegations. Further in-depth investigation will undoubtedly show an increase in both 'targets' and 'charges' ..."

As soon as I had completed the long task of developing Goldstock's contrived investigative plan, I had Lehrman review it also.

After he had studied it carefully and handed it back to me, he commented, "I don't know what the hell he wants in an investigative plan, but it looks like you've got all the points covered that he asked for."

"What he wants," I answered brusquely, "is to slow me down enough to block my investigations — and there's not a damn thing I can do to stop him."

Unfortunately, I was to prove myself right. Ten days after I had submitted the investigative plan to Goldstock, it was rejected and returned. There were no guidelines as to what he wanted to see, just to "redo it."

On October 26, I submitted an even more detailed supplemental memorandum to him.

It, too, according to Goldstock's memo of November 2, was deemed unacceptable. Again, there was no guidance, written or otherwise, as to what he wanted.

Lehrman, who from the sidelines had witnessed my growing frustration, now, also, became directly involved.

After a particularly derogatory response to my second *plan,* Goldstock stated that because of my lack of investigative experience, I was unable to give him what he wanted. He, then, contacted Lehrman to say he wanted him to become personally involved in the preparation of what was known to Lehrman and I, as a *hypothetical* investigative plan.

Both of us knew that no such plan had ever existed before in the I.G.'s Office, nor had we ever heard of one.

"He must be getting this information from somewhere," Lehrman insisted, "because he keeps harping on it."

"I've asked some of the other guys already," I stated, "and nobody knows what the hell he's talking about either."

"Let me do some extra digging, before we start a third plan," he suggested.

"Be my guest," I said. "But it won't make any difference no matter what you find."

Lehrman, however, did come up with some interesting information, a book that Goldstock, himself, had written in collaboration with another author. When he showed me the book, he pointed out a section that mentioned our elusive *investigative plan.*

"That sneaky sonuvabitch," I said, "he never once referred to this book."

"I guess you're supposed to be a mind reader," he said lightly. Because I had already devoted so many hours in the workup of my plan and because I was so knowledgeable of the potential defendants, Lehrman wanted me to continue what I was doing, even though I was fed up with what I considered to be an exercise in futility.

"Just hang in there, buddy, we'll get this through him yet," he said optimistically, "now that we've got the guidelines."

I read the particular section carefully and then adapted it to the third draft of the investigative plan. This time however, Lehrman suggested we narrow our charges down to five "criminal charges," and five "subjects," and I opened my revised six-page memorandum accordingly.

Under *Criminal Violations,* I listed what we had decided were the most important, and were more easily proven:

"• 18 USC 665(b) — Improper Inducement

"• 18 USC 1001 — False Statements

"• 18 USC 1341 — Mail Fraud

"• 18 USC 371 — Conspiracy

"• 18 USC 600 — Promise of Employment or other benefit for Political Contribution."

The second section, Subjects, identified the five potential defendants. The pared- down list included the former personnel director, the former Secretary to the City Council, a former Chairman of the City Council, the present Chairman of the City council, and, of course, the Mayor, who while a city councilman, himself, had allegedly violated two, and possibly three, of the federal criminal statutes.

The third section, under *Synopsis,* then capsulized the allegations — and evidence — gathered on the five subjects.

The fourth and final section, *Investigative Plan,* then spelled out precisely what investigative actions would be undertaken to cement the cases against all the defendants.

The closing statements of this academic exercise to satisfy Goldstock's repeated cry of an investigative plan stated:

"At the present time there are many alternative modes of investigation which can be used. However, at this time the investigative effort will be directed towards obtaining information to prove or disprove the allegations through interviews of victims, witnesses etc, and obtaining official records and documentation needed to support the objectives.

All alternative modes of investigations, i.e., surveillance, undercover work, electronic devices, etc. will be approved in advance on a case-by-case basis by the U.S. Attorney and the Department of Labor. This is in no way intended to impede any investigative initiative, but is designed to ensure that any change to this basic investigative plan is agreed to by the federal officials involved and the relative merits of each change are fully explored."

Before it was submitted to Goldstock, *again,* Lehrman reviewed it, and then compared it to the investigative plan in his book. "If that doesn't satisfy him," Lehrman noted, "nothing will."

"I hope you're right, Paul," I said slowly, "but ..."

He looked at, waiting for my comment.

I decided to keep my mouth shut.

However, within a few days, my unspoken words became apparent to both of us.

The third draft, minutely supervised by Lehrman, was also rejected by Goldstock. When he learned of Goldstock's response, he threw up his hands in disgust. I didn't want to rub it in and say *I told you so,* but I did step in and say "I'm gettin' tired of this fuckin' bullshit."

"What now?" Lehrman asked dejectedly.

"I'm gonna write Knowles again," I said, "and let her know exactly what's going on."

"You think she doesn't know already," Lehrman said sarcastically.

"I'm sure she does," I added, "but I also want her to be aware of where this whole 'cover-up' is headed."

In my two-and-a-half-page memorandum to her on November 13, on the same subject, *Interference with Official Investigation,* I mentioned Goldstock's "personal attack" on me and stated that he had, "become increasingly paranoid about his unrealistic mandates to write up an 'Investigative Plan' ..." I also wrote that, "his insistence had effectively 'bogged down' my investigation by pulling me into the office for several weeks ..." I also noted that after Lehrman was assigned to write up a *new* plan, he, then subsequently located a book titled, *"Rackets Bureaus: Investigation and Prosecution of Organized Crime,"* that had been co-authored by Goldstock under the auspices of a LEAA grant. I mentioned further that based on the reference to an investigative plan found in the book, that a detailed memo was again submitted. I reminded her, that it, too, was unacceptable, and that a new *plan* was required. I asked her, "again, at what expense to the successful investigation of these cases."

I hammered away at the ludicrousness of the entire exercise that was imposed on us by Goldstock, and pointed out the pitfalls of his actions — and her inaction:

"My objections to his hypothetical 'plan' were

voiced in my October 15 and October 26 memos to him. It should be noted that even in the book that he co-authored that these same type of objections appeared.

"This information was unknown to me at the time but reiterates my concern for the danger that this type of unrealistic approach takes. It is reminiscent of a Junior College 'INTRODUCTION TO CRIMINAL JUSTICE 1A' course or of the stilted introduction in Law School on 'How to brief an Examination.' It is indicative of a lack of 'street experience' and is an exercise in academia that will not only bog down an investigation, but as indicated on page 49 of the book, might jeopardize prosecution of the case.

"It is noteworthy to comment upon, that in Mr. Goldstock's treatise of an 'Investigative Plan,' he is equating a long range 'plan' dealing with 'organized crime' with a short range plan dealing with 'fraud.' Further, in Mr. Goldstock's personalized response of November 2, 1979, he 'lifted verbatim,' from the book, his entire paragraph 5 and paragraph 6 of his memo. He did so without benefit of citations indicating his source, which is the customary method utilized in pieces of this nature. Mr. Goldstock, however, did not bother to cite the opposition's view point — which happened to coincide with mine.

"Mr. Goldstock further states in his memo to me that a written investigative plan is a 'practice of this office.'

"This is a deliberate false statement. An investigative plan has not been, nor is it now, a practice of this office. If, as he says, that it has been his 'practice,' then it behooves him to properly and administratively implement his 'practice' so that all investigators can understand the workings of his mind.

"In reviewing my extensive memos to him during the past eight weeks, it is obvious that his words are not consistent with his actions and have succeeded in 'keeping me off the street' to pursue my cases.

"My concern with 'obstruction' should become your concern because, as you are well aware, you as the Inspector General are charged by Congress to investigate criminal violations and other abuses within the jurisdiction of the Department of Labor. Any course of conduct that is inconsistent with this mission is dangerous as we have all noted from the events that have occurred relative to the handling of PRIDE by HUD.

"In view of the serious nature of this memorandum, your personal response is requested."

The mention in my memo, of "events" concerning PRIDE at HUD, the U.S. Department of Housing and Urban Development, referred to a very recent newspaper article. The November 11 issue of the Local Star, an insert to the *Washington Star*, noted that the U.S. Attorney's Office had begun a grand jury investigation into allegations that the Mayor's former wife, Mary Treadwell, and others had systematically misappropriated at least $600,000 between 1974 and 1978 from P.I. Properties, an apartment project which was a subsidiary of PRIDE.

Although the Mayor was apparently not implicated in this particular phase of PRIDE, it was a name that I had become very familiar with earlier in the summer because of the proposed audit by Lehrman and Peterson, the former Chief of the Audit Division. It was also a name, that would figure heavily in my continuing investigation of cover-up in D.C. government by our own I.G.

Within two weeks, I would have a sworn affidavit attesting to the fact that Marjorie Fine Knowles would not investigate Youth Pride because of Mayor Barry's connection with it.

In spite of my warnings to her in my November 13 memo, she would blatantly ignore them, and would also fail to respond to my charges about Goldstock. However, at that time, being unaware of her future intentions, I was taking one day at a time.

The following day, on November 14, I learned that I was to

be excluded from a meeting with U.S. Attorneys who would be discussing my cases. Although Lehrman questioned Goldstock as to my non-attendance, he wasn't given a satisfactory answer and apologized to me for it afterward.

"Why that no-good son of a bitch," I said. "How can he exclude a lead agent from the cases, cases that I've been working on for eight months?" I demanded to know from Lehrman.

He shrugged his shoulders. "You know by now, that he's doing whatever he wants."

I sent Goldstock a memo asking the same questions. It, too, as so many memos before it, went unanswered.

Barron, who had also been following my confrontations with interest, stopped by my desk that same day.

"Here, Nickolai, I thought this might cheer you up," and he dropped another article in front of me to read.

In Joseph Young's *Federal Column*, there was a long article, "Plans Aim to End Sexual Harassment in Federal Service."

Before I even read it, I looked up at Barron, "Bullshit," I said. "It's not going to happen here."

"Just read it, paisan, and you'll see what I mean," Barron continued.

I read further and noted that the "House Civil Service Investigations Subcommittee headed by Rep. James Hanley, D-NY has been holding hearings on sexual harassment of women employees."

"Yeah, my buddy," I said sarcastically.

"But," Barron interrupted me, "they're holding hearings on it. Maybe you did get through to somebody."

"Yeah," I added. "That's why they called me to testify."

"You're bound to be making some impact," he noted, "with all the stink you've been raising."

"Not enough, Cam," I said. "It's still being swept under the rug."

Lehrman, who had been listening to the exchange, stepped in with a comment.

"If not, now," he tried to say reassuringly, "someday."

For the next week or so I was just spinning my wheels, and going through the motions of trying to do something constructive. Finally, fed up with my inaction and the status quo of my stagnant situation, I sent Goldstock another memo on November 20, and requested a "transfer back to the Washington Field Office."

In it, I reminded him that my detail, which initially had been 90 days and then was extended another 30 days, had expired on *October 7*. There had been no personnel actions, officially extending me the additional six weeks. I also advised him that I had submitted two previous memos, on October 23 and on October 30, requesting the same thing. I stressed in both of those memos that "my working area was not conducive to conducting sensitive investigations."

Although I did receive a vitriolic memorandum from him on November 2, he did not address the issues that I raised in my two memos cited. Instead, he noted that he was "not aware of any factors" in my investigation which made my working area "inappropriate." His non responsive comment was typical of a remark made by someone who does not want to be bothered by facts — just disregard them.

In spite of the fact that he deliberately ignored my initial complaint in June that my working space was totally inadequate, I renewed that notice again because of recent developments:

> "On or about November 9, 1979, I together with PAUL LEHRMAN, my Acting Supervisor, were relocated to another 'working area' because of major renovations being undertaken in our area. This new section is no better. We are in the office that comprises automatic data processing personnel — that is a far cry from our own restricted 'investigations.' We have a single telephone between us and our line is part of the 'ADP' extensions. We do not have clerical help to answer the telephone if we are away from our desks and therefore important telephone calls are either delayed in reaching us or do not reach us at all. There have been at least two occasions in which 'informants' have tried unsuccessfully to reach me only to have the telephone answered by an individual identifying the telephone number as 'ADP.' In addition, the low partitions, that are in close proximity to other personnel, make

conversations about sensitive matters a virtual impossibility. The clearly inappropriate 'working areas'
and the complete lack of responsiveness or concern
about my investigations would, I believe, negate
your unfounded remark in your memo of November 2, 1979, that my complaints are without merit."

In addition to my continuing complaint about our poor investigative space and my ongoing request to be transferred back to
my original office, I tried a new approach:

"If my requests are inconsistent with the desires of the 'front
office,' then I hereby request that I be granted a full IPA detail to
the U.S. Attorney's Office so that I can continue my investigations
unimpeded by that which has gone before me."

I knew I would be wasting my breath by just asking for an
Interpersonal Act detail to U.S. Attorney's Office, but I figured I
had nothing to lose.

Goldstock's non-responsiveness to my latest memo, and his
continuing disregard — as well as that of Knowles — toward my
investigations, left me with no alternatives other than to expose
them for their wrongdoing.

... **10** ...

The morning of November 26, I received a tip that if I wanted to know why Youth Pride was permanently off limits for an audit, then Peterson was the one to ask.

By that afternoon, I had done just that, and to boot, had obtained his sworn affidavit directly implicating our Inspector General in covering up for the Mayor. Now, that I had hard proof of a cover-up, I debated exactly what to do with it. There was no one above me I could relay my information to, because they, themselves, were directly involved. The only one above the I.G. and her Deputy was the Secretary of Labor, and I didn't feel confident relying on him. That left only the U.S. Attorney's Office, and there was no one in the felony section that I felt I could rely on. None of them really knew me, and, furthermore, I was excluded from a recent meeting with them. I didn't know what Goldstock had said behind my back to them. Although I knew that I could thoroughly trust Owens, I held that thought in abeyance.

When I showed Lehrman the affidavit, he said, "Careful what you do with it. You've got a tiger by the tail."

Barron, whom I also confided in, asked, "What are you going to do with it?"

When I shook my head, he added the same type of cautionary note that Lehrman did. I added, however, "I've got to do something. I can't let these sonsabitches get by with this."

During the next 24 hours, I slept on it. When I finally came up with a solution, I considered it the only possible answer to the problem. I felt that the U.S. Attorney General was the only one who could be trusted. I still believed in the *system* and felt that, in his capacity, he was the single authority who had jurisdiction over the political hire of an Inspector General. In theory, it was a good solution, but in practice it was not to be resolved that way.

When I made up my mind that it was the only path I could take, I rapidly moved forward. I didn't consider the consequences of my planned course of action. I knew I was right and also knew no one else would expose those superiors. I had taken an oath of office to enforce the law. To me — however naively I believed — no one was above the law. Not the mayor of a city, even if it was the capital, and certainly not my superiors who, themselves, had sworn to uphold the law.

Accordingly, I wrote up a brief cover letter explaining my actions, and then prepared a detailed affidavit that I had notarized. In that sworn affidavit, I recapped all of the events of the past seven months that led me to believe that my investigations were systematically being obstructed:

> November 28, 1979
> The Honorable Benjamin Civiletti
> Attorney General
> Department of Justice
> Washington, D.C.
> Dear Mr. Civiletti:
>
> My superiors at the Department of Labor, MARJORIE FINE KNOWLES and RONALD GOLDSTOCK, the Inspector General and the Deputy Inspector General, respectively, have conspired together to prevent me from fulfilling my official duties as a Special Agent and have thereby obstructed my criminal investigation of highly placed officials within the District of Columbia government. Lesser DOL officials have also acted in concert with this obstruction. My initial investigation centered mainly upon 18 USC 665 (b) Improper Inducement; however, the potential criminal violations now are numerous and varied involving additional potential "targets."

Attached find my sworn statement which contains events that are the basis of my allegations.

As indicated therein, documentation is available for verification.

Sincerely,
Nicholas J. Mangieri
Special Agent
Fraud Division
Washington Field Office
OIG - DOL
Attachment (as stated)

AFFIDAVIT

NICHOLAS J. MANGIERI, being duly sworn and deposes says:

I am a Special Agent with the Office of the Inspector General for the U.S. Department of Labor, assigned to the Fraud Division of the Washington Field Office located in Arlington, Virginia. I have been "detailed" to the National Office in Washington, D.C., since early June 1979.

For several weeks prior to my detail to the National Office, I was investigating allegations of sexual coercion of CETA females in the District of Columbia government by highly placed city officials.

On or about May 2, 1979, following an article in the *Washington Star* newspaper that the Department was looking into "CETA sex charges," I was told by my supervisor, that my investigation could endanger the Senate confirmation of the new nominee for the recently established Inspector General position, MARJORIE FINE KNOWLES. My attempt to ridicule that contention went unheeded on that occasion, as it did on several other occasions during the following month. In addition, during this same period I was constantly reminded of the Inspector General's "concern" over my case and the resultant publicity that has attended my investigation of it.

On or about June 5, 1979, my supervisor prepared false and malicious allegations in a written "proposal" to suspend me from duty for three days. These allegations were written in collusion with the then Acting Chief of Investigations, who had told me in an earlier meeting "to wrap up (your) case as soon as possible."

On or about June 6, 1979, I received what appeared to be reliable information that MAYOR MARION BARRY, while still a City Councilman, allegedly sexually harassed a female in City Hall. That allegation was transmitted to the National Office by one of the agents working with me without my knowledge or concurrence, although I was "lead agent" on the case.

On or about June 7, 1979, I was quickly detailed to the National Office, without the preliminary official documentation and without the customary advance notification of a new change in station. The unofficial reason given by the Acting Chief of Investigations was that it was done because of the "extreme sensitivity" of my case. (Subsequent documentation indicated that the 120 day detail was "NTE 10/7/79.)

My new working space in the National Office was totally unsuited to conducting a sensitive investigation. It was in a cramped, public area surrounded by personnel who were not criminal investigators. Repeated attempts to obtain a "certain modicum of security" to continue with my investigation were ignored and eventually ridiculed as unjustified complaints by the Deputy Inspector General, RONALD GOLDSTOCK. The two agents who had previously assisted me in the field office were removed from me upon my detail to the National Office, although they had no pressing workload to dictate it, and it was common knowledge that the scope of my investigation was ever-increasing.

On or about September 14, 1979, my supervisor rescinded his June 5, 1979, proposal to suspend me from duty for three days. His complete reversal followed an extensive in-depth expose by myself of his false and malicious allegations. My exposure of his activities also indicated collusion between him and the Acting Chief of Investigations. My expose also was brought directly to the attention of the Inspector General and the Deputy Inspector General. However, neither the Inspector General nor her Deputy chose to delve into my allegations of collusion nor to pursue my contention that it was done by design to hamper my investigations.

On or about September 15, 1979, I dispatched a Confidential memorandum to the Inspector General advising her of a "subtle cover up" of my investigations into D.C. Government and into City Hall, especially because of its political ramifications. I referred to a specific incident involving the then Acting Deputy Assistant Inspector General for Investigations.

On or about October 1, 1979, I received a response from the Deputy Inspector General. Although he acknowledged that my allegations were "obviously extremely serious," there were no denials nor any indications that any independent investigation of my charges would be launched. Instead, I was directed to prepare a lengthy detailed analysis of my investigations to be submitted to him in written form. I complied, but in my first written analysis to him pointed out that such a procedure was unwise and dangerous and could compromise my cases.

Other detailed memorandums were directed to his attention but were unsatisfactory. His unending requests effectively kept me "tied to my desk" and unable to pursue my investigation "on the street." During that month-long period, I also queried him officially on at least two occasions to transfer me back to my field office so that I could work undisturbed. I also reminded him that my detail had expired on October 7, 1979.

On or about November 2, 1979, I received a scathing unprofessional memorandum from the Deputy Inspector General removing me as "lead agent" and assigning my investigations to my Acting Supervisor in the National Office.

On or about November 14, 1979, I was precluded from attending a meeting in the Deputy Inspector General's office at which representatives of the U.S. Attorney's office were present to discuss my cases.

On or about November 15, 1979, I dispatched a memorandum to the Inspector General advising her that her Deputy was obstructing my criminal investigations. As of this date, I have had no response from her regarding my memorandum although I specifically requested a written reply.

In addition to my own personal experience with the Inspector General and her subordinates I have also come across a similar "cover-up" unrelated to my own investigations.

Documentation is available to support all of the allegations cited herein.

NICHOLAS J. MANGIERI

I, then, hand-carried, my letter and affidavit over to the Department of Justice and had one of the secretaries in the Attorney General's Office date-stamp it in.

I felt like the weight of the world had been lifted off my shoulders after I had accomplished my mission.

I swung by Jim Owens' office and related what I had just done.

"I hope everything works out for you," he said solemnly. "You know they'll be gunning for you now."

"I did what I had to do, Jim," I replied. "I'd do it again."

"I'll give you whatever support I can from this office," he assured me.

I thanked him and returned to my own office where I informed

Lehrman, also, of my recent actions.

"The shit's gonna hit the fan now," he unceremoniously announced.

He was right, of course, but it wouldn't happen for a few days.

After I had filed with Civiletti's office, I half expected an immediate response because of the seriousness of my allegations. When, after a few days, there was no word forthcoming on my disclosures, I became impatient with the delay. I didn't want to believe the worst about the Attorney General's Office, so I decided to carry my plans a step further.

On December 3, I called Ken Walker of the *Washington Star*, the same reporter who had done extensive investigative reporting on sexual coercion within D.C. government, and had also provided me with information in the early stage of my probe. When he heard my voice, he recognized who I was and asked, "What can I do for you today?"

"It's not what you can do for me," I replied, using the same line that he had used with me months earlier, "it's what I can do for you." I briefly explained what occurred the previous week.

"When can we meet?" he asked excitedly. We set a mutually agreeable time for later that day in a small room that he used as an additional office in the same building as the U.S. Attorney's Office. I didn't want to be seen going into the *Washington Star* newspaper complex.

"Good to see you," he said, as we met. "What's going on?"

In response to his question, I silently took out a copy of my letter with the affidavit I delivered to the Attorney General's Office. I rose and placed it on my chair.

"I'm going down the hall to get a drink of water, Ken," I said. "How long should I take?"

He looked at me and smiled. "I think that five minutes should be long enough."

When I returned, I picked up my copy and put it back in my folder.

"In case I'm asked by any of my superiors," I said, "I didn't *give* you anything."

Before I had a chance to ask him about when it would hit the papers, he anticipated my question.

"This is news," he said. "It'll probably be in tomorrow's edition."

He was right. The next morning I saw the article that would soon shake the Department of Labor — and me with it:

TWO ACCUSED OF 'OBSTRUCTING' SEX PROBE

By Kenneth R. Walker
Washington Star Staff Writer

"The U.S. Labor Department's inspector general and her deputy have been accused of 'obstructing' the department's probe of allegations that several District government officials used a federal jobs program to extort sexual favors from young women.

"Nicholas J. Mangieri, the Labor Department agent in charge of the investigation, filed a sworn complaint of the obstruction allegations with Attorney General Benjamin Civiletti last week, The Washington Star has learned.

"In the complaint, Mangieri alleged that Inspector General Marjorie F. Knowles and her deputy, Ronald Goldstock, 'conspired together' to obstruct the criminal investigation.

"In his affidavit, Mangieri claimed that the alleged obstruction began last May, when he said he was told by supervisors that his investigation could jeopardize the then-pending Senate confirmation of Knowles as inspector general.

"Following Knowles' confirmation, Mangieri stated in the affidavit, his assignment was 'quickly changed' following the receipt of information that a high District government official had 'allegedly sexually harassed' a female city employee.

"As reported in The Star last spring, Labor Department investigators uncovered evidence that one former and two sitting members of the D.C. City Council had allegedly engaged in the practice.

"The Labor Department investigation began after The Star's publication last April of allegations that female city government employees hired temporarily under the federal Comprehensive Employment Training Act were coerced to provide sexual favors in exchange for permanent jobs, promotions and other privileges.

""Mangieri stated in his complaint that while the investigation had centered on a federal statute barring improper inducement, 'the potential violations now are numerous and varied involving additional potential targets.'

"Mangieri stated in the complaint that he first informed Knowles on Sept. 15 that a 'subtle cover-up' of his investigation was under way.

"On Nov. 2, the complaint stated Mangieri was removed as the agent responsible for the investigation.

"In a statement released by a spokesman, Knowles rejected Mangieri's charges as 'totally frivolous allegations by a disgruntled employee facing supervision.'

"In a telephone interview, Mangieri declined to comment directly on the suit."

Lehrman's excrement forecast was accurate. However, it was more than just the shit hitting the fan, it was the whole damn pot.

As soon as I entered the building on the morning of the 4th, the reactions were as varied as the individuals, themselves. Those below supervisory rank were either patting me on the back, or making other appropriate remarks:

"I'd put in for a transfer if I were you."

"You do like to live dangerously, don't you?"

"Are you crazy, man?"

"You running for Congress, Mangieri?"

Those in the supervisory capacity and up, with the exception of Lehrman, all had a stony silence. Nothing was said to me by any of them. In fact, I was avoided like the plague.

Lehrman, who noted all the various responses, was amused by the situation.

"They're all acting like a bunch of kids," he said.

Barron, who had stopped by to see how I was faring, was more down to earth in his remark. "They're all acting like a bunch of pussies," he exclaimed.

Both he and Lehrman agreed on one thing though, "I'll bet they're planning something right now," one of them noted.

The next morning, on December 5, I received a very short memo from A.M. Statham, the new Assistant Inspector General for Investigations:

"This is to notify you that, pursuant to your request, your detail to headquarters has been terminated effective December 5, 1979."

It then added that a copy of Standard Form 52, Request for Personnel Action, would be forthcoming.

"It's about damn time," I said when I received it.

"Don't get your hopes up, buddy," Lehrman commented. "You know they're not going to let you get by with this."

I agreed, but also added that anything was better than being there.

Shortly after our conversation, Lehrman, who had been casually looking at the *Washington Post,* suddenly stopped.

"I'll be a sonuvabitch," he said, "I made the papers this time," and pointed out an article about Youth Pride:

EX-LABOR AIDE SAYS AUDIT OF PRIDE VETOED

In the two-page article it noted that:

"The Inspector General of the U.S. Department of Labor vetoed a planned audit of Youth Pride Inc., which has received over $20 million in federal funds, out of concern that the probe might be potentially embarrassing to D.C. Mayor Marion Barry, according to an affidavit from the Labor Department's former top auditor."

Although the in-depth account gave verbatim contents of the affidavit that I had obtained from Peterson on the prior week, it failed to mention that I had been the one who obtained the incriminating document from him.

When Lehrman called my attention to it, I shrugged it off but I did think it was rather odd that I was not cited as having initiated the contact with him. Lehrman's name appeared in the article, as did that of Wendy Rhea, the former program analyst who had worked with Lehrman and Peterson on the proposed Youth Pride audit. In a direct quote from Rhea, the Post reported that in an interview with her, that she stated that Knowles was "politically extremely sensitive." The Post also noted that:

"The auditors had already been in touch with Marion Barry," Rhea said. "He was already touchy because of a case about improper hiring by the City Council."

The *improper hiring* by the City Council was a result of allegations that I had already been pursuing.

The article in the paper then continued with further quotes from Rhea:

"Then we raised Youth Pride and we were told by Knowles that 'it looks like you're picking on Marion Barry and we're trying to work with him.' "

It was her final comment that made me sit up and take notice, because until then I really wasn't fully aware of the political handholding that went on in Washington — nor the trouble that I was causing with my naive concept of justice being equal for all:

"At that point, Barry was doing well with Congress and the [Carter] administration and Knowles didn't want to come up against him," Rhea said.

The balance of the apparently well-researched article then indicated that as a result of an examination of Labor Department records on Youth Pride, it revealed not only very sloppy bookkeeping, but outright questionable expenditures. It also cited apparently unnecessary spending for supplies that were either unsupported or unauthorized.

Although this article was the first attempt by the *Washington Post* "to get into the act" concerning District Government and the ongoing investigations that the *Washington Star* had initiated, Lehrman and I nevertheless congratulated ourselves for their appearance.

"Maybe next time, you'll be in," Lehrman said playfully, alluding to some future article.

The *next time* was to be soon, but unfortunately, the type of coverage that I anticipated was not to be forthcoming.

December 4, the previous day, proved to be as eventful as December 5 had been. Statham asked to see me in his office. He had recently assumed control over all investigations as the new Assistant I.G. for Investigations. As such, he had replaced Gotsch, the Acting Assistant Deputy, who initially had supervision over my cases. Gotsch was the newly selected bureaucrat, who three months earlier, insisted that I work on one target at time instead of the three or four proposed by one of the Assistant U.S. Attorneys.

In Statham's curt conversation with me over the phone, he advised that I should give him my entire case so that he could read it over.

When I suggested that perhaps I should go over it with him, or be available should he have any questions, he coldly replied, "That won't be necessary."

You've gotta be kidding, I told myself.

"It's starting," Lehrman commented afterward.

The next day, Statham informed me that my case consisted primarily of allegations, nothing more.

When I relayed to Paul, what shouldn't have been surprising news to me at all, he simply turned his palms upward as he looked me directly in the eye.

"You really didn't expect him to do any differently, did you?"

I didn't want to hear the obvious.

"That's bullshit, Paul, and you know it. He couldn't have read any of it. I just gave it to him yesterday."

"I know it, and you know it," he answered, "but we're in the minority. You better keep your back covered from here on out, buddy."

On the morning of the 6th, I was back in my Arlington office. Juliano had been transferred to the National Office six weeks earlier, and "Pete" Castro had been named the Acting Supervisor. Charmayne, however, and Peter Ives greeted me and were happy at my return. In spite of the still-strained feelings between Castro and myself, I was equally happy to be back in my own small office.

That feeling of satisfaction was short-lived, however, for on that same morning, I received another brief memorandum. This one was from David R. Coffman, Special Agent Supervisor of the Philadelphia Division, and referred to my primary case:

"Effective December 6, 1979, I am assuming the role of Lead Agent on the above matter. Stu Hannon will be joining me in this investigation. Pending our review of the entire file and formulation by us of our investigative plan, you are hereby instructed to take no further investigative actions in this matter such as interviews of witnesses, discussions with the United States Attorney, etc ..."

The memo then stated that I "should plan to meet with him and Stu," another supervisor from the Boston office, on December 12 "to fully brief us on this investigation, and to turn over all field documents, agents' notes and any other material which is in any way related to this case."

Before I had a chance to catch my breath from that new announcement, both he and Stewart Hannon appeared suddenly in the Arlington office.

Coffman, the younger of the two supervisors, appeared to be in his mid-thirties. He was the fidgety-type and acted as if someone were forever pulling his strings. Hannon, on the other hand, appeared to be in his late thirties, or early forties, and had some prematurely grey hair. He seemed to be okay, but as time went on, my feelings about him would change, and he would be put in the same category as all the others who were trying to bury my case — and me.

Their stay was short. Jumpy Coffman wanted to make sure that I understood his memo to me and that I would cooperate fully.

I nodded. "I understand *fully*," I said.

To myself I said, *yeah, it's started,* repeating Lehrman's earlier admonition to me.

The shit was still coming.

On the next day, December 7, I received still another piece of disconcerting correspondence. That letter was from a Lovida H. Coleman, Jr., a Special Assistant to the Attorney General:

> "Your letter and affidavit of November 28, 1979, have been received in the Office of the Attorney General. I have reviewed your affidavit and although, on its face, it fails to substantiate any charges of a criminal nature that you have made concerning employees of the Department of Labor, I have forwarded them to the General Counsel of the Merits System Protection Board and the Public Integrity Section of the Criminal Division in the Department of Justice. Those offices will review your letter and affidavit and determine what action, if any, should be taken."

I read it, re-read it, and then read it again.

What the hell does she mean, "it fails to substantiate any charges of a criminal nature ..."

Goddamn it, what the hell did she think I was doing?

In disgust, I threw the letter down on the desk, took a deep breath, picked it up, and then read it again.

I noted that she had forwarded it to the Merits System Protection Board and to the Public Integrity Section within the Department of Justice. My first reaction to the mention of the "Merits System Protection Board" was, *why the hell is she sending it there? What are they going to do, slap her wrist? What kind of a whitewash is this?*

However, when I calmed down, I saw that it also went to the Public Integrity section. *Maybe they'll do something about it,* I thought hopefully.

Not having heard much about a "Public Integrity Section," I assumed it was like the Internal Affairs Divisions in existence in most large police departments, where cops investigate other allegedly bad cops who have had complaints registered against them. The thought buoyed me up temporarily, but, in reality, I was expecting much more. Because of my superiors' high positions, that of Inspector General of an agency and its Deputy Inspector General, and because of the seriousness of the charges — conspiracy and obstruction of justice — I believed they would fall under the Congressional provision calling for a Special Prosecutor to investigate them. I soon learned, though, that the Inspector General concept was so new, there was no provision to include them in any Special Prosecutor probe.

It took me a couple of days to get over the disappointment of the Special Assistant's letter. The more I thought about it, the more it bothered me. *There must be something else I can do to get the Attorney General's attention,* I thought.

The only thing that came to mind was another letter to him, and three days after the receipt of the Coleman's letter, I sent my reply:

Office of Inspector General
U.S. Department of Labor
Fraud Division
4040 Fairfax Drive, Suite 1002
Arlington, Virginia 22203
December 10, 1979

The Honorable Benjamin Civiletti
Attorney General
Department of Justice
Washington, D.C.
Dear Mr. Civiletti:

I am in receipt of a December 7, 1979, letter from your Special Assistant, Lovida H. Coleman, Jr., advising me that my letter and affidavit of November 28, 1979, to you, concerning obstruction of justice were reviewed by her. I am appreciative of her action forwarding those items to the General Counsel of the Merits System Protection Board and to the Public Integrity section of the Criminal Division in the Department of Justice for their respective reviews.

I am, however, concerned with the negative connotation that her letter implies; that, "although, on its face, it fails to substantiate any charges of a criminal nature ..." they were referred to the above offices. The phraseology is weak and inappropriate and, I hope, is her comment as an individual and does not reflect the official position of your office.

The allegations made in my letter and in my affidavit are very specific and based upon hard fact. The substantiation can be obtained, as my affidavit very explicitly states, by the documentation in my possession. An in-depth investigation by the Department of Justice will verify my allegations, as well as those of a similar nature.

In view of the seriousness of the allegations against these two officials, your personal intercession is requested to preclude this investigation from being "lost by the wayside."

Sincerely,
Nicholas J. Mangieri
Special Agent
Fraud Division
Washington Field Office
OIG - DOL

Timeliness, not being a notable governmental attribute, I received no response from that letter for many weeks.

Meanwhile, I had to respond to Statham. It had been almost a week since he had told me I *had no case*, so I felt compelled to answer his inaccurate allegations. During that week, I had been fully involved with analyzing the newspaper articles with Coffman, and finally with letters to and from the Attorney General's Office. It left me little time to do all I had to do. It seemed as if a *new front* were being opened up on me every day. Each day was a constant battle.

Barron who had invited me out for a beer after work one day commented, "Why don't you give it up, Nick? You know you can't fight the whole department."

"Whole department, hell," I admitted. "It feels like I'm up against the whole fuckin' government."

"That's what I said, paisan," he added softly. "You can't fight them all."

"It's not over yet, Cam," I said. "I gotta keep trying."

"All the guys are behind you," he said, "for whatever it's worth."

On December 11, I sent a detailed memorandum to the new honcho in the sky, A.M. "Mac" Statham, including the nickname he always used. It was one he always used to engender camaraderie among the troops. I uncompromisingly titled the subject matter of the memo, "Obstruction of Criminal Investigation." It was no sense pussy-footing around any of my superiors, now, because they all knew where I was coming from. I didn't want to go with my head bowed in front of any of them. I was fed up with the continuing blatant cover-ups used by all.

My lengthy chronological memorandum to him left nothing out and was specifically phrased to cover an even wider interested reading audience.

> "It appears that your actions following the filing of my criminal complaint with the Attorney General against Marjorie Fine Knowles, the Inspector General and Ronald Goldstock, her Deputy, are retaliatory and punitive in nature and are merely a 'smoke screen' of propriety.
>
> The following events are self-explanatory:

• On November 29, 1979, my criminal complaint was filed, charging them with obstruction of justice and conspiracy.

• On December 4, 1979, that information appeared in an article in the *Washington Star* newspaper.

• On that same date, you requested and received from me all of my investigative reports concerning my case at City Hall and the District of Columbia government.

• On December 5, 1979, you advised me that:

(1) You had read over my entire case and that they were primarily 'just allegations with very little substantiation.'

(2) The agents in charge of the Philadelphia and Boston fraud offices were coming in immediately to 'work the cases.'

• On December 6, 1979, I was transferred back to my field office in Arlington, Virginia.

• On that same date, I was met by Dave Hoffman, Agent-in-Charge of the Philadelphia office and Stewart Hannon, Agent-in-Charge of the Boston office and advised that:

(1) Upon their return to the Washington area on December 12, that I was to turn all case material over to them.

(2) I was to do no work at all on my cases until their return.

(3) I was forbidden to contact the U.S. Attorney concerning my cases.

Upon reflection of the above and based upon the following, it would further appear that my contentions have considerable merit:

(1) You have never solicited information from me concerning my allegations although you have been cognizant of them for at least six weeks.

(2) It was a virtual impossibility for you to read and understand my voluminous case material in less than a 24-hour period. (That material compressed

to a one-and-a-half-inch thick file. It involved six different agencies and mentioned approximately 200 names of suspected, victims, witnesses and others knowledgeable of information. It contains various types of documentation and made reference to other types.)

(3) The agents from the Boston and Philadelphia offices are not 'street agents' but supervisors. Presumably they have sufficient work in their own offices to keep them fully occupied.

Therefore, it would appear that the detailing of supervisory personnel from other cities is an impractical, contrived move that will accomplish little or nothing and was done as a 'stop-gap' measure to force me out of an effective investigation.

It would further appear that your actions, or lack of actions, are less than objective and are self-generated — thereby implicating you in the scheme devised by the Inspector General and her Deputy.

If my assessment of the situation is wrong I will apologize to you, but an analysis of the facts indicates otherwise."

I reviewed my accusatory memorandum, and was satisfied with its content.

I then decided to send four copies to appropriate sources. The first copy was sent to: Ray Marshal, Secretary of Labor. The second copy to: Benjamin Civiletti, Attorney General, again, and the final two copies were sent to the: *Washington Star* and the *Washington Post*.

As I mailed them all, I told myself, *if that doesn't get their attention, nothing will.*

... 11 ...

The Christmas holidays came and went. While I tried not to let all of my troubles at work dampen the festive occasion with my three kids, it was a cloud that hovered during the season.

Just before taking some annual leave for Christmas, Coffman and Hannon arrived at the Arlington office to relieve me of my case material. At the conclusion of the turnover, Hannon had an "Inventory of Items Submitted" and then signed it for me.

The inventory noted there were eight folders bearing names, five case jackets, numerous reports, letters, statements and memos, and "three lists of names and addresses of D.C. CETA employees." In addition, the inventory included sixteen tapes with a list of the individuals recorded and dates the tapes were made. Some had been transcribed by the typist, and some had not.

In spite of this extensive accumulation of case material, Mac Statham, our illustrious Assistant Inspector General for Investigations, had told me just one week earlier that he had read over my "entire case," and that all I had were "just allegations with very little substantiation."

His reference to *a* case obviously was inaccurate because I had *six* open cases. Undoubtedly he wanted to minimize the extent of my investigations by referring to a single case in lieu of the multiple cases I possessed. Further, his self-serving statement failed to take into consideration the additional material I had — nor did he ever ask what else I may have had. If he was ever embarrassed by the amount of case material that Hannon and Coffman confiscated from me no one knew. Either he buried it or the individuals he reported it to buried it to minimize the appearance of wrong-doing within the District of Columbia. Further, the Felony Division within the U.S. Attorney's Office would have little or no knowledge of the scope of my investigative matter because not only was I precluded from meeting with them, but any input to their office would, of necessity, come from our Assistant Inspector General for Investigations. Their plan was ingenious in its simplicity but very effective.

I, however, had other plans. I wasn't holding my breath waiting for the Public Integrity Section of the Department of Justice to do its job regarding my allegations against Knowles and Goldstock.

I heard that under the recently enacted Civil Service Reform Act that I, as a federal employee, was protected against "prohibited personnel practices, including reprisals against whistleblowers."

I don't believe, in my twenty years of federal service, I ever heard that term used before in the context that it was being used, nor did I think that the choice of such a phrase was sufficiently strong enough. To me, it was an innocuous description of someone just *doing his duty*. Over the years, my feelings have not changed in the use of the "whistleblower" term.

In early January, I wrote the Office of Special Counsel within the Office of Personnel Management a detailed letter requesting intercession in accordance with the provisions of that Civil Service Reform Act. I enclosed my affidavit to the Attorney General and four exhibits I considered relevant for consideration: the Lovida denial letter of December 7, my reply to the Attorney General of December 10, my December 11 accusatory letter to Statham, and finally, the December 5 memo to me from Statham terminating my detail — *two months* after it should have ended.

In my lengthy letter I also mentioned that "I not only was - removed from my case as 'lead agent' but removed from any participation at all." I further noted that "my removal from the case is punitive and designed not only to impede the case but to impede my career growth in the Department of Labor."

In the days that followed my letter, the minor workmen's compensation cases doled out to me did little to fill my time. The days dragged out slowly as I awaited some type of reply or action from the Office of Special Counsel.

On January 11, I received a call from Lehrman.

"Have you seen today's *Post*?" was the first question out of his mouth.

"No, Paul," I answered. "That's your paper, not mine."

"I think you'll want to see *this* issue," he stressed.

"Why? What's in it?"

"I'm not going to tell you," he answered, "but when you read it, you're not going to be happy."

"Goddamn, Paul! Don't keep me in suspense. Where do I look?"

"Check the Letters to the Editor section. You can't miss it," he said, then hung up.

I located a copy of the *Washington Post* in front of our building and took it back to my office to read.

As I opened it to the section Lehrman mentioned, a large caption immediately caught my attention:

SECRETARY MARSHALL ON A 'FALSE ALLEGATION'

"On Dec. 21 *The Post* reported a false allegation by a former employee of the Office of Inspector General at the Department of Labor that the inspector general had rejected an "investigation" of Youth Pride, Inc., a District of Columbia CETA subgrantee, for "political reasons." The same allegation had been printed in a front-page article of *The Post* on Dec. 5 and was mentioned in a front-page article on Dec. 12. The facts, which have been made available to *The Post* but have not been printed, belie this allegation. Because I believe the integrity of inspectors general to be of critical importance in their fight against waste, fraud and abuse, I want to set the record straight.

"Inspector General Marjorie Fine Knowles did indeed make a management decision to reject a proposed review of Youth Pride, Inc., in June 1979. However, the proposed review was neither an audit nor an investigation. It was, instead, part of a new program called Fraud and Abuse Prevention Sur-

veys (FAPS). These surveys are used as management tools to identify any systemic weaknesses that
might lead to waste, fraud or abuse. The FAPS program was designed as an experimental program to
develop methods for preventing fraud and abuse.
It was not designed as an investigative program.
The FAPS program was, and still is, in an early stage
of development.

"At the time the review of Youth Pride, Inc.,
was proposed, the Office of Inspector General was
interested in testing the FAPS guides in a CETA
subgrantee — any subgrantee. It is important to
understand that FAPS are not a substitute for the
Office of Inspector General's regular audit and investigative activities.

"In fact, at the time of the proposed FAPS,
Inspector General Knowles had no information to
indicate wrongdoing or even allegations of wrongdoing, at Youth Pride, Inc. The decision not to proceed with a FAPS of Youth Pride, Inc., was a management decision based upon the discretionary
nature of a FAPS review and the need to rationally
allocate limited resources throughout the country.

"At that time, two major audit activities of the
District of Columbia CETA program were already
getting under way. First, a financial compliance audit
was scheduled that would cover the D.C. CETA
prime sponsor as well as subgrantees. Second, a special audit review of the D.C. Summer Youth
Employment Program was scheduled as part of a
nationwide project. In addition, the Office of Inspector General was involved in activities concerning
use of CETA funds for inmates at Lorton. Even in
hindsight, it was a logical decision at the time to
have conducted the proposed FAPS on another
CETA subgrantee in an area receiving less Inspector General attention.

"In addition — and critical to the issue at hand
— an investigation into possible misuse of CETA

funds by Youth Pride, Inc., was promptly begun in October 1979, when information indicating possible problems emerged. That investigation is ongoing. Also, an audit of Youth Pride, Inc., is being undertaken by the prime sponsor, whose responsibility it is to audit its sub-grantees.

"Finally, let me state that Marjorie Fine Knowles was nominated to be the first inspector general of the Department of Labor not only because of her outstanding professional background as a lawyer, prosecutor and manager, but also because of her unquestioned integrity. Rest assured that neither she nor I will condone fraud, abuse or waste for any reason, including political considerations.

RAY MARSHALL,
Secretary of Labor

While I was reading his letter I could feel my blood pressure rise and my stomach knot up.

What is this crap? I muttered to myself.

I called Lehrman back, and was boiling when he picked up.

"Either someone's been feeding him a load of shit, and he's buying it, or he's whitewashing Knowles," I bellowed into the receiver.

"I told you you'd be unhappy," he tried to answer calmly.

"He's calling Peterson a liar," I said, unbelieving.

"In effect," Lehrman said. "He's doing the same to me and to Wendy. If you remember she gave an interview to the *Post* reporter, as well."

"I know," I agreed.

"I don't really think he's involved with them though," Lehrman mused aloud. "I think they just gave him a snow job, and he bought it."

"This shit just keeps getting deeper all the time," I said. "There's no end to it."

Lehrman grunted an acknowledgment. "There's nothing you can do about it either. She's got all the right contacts."

"Well, I've got to set the record straight," I insisted. "If that letter is believed, that sets everything back we've done."

"How're you going to do that?"

"Another Letter to the Editor," I said, "only this time, complete facts and answers to what the Secretary brought out in his biased letter."

"Can't say I disagree with you, buddy, but your guess is as good as mine as to how successful you'll be," he said pessimistically.

"Nothing ventured, nothing gained, Paul," I continued. "I just can't sit on my hands and do nothing."

"You're probably right," he conceded. "Good luck."

Over the next ten days or so I wrote and rewrote a detailed response to Secretary Marshall's letter. Finally, on January 24 I submitted my final amended product to the Letters to the Editor section of the *Washington Post:*

> "Dear Sir:
>
> "On January 11 the Post carried a response by Secretary of Labor, Ray Marshall, to articles appearing on the front pages of both your December 5 and December 12 editions. The gist of Secretary Marshall's letter was one of defense of the DOL Inspector General, Marjorie Fine Knowles, of allegations that she blocked a probe into Youth Pride, Inc., because of potential political embarrassment to D.C. Mayor Marion Barry.
>
> "I have no quarrel with the Secretary nor any reason to believe that he was aware of I.G. Knowles' decision to block that probe last spring. However, I feel that the Secretary has been misinformed and should and must be presented with all the facts before he reaches a point of no return.
>
> "Knowles, contrary to what the Secretary was told, was not so deeply inundated in investigations within the District of Columbia that would have precluded her from approving a Fraud and Abuse Prevention Survey (FAPS) of Youth Pride, Inc. The two "major audits" mentioned in the Secretary's letter of January 11 were merely scheduled. They were not ongoing. The "involvement" with CETA funds at Lorton was merely at a superficial stage.

Although the original allegation came into the I.G.'s office from Congressman Cavanaugh's office, the in-depth review of the prisoner's being paid CETA funds was handled by ETA (Employment and Training Administration) within DOL and not by the I. G.'s office.

"If Knowles needed a valid excuse for not commencing a new investigative effort into the District of Columbia that was proposed by her audit staff, why wasn't my case cited? I was the lead agent on a full-blown criminal investigation into sexual coercion by highly placed officials in D.C. Government and within City Hall. An investigation that began a full six weeks before Knowles stopped the Youth Pride probe. One that had made the news and one that Knowles and her key staff were painfully aware.

"If, as the Secretary's letter states, Knowles' June 1979 decision not to probe Youth Pride, Inc., because FAPS was merely a "management tool," why wasn't the Secretary told of the more enlightening contents of a May 18, 1979, memo from the audit division to Knowles. That memo advised Knowles that a "new" surveillance audit was devised beyond the original FAPS concept that could flush out fraudulent acts that had occurred "with or without collusion'" and could even spot sophisticated fraud "even though internal controls may appear to be strong."

"If, as Knowles told the Secretary, the District of Columbia was being saturated by investigations, why didn't she reject the new probe immediately subsequent of the May 18 memo when her audit division explicitly told her of their plans? Why did she wait until after the June 11 Memo to her that Youth Pride, Inc. had been chosen and that Mayor Barry's office was in the process of being contacted?

"If, as was commonly known throughout OIG, there was an austerity move to conserve travel funds, why were the two investigators and three auditors diverted from the local Youth Pride probe to spend approximately three months in Milwaukee on another FAPS probe?

"Contrary to what the Secretary was told by Knowles an "investigation" was not promptly begun by Inspector General Knowles in October 1979 into possible misuse of CETA funds by Youth Pride, Inc. Her "investigation" was merely a monitoring effort of the FBI's activities and this was officially done on October 22 when Youth Pride made *Post* headlines and not before.

"Congressional sources were also misled by Knowles. She misadvised them, as well, that DOL had an "ongoing" investigation.

"Is this lack of candor indicative of her alleged "unquestioned integrity?"

"In addition to the allegations concerning blockage of the Youth Pride probe, my own criminal investigation into D.C. Government, and particularly into City Hall, has been continually subjected to interference, and, myself, to constant harassment. Initially there were covert attempts to cover up my investigation by my superiors. Then more overt attempts by Knowles and her Deputy, Goldstock. On November 19, 1979, I filed an obstruction of justice charge with the Attorney General. That complaint is now being reviewed by the Department of Justice.

"Knowles' tendency to cover up politically sensitive investigations is not unique to her present assignment. A reliable source at HEW informed me that while Knowles was General Counsel to the I.G.'s office there, she allegedly stopped a criminal investigation at Eppley Institute, a Cancer Research Center, in Omaha, Nebraska.

"Deputy I.G. Goldstock, too, has allegedly been involved in current improprieties while at DOL. A reliable source also has revealed that audit work performed at Cornell University, for Goldstock, was not government work.

"These allegations and others could be verified if a Congressional Committee or any other impartial investigative group would interview OIG employees at both DOL and HEW.

"It would appear that Knowles is more interested in her self-interests than in making the Inspector General's role at DOL more effective. Last summer, she relocated several investigators from her office to make way for her $18,000 private bathroom. A move that was reported in the *Star's* "Ear Column" on 6/28/79.

"If myself and other investigators are to conduct meaningful criminal investigations, we cannot be shackled to the self-serving interests and ambitions of a few who consider our work a threat to their own political futures. Protection of political figures cannot be permitted, nor can cover-ups of investigations into their activities be tolerated, if the public is to have renewed faith in the government.

Nick Mangieri
Special Agent
Fraud Division
Washington Field Office
Office of the Inspector
General
Department of Labor

I waited a couple of days for it to appear in print, then three, and finally on the fourth day I called the paper to get status on it. I was put through to the editor who handled that department and explained who I was and that I had written a response to a letter by the Secretary of Labor. He hesitated and then said that he would look into it and get back to me.

He called as he said he would, but his reply was not what I expected.

"I'm sorry. We can't run it," was his quiet response.

Somewhat taken aback by his answer, I inquired why the paper would not run it. He didn't give me a satisfactory reason. All he would say was that he had taken it higher and the decision was not to use it in the *Post*. I pressed him about whose decision it was, and why my factual, accurate response to the Secretary's misinformation was not given the same space and consideration. He avoided the first part of my question but conceded that my letter should have been carried. He apologized and indicated that if it was left up to him, my letter would have appeared.

After I hung up on the editor, I cursed a blue streak and stomped around my office in anger. Barron, who was in an adjoining office, heard me and poked his head in the doorway.

"Something wrong?" he asked.

When I explained what I had just been told over the phone, he looked as surprised as I had been a few moments earlier.

"I didn't know they could censor the news," he replied naively.

"I didn't either," I said. "We must both be living in another world."

I called Lehrman to tell him what happened.

He was silent for a minute and then spoke.

"The whole city's controlled under this administration," he said slowly. "There's a Democratic President, a Democratic Congress, a Democratic Mayor, and even our I.G. is a Democratic appointee." He stopped to let the words sink in. "You're buckin' the whole system. They can pull strings and call in favors that we wouldn't believe were possible."

"The whole fuckin' system stinks then," I said disgustedly.

"You did your best, buddy," he tried to soothe me. "I don't know what else you could have done. They've got the deck stacked against you."

His words were small consolation in light of what had been happening to me on an almost daily basis.

Norman Romney, another agent who had recently been reassigned to Arlington with Barron, overheard the heated conversation within my office. Ives and Castro were both out of the office and Charmayne, who was transcribing, was oblivious to the minor commotion.

Romney stepped into my room.

"What's up, Nick?" he asked in a concerned tone.

I didn't go into the details with him, although as I grew to know him, I realized I could have.

"Just political bullshit, Norm. I'll tell you all about it someday."

Romney was a retired ex-cop from New York, probably in his mid-fifties and still as perceptive as he had been when he was a beat cop.

"I ran across it all the time when I was in Manhattan," he said.

A leisurely conversation ensued between the three of us and it relaxed me — until Castro returned.

He handed me an "Authority for Release of Information" form from the U.S. Civil Service Commission.

"What's this for?" I asked.

"We all have to sign one," he said, as he handed them out to Barron and Romney as well. "It gives the department permission to check all of our backgrounds."

Barron and Romney looked at each other and then back to me before they addressed Castro.

"We've already had our backgrounds checked before we were ever hired," Barron noted.

"Yeah, that's true," Castro admitted, but the I.G. wants it again."

I read the single-sided form quickly, did a quick deletion, initialed my change and gave it back to Castro after I signed and dated it.

"What are you doing, man?" he asked.

"I'm deleting the liability section," I said. "I don't trust the system."

Castro read aloud where I had lined through on the form:

"I hereby release any individual, including record custodians, from any and all liability for damages of whatever kind or nature which may at any time result to me on account of compliance, or any attempt to comply, with this authorization."

Barron and Romney couldn't help but laugh at what I had done.

"I'm not releasing anybody for any damages done to me," I said firmly, and resumed the work on my desk.

The balance of January was uneventful, but on February 8, the other shoe dropped. I received a short letter from John C. Keeney, the Deputy Assistant Attorney General, for the Criminal Division:

> "This letter is in response to your letter to the Attorney General of November 28, 1979, and enclosed Affidavit and your letter of December 10, 1979. I have discussed the matters raised therein with members of the staff of our Public Integrity Section who conducted a thorough review of the situation. In accordance with their recommendations, the Criminal Division is closing this matter without further action.
>
> "The criminal investigative resources of the Department of Justice can be utilized only in circumstances where the facts indicate that a federal criminal law may have been violated. The information you have brought to our attention and the information gathered by members of our staff does not provide an adequate basis for further consideration of this matter by the Criminal Division.
>
> "We appreciate your bringing this matter to our attention and your courtesy in providing additional information and in responding to the questions of the Public Integrity Section attorney."

To say I was shocked, or even surprised, at the content of the official reply would no longer be an appropriate description of my feelings. I had been on the receiving end of so many letters, memos and other forms of *official* documentation that I was becoming desensitized to them. To say I was disenchanted or disillusioned by the federal bureaucracy would be much more accurate.

After the initial wave of frustration passed, I tried to analyze the words used in this new rejection. He mentioned that the Public Integrity Section "conducted a thorough review of the situation." *How the hell could they conduct a thorough review,* I said to myself, *if all they had were my two letters and my affidavit?* That correspondence from me was merely to point out to the Attorney General that there was *probable cause* to believe that "obstruction of justice" had been committed. That *probable cause* was merely a reasonable ground for belief in certain alleged facts, or as legal texts would point out:

"A set of probabilities grounded in the factual and practical considerations which govern the decisions of reasonable and prudent persons and is more than mere suspicion but less than the quantum of evidence required for conviction."

Certainly my affidavit had raised more than a "mere suspicion" of my superiors repressive antics but had delineated their actions in a step-by-step sequence that strongly indicated they had engaged in violations of several federal statutes.

The edition of the U.S. Code in usage, at that time, gave 18 USC 1510(a) "Obstruction of Criminal Investigations," as: "Whoever willfully endeavors by means of bribery, misrepresentation, intimidation, or force or threats thereof to obstruct, delay, or prevent the communication of information regarding to a violation of any criminal statute of the United States by any person to a criminal investigator ... ."

All of my superiors, up to and including the Deputy and the Inspector General, *misrepresented* to the U.S. Attorney's Office the scope and the depth of my investigations. These actions effectively "kept me off the street," thereby *preventing* and *obstructing* witnesses from *communicating information* regarding violations of criminal statues to me.

In addition, the repressive actions against me by my superiors *intimidated* witnesses and kept them from coming forward to give me the information I sought.

These elements were the basis for investigation — and prosecution — of my superiors.

The U.S. Code at 18 USC 1505, "Obstruction of proceedings before departments, agencies, and committees" also described in part:

"Whoever corruptly ... impedes or endeavors to influence, obstruct ... the due and proper exercise of the power or inquiry under which any inquiry or investigation is being had by either House, or any committee of either House or any joint committee of the Congress ... ."

As noted, my superiors, specifically at the top level, had *impeded* my invitation to appear before the House Subcommittee on Investigations. That request was a *due* and *proper inquiry* conducted by the House of Congress. My superiors, however, unquestionably obstructed my appearance before that group, and again, the elements were met.

In view of the substantial detailed content of my affidavit to the Attorney General's Office there would no doubt appear to be *probable cause* that potential violations had, indeed, occurred in 18 USC 1510(a), and in 18 USC 1505, as a result of my intensive investigations. The "1510" violation would apply to all of my investigative efforts as a whole, and the "1505" violation would specifically apply to preventing me from testifying before the congressional committee.

For that matter, there were also reasonable grounds to believe that a conspiracy was involved to interfere with my investigations. The U.S. Code at 18 USC 371, "Conspiracy to commit offense or to defraud United States," gave the elements of the crime in its description:

"If two or more persons conspire either to commit any offense against the United States, or to defraud the United States, or any agency thereof in any manner or for any purpose, and one or more of such persons do any act to effect the object of the conspiracy ... "

Again, it would appear that my superiors met the elements of 18 USC 371, when they *conspired,* or in layman's terms "planned in secret," to commit the offense of 18 USC 1510(a), "Obstruction of criminal investigations." My documentation would undoubtedly be rife with their continuing *acts* to effect the object of the conspiracy.

Even more on target would be the wording of 18 USC 372, "Conspiracy to impede or injure officer:"

"If two or more persons in any State, Territory, Possession, or District conspire to prevent, by force, intimidation, or threat, any person from accepting or holding any office, trust, or place of confidence under the United States, or from discharging any duties thereof, or to induce by like means any officer of the United States to leave the place, where his duties as an officer are required to be performed, or to injure him in his person or property on account of his lawful discharge of the duties of his office, or while engaged in the lawful discharge thereof, or to injure his property so as to molest, interrupt, hinder, or impede him in the discharge of his official duties, each of such persons shall be fined not more that

$5,000 or imprisoned not more than six years, or both."

My memoranda and letters constantly referred to my superiors' actions to *prevent* me from *discharging my duties*. Their coercive and domineering methods certainly met the criteria for *intimidation*. Further, there would be even more proof to show that there was *injury to my person or property* while engaged in the lawful discharge of my duties.

Of course, none of these potential felony violations — which carried up to five and six years imprisonment — were pursued because, as the Keeney letter stated, "The information you have brought to our attention and the information gathered by members of our staff does not provide an adequate basis for further consideration ... "

This conclusionary remark fell on the heels of his written comment that criminal investigative resources at the Department of Justice could only be used when the facts indicate a federal criminal law may have been violated.

His use of the word "may," arguably put it into the parameters of the definition of *probable cause,* wherein a "reasonable ground" existed in alleged facts rather than a certainty required for a conviction.

After thoroughly digesting his letter — knowing what I knew and could prove — I still couldn't believe the type of reply that I received. None of the documentation I had compiled, beginning with Juliano, then Eder, Gotsch, Statham, and up through Goldstock and Knowles, was ever examined for corroboration of my allegations.

To my knowledge, Lehrman was never questioned by the Public Integrity section. If he were, I feel confident he would have mentioned it to me.

In addition to my obvious concerns about the lack of interest by that section in the material they already had, I became equally concerned about one of my suggestions to them. I had volunteered to wear a wire to extract any pertinent information from my new supervisor, Dave Coffman. I raised this issue with them knowing Coffman's tendency to say something without thinking it through would have resulted in something incriminating. My request was never granted if, in fact, it was ever considered.

Inasmuch as that door was now closed to me, I decided to concentrate on the civil aspects of my ongoing battle. Obviously, the Criminal Division would be of no help to me in the future, because as the letter conclusively stated, they were "closing this matter without further action." There were no contingencies left open, as I might have expected. The issue of criminality regarding my superiors was dead in the water with no possibility of revival.

Apparently the word had gotten back to those same superiors because they continued business as usual in their dealings with me. However, although I had lost another battle, I wasn't going to lie down and die for them.

On February 14, I sent a memorandum to Coffman, who although my official supervisor, was still operating out of the Philadelphia office. In that memo I requested that I be detailed to fill the position of Acting Team Leader of our office, which, in effect, was also considered to be the Acting Supervisor. I further advised Coffman in that memo:

"You are aware that although the present Acting Team Leader, Osvaldo "Pete" Castro, was officially designated to that position in a memo dated October 24, 1979, he was in effect the Acting Supervisor long before that date."

I notified Coffman that OPM regulations, and those adopted by DOL, specified that details to any position were not to exceed a four-month period. I then reminded him that Castro had exceed that time limit and that my "administrative, investigative and academic backgrounds" were superior to Castro's.

When I told Barron over a cup of coffee what I had just requested of Coffman, he responded with, "You gotta be kidding, paisan. You know how much he hates your guts."

"I know," I replied calmly.

"Do you think he'll give it to you?" he asked in a half-serious tone.

"Hell, no," I answered.

"What have you got up your sleeve then?" he asked.

"Then I'll grieve it to personnel," I said.

I didn't have to wait too long. On February 21, I received a two-word response to my "Career Development" memo. In it, Coffman simply wrote, "Request Denied."

You stupid son of a bitch, I said to myself.

I then went to Castro to advise him that I wanted to go over to the National Office to file a grievance. He, in turn, refused to give me permission to do so, saying permission had to come from his supervisor.

Rather than argue with him and tell him what I thought of him I decided to put my request in writing — for the record:

"On February 25, 1980, I advised you of the necessity to visit our personnel office for the purpose of filing a Formal Grievance. You orally denied me that 'right' and in addition refused to respond to my request in writing, although I specifically sought it. Further, you advised me that I would have to contact the next level of supervision for that permission, Dave Coffman, Special Agent-in-Charge of the Philadelphia Division.

Be advised that Chapter 19 of the Employee Handbook states that: 'your immediate supervisor does not have the right to keep you from visiting your personnel office or seeing a higher level management representative, but does have the right to require you to delay your visit to a later time, or day, because of workload or another good operational reason.'

Inasmuch as this operational decision to grant me the right to visit personnel does fall within your bailiwick as my immediate supervisor, kindly advise me when I can visit my representative."

To throw in a kicker by reminding him of a memorandum that he had previously circulated to our office staff, I added the following sentence:

"Attached find a copy of your January 28, 1980, memo advising our compliance with Chapter 19 of the 'Handbook' before we visit our Personnel Office."

In spite of my written request with its supportive documentation Castro still refused to permit me to visit that office. I then called Coffman in Philadelphia to renew my request as per regulations. At first, he also refused because Castro had already told him I was "disruptive to the office" as a result of my visiting personnel "two or three times per week."

"What?" I said in disbelief.

He repeated himself.

I was tempted to bellow, "bullshit" into the phone, but held myself in check.

"False info," I said firmly. "I haven't visited our personnel office in weeks."

He asked that Castro be put on another line, and a three-way conversation ensued. When he asked Castro to check the log he sheepishly admitted that it showed I had last visited personnel on January 21, 1980, — five weeks before — not the "two or three times per week" that he had initially alleged.

I was then granted permission, and on the following two days, briefly stopped in at personnel on two separate occasions. On the first trip there I picked up a copy of the Grievance Procedure. On the second trip I sought to obtain specific information from one of the personnel technicians in order for me to perfect my grievance. While waiting for the technician to research the issue, I decided to visit our finance section to follow up leads given me by a very reputable source. That source not only was a Supervisory Criminal Investigator but held the position of SAC of the Eastern District in New York in DOL's Office of Organized Crime and Labor Racketeering.

That fateful decision to pursue leads against Goldstock and another one of his Special Assistants involved the alleged fraudulent filing of travel vouchers to obtain illegal reimbursements from the federal government. It was a decision, that while opening a new Pandora's box of charges against our Deputy Inspector General, would be the beginning of doors being slammed shut on me.

... 12 ...

Although my arrival in the travel section to check vouchers might have raised some eyebrows, on the whole there was cooperation by the employees because, as a Special Agent, I was working within the scope of my duties.

The source of the tips that I was investigating came from Barry Silvers, the SAC of the New York office, and it involved Robert Nicholson, a Special Assistant that Goldstock personally had hired from New York. Even though Nicholson originally was hired as a GS-12 by DOL in the Organized Crime Division of New York, he magically rose to a GS-15 through Goldstock's direct intervention with the Office of Personnel Management.

The specific tip concerning Nicholson centered on alleged improprieties in his travel vouchers. A cursory inspection of those vouchers, for travel that occurred between July and December 1979, revealed that there was, indeed, possible misuse of government vehicles and his own private vehicle for which he was reimbursed by the government. I also noticed that Nicholson's travel vouchers were either approved by either Ronald Goldstock or Stuart Eder, who had since moved to head up the Internal Affairs Section.

I made a mental note to come back and make copies of all those documents and then analyze them more thoroughly. If my suspicions, and those of my reliable informant, proved correct there were numerous possible violations of both 18 USC 286 and 18 USC 287.

The latter statute, that of "false, fictitious or fraudulent claims," would, if true, involve the travel vouchers of Nicholson. The former statute, that of "conspiracy to defraud the Government with respect to claims," would possibly implicate both Goldstock and Eder.

In addition to examining the Nicholson vouchers, I also briefly inspected Goldstock's travel vouchers for the same general period. My purpose in doing so was in regard to my informant's tip that Goldstock had made trips to Hawaii and Miami for personal reasons, not government business.

When I noted that the travel vouchers from October 1979 to February 1980 were not in that same working area, and inquired where they were, I was told they were on another floor. However, because I had been gone from the Arlington office a little longer than I had initially signed out for, I decided not to visit that part of the building.

Just before leaving the travel section, I spoke to Joe Duffy, a supervisor there. Conversation with him revealed the fact that Goldstock had been paid $6,000 for travel expenses subsequent to being hired by Knowles. Although she allegedly "fought to get him to retain it," she was advised that it was against federal regulations because he was not a prior federal employee and therefore not entitled to the receipt of moving expenses.

In a "Memo for the Record" on that same day, I made an additional brief notation to myself: "Have the FBI check the double billing (pay by the institutions that Goldstock lectured at, and pay by the Department of Labor)."

En route to Arlington from the National Office, I was feeling very pleased with what I had seen and even more optimistic about what I had yet to uncover. However, that feeling of elation would vanish shortly after I returned.

At approximately 3:30 p.m., I walked into the office, greeted my fellow agents and entered my own room. There were no messages, and in spite of the fact that we were all there, it was unusually quiet. I made an off-hand comment to Barron about it. He jerked his thumb toward Castro's office and entered his own room.

Within the hour Castro called us all together – Barron, Romney, Ives and myself – to tell us that Coffman was flying in that evening as we had a "hot bribery going down" and he wanted us all to be there when he arrived on the 6:15 p.m. flight.

We all looked at each other, wondering what the hell was going on, but none of us had an inkling. Castro was of no help, either.

"You'll all just have to wait until he comes to find out," was all he would say.

"They're making a big deal out of nothing," I said to the others. They all made appropriate comments and retreated to their own rooms again.

At 7 p.m., a stony-faced Coffman arrived and entered Castro's office. After about five minutes, he emerged to give us our anticipated "briefing." He apologized to us for having us all stay but said he and Castro could handle it. We looked at each other and shook our heads at what we all perceived to be a ridiculous scenario. Coffman then excused all the other agents except me. Barron looked at me questioningly, and I just shrugged my shoulders. As soon as they all left, it started.

For the next two hours, I was wildly questioned by Coffman as to who my informant was, who I was investigating and why. He ranted and raved at the top of his voice and alternately pounded on a table to get me to tell him what he wanted to know. I was threatened with termination if I did not respond to his questions and threatened with detention by the guards in the lobby if I tried to leave the building. A phone call was even placed to them in an attempt to have them visit our floor to somehow restrict my movements within the office. Apparently Coffman used that threat in an effort to intimidate me even further. As I later learned, the civilian guards refused to accede to his demand and instead referred him to a supervisor in the Federal Protective Service.

When I finally answered Coffman's insistent questioning, I advised him that he, himself, could not be trusted for two reasons. The first reason was that he would then report directly to his superiors, the very ones I was investigating. My second reason was equally strong. I told him in no uncertain terms that he also was directly involved in the cover-ups of my City Hall investigations and that I would turn over my information to the FBI, no one else.

With my adamancy and my refusal to cooperate with him, he became even more volatile. He demanded I turn over my credentials to him. When I refused, he resorted to a turbulent tirade against me and became even more violent in his pounding the furniture. Castro, who had passively observed the situation the whole time, interjected that I should surrender my credentials in an effort to quiet the scene down.

Finally, when Coffman saw the futility of his demands, he summarily told me I was being placed on immediate administrative leave and was to turn over my key to the office and the key to my own individual safe. I handed him the office key, but before I gave him the key to my safe, I opened it to extract my personal papers and effects. When he saw me do so, he very slowly and methodically read everything that was mine with appropriate malicious remarks concerning the content. Although I continually pointed out that the papers were obviously of personal nature, he ignored me. At one point, while I was going through my briefcase, Coffman even reached in without my permission and took out various small items that were not discernible without physically delving into corner recesses. When I told him specifically to replace those items that were my personal property, he again ignored me. All the while, Castro was supporting Coffman and did, or said, nothing to stop him.

During the course of these bizarre antics by Coffman, he also tried to pat me down for a weapon. I brushed his hand aside and emphatically told him I was not carrying one. It was even more obvious that I was not armed because I wasn't even wearing a jacket to conceal a weapon.

At the termination of my two-hour ordeal with Coffman and Castro, I was instructed not to visit the National Office on the following day but to remain by my phone at home to answer Coffman's calls. I also was told not to leave between the hours of 8:30 a.m. and 5 p.m. so he could "check on me," whenever he "could find the time." He also advised me that if he did not find me at home during the hours specified I would be labeled AWOL "with additional charges to be filed."

As unreal as the situation was that evening, events from that point onward would only intensify

In an attempt over the next few days to somehow respond to a supervisor's actions that were even more outlandish than I had experienced under Juliano, I decided that my only recourse was to stay within the civil service system.

In a detailed memorandum I wrote to A.M. Statham, as Coffman's immediate superior, I headed it up with:

"Misconduct, Conduct Unbecoming a Supervisor and Harassment by David Coffman, SAS."

Although I knew that writing to Statham would be tantamount to asking a fox to watch the chickens, I did so, in order to build the *perpetual record* I knew I would need. I commenced with the National Office events of February 27, where "pursuant to prior information received from a reliable confidential informant, I inspected the travel vouchers of an official within the Inspector General's Office and that of one of his assistants."

At this juncture, I also knew Statham and everyone else for that matter in Knowles privileged "Immediate Office" were aware that my targets in the travel section were Goldstock and Nicholson.

In my lengthy memo, I chronologically and graphically described the incidents that occurred in the Arlington office the evening of the 27th. In addition, if there was to be any question as to Coffman's use of heavy-handed methods, I also related an episode that happened when he subsequently came to my home:

> "On March 3, 1980, Coffman, in the accompaniment of Agent Romney, continued his further harassment of me. On or about 6 p.m. he personally visited my home and intimidated my two young daughters to admit him into my house without my express permission to do so. (My daughters aged 10 and 15 years were in awe of his insistent request to see me and admitted them.) They were in no position nor felt able to deny his entrance. Upon my descent from a second floor they were both standing inside my hallway. In answer to Coffman's question as to whether I 'was busy,' I replied in the affirmative. He ignored my remark, proceeded to a kitchen table in an adjoining room and stated that he had something for me in his briefcase. Without giving me time to further object to his unannounced and uninvited presence in my home, he laid his briefcase down on my kitchen table and extracted a letter from Ronald Goldstock, Deputy Inspector General, DOL, dated February 19, 1980. The let-

ter stated that I was relieved of my duties and responsibilities as an investigator and instructed me to turn in my credentials. I was further advised by Goldstock that I was detailed to an administrative management desk position for a period of 120 days.

"There was no urgency in a personal visit at my home other than continued harassment. The letter could have been mailed. If I was unable to have been reached by phone a telephone message could have been left with anyone to relay the 'urgent' information to me.

"I was further informed by Coffman that my office had been stripped of all my personal effects and crated. I objected to his highly improper method utilized and specifically objected to my non-presence to be able to examine, determine that which was mine and then retrieve my personal effects."

In that same memorandum, I called attention to an additional visit on the following day that also distressed me:

"On March 4, 1980, Agent Romney delivered a carton which purported to contain all my personal effects. A receipt was tendered with the wording indicating that 'all' of my personal effects were included therein. A quick inspection of the carton indicated that it was only partially filled and I placed a disclaimer on the receipt. Closer subsequent inspection not only verified my contention but showed that my privacy was further invaded by Coffman's perusal of highly personal papers (including but not limited to my divorce decree and related papers and correspondence)."

Romney apologized profusely for having to disturb me at home and for the manner in which Coffman was handling the whole situation.

"I'm sorry, Nick," he said, seeing how agitated I was becoming as I searched through my personal effects.

"That no good son of a bitch," I said tightly.

"None of us knew, buddy," he added, "or we would have never left you."

I nodded, understanding, but Romney still had a tense expression.

"Don't sweat it, Norm," I said. "He won't have the last word."

My memo to Statham was the first of many. So that he would know there would be more coming, I advised him that my letter was in accordance with DLS Subchapter 3-19, FPM-771 and would constitute an *Informal* Grievance Procedure. This procedure, as he would learn from personnel, was the first step in a formal grievance process. I also did it to let him know that, as Coffman's supervisor, he officially was being put on notice that his subordinate's actions were perpetrated against me "while I was lawfully engaged in the pursuit of my duties as a Federal Agent."

The Goldstock letter that Coffman felt the need to hand-carry to me gave Goldstock the added impetus to attack me. In that self-serving document he pretentiously wrote, "I feel it to be my public obligation to relieve you of your duties and responsibilities as an investigator in the Office of the Inspector General." His statement came after he noted that I failed to report to my direct supervisor official business that I "claimed to be pursuing," and failed to answer questions about that investigative activity.

I'll bet that slimy son of a bitch really thinks he's covering his ass, I thought to myself.

His letter further advised me that I was being detailed back to the National Office for a period that was also "not to exceed 120 days."

Standard terminology when they want to bury you.

My new detail was to be to the Administrative Management Staff, in the Office of Loss Analysis and Prevention where I was to perform duties related to legislative and regulatory review.

Bullshit, I said to myself. *A goddamn desk job.*

The part of the letter I didn't want to see, appeared at the bottom:

"You are to turn in your credentials by close-of-business March 3."

I was further instructed to "relinquish" to Coffman "all official information and documents related to these investigations."

I took a deep breath as I read it and then tossed it aside.

"There goes all my fuckin' work down the drain," I muttered. "No one is going to do a fuckin' thing to stop him."

I went out for a drink – maybe it was two.

Monday morning, March 3, I reported to my new supervisor, Don Hehir, in the AMS section. He was a nice old guy, thin, gray-haired, wearing glasses that constantly slipped down on his nose. He reminded me of some harried accountant who had his nose in his ledgers for years. However, as pleasant as he was, and would be, I was in no frame of mind to appreciate it. My attitude especially didn't change when I was assigned to my new "office," a five-foot-square cubicle with five-foot partitions on all sides. It felt like I was in a padded tomb.

Great! I said to myself.

I told Hehir I had to turn in my credentials, and he said he understood. Apparently, he had been briefed on the reason for my detail, but in the time that I would be assigned to him, he never brought the matter up, or let any of the I.G.'s actions cloud his judgment or his dealings with me. For that I was thankful, because he never interfered with the myriad of personnel actions I initiated. Hehir was well-satisfied as long as I did the tasks doled out to me. Although on paper, I was still classified as a Criminal Investigator, my new duties were totally inconsistent with that position description. A brief statement of duties given to me when I reported for duty were to, "review existing and proposed legislation and regulations to assess their impact on the detection and prevention of fraud, waste and abuse in DOL programs and operations."

In time, my new position description would be changed to reflect my new meaningless duties. No matter how much time I devoted to analyzing legislation and writing about it, it would either be ignored or never used, for I would never hear of the results of my written work after I turned it in. In spite of the fact that Hehir sporadically gave me an assignment, he had to turn it over to his supervisor, and who knows what happened to it afterward.

The morning I had to turn in my credentials – a small gold and blue badge with my identification – I did so with a heavy heart. I had thoroughly enjoyed my work. I was good at it, and I produced results. However, in exchange for that effort, I was given a receipt for number 018, a designation meaning I was one of the first to be employed as a Criminal Investigator for the Department of Labor. Subsequent to my own hire there were at least 200 more agents hired, with chronologically numbered I.D.'s.

From the front office on the first floor, where I turned in my credentials, I went to Lehrman's office now located on the other side of the building on the fifth floor. He had since transferred out of the OIG's office and had a new position that he liked. His new space was a medium-sized room that had a window overlooking downtown Washington.

"Classy, Paul," I announced when we met.

"Not like our old space, is it?" he quipped.

"Naw, but my new one is," I said.

"I heard."

"Word gets around fast, doesn't it?" I responded.

After he commiserated with me for what Coffman and Goldstock had both done, he added, "You come at them face on, buddy. I use a knife from behind."

"That's always the way I've operated," I said defensively.

"Yeah, I know," he conceded, "but my methods are always effective because they never knew what hit them."

"It's a little late to change my methods of attack," I said.

"I know," he said. "That's what makes you the way you are."

I smiled weakly at the left-handed compliment.

"Just hang in there, buddy. You'll be okay."

Once back in the solitude of my small cubicle, I decided I better make my time as productive as possible. I had no workload awaiting me and wouldn't have for several days. Even when something was assigned to me, there was an unnecessarily long return date for its completion. What I could realistically accomplish in hours was not due back for several days. I'm sure Hehir's supervisor was dancing to the strings of the I.G.'s office. I was given enough work to make it appear I was doing something important to substantiate my detail to the AMS office. In reality, it was a waste of time and money, if ever that was considered in government.

On March 5, I sent a memo to Statham that involved the formal grievance procedure concerning my "denial of career development" because Coffman had arbitrarily refused to consider my being assigned to the Acting Team Leader position in Arlington. I not only reiterated that Castro was beyond his 120-day detail in that office, but that Castro had deliberately alleged I had visited personnel more times than I had.

I knew there was a snowball's chance in hell of Statham conceding my qualifications for the slot, but I was "going by the book." I was going to make Statham officially respond to my formal grievance. I was going to bury the bastard in paperwork.

I reminded Statham that the planned management action "to mold Acting Team Leader Castro for a future permanent position" was not only inequitable but fell "under a prohibited personnel practice of the Office of Personnel Management." To really get his attention, I also advised him that "as deciding official in accordance with Section F" of the FPM, that the decision had to be made by him.

Not content that I had done everything possible, in addition to the March 7 memo to Statham about Coffman, I also sent a memorandum to Alfred M. Zuck, Assistant Secretary for Administration and Management. I was told earlier by Joe Duffy in the travel section that Zuck was the individual who had called Knowles' attention to the improper payment of Goldstock's moving expenses.

In my memo that I identified as "Bias and Misconduct of, and Harassment by, Ronald Goldstock, Deputy Inspector General," I noted in detail that:

> "Ronald Goldstock, the Deputy Inspector General, acting in his official capacity, in a letter dated February 29, 1980 (Exhibit 'A'), stripped me of my credentials because he learned I was investigating his activities and examining his travel vouchers and those of one of his assistants. My investigation was consistent with my duties as reported in my informal grievance to A.M. Statham, Assistant Inspector General for Investigations (Exhibit 'B').
>
> "SAS Coffman's highly improper method of questioning me concerning my activities was also reported in that informal grievance. Coffman was acting at the direct orders of Goldstock, of which Marjorie Fine Knowles, the Inspector General, should have been aware. All of these individuals

have compromised the integrity of the Department of Labor and have now made the Department civilly liable for actions committed within the scope of their employment.

"Therefore, in accordance with the Informal Grievance Procedure specified in DLS Subchapter 3-19, FP 771, subject memorandum is being forwarded to you for whatever action you deem appropriate at this time. It should be obvious that if remedial action is not instituted immediately to stop Goldstock or his subordinates from further misconduct the damage to the Secretary and to the Department could be irreversible.

"It is common knowledge that I initiated an obstruction of justice charge against both Goldstock and Knowles for their effort in preventing me from my criminal investigation into the activities of some highly placed officials within the District of Columbia Government (Exhibit 'C').

"Goldstock's biased behavior toward me is best reflected in my Nov. 13, 1979, memorandum to Knowles concerning his actions (Exhibit 'D'). His inflammatory prejudicial remarks are also found in paragraph #1 of Exhibit 'A' and indicate a continuing attempt to justify an indefensible position.

"It also would appear that because of Goldstock's blatant abuse of power in preventing me from performing my duties as a Federal Agent that he has opened the door for the filing of civil rights violations as well.

"The Secretary is being apprised of this memorandum because of the immediate importance to him and to the Department. However, because some measure of the resolution of this grievance lies within your jurisdiction according to the above-cited Federal Personnel Manual source, it is directed to your attention.

"Specifically:

"(1) Restoration of my credentials, improperly

taken for personal reasons.

"(2) Transfer back to my field office.

"(3) Resumption of my AUO arbitrarily and capriciously terminated.

"Attachments"

The reference made of "resumption of my AUO" in my memorandum referred to Administrative Uncontrollable Overtime. It amounts to an additional 10 percent of one's salary because of the overtime usually required in investigative work. When I was removed from my field work, I lost that extra pay. Any loss in pay with a family to support hurts.

I still had one more bit of business to do before I left for the weekend.

I sent one final memo to Paul Jensen, Executive Assistant and Counselor to the Secretary of Labor. In that brief memorandum, I attached copies of my informal grievances about Goldstock and Coffman and advised that I believed the Secretary should be made aware of those actions as soon as possible.

As I reviewed what I had done on that Friday, I thought to myself, *not bad Mangieri, you've done a good day's work*. For the first time in what seemed like a long while, I had something to look forward to again, especially the memo to Zuck who I thought might be sympathetic. As for the Jensen memo, and the request to show it to the Secretary, I thought I had better than a 50/50 chance. At least there was hope, or so I felt on that Friday afternoon.

Monday came and went with no responses, as did Tuesday, Wednesday and Thursday. When Barron stopped by at the end of the week, we went out for lunch.

"How you doing?" was his first question.

"You mean what have I been doing?" I answered.

"Okay, I've got a feeling you're gonna tell me without me even asking."

I filled him in on the events of the prior week.

"They're gonna be sorry they detailed you here too," he said with a laugh.

"That's what I thought when I sent those memos out last week."

"You mean you haven't heard anything yet?" he asked incredulously.

"Nothin'," I replied." Not a fuckin' thing."

"I still can't believe they're ignoring what you're saying," he said.

"Right up to the top," I said. "But, as they say, the battle goes on."

"Is it worth it?" he wanted to know.

"It is to me," I replied.

On the following day, March 14, a full week after I sent the memos to Statham and Zuck, I was advised by personnel to amend both of them to a more explicit grievance that could be easily resolved. Accordingly, I did so.

In Statham's, I changed the wording to:

"Amendment of Grievance Concerning the Conduct by David Coffman on February 27 and March 3, 1980, and Concerning an Illegal Administrative Leave Order of February 27, 1980."

The body of the grievance stayed basically the same, with the exception that the specific points I wished to bring out were numbered. There were 13 in all. The final paragraph contained, as per personnel's advice, exactly what it was that I wanted:

"As a relief, I request (1) that my personnel file be amended to reflect the fact that the administrative leave order of February 27 was illegal and unwarranted; (2) that a letter of reprimand be issued to David Coffman; (3) return of all my personal papers and (4) a letter of apology from the Agency."

In Zuck's memo, the new wording of the subject matter was slightly different:

"Amendment of Grievance Contesting My Removal from My Position as an Investigator from the Office of the Inspector General (DOL), and My Detail to the Administrative Management Staff."

The body of the amended grievance was much more detailed and highlighted all of the repressive actions that had occurred, thereby substantiating my strong belief in a cover-up of my investigations. Again, at personnel's advice, I was more explicit in the resolution of my grievance:

"As relief, I request that I be returned permanently to my post as Criminal Investigator, that my credentials be returned to me, that I be reassigned to the case from which I was removed, and that my superiors be enjoined from hindering my investigation."

This time there was an immediate response to my last memo, which amended my grievance to Zuck. It was not what I had hoped for, but it was an answer, and it did direct me what to do next. It was not only typical bureaucratic gobbledygook, but it really "passed the buck."

In that long-winded reply, the Assistant Secretary for Administration and Management informed me that in the departmental organizational hierarchy, he was not the next higher authority for the Office of the Inspector General, but that the Undersecretary was that authority. To further confound his explanation before he got to the bottom line, he advised me:

> "The administrative grievance procedure provides further, that if the person to whom the grievance is first presented does not have the authority to make a determination, it shall be immediately forwarded to any level below the first step of the formal grievance procedure at which such authority exists. If it is determined that no person below the first step has such authority, the grievant shall be so notified, and advised to proceed under the formal grievance procedure.
>
> "In this instance, there is no official below that is normally the first step of the formal grievance procedure with authority to rescind actions directed by the Deputy Inspector General in his letter to you dated February 29, 1980, which is the subject of your informal grievance. Therefore, in accordance with established procedures you are advised to proceed under the Department's formal administrative grievance procedure - - -.
>
> "If you decide to file a formal grievance, it must be filed within ten (10) workdays of receipt of this letter, with the Inspector General, Marjorie Fine Knowles, who is the appropriate first step official in this instance."

I shook my head at the ludicrousness of the whole system. Here I was, back in Knowles' ball court having to officially complain to her – as I had done unsuccessfully all along – about Goldstock's actions.

The balance of Zuck's memorandum to me then gave me the option to proceed under, in the event that any "acceptable adjustment is not reached." The option that he cited was to request a grievance examiner through the Federal Mediation and Conciliation Service. That examiner's finding and recommendations would then be submitted back to Knowles, then on to the Undersecretary, and then finally sent to the Secretary of Labor.

Unbelievable, I said to myself. However, I knew I had to play by the rules, as stupid as they seemed, if I wanted to come out on top. Therefore, in accordance with Zuck's instruction to me, I merely changed the wording on the "Amendment of Grievance" to Zuck on the 14th, to "Formal Grievance" to Knowles. I, then, hand-carried my formal grievance down to the Immediate Office, and had it acknowledged as being received on March 21, by Mazie Haley, the pleasant-looking blonde secretary who sat by the entrance door. I'm sure my continued appearance was not a subject of joy to her any more than it was to the rest of her superiors in that elitist office. I, nevertheless, gave her a big smile, as if I were enjoying the whole exercise. My smile was hardly ever reciprocated.

My strict adherence to personnel rules must have gotten the attention of those in the head office, because on the 21st, Statham answered my memo of March 7 concerning my "denial of career development" by both Castro and Coffman. In that response, he rejected any possibility that I should have been considered to fill a detail to the acting Team Leader's position, because, as he stated, mere status as an employee in an organization did not entitle me to a tour of duty in that slot. He also blindly followed Castro's and Coffman's allegations that "workload or other operational reasons" must have required me to delay my visit to the personnel department to file the grievance against Castro. The issue of my being more qualified than Castro, which I addressed in my memo, and of his time limit being exceeded, was never discussed. In an effort to make his stance on the matter even stronger, even though he had no documentation or justification to support his position, he wrote, "I am convinced your visit was delayed because of your workload ... "

Apparently, Statham didn't read that Castro's *delaying* me was more than just that, it was *refusing me*. In addition, Statham totally ignored the fact that Castro had deliberately lied to Coffman when he said I had been visiting personnel two or three times per week.

Based on Statham's failure to note, or consider, factual situations, he then found "no basis" for a remedy and advised me that if I didn't like his response I could refer it to a grievance examiner. His reply to me, that date, was no different than the denial I would receive from him on the 28th. That very brief memo was in direct response to my March 14 "Amendment of Grievance." He erroneously stated in that memo that I would have to resubmit to him for it to be subsequently entered at the *formal* grievance level. Although I specifically called attention to the fact that Coffman's administrative leave order to me was illegal (as per personnel's advice) and that I wanted my personnel file amended, he ignored my request. He also ignored any reference to the return of all of my personal papers, and, not surprisingly failed to mention anything about a letter of apology from the Agency.

If they thought that by continually throwing up roadblocks to delay or frustrate me I would be discouraged from proceeding further with my grievances, they were wrong. I was just getting started.

Fortunately, the individual they assigned me to in the Office of Loss Analysis and Prevention, Don Hehir, didn't jump when any of his superiors pulled any strings. He was just biding his time until retirement, and really could care less about internal politics. He never interfered with the time involved in my legal responses.

Lehrman, although not in the OIG any longer, still tried to assist me in the recommendation phase of my career. Any promotional positions that would appear, he would in glowing terms, recommend me for any GS-13 slot that I saw in the announcement bulletins. The first one I applied for in late March was within the Office of Professional Responsibility. It was similar to an Internal Affairs Office. Although neither I, nor Lehrman, were optimistic about my getting the position, he nevertheless filled out a three-page Merit Staffing Plan Appraisal for me. In the 34 categories that an individual is ranked under, he checked the highest block possible in the majority of the categories. On the last page under supervisor's comments, since he had been my last one, he wrote:

"Mr. Mangieri is an aggressive professional investigator who perpetually seeks truth and honesty in Government. He is dedicated to the exposure of corruption and is adept at uncovering it.

In my opinion, he would be ideal for a supervisory position in your office of professional responsibility."

As he signed it and handed it to me, he remarked, "Anywhere else that this is received, you'd probably be a shoo-in, but ... ," and he hesitated, "not here."

"Maybe, they'll promote me somewhere, just to get me out of their hair," I said jokingly, trying to sound optimistic.

"Good luck, buddy," he said somberly.

Over the next few months, I would file for a dozen or so jobs whenever they were posted. However, word must've filtered down from the top that I was a pariah, and not to be touched, because I was never considered for any of the positions. In fact, nothing was being spared to pull the noose tighter on me.

... 13 ...

Statham, in his letter to me of March 28 concerning my prior amended informal grievance to him about Coffman's conduct, had misinformed me as to my next step. He initially told me that *he* also was the next step in the formal grievance procedure. In a new memo to me on April 1, he advised me that Goldstock was the proper party to file at what was called the Step I level.

Back to the fox watching the chickens again, I thought, but I did what he said. All I had to do to make it a *formal* grievance was merely change the wording on the "amendment of grievance" subject matter sent to Statham on March 14 to "formal grievance." I wished the rest of my grievance procedure would be that easy, but I knew it wouldn't.

On the day I made my perpetual trip to the front office to hand-deliver my new formal grievance, I received the first bit of information I considered newsworthy. It wasn't anything momentous, but it did point out that favoritism existed in the upper ranks and that regulations were being bent, if not broken.

Joe Duffy, the supervisor in the travel section who had confided in me about Goldstock's improper receipt of the $6,000 moving expense, stopped me in the hallway. He reminded me that our Deputy Inspector General still had not repaid the money. His information not only confirmed what I had thought about improprieties in the front office but would serve me in good stead within the very near future when repayments were directed against me for money I had received validly.

With my constant filing of grievances and my adherence to time limits, events in that area were moving rapidly. I received notification from the Personnel Officer, Patricia Lattimore, that because Knowles was out of town, she could not respond to either my informal or my formal grievances in a timely fashion, but would do so upon her return on April 7. On that date, I received two short responses from her. The first abbreviated reply was to the termination of my AUO pay. She upheld it as proper. Her second brief answer was in response to my five-page formal grievance, which was in reply to my complaint of removal as an Investigator and my current assignment detail. Although my grievance covered nineteen items, minutely, she replied to none of those. All she covered was the allegation that I refused "to obey the requests" of my supervisor and, therefore, could find no basis for the remedies I requested. There was no attempt to discuss any of the specific episodes cited in my grievance, which underscored my belief that my investigations were being hindered. Instead, she answered my charges by merely stating that Coffman would handle my caseload, as if that would automatically resolve my allegations. In the future, his blatant cover-up of my caseload would bear out my ongoing contentions. As to my investigation of the travel vouchers of both Goldstock and his assistant, Nicholson, her only comment was that I should turn it over to another appropriate body.

In her broad-brush whitewash remark with which she intended to swiftly close out my grievance, she noted pretentiously:

"This indicates that every possible effort was made to ensure that all allegations were properly investigated."

What a load of crap, I muttered. *Who's going to believe this stuff?*

Two days later, I found out the Secretary was one of those who believed her, or at least said he did.

In an "Immediate Release" from DOL's Office of Information, on April 9, a startling news release was disseminated throughout the building:

"Marjorie Fine Knowles has resigned as the Department of Labor's Inspector General effective May 2, 1980, Labor Secretary Ray Marshall announced today.

"Knowles, who was sworn into office last May

18, will become a consultant to the Ford Foundation.

" 'As the Department's first Inspector General,' Marshall said, 'Marjorie Knowles did an outstanding job in organizing the new office and moving to improve Labor Department programs. I wish her every success in her new endeavors.'

"Secretary Marshall said a search for a new Inspector General is under way. Pending the naming of a permanent replacement for Knowles, Deputy Inspector General Ronald Goldstock will serve in an acting capacity.

"Until a successor is named, the Secretary said Undersecretary John N. Gentry will oversee the management activities of the Office of the Inspector General."

When I read it, I was as taken by surprise as the rest of the building. *No wonder she wanted to wrap my grievance up as quickly as possible,* I thought. *She knew she was leaving.*

I didn't know whether to applaud or do handstands. Then, I realized that Goldstock was to be the Acting I.G., and in my book he was worse than she was.

I called Lehrman to congratulate us, and the I.G.'s office, for her resignation. His feelings also were mixed because he knew Goldstock was remaining and believed, as I did, that he was more insidious. When I questioned Lehrman about Knowles' sudden resignation, he responded with, "I heard she was fired by the Carter Administration but was allowed to resign."

I must've been speechless for a moment, because I was expecting that remark even less than her sudden resignation.

"Well, I'll be damned," I said in disbelief.

"That's the word," he said, and it wouldn't surprise me because of all the unfavorable publicity she's been getting."

"Then, goddamn it, we should be slapping each other on the back," I said loudly.

"Just remember Goldstock will be the I.G. soon," Lehrman warned me, "so you've really got to watch yourself, buddy."

"So far, so good, Paul," I answered him.

However, it wasn't *so far, so good* for long. The next day, on April 10, the screws were tightened even more. I got a call from Walter McDonough, the new Chief of the Administrative Management Staff, reminding me of a memo that he had sent to me on April 3. That notification instructed me that I would have to repay an outstanding travel advance of $1,048.76 because I was no longer an agent in need of travel monies. When I advised him that an immediate payment would be a hardship because I had three kids, he said to work out an arrangement with Payment Services. Accordingly, I contacted Helen McConchie, the Chief of that section and explained my personal situation. She agreed to a payment schedule every two weeks until the full amount was satisfied. She requested that I instruct her in writing what amount should be deducted from each paycheck and she would, in turn, advise payroll. I then directed a memo to her telling her to deduct $75 from my paycheck on a bi-weekly basis until the settlement of the travel advance. She agreed. To complete the paperwork, I wrote McDonough telling him that I had made arrangements with McConchie in Payment Services. Upon receipt of my memo, he called to complain about my repayment schedule. After I listened to him hound me regarding my payment, I mentioned Goldstock's foot-dragging in making the repayments of his own travel expenses, which I could not fail to mention were "improper." At the termination of our conversation, which did not appear to dissuade him, I wrote him a sarcastic, but appropriate, memo:

> "In confirmation of our discussion this date of the $6,000 moving expenses given Ronald Goldstock on his appointment as Deputy Inspector General, this memorandum will serve as a reminder of that overpayment.
>
> "I am sure that your office will apply the same standard toward our supervisors in requiring their repayments as it does of its employees. Undoubtedly a suitable amount per payday can also be worked out in his repayment plan as well."

As I expected, McDonough was not satisfied with my proposed repayment schedule and on April 18, wrote McConchie that because

I had not repaid the full amount as he had demanded, that she follow his recovery schedule. He told her that effective the next pay period to withhold $175 from my paycheck — not the $75 that I had agreed to pay — every two weeks.

When I mentioned to Barron what they were now pulling on me, he became as agitated as I did.

"He can't do that," he insisted. "Doesn't he know that you've got a family and even the $75 per payday would have been a hardship?"

"He's at the beck and call of the I.G., " I said, "and you know he does exactly as he's told."

"They're never going to let up on you, are they?"

"It looks that way, Cam."

However, I wasn't going to take it lying down, so I sent McDonough a second memorandum:

> "On April 11, 1980, I voluntarily agreed to repay the $1,048.76 outstanding on my travel advance. This action was accomplished by the submission of a written request to Helen McConchie, Chief, Payment Services to deduct $75 from my paycheck, per payday, until that amount is satisfied.

> "Your letter of April 18, 1980, to Helen McConchie, directing her to withhold $175 from my paycheck, per period, until satisfied, is not only an unnecessarily harsh schedule and a hardship as previously discussed, but also is inconsistent with the regulations. Section 145d(3) under the General Travel Regulations states that the initiation of payroll withholding should be accomplished only, 'if the employee does not enter into a reasonable agreement to repay amount owed.'

> "The amount of $75 requested by myself to be deducted per payday is reasonable.

> "You have offered me no compelling reason why I should have to repay the $175 per payday, other than the fact that you were doing so at the direction of your immediate supervisor, Marjorie Fine Knowles, the Inspector General.

"Further, to my knowledge, no other OIG employee nationwide has been faced with the same mandates as I have described above.

"Kindly advise Helen McConchie in Payment Services that the payment schedule specified in my April 11 letter is acceptable."

I was, as usual, to receive no answer to my memorandum, and on the advice of friends decided that I might need an attorney to speak for me. Someone suggested I contact a couple of different sources, and eventually wound up with a female attorney who had successfully handled various types of civil service cases. Her name was Bridget Mugane. For a slight-of-build bookish-appearing female, she proved to be exceptionally aggressive and very effective.

When I related my travel advance dilemma to her at our first meeting, she agreed to send a letter to John Gentry, the Undersecretary of Labor, requesting his intervention "to prevent a politically motivated retaliatory action by Walter McDonough" against me. She reiterated the forced deduction of $175 that McDonough had arranged, and advised the Undersecretary that inasmuch as I was a single parent responsible for the support of three children that it was "obviously an extremely punitive measure which is certainly not justified by the circumstances."

She further advised Gentry that, in addition, McDonough also had violated the Department's own travel regulations.

In part, those regs state that the collection of outstanding balances from employees being transferred or separated should be "no less than 15 percent or a minimum repayment of $15 per pay period on overdue balances if the employee does not enter into a reasonable travel agreement to repay the amount allowed."

My attorney then pressed home the fact that since I had "neither been transferred or separated," that the specified terms for repayment did not apply to me. She advised the Undersecretary that inasmuch as there was no overdue balance from me, as stipulated, the regulation also did not apply to me.

If Gentry would fail to understand the terminology of the regulations that she cited, she also noted:

"Mr. Mangieri has agreed to have $75 per pay period (i.e. $150/month) withheld ... this constitutes a 'reasonable agreement to repay the amount owed.' The specified minimum in the absence of such an agreement is $15, which is far less than the $75 offered by Mr. Mangieri (the regulations wording does not require 15 percent of the amount, but either $15 or 15 percent)..."

Neither the abidance of regulations, nor equity, would apply in either my prior memos or in my attorney's letter. On the same date that Mugane wrote Undersecretary Gentry, McDonough wrote me again. In it, he was adamant that his prior "memorandum to Helen McConchie stands." It wasn't until three weeks had elapsed, on May 16, that Mugane had a reply to her letter to Gentry. However, instead of his direct response to her, he gave it to Alfred Zuck, the Assistant Secretary for Administration and Management, to answer. I already had realized that Zuck was a team player, and his response was no surprise to me. The gist of his letter was that the Department would support the position taken by McDonough for the Inspector General. In an absurd closing remark in his letter, he wrote an even more incredible comment, "This is not a punitive measure but a compassionate one on behalf of the Office of the Inspector General."

As Mugane reread that section to me, she snickered, "If that's compassionate, I'd like to see what punitive is."

We agreed after the receipt of that response that the only solution to resolve all of their actions against me would be to request a formal hearing before an examiner.

Subsequent delving on my part revealed that Walter McDonough came on duty with the Department on March 24, 1980, just ten days before he sent me his first dunning letter. Presumably, he knew nothing of me, nor the fact that I had an outstanding travel advance. He undoubtedly *discovered* that information only after being told by either the I.G. or her Deputy. However, in a general memo issued by Knowles concerning "travel advances," she stated that all "assessments" of outstanding advances should be forwarded to her by *April 30, 1980*. In other words, McDonough had jumped the gun on the return date by almost four weeks. There would appear to be little doubt that the specific instruction was to pressure me where I was most vulnerable.

McDonough, at the direction of the front office, was not the only one on my back at that particular time. Coffman also was brought back into the act. Inasmuch as he and his supervisors were aware that I had been continually filing for supervisory positions at the GS-13 level, they made sure that I would never be considered for any of those openings. It apparently was decided that because Coffman had been my supervisor for a short period of time an appraisal from him had to accompany all of my promotion applications. Accordingly, he completed a four-page form on April 23 that was unquestionably the worst I had received in all my 22 years of service. I would not, however, be aware of its contents for over a month. In that appraisal, he not only indicated that I "needed improvement" in some areas, but also checked the lowest possible category in others – that I had "insufficient knowledge" in my job. To further point out my inadequacies to anyone reading my application, he even wrote additional in-depth derogatory comments about my abilities.

When I first read it, I was livid, and my hands were shaking.

"Why that no-good son of a bitch," I said, and then repeated it in an effort to calm myself down.

As I read it in even more detail, I noted that for the "period covered by this appraisal," he had marked from "12/1/79 to 4/22/80."

Bullshit, I said to myself. *I've been over here since March 3 and Hehir's been my supervisor since then.*

I called personnel to complain about the gross inaccuracies.

"You're entitled to place a comment about his appraisal to rebut whatever you believe is inaccurate," was their noncommittal reply.

After listening to their innocuous remark, it seemed as if even the personnel people were on the I.G.'s side. In all the years I had worked in the federal system, I always thought they were impartial. As time passed, I found out the full extent of their partiality. They were unquestionably management-oriented and did little to hide it.

Before doing what they suggested, however, I did some additional research. I located a personnel manual that specified exactly what I wanted to know concerning my retort. In reading the material, I noted that the minimum period for a performance appraisal was "90 days." I knew Coffman had grossly exaggerated his period of supervision over me, but I checked back into my own records just to make sure. I discovered that he officially became my supervisor on December 6, not December 1, as he had indicated. I, then, counted the actual days that he was my supervisor. In doing so, I

logged 89 days, not the "minimum" 90 days that were required.
Gotcha, you lying son of a bitch, I said to myself.

Referring to the personnel regulations under DLS Appendix
A, FPM 335, Subchapter A5, paragraph (b), I pointed out the
shortfall to personnel in my reply in late May. I particularly stressed
that fact, when I stated:

"He is well aware that he was my supervisor from 8:30 a.m.,
December 6, 1979, to 5:30 p.m. March 3, 1980, and not the period he cited."

I reminded personnel in my rebuttal memo that, "he therefore
overstated by eight weeks the period that he supervised me in an
attempt to enhance his credibility as a supervisor."

I further advised them that Coffman's appraisal not only was
biased and inaccurate but was instigated, "as a direct result of my
initiating an investigation into the alleged unlawful activities of his
superior, the present Acting Inspector General Ronald Goldstock."

I also told personnel that inasmuch as his office was located in
Philadelphia, which was some 90 miles distant from my own office
in Arlington, that he had not been in any position to give me the
"close and detailed" supervision he alleged.

If the ammunition I supplied personnel was not enough to
scuttle Coffman's efforts to down me, I called their attention to a
more vital area. He had, contrary to regulations and instructions,
failed to discuss the appraisal with me, as required. In fact, before
handing me the appraisal, he had advised me that he had no intention of changing the wording. His actions, I stressed, were for the
purpose of precluding my name from being placed on a "CERT
List" of highly eligible employees identified for promotion.

In closing out my "employee comment," I noted that because
Coffman was unable to give me a valid written performance appraisal
based on his failure to meet the "minimum" supervisory period
required, — his form should be withdrawn.

After it was sent to personnel, I called to check on its status.

I was informed, in no uncertain terms, that the appraisal would
remain because while I was on a *detail,* I was still considered attached
to the Arlington office, and consequently Coffman was still my
official supervisor.

The hack in that office obviously had her mind made up and did
not read nor understand the contents of my retort, and while I was

tempted to be less than civil to her, I was not. Instead, I tried to reason logically with her.

"How can I still be a Criminal Investigator? I not only was told prior to my detail that I was no longer to consider myself one, but also had my credentials officially removed?"

"I don't know anything about that," she said dumbly. "All I know is what the regulations say."

"Let me put it this way," I continued, "for purposes of an invalid appraisal, I'm still a Criminal Investigator, but for purposes of my career, or my career development, I'm not."

"I can't answer that," she said.

"Getting a little exasperated with her robot-like responses, I asked her, "Aside from the time element, did you, or anybody, read what I put in my reply?"

"That's really of no concern, at this particular time," she insisted. "You have the right to grieve anything that you think is unfair."

I could see I was getting nowhere with the conversation and hung up the phone. In addition to the "employee comment" memo that I forwarded to personnel, I also sent a short memorandum to Coffman calling his attention to his "inaccurate period of supervision." I wanted him on record that I was aware of what he was pulling, and I also wanted to have a trail of documentation that would be used when I appeared before a hearings examiner.

Weeks earlier, after conferring with Mugane, who was to be my attorney, we agreed that the only recourse left to me was to officially request a hearing. At my request, personnel had supplied me with a list of five arbitrators from the Federal Mediation and Conciliation Service. I had, at her suggestion, also requested that personnel consolidate my three separate grievances into a single grievance. She recognized the same events and personnel were responsible for all of the grievances. She also realized that if those three grievances were processed separately, there might be conflicting findings of fact and conclusions of law by respective examiners. This explanation also was offered to personnel and they acquiesced. It also was called to our attention that subsequent to a hearing examiner's decision, his recommendation would be submitted to John Gentry, the Undersecretary of Labor. We agree to that procedure.

There were two other incidents of significance, however, during the latter part of the month of April. The first of these was my reminder to Goldstock that I had not yet received all of my personal effects from my Arlington office although I hadn't been there for six weeks.

In my memorandum to Goldstock of April 25, I notified him, in part, that:

> "As I stated in my amended grievance of March 14, 1980, to A.M. Statham, the carton of material delivered to me in the National Office did not contain all of my personal effects. I indicated that information on the receipt because the wording purported that 'all' of my effects had been removed and returned to me.
>
> "I never received the 'inventory list' from Coffman prior to my lock-out from my office on February 27, 1980, nor was I present when all of the effects in my desk, in my safe and on my walls were stripped and subsequently delivered to me on March 4, 1980, in a partially filled carton. The contents of my office would have filled several cartons. If there was a question as what constituted 'personal' effects, then an independent observer should have been present and not Coffman's employees. Further, there was no compelling reason to exclude me from being present from my office while all of my effects were systematically examined."

Although I knew that my detail to National was a result of punitive measures, a fact that was to be brought out successfully in the upcoming hearing, I also wanted on record what had occurred in my office prior to my removal:

> "It should also be noted that it is not customary procedure to completely strip an employee's office when he is on a 120-day detail, as I am now. Further, my office space was not urgently needed at that time, nor is it needed now."

In the balance of my extensive memo, I then listed eighteen personal effects that were not returned to me. The list was more than just eighteen individual items, it was a compilation of items that were grouped together for purposes of general identification. They included, but were not limited to, the following:

- A folder with my annual or sick leave.
- A folder with copies of my SF-171s.
- A folder with copies of various letters of recommendation.
- A 1979 desk calendar (with numerous attachments thereto and personal notations thereon).
- A 1980 desk calendar (with numerous attachments thereto and personal notations thereon).
- Numerous folders containing handwritten memos and notations of assorted subjects."

By mid-May, I still had not received delivery of any of the items I listed or a response from Goldstock.

The other incident of significance, at the end of April, was disappointing news from the FBI concerning my allegations of Goldstock's questionable travel vouchers. According to their memo to me, they had checked with Knowles about the propriety of his travel. She naturally supported him. They then advised me that, "inasmuch as the foregoing allegations are not substantiated ..." they would conduct no further investigation.

Again, no surprise to me for their lack of investigative interest. What disturbed me greater was that the scales of justice were tipped in favor of those in power. It was a concept I long ago had been aware of, but when the possibility became a close-up reality, I became disillusioned with justice as I perceived it should be.

I showed Lehrman their response.

Ever the cynic he replied, "Did you expect it to be any different?"

Ever the optimist, I answered truthfully, "Yeah, Paul, I really did. I thought the Bureau would delve into it."

"It was your word as a disgruntled employee against that of the Inspector General of an agency," he countered.

"Disgruntled, hell," I said.

"Take it easy, buddy," he said. "I'm just repeating the *party line*. You recall what Knowles said in response to the *Star's* article after you filed charges against them?"

"Yeah," I had to admit.

"You're not only labeled a 'disgruntled employee' by her, but you're also facing charges by her and her underlings. Who do you think the Bureau's going to believe?"

"I gave them more credit than I should have."

"This is not the movies," he said. "They put their pants on one leg at a time, just like we do. Besides," he continued, "they wanted more proof."

"How much could I give them in less than an hour's inspection of the travel vouchers?" I wanted to know.

"I agree they could've probed deeper," he said, "especially if they looked into his consultant background."

I hadn't heard that comment before.

"What do you mean, Paul?"

"Well, if, as a consultant, he was also paid out of federal funds, then that's a conflict of interest," he said. "And," he continued, smiling, "that's illegal."

I looked at him with renewed interest. He had definitely gotten my attention.

"What else?"

"Well," he went on nonchalantly, "they could've checked with the bookkeeper at the Organized Crime School in Cornell University where he was ostensibly its Director to see if there was double payment by Cornell and the Department of Labor."

"What do you think they would've found?"

"I don't know, but it wouldn't have involved a great deal of effort." He paused. "It's just good investigative technique."

"Anything else I should know?" I inquired in a low key manner.

"Only that I heard he bid on a CETA contract," he said.

"Where are you getting this information?"

"I've got my sources, too," he said, and then he smiled, "You're not the only one doing your job."

"Is that it?"

"Well, that's about it, although I did hear something about ten LEAA contracts and something about a partner in his consulting business."

"You're a fountain of information yourself," I complimented him.

"I try," he said, giving me another quick smile.

As I turned to leave he said, "Remember, they've already done a number on you On the Hill, and now probably the same thing with the Bureau, and all behind your back. They're destroying your credibility, and I don't know how the hell you can stop that."

"I don't either, Paul," I confided, "but there has to be a way."

"All I can do is wish you good luck in what you're doing. I hope you get the break that you've been looking for, and deserve, but," and he hesitated, "it looks like you're just pissin' in the wind."

His remark brought back a comment by one of Rocky DeMarco's former Special Assistants, Walter Evanoff. He was a retired sergeant from the Washington, D.C., police department and not only looked like, but talked like, the gruff actor from the classic movie "For Whom the Bell Tolls," Akim Tamiroff. Evanoff, like the actor, was a Russian, and a personable, very likeable individual. He was especially comical when he was describing something.

On one particular occasion before he transferred out of the I.G.'s Office, seeing the handwriting on the wall, he commented in his gravelly voice:

"See that light at the end of the tunnel, Mangieri," he said referring to some favorable temporary resolution I had managed to accomplish. "Well," he continued, "that's just a train bearing down on you."

It was a humorous remark at the time and one I thought only applied to a particular incident we were both discussing. However, as the months rolled by, I was reminded of it often.

With the departure of Knowles on May 2, there was little, if any, change as far as I was concerned. If anything, Goldstock's actions only intensified, as did the attitudes of all those other supervisors between him and me.

One such example involved that favorite of mine, the Assistant Inspector for Investigations A.M. Statham. In a Memo for the Record I entered on May 23, I noted a comment from Lafayette Vance, an agent who had once worked at the Arlington Office, and one with whom I remained on friendly terms since his transfer to the National Office. He informed me, "that Ray Bailey of the San Francisco Fraud Office told him that an *unnamed employee* who had applied for the vacant GS-13 positions in National Office would not make the CERT because of an unfavorable Performance Rating."

I learned *I* was that *unnamed employee.*

In that memo, I also briefly wrote, "Vance also told me that Statham had told Floria Jones that since the employee was going to receive an unfavorable rating, why couldn't a CERT be issued without his name on it. Floria Jones refused saying that it was improper."

Floria Jones was a personnel technician. She was one of the few who had any scruples and whom I liked because I felt she was honest and could be trusted. Obviously, Coffman and Statham had planned their actions in advance and had put into effect those plans that were against regulations. A conspiracy by any other name is still a conspiracy.

Events from early June onward moved rapidly, and it seemed for a while that the light at the end of the tunnel was going to be a ray of hope.

In response to a prior memorandum from Patricia Lattimore, the DOL Personnel Officer, I, in conjunction with my attorney, ranked by preference the list of five examiners that the Federal Mediation and Conciliation Service had provided. Donald P. Rothschild was our third choice, but he was the one chosen to be the hearings examiner. Also, I officially advised personnel that Bridget R. Mugane was to be my legal representative.

Shortly after that notification to Lattimore, I forwarded a copy of my "Employee's Comments" re the Supervisory Appraisal of Performance by Coffman. I wanted to make sure that not only was some technician in the personnel department aware of my complaints regarding the appraisal, but that the Personnel Officer herself was cognizant of my specific points. In addition, to make doubly sure that the top brass at the Department of Labor knew exactly what was going on, I sent a copy to Undersecretary of Labor John N. Gentry.

The day following the transmission of my memos to both Lattimore and Gentry, I sent a new memorandum to Statham, with personnel's knowledge and approval. That subject heading read:

"Request to Travel to Philadelphia Area re: Credibility of David Coffman."

In that memo, I made some unnerving comments that I am sure made Statham — and undoubtedly Goldstock — wary of my sources and the information I possessed about Coffman:

> "Pursuant to the provisions of the Federal Personnel Manual which states that a reasonable amount of time will be granted to an employee to pursue a grievance against his supervisor, a reasonable request is solicited.
>
> "Request is made to travel to the Philadelphia area, via Government authorized travel and expenses, to interview several Department of Labor officials who allegedly have pertinent first-hand knowledge concerning adverse information about David Coffman, my former supervisor.
>
> "The purpose of this trip is to present to the grievance examiner, at my upcoming hearing, testimony of a corroborative nature. This testimony or evidence will indicate that Coffman's abusive and improper actions toward me the night of February 27, 1980 — as well as his future actions — are consistent with his past course of conduct in relationships with others. Also, this discovery process is not limited to the discovery process cited above, but to present and former employees of the Philadelphia Field Office, to the Office of Personnel Management, and to the Wilmington, Delaware, area to interview a former neighbor of Coffman's.
>
> "The duration of the trip should not exceed two days as I have specific individuals to see and will organize my itinerary prior to departure.
>
> "Your concurrence is necessary in this request to assure that equity will prevail and will further demonstrate that the Department of Labor is not biased in its relationships with any of its employees but is impartial and objective toward all."

I, naturally, sent a copy to the Undersecretary, as well.

The travel request was sent to Statham with the slim hope that it would be honored, although I harbored no realistic illusions about any type of assistance from the department. Inasmuch as there was no possible way I could afford the Philly trip because of my recent sizable cut in pay, due to McDonough's efforts, I thought I would try the "equity" approach, anyhow.

Although my memorandum to Statham stated that I wanted to "interview" individuals concerning adverse information about Coffman, I already had gathered substantial damaging information about him from other agents. Two of them had confirmed that he "couldn't control his anger" and related a couple of incidents. In one of those episodes there was a blatant confrontation in a restaurant, in November 1979. In another, there was a domestic blowup at his house, with at least one of the agents in attendance. In still another allegation of a physical encounter, there was a report of a confrontation with one of his former neighbors in Wilmington, Delaware. That neighbor was reportedly an FBI agent. Another allegation from one of his former employees stated that not only was he "by far the worst supervisor that he ever had," but that he was "not experienced enough to be a criminal investigator." That same employee referred to other "confrontations in his office." That derogatory information also confirmed his behavior toward one of his female employees. That girl had reportedly worked for him a few days and then left to return to law school. After her departure, he allegedly sent a scathing letter to the Dean of the school about her lack of competence. However, his own competence was also allegedly questioned by an Assistant U.S. Attorney in Pittsburgh, for his ineptness in handling a case in that jurisdiction. There were still other reports that kept coming in about him.

The response from Statham, on June 12, was expected. It was denied. He then explained that, "Notarized statements can be supplied by individuals for submission with your grievance."

Not happy with the content of his denial letter, I filed a formal grievance for that denial of travel, with Goldstock, as Statham's superior.

My reply, in part, stated that:

> "It is my contention that such travel is necessary to obtain first-hand information derogatory to Coffman. Such information is pertinent and supportive to my allegations of Coffman's conduct in my formal grievance covering his actions in the dates

cited above.

"It is poor investigative practice to attempt to interview prospective witnesses by phone in order to produce notarized statements. Further, it is impractical and an impediment to the preparation of pertinent material, to confirm an investigation of a defendant in an action solely to the use of a telephone. Therefore, my request to travel to the Philadelphia area, at Government expense, is reasonable and is the specific relief which I seek."

However, fully anticipating Goldstock's support of Statham, I added the following sentence:

"If you do not grant the relief sought, then it is my request that this grievance be consolidated with my other formal grievances to be heard before the hearings examiner."

Also, on the following day, on the 17th, I initiated two new formal grievances with the explicit instruction, that if not granted, to have them consolidated with my other grievances to be heard before the hearings examiner.

The first formal grievance was to Walter McDonough regarding the recovery of my travel advance. It was directed to McDonough in accordance with a telephone conversation I had with Judith Peterson, the Chief, Policies and Special Programs Group, with the personnel department.

In that grievance, I repeated what I had already informed him in prior memoranda, that his deductions from my paychecks were, "all indicative of an ongoing retaliation against me," and, as relief, requested cessation of those deductions. I also referred to Goldstock's improper receipt of $6,000 on his moving expenses when I incorporated in my list of specific relief, the demand that, "Equal application of the repayment of travel or other expenses to all employees, including the Acting Inspector General."

In addition, I called explicit attention to his questionable methods when I cited:

"Your actions of forced and excessive recovery are biased and are not compatible with the manner in which other individuals, similarly situated, have

been treated. Further, the immediacy of the recoup-
ment method — that of being hand carried and
implemented 'on-the-spot' — is totally inconsistent with the normal procedures in existence within the payroll department to add, or to deduct, from
an employee's paycheck."

The second formal grievance was submitted to Statham, as
Coffman's supervisor, and concerned the highly improper supervisory appraisal of my performance by Coffman. As previously
requested, the specific relief stated was not only the withdrawal of
that appraisal and a letter of reprimand to Coffman, but a letter of
apology from the department.

Within the next ten days, or so, responses came back from
Goldstock, McDonough and Statham.

Barron, at a late afternoon beer after work, commented on my
constant stream of grievances to the front office, and to McDonough.

"You must be drivin' 'em crazy Nikolai," he laughed.

"Yeah," I replied, "but it's too bad I'm not getting better replies
from those bastards."

"But you are keeping them on their toes, paisan," he said.

"There's no question about that," I smiled. "Besides, it gives
me great documentation for the hearings."

The first response came from Goldstock concerning my travel
to the Philadelphia area. In typical bureaucratic musical grievance
shuffling, he decided that he was not, in fact, the appropriate official with whom to file a formal grievance on the matter. In a detailed
two-page mumbo jumbo of explanation, he advised me that McDonough was really the proper Step I official at the formal level. He
advised me that he was reforwarding it to him. The next reply I
received was from McDonough, who wrote that inasmuch as I
could receive the necessary documentation I sought "through other
means," it was not necessary for me to travel to Philly. Accordingly, he was denying my request.

The Statham response came next in regard to my formal request
to have Coffman's supervisory appraisal withdrawn. Again, not surprisingly, he denied my grievance, based on the premise that the
Federal Personnel Manual states that supervisory evaluations for

periods less than 90 days are allowed "when made in conjunction with a merit staffing action."

Apparently, they were alleging that the FPM supported their position *because* I was applying for a promotion under the merit staffing action. To prove his point, Statham even included that Department of Labor supplement, DLS, at Appendix A, subchapter A5(b) to FPM 335.

I read what he attached, but it did not back him up.

> "Ordinarily, no performance report should be made on an employee who has occupied his position for less than 90 days. However, if a performance report is needed in connection with a merit staffing action on such an employee, the Personnel Office or Regional Administrative Office should see that the rating panel is provided with the most accurate and up-to-date performance information available. If the current supervisor feels he is well enough acquainted with the work of the employee to complete a report, he should do so."

Obviously, because Coffman was 90 miles away in the Philadelphia office, and had been for the duration of his "supervision" over me, he was unable to become acquainted with my work on a daily basis. None of it was sent to him for his approval, nor was any of it discussed with him on any ongoing basis. The balance of the regulation was even less supportive:

"The opinion of the employee as to his supervisor's knowledge of his work is, of course, a factor to be taken into consideration."

Again, my "opinion" was never considered, in spite of the fact that I strongly objected to his evaluation and gave pertinent details as to why I wanted it withdrawn. The rest of that specific regulation supportive of my stance stated if a current supervisor has not supervised an employee long enough "to complete an accurate report," then "a report may be secured from a previous supervisor." Lehrman, my previous supervisor, had already done so. However, because that appraisal was highly favorable of me, and was in the "exceptional" range, none of *my* superiors would accept it.

In spite of Statham's attempt to justify his position as to why

Coffman's appraisal was valid and would not be withdrawn, he nevertheless, changed the dates of the performance appraisal, by Coffman, "from December 6, 1979, to March 2, 1980," in lieu of his initial dates "from December 1, 1979, to April 22, 1980."

Although I had admittedly won a point when I challenged Coffman's improper reference to an inaccurate time period, Statham undoubtedly had personnel's support and consequently refused to back off.

It was because top personnel officials repeatedly acceded to Goldstock's wishes that I decided to re-contact the Merit Systems Protection board, within OPM, to advise them of the violation of 5 USC 2302, *Prohibited Personnel Practices.* Accordingly, in mid-June, I spoke to a Rob Stern in their Office of Special Counsel and advised him of continuing retaliations against me, especially in regard to the improper supervisory appraisal form. His response and those of another individual on the following day, indicated that it did appear that 5 USC 2302 was being violated and to send them a memorandum on it. I did so on June 26.

In that detailed memo, I referred to apparent violations in the following sections:

- 5 USC 2302 (b) (4)
- 5 USC 2302 (b) (8) (A) & (B)
- 5 USC 2302 (11)

I named not only Coffman and Goldstock but also the Personnel Officer, Patricia Lattimore, and Judith Peterson, her Chief, Policies and Programs Group.

Under 5 USC 2302 (b) (4), it stated that:

"Any employee who has authority to take, direct others to take, recommend, or approve any personnel action, shall not, with respect to such authority — deceive or wilfully obstruct any person with respect to such person's right to compete for employment."

Applicable provisions under 5 USC 2302 (b) (8) (A) & (B) provided in part that those employees who had the authority cited above, should not:

"take or fail to take, or threaten to take or fail to take, a personnel action with respect to any employee or applicant for employment because of — 'any disclosure of information by an employee or applicant (which) evidences ... a violation of any law, rule, or regulation,' or 'any disclosure to the Special Counsel, or to the Inspector General of an agency' ... for the same violations cited."

Under 5 USC 2302 (11), it also noted that those who had such authority should not:

"take or fail to take any other personnel action if the taking of or failure to take such action violates any law, rule, or regulation implementing, or directly concerning, the merit system principles contained in section 2301 of this title."

Section 2301 provided, in part, that employees should be protected against "arbitrary actions," and "against reprisals for the lawful disclosure of information."

In the body of that June 26 memorandum to the Merit Systems Protection Board, I pointed out the history of events that convinced me of the strong possibility of collusion not only within the I.G.'s office, but with, and within personnel, as well:

> "On June 9, 1980, my official comments were attached to the appraisal form and submitted to Personnel requesting that the form be withdrawn because it was invalid. I cited not only the fact that Coffman was unable to objectively appraise my performance but that he was guilty of a deliberate gross inaccuracy in citing his period of supervision over me. He expressly stated that he was my supervisor for a five-month period, whereas it was less than three months. Accordingly, I advised Personnel that the regulations precluded an appraisal of less than 90 days.
>
> "On Friday, June 13, 1980, I was notified by the staffing specialist who was responsible for reviewing the applications, that a meeting had been held within Personnel and it was decided to 'throw out' the appraisal because of the insufficient time factor. Also, the fact that I had submitted an unofficial appraisal from a prior supervisor, Paul Lehrman, for a six-month period, and also three other recent letters of commendation, they would suffice regarding my qualifications.
>
> "On Monday, June 16, 1980, I was told that when Goldstock learned that Coffman's appraisal

was being left out, he was very upset. Apparently, he relayed his displeasure to Judith Peterson, Chief, Policies and Programs Group within Personnel and she in turn advised the others within Personnel, who had 'thrown out' the appraisal, to retain it. Upon being advised of their immediate 'about face' because of pressure from Goldstock, I sought a reconsideration of what I considered a blatant abuse of the regulations.

"On the morning of June 17, 1980, I sought guidance from your office as to the approach to use. However, because of non-availability of personnel to advise me, I contacted an office within OPM. Their response was that it appeared that 5 USC 2302 was being violated. In-depth review of this section then confirmed this information.

"In early afternoon, of June 17, I left a note with the staffing specialist advising her to tell Patricia Lattimore, the Personnel Officer, that in their upcoming meeting concerning the retention or withdrawal of that appraisal form, that 5 USC 2302 was being violated. However, in spite of a warning to that effort, Lattimore chose to ignore it and decided to retain the appraisal form. I immediately directed a memo to Lattimore requesting her rationale, but have not yet received a response.

"Not only will retention of that inaccurate and invalid appraisal impede my consideration for those — or any other — promotional positions, its retention in my personnel file will have further adverse effects on my career, the most impending of which is a within-grade step increase due in the very near future."

I also reminded Stern, the individual to whom I was directing my memo that:

"In addition, Goldstock is either the actual selecting official, or the de facto selecting official, on all the vacancies for which I have applied and for which Personnel is currently rating the performance appraisals of applicants."

My well-founded concern about our personnel department intensified during the month of July, especially in regard to the Personnel Officer.

In her first memorandum to me on July 1, in which she finally explained her rationale for retaining the Coffman appraisal, she relied on the same line that Statham did. DOL regulations, according to her interpretation, stated that, "if the current supervisor feels he is well-enough acquainted with the work of the employee to complete a report, he should do so."

She never referred to the conditions that succeeded that discussion in the regs, which unwittingly Statham forwarded to me. Perhaps they were of the impression that either I would take them at their word or that I couldn't read.

Ten days later, on July 11, she responded to my "informal grievance" on that same issue. In that memo, she stated that DOL regs do not have the option of having a rating "withdrawn," as I requested. Rather, she informed me that a statement, by myself, could accompany that unfavorable appraisal when it is sent to the panels. She reiterated, unconditionally, "Therefore, the retention of your merit staffing report was necessary and proper."

At the conclusion of her memo, she advised me that if I wasn't satisfied with her response, I could file a formal grievance with Director of Personnel Frank Yeager.

On that same date, I received a second memorandum from her in response to an informal grievance about my non-certification of two Criminal Investigator positions at the GS-13/14 level. In my grievance to her, which I conducted orally on July 1, I told her that the panel members on the promotion board were subordinates of individuals against whom I had previously filed grievances. As a remedy, I requested that my application be re-evaluated by panel members who were not subservient to those same individuals. Her response was that since a Qualified Rating Examiner had approved those panel members as to their use of all of the information at their disposal, it was both fair and reasonable.

However, she did unwisely note that the information used was based upon my SF-171 and performance evaluation. Since that performance evaluation was Coffman's appraisal, there could hardly have been a fair and reasonable review by a biased panel.

She again advised me that if I was dissatisfied, to file another formal grievance with the Director of Personnel.

On July 15, I did just that. I filed my first formal grievance concerning my non-placement on the CERT list for the two positions. In my very explicit memo to Yeager, I stated in part:

> "Two separate 'panels' were used to establish the CERT lists into which highly qualified applicants were placed. Michael Treworgy, the Deputy to Assistant Inspector General for Investigations, A.M. Statham, was on both panels. Tony Rossi of the Office of the Inspector General was on one panel, while Graham Schatz was on the other, also of the OIG.
>
> "Schatz, in the Summer of 1979, participated in a pattern and practice of retaliation against me initiated by Stuart Eder, the former Acting Chief of Investigations. Eder has since divorced himself from being involved on a panel before which my name has appeared. Schatz has not.
>
> "It is my contention that the members of the rating panel were biased in their selection of highly qualified applicants for both of these positions and should not have participated. Treworgy, because of his subordinate roles to both Statham and Goldstock, who both have been the subject of several of my grievances. Rossi, because of equally subordinate roles to not only Statham and Goldstock but also to Treworgy, as well, cannot truly make an independent decision as he is subject to their displeasure.
>
> "Further, my initial selection as a Criminal Investigator, GS-12, with the Department of Labor back in July 1978 was as the result of being 'highly qualified' for the position. I and six other Investigators, were the nucleus of the Office of Special Investiga-

tions which became the Office of the Inspector General in October 1978. We seven Investigators were chosen from a field of 200 applicants for the positions. Now two years later, I not only possess those same qualifications,but have had the 'in-house' specialized experience of an additional two years on Department of Labor criminal violations.

"The use by the above-mentioned panel members of my improper and derogatory performance appraisal, executed by David Coffman, my former supervisor, severely inhibited my being considered to be 'highly qualified' for the positions described above. Further, the lack of proper 'weighting' given to the Paul Lehrman appraisal of me virtually guaranteed that I would not be placed on the CERT list. Coffman was my supervisor of brief and sporadic tenure (perhaps once a week for an 89 day period). Whereas, Lehrman was my daily supervisor for a six-month period. (Note: Coffman's office was located in Philadelphia, Pennsylvania, 90 miles from our office.)

"The whole process was a direct result of reprisals and retaliation against me for my investigation and complaints against Goldstock — all of which is a violation of 5 CFR 771.205.

"The use of a Qualified Rating Examiner subsequent to the panel's review of my qualifications was not 'both fair and reasonable' as stated in Lattimore's response to me of July 11, inasmuch as the improper and derogatory performance appraisal by Coffman was also used to rank my qualifications by that QRE."

On July 16, I filed my second formal grievance with Yeager concerning the, "improper retention of performance appraisal in a job application files."

In that equally lengthy memo, I reviewed events that preceded Coffman's actions leading to his performance appraisal of me. I also repeated the information that although Floria Jones of personnel had caused the Coffman appraisal to be withdrawn, her supervisor, Judith Peterson, ordered it reinserted at Goldstock's behest.

I, then, wrote:

> "I challenged this reinsertion of the Coffman evaluation in the job application files; the intervention of Mr. Goldstock was improper because he intervened in order to shape my application file in a prejudicial manner, thus influencing the decision of the rating panel and preventing my placement on the list of certified eligibles.

> "This willful obstruction by Mr. Goldstock of my job applications was a Prohibited Personnel Practice under 5 USC 2302 (b) (4) which provides that 'any employee who has authority to take, direct others to take, recommend, or approve any personnel action, shall not, with respect to such authority deceive or willfully obstruct any person with respect to such persons right to compete for employment.'

> "Mr. Goldstock's motive in obstructing my applications was part of a pattern and practice of retaliation as evidenced by the substance of my other pending grievances against him."

> "Because the purpose of the formal grievance was to request specific relief for the improper retention, and consideration, of the Coffman appraisal, I also stated:

> "Due to the aggravated nature of this Prohibited Personnel Practice, i.e. – the willfulness and bad faith of Mr. Goldstock's intervention, I request that:

> "(1) the Coffman evaluation be removed from all Department files with retroactive effect to the date of its original insertions; and

> "(2) a neutral rating panel outside the OIG review my application file after removal of the Coffman evaluation and determine whether I am high-

ly qualified for Vacancy # OPS-80-116. If I am so
deemed, I request that I be appointed to this promotion without review by the Selecting Official
because of his demonstrated bias against me."

My reference to Vacancy #OPS-80-116 dealt with the promotional opening in Internal Affairs and was a position for which I
was not only uniquely highly qualified, but one that I wanted. The
likelihood of being selected was remote because that position, too,
reported to Goldstock. However, inasmuch as Knowles allegedly was
forced to leave, that same possibility undoubtedly would happen to
Goldstock. Hence, my constant flow of memos to personnel were
necessary documentation for my personnel file. Also, my grievance
to Yeager on the 15th, mentioned "a violation of 5 CFR 771.205."
That specific cite in the *Code of Federal Regulations* dealt with a
"Review by the Office of Personnel Management," which provided that they "shall review from time to time agency administrative
grievance systems ... to determine whether the systems meet the
purpose and requirements of this part," and that, "the Office shall
require corrective action to bring a system which fails to meet the
purpose and requirements into conformity." Although I was to
receive denials from Yeager on July 22, to both of my formal grievances, using the same indefensible explanations Lattimore had
offered, they were forwarded to Donald Rothschild, the Hearing
Examiner, for his future consideration.

The balance of the month of June was fully occupied with a
myriad of actions and activities. Undoubtedly, the various hornet's
nests I stirred up, generated a lot of reactions. By and large, they were
all united in their plan to succeed over me, but it wasn't to be as easy
as their planned initial attack strategy.

The first back-peddling came from Coffman. In a short memo,
to me, that he wrote grudgingly:

"I have been advised by Don Hehir, your supervisor for your
present detail that your work has been of an acceptable level of performance in the capacity of commenting on pending legislation
relating to a variety of areas. I am therefore obligated to approve your
upcoming within-grade increase."

As galling as that notification must have been for him to
acknowledge, it unquestionably came as a result of my constant

memos to personnel. Not to be shut up completely by the system, and in an effort to flaunt his authority, again, he, however, reminded me that my performance as a Criminal Investigator was still "totally unacceptable" to him.

At the same time I received Coffman's memo, I received other personnel actions. The first was from Goldstock to Yeager, to the attention of Lattimore. It requested that a new detail be initiated for me to include "additional duties beyond the statement of duties to which he has been assigned." Before I had a chance to react, additional paperwork from Yeager to Lattimore informed me that the request to extend me for an *additional* 120 days was approved. Immediately thereafter, a copy of a memo form Lattimore to a Larry Goodwin advising him of the extension, was placed in my in-basket. That memo also stated that I was to be detailed to a Program Analyst's position because of a previously stated need for my services in OLAP, the Office of Loss Analysis and Prevention.

Bullshit, I said to myself. *There's no need for my services here. They just want me out of the way permanently.*

There was little I could do to counteract what they had done, officially. I knew I would have to wait for the Hearing Examiner to take note of all that had transpired, and then issue his recommendation.

However, I still had an ace-in-the-hole. That card was the Government Accountability Project, a non-profit, public-interest organization that had been well-briefed on my case and was eager to see justice done. For the next two years, members would fight relentlessly in my behalf, much to the dismay of the Department of Labor.

... 14 ...

On June 25, 1980, the Government Accountability Project filed a notarized official, "REQUEST FOR INVESTIGATION PURSUANT TO 5 U.S.C. 1206 (b)3," with the Office of Special Counsel at the Merit Systems Protection Board. Attached to that eleven-page document was my own notarized thirteen-page AFFI-DAVIT that detailed not only my own background and assignments with the Department of Labor, but specifically covered my perceptions of cover-up and the retaliation that followed.

The two individuals with whom I worked very closely prior to the submission of the extensive material were Louis Clark and Thomas Devine, the Director and Associate Director, respectively, of that public interest group. Never have I had the privilege of working with a more interested, sympathetic and dedicated pair of individuals than I had with those two. In addition, all of their staff who participated in the review, investigation and research into my allegations were equally amazing.

As Clark was to point out in a letter of support for me years later:

> "As Executive Director of the Government Accountability Project, my association with Nick was close and intensive for over a two-year period. His allegations of corruption, cover-up and retaliation were examined and followed up by our Legal Director. Our conclusion, at that time, was that

Nick was subjected to the most extreme forms of harassment and reprisals by his supervisors and superiors, for doing his job and for attempting to curtail their violations of duty. Our concerns were fully documented and submitted to the merit Systems Protection Board and to the Office of Special Counsel ... .

"Our public interest group receives hundreds of similar requests for assistance from whistleblowers, or those who perceive themselves to be. Our resources are limited and our selection process is consequently quite stringent. The fact that Nick survived that initial screening attests to his truthfulness and to his integrity. The intensive follow-up that accompanied our verification only served to strengthen our faith in him and to enforce our realization that management will stop at nothing in its retaliation, especially if they themselves are 'targets' of investigation."

In GAP's "Introduction" to its formal REQUEST, the organization stated:

"The purpose of this memo is to request an official investigation by the Special Counsel, pursuant to 5 U.S.C. 1206(b)3. [Authority and Responsibilities of the Special Counsel].

"The whistleblower is Nicholas Mangieri, a GS-12 Criminal Investigator with the Department of Labor's Office of the Inspector General. (Hereinafter, DOL/OIG). His charges all focus on officials within the OIG and do not extend to other divisions of the Department of Labor.

"Mr. Mangieri consents to the release of his identity, both during your review of his charges, and during any subsequent investigation or referral of the allegations below.

"Mr. Mangieri has come gradually to a firm belief that the DOL/OIG is acting in violation of its mandate pursuant to the Inspector General Act of 1978 — U.S.C. His attached affidavit describes prolonged and frustrated attempts to compel his superiors to pursue their duty to conduct investigations and to report to Secretary of Labor Marshall and the Congress whenever there are 'problems' or 'deficiencies' in administration of DOL programs; here, CETA.

"He alleges the following instance of misconduct by OIG employees:

"I. Mismanagement by numerous supervisors displayed by their failure to conclusively investigate and report on allegations of potentially criminal abuses in District of Columbia CETA program administration.

"OIG officials who thus failed to exercise their affirmative investigative duties pursuant to 5 U.S.C. §4(a)(4) and (5) of the Inspector General Act are:

"1) Marjorie F. Knowles, (former Inspector General for the DOL)

"2) A.M. Statham, (Assistant Inspector General for Investigations)

"3) Ronald Goldstock, (former Deputy Inspector General/currently interim Acting Inspector General)

"4) Stuart Eder, (former Acting Chief of Investigations)

"5) Arnold Juliano, (Agent-in-Charge: Washington Field Office, Arlington, Virginia)"

The REQUEST then specified the areas in which the officials mentioned had violated their duties:

"I. *Mismanagement* per 5 C.F.R. §1250.3 *by Inspector General Marjorie Knowles and other DOL OIG Officials.*

"As demonstrated by a combination of:

"1. Unwillingness to investigate charges of improper sexual inducement by DOL/CETA supervisors and

"2. Lack, to date, of resolution of those charges in derogation of the duties and responsibilities delegated by the Inspector General Act of 1978.

"II. *Abuse of Authority by Marjorie F. Knowles, Ronald Goldstock, Stuart Eder, Arnold Juliano, A.M. Statham*

"In arbitrary use of powers to cover up a "sensitive" investigation, motivated by a concern for the political advantages to themselves and the parties accused; or to retain the favor of their supervisors.

"III. *Abuse of authority by David Coffman* (Agent in charge of Philadelphia Field Office to which the Washington Field Office now reports).

"A. Exercised his powers of supervision to intimidate Investigator Mangieri intending to dissuade his probe of allegations by misuse of DOL travel vouchers by officials.

"B. 'Relieved' Mr. Mangieri of his investigation duties for the purpose of preventing him from further exploring the charges of travel voucher misuse by DOL supervisor Ronald Goldstock.

"After careful review of his charges and an independent reference check, the Government Accountability Project has offered to represent Nicholas Mangieri. It is our position that the Office of the Special Counsel has jurisdiction (see infra) and, upon a finding that there is a substantial likelihood of truth in the charges, can compel the Secretary of Labor to conduct an investigation. However, the normal procedure of referral by the Secretary to the DOL/OIG is obviously of questionable value here since the OIG is *itself* the department under scrutiny. Therefore we suggest that an impartial and objective investigation be conducted by: (1) DOL staff not closely associated with the OIG, (2) An outside staff, or preferably an investigator."

In its formal REQUEST, the Government Accountability Project then set out the "Jurisdiction and Standard of Proof" under which the Office of the Special Counsel could operate:

> "5 U.S.C. 1252.2 states that the Special Counsel 'will' require an agency investigation pursuant to 5 U.S.C. 1206(b)(3) if there is a 'substantial likelihood' information provided by an agency employee or former employee 'discloses a violation of any law, rule or regulation, gross waste of funds, abuse of authority, or a substantial and specific danger to public health or safety ...' Since Mr. Mangieri is a Department of Labor employee, the Special Counsel has jurisdiction for his disclosure.
>
> "The regulations do not define 'substantial likelihood,' the standard of proof that a whistleblower must satisfy. We propose that Mr. Mangieri's disclosures be tested under the following definition of 'substantial likelihood':
>
> " 'Sufficient basis in fact that a reasonable person might conclude that the material elements of the complainant's charges probably disclose the illegal or improper activities listed in 5 U.S.C. 1206(b).'...' "

The REQUEST then cited numerous precedents upon which the Office of the Special Counsel could be guided in its determination of "substantial likelihood."

Under the next major category of a "Standard of Review," the REQUEST noted that:

> "5 U.S.C. §7703 (c)(1) requires the court to set aside any Merit Systems Protection Board decision that is 'arbitrary, capricious, an abuse of discretion or otherwise not in accordance with law ...'

Numerous court decisions were then referenced by GAP again, to bolster its contention.

In the next all-encompassing section, entitled "Mismanagement by DOL Officials: Knowles, Goldstock," the REQUEST also appropriately noted that:

"5 C.F.R. §1250.3[11] (e) provides a definition of 'mismanagement' which should give rise to Special Counsel investigations.

"'Mismanagement' means wrongful or arbitrary and capricious actions that may have an adverse effect on the efficient accomplishment of the agency mission.

"Mr. Mangieri contends that I.G. Knowles mismanaged through her inaction in the face of his repeated complaints that the D.C. Government investigation was being improperly conducted. By this, she implicitly condoned the actions of her subordinates and possibly even ordered them to delay his progress on the case.

"For Ms. Knowles to fail to promote an expeditious inquiry into such serious charges as 'improper sexual inducement' in the CETA program administration she must ignore her mandated duties under the 'Inspector General Act of 1978.' In pertinent part only it provides:

"§4(a) "It shall be the duty and responsibility of each Inspector General with respect to the establishment within which each office is established ...

"(4) to ... supervise or coordinate relationships between such establishment (DOL) and ... local government agencies (here D.C. government) ... with respect to

"(A) all matters relating to ... the prevention and detection of abuse in programs administered or financed by such establishment, or

"(B) the identification and prosecution of participants in such ... abuse'

"Mr. Mangieri contends that allegations of improper sexual inducement meet the definition of 'abuses' within a DOL financed program, CETA. The mission of the Department of Labor with respect to CETA is the provision of employment basically for the unemployed, underemployed, and economically disadvantaged. To have such a program tainted by practices of sexual inducement is bound to hamper the 'efficient accomplishment of the agency mission.' Unpleasant as the task might be, it was Ms. Knowles duty to determine if the CETA program was subject to such abuse. To date, the D.C. case has not been expeditiously investigated. (Fourteen months have passed since the initial allegations.) Mr. Mangieri contends that there is no conclusion of the case because it is not being actively pursued by those assigned to replace him when he was removed from the investigation.

"The overall responsibility here rests with the Inspector General. But her subordinates have also contributed to the failure to investigate the alleged D.C. CETA abuses. Among them:

"*Arnold Juliano,* who brought an insupportable personnel action against Mr. Mangieri just after Mr. Mangieri accused him of impeding the early stages of the investigation. (See p.4 of affidavit and especially note the time expended in resolving the action.)

"*Ronald Goldstock,* who halted the investigation during fall '79 by repeatedly demanding 'investigative plans' and failing to give good faith guidance to Mr. Mangieri so that he could comply. (p. 7 affidavit)

"*Gerald Gotsch,* who ordered Mangieri to slow the conduct of the D.C. case investigation despite advice of the U.S. Attorney to the contrary. (p. 6 affidavit)

"*A.M. Statham,* who removed Mangieri from the national office the day after the news that Mangieri's complaint of obstruction of investigation was made public. (See p. 10 affidavit)

"In sum, all of these official's actions in consort with inaction by the Inspector General combined to prevent the efficient performance of the DOL/OIG mandate."

The following section, "Abuse of Authority/Failure to investigate for purpose of personal gain," that GAP noted in its detailed request, was equally damaging to the OIG hierarchy:

"5 C.F.R. §1250.3(f) defines 'abuse of authority' to mean;

"'An arbitrary or capricious exercise of power by a Federal official or employee that adversely affects the rights of any person or that results in personal gain or advantage to himself or to preferred other persons.'

"Mr. Mangieri contends that Ms. Knowles sought to cover up the D.C. government investigation because of its implications for her Senate confirmation to the I.G. post (see affidavit p.3)

"The facts show that Mr. Mangieri's supervisor, Arnold Juliano of the Washington Field Office, was unwilling to have the Labor Department visible in early inquiries by the U.S. Attorney's Office. This gave the definite appearance of 'higher up' discomfort with the investigation.

"Secondly, affiant Gerald Peterson (p. 10 affidavit) corroborated this impression based on his instructions not to proceed with an audit which also carried political overtones. (The Pride audit is still in the news.)

"Mr. Mangieri contends that Ms. Knowles complied with her subordinate's decision to 'cushion' her from 'bad' publicity even if she didn't herself order it as the Peterson affidavit suggests. (see affidavit exhibits 41 and 42) Nonetheless, she consistently deferred any action to her Deputy, Ronald Goldstock or simply failed to respond at all. (see p. 8 affidavit and incident of September 13, 1979, at p. 7)

"In addition to Mr. Mangieri's personnel grievances which we do not address here, the parties whose 'rights are adversely affected' (per the language of the Inspector General Act) are those CETA employees whose positions might subject them to improper sexual inducement. Without expeditious and effective investigatory response to their complaints, they risk a great deal for nothing. The DOL should respond to abuses within its own programs. If the top-most official is preoccupied with political favor, who will prevent continuing abuse?"

With that very pertinent last question concerning political sensitivity rather than doing one's job, the REQUEST then launched into the final descriptive section, that was perhaps even more detrimental to the officials named:

"Abuse of Authority/Intimidation and Termination of Investigatory Duties: David Coffman and Ronald Goldstock"

That extensive section of the submission to the Office of the Special Counsel then stated that:

"Mr. Mangieri contends that his removal from all investigatory duties by Ronald Goldstock was a reprisal, but more importantly a final constraint on his professional activity. His affidavit (pp11,12) describes that he began an investigation of misuse of travel vouchers within the DOL/OIG itself. The very unprofessional response by his superior, David Coffman, is described in some detail there. In sum he was called to an 'after-hours' meeting where he was threatened with job loss, interrogated and generally harassed for several hours. Building guards were sought to prevent his departure and his file contents were examined despite his objection that personal papers were included. The actions described are not only highly questionable personal infringement but also constitute the sort of reprisal which 'chills' employee criticism. Meanwhile the advantage (here, to Mr. Coffman) is that he has prevented further inquiring into the questionable activities of a superior.

"Certainly Mr. Goldstock's action in removing Mangieri from his investigatory duties several days after this incident can only suggest that he wished to control Mangieri further. Particularly when he himself was the accused abuser of the travel voucher privilege.

"Even in the event that there was no abuse of the voucher privilege, Mr. Coffman and Mr. Goldstock's actions cannot be condoned. Both acted to restrain the appropriate investigative activity of an investigator. Thus both abused their given authority for personal gain."

In the Government Accountability Project's "Conclusion" to its memo, it very succinctly identified the problem that I had faced ever since I had initiated my investigation into D.C. politics and brought into bearing why it was imperative that the Office of Special Counsel should conduct an investigation:

"To date, Mr. Mangieri has taken the approach most administrators applaud where there are questions of 'in-house' abuses. He has been forthright and candid regarding his concerns and has expressed them to the appropriate individuals in the 'chain of command.' Obviously his method did not work.

"His personnel grievances pursuant to §5 U.S.C. 1206(a) are being addressed to the Office of Special Counsel in a separate action. Our concern here is that the serious improprieties alleged above not be allowed to stand unquestioned.

"Mr. Mangieri, as a criminal investigator, has been trained to make careful observations and from them to draw prudent conclusions. More than the average person, he has been taught to distinguish between substantiated belief and mere suspicions. Because he is a prudent individual he did not jump to the conclusion that the DOL Inspector General was consciously attempting to slow or halt his assigned duty to investigate allegations of improper sexual inducement by upper-level D.C. Officials. Only after four months of increasingly obvious reticence did he conclude that the very Inspector General herself might be in support of a cover-up. Taken as a whole, the events he describes brought him to a reasonable belief that the Office of the Inspector General is not serving the public as intended. Here, there is an affirmative duty to act. A failure to do so establishes a substantial likelihood that there is wrongdoing. This likelihood is amplified by abusive questionable personnel actions against the party who objected clearly and repeatedly. Finally, the timing of various sanctions against Mr. Mangieri repeatedly suggests that his insistence upon doing his investigative duty was at odds with the interests of his superiors.

"The success of the I.G. Act of 1978 depends upon the independent and objective conduct of each Inspector General and his/her staff. The I.G. must adopt a style for self-interest. The integrity investigation depends on it.

"Here we have a situation where the Inspector General has failed to serve by her very inaction. Absent the authority of the Special Counsel to intervene, there will probably never be a final and in-depth report on the results in the 'D.C. Government case' and the charged abuse of travel vouchers. We urge the Office of Special Counsel 'to help clear the record.' In an even broader sense, we urge your action as an on-going reminder of the influence of 'checks and balances' even in our sprawling governmental system."

After I had reviewed the in-depth memo that GAP had done, following weeks of intense preparation and assimilation of all my documentation, I was astounded at the thoroughness of the final product.

"I can't thank you both enough," I said to Clark and Devine

who were both in attendance at our final session before it was to be mailed out.

"Don't thank us," was their reply. "You did it all. We only compiled it."

In spite of their modest disclaimer, I knew the amount of work that went into their product, and continued heaping praise on them and their organization.

"We're only too glad to be able to be of assistance to you," they insisted. "The government needs more people like you to come forward," they said.

Their effort was to be recognized — if only temporarily — within the near future.

As eventful and promising as June had been, July was turning out to be rocky. For a start, I had to write the Personnel Officer a memorandum on July 3 questioning the unsettled scheduling of Donald Rothschild, the Grievance Examiner, as a result of an indefinite letter that she had just sent him. I advised Lattimore that Sally Wagner of her office had given us a date firm, of July 23, for the hearing, and that my attorney had set aside that time in reliance of her word. On July 8, Lattimore responded and advised me that because Walter McDonough was "unavailable to testify" on that date that the hearing was to be rescheduled for July 28.

On the same date that Lattimore sent me her memorandum, I decided to send one of my own to McDonough. I was fed up with not only his constant harassment of my travel repayment, but of his refusal to deal similarly with Goldstock on his own illegal receipt of moving expenses. My memo on the 8th was in direct response to a four-page memorandum that McDonough had forwarded to me at the end of June. He reiterated that his action to recover my outstanding travel advance "was as directed by department regulations." However, as I, and my attorney, Bridget Mugane, had constantly reminded him, it was improper and retaliatory of him to take action against me and not against Goldstock who had received the $6,000 moving expense reimbursement, which was definitely against regulations.

McDonough, in an effort to justify his own inaction against Goldstock, stated that the matter had been referred to the DOL Solicitor's Office, for an opinion. He also advised me that Goldstock had told him, "that if it were decided that immediate repayment were appropriate he would immediately repay the amount in question."

When I saw that self-serving comment I couldn't contain saying another, "Bullshit," out loud. The reference to an *immediate* repayment was only after I had repeatedly raised the red herring issue, and, of course, *eight months* after he had come on board. In my memo to McDonough, I couldn't resist pointing out to him what I thought of his last reply to me:

"Inasmuch as the impropriety of Goldstock retaining the $6,000 on his PCS move was apparently resolved approximately five months ago, your information is of considerable interest to me."

I then followed up with a series of five questions to him that I requested "answered as soon as possible":

"(1) What was the basis of the request to review Goldstock's $6,000 overpayment?

(2) Who approved Goldstock's initiation for review?

(3) What date was it submitted to the Solicitor's Office?

(4) Who within the Solicitor's Office is responsible for its resolution?

(5) What is its present status and when is a final determination expected?"

My memorandum must've hit a nerve with McDonough because within a few days, he responded to me. Apparently an implication in my memo, or so McDonough interpreted, that Goldstock had initiated his own referral to the Solicitor's Office, brought his immediate brief denial on that particular issue. Of course, any other specific answers to all my questions were not to be included in his terse memorandum. All he would say was that:

"The Solicitor's Office is drafting a bill for the relief of Mr. Goldstock and other OIG employees who were told by officials of OIG prior to their employment that relocation expenses would be paid."

He also mentioned that a "Mr. Seth D. Zinman was the individual in that office with whom he had discussed the matter."

DOL's blatant solution to anything improper, or illegal, just "draft a bill" okaying it. I wonder, now, if the GAO would look as favorably on those actions as DOL had then. However, because I was so deeply ensconced in my own work, I didn't have the time, nor the inclination, to find any other governmental agencies who could check into it. I was beginning to lose faith in the system. It was a feeling I tried to suppress.

Although my initial concern had been with Goldstock illegally receiving relocation expenses, I was unaware of any others. McDonough, in his brilliance, had alerted me to that abuse when he referred to, "other IG employees." Either Knowles also had brought them aboard, or Goldstock had. Not only had they knowingly broken the regulations, but they now had the Solicitor's Office condoning it. *How far up the ladder, does this shit go?* I wondered.

It wasn't too long before I would find out.

In spite of the fact, that I tried to be like the fabled Dutch boy who held his finger in a hole in the dike to stem the inevitable flood — a comparison, I had always liked and would use often — it was becoming useless.

On July 16, a brief letter was sent by Timothy J. Reardon, III, Assistant U.S. Attorney, in the Washington U.S. Attorney's Office, to Coffman in Philadelphia:

"After having scrutinized your thorough investigative report in the matter of possible violations of 18 U.S.C. §665(b) involving the alleged sexual harassment of CETA employees which was submitted to us on or about May 7, 1980, we declined prosecution of the matter on May 29, 1980, due to clearly insufficient evidence.

As you know we have developed the theory of attaching criminal conduct involving sexual harassment of CETA employees through the rather innovative use of 18 U.S.C. §665(b). When the facts merit it we remain prepared to apply this statute."

"What thorough investigative report," I said. "What the hell is going on?"

I couldn't keep my annoyance down. There was no mention of any of the eight felonies that I had been investigating, only the Improper Inducement misdemeanor at 665(b).

What a goddamn cover-up, I said to myself.

I believed that Coffman in his inept supervision of my cases would do a lousy job in organizing what I had already done, but I didn't think that he would deliberately disregard, or hide, the felony allegations. Because the Reardon letter had only cited the sexual harassment of CETA employees, I knew that none of the other evidence I had accumulated could have possibly been sent to the U.S. Attorney's Office for consideration. If anybody could easily have been prosecuted for obstruction of justice, Coffman could have, and should have. Subsequent discovery, months later, by the Government Accountability Project revealed just that omission.

Before I finally put aside that denial letter, however, I couldn't help but deride the comment made about *their* developing an innovative theory of using 18 U.S.C. 665(b) for violations against CETA females.

I had been the one who had effectively used it in Florida for the first time, and then suggested and used it on all my cases in the District of Columbia.

A subsequent FOIA request, by myself, months later also confirmed what I believed about his cover-up. What I found even more unbelievable, however, after I had read his "thorough investigative report," was that it had been accomplished with the use of *eight* other agents and *three* other investigative aides.

Shit, I said to myself, *if I had that many working for me, there's nothing that I couldn't have found out.*

As it was, the best his in-depth saturation investigation could uncover, he noted as:

"The results of this inquiry produced the names of eight CETA employees who may have been potential victims of sexual harassment. Of those eight, five denied any knowledge of sexual harassment while they were CETA employees, one refused to talk, one was not located and one admitted that she was the victim of sexual harassment."

After I read that phony report, I was even more fed up with the scope of the supposed effort to pursue my investigative leads. When it was eventually learned, in the city, that DOL had abandoned its investigation into City Hall, GAP received calls of dismay from D.C. employees who also complained about the ineptness of Coffman's superficial investigation. There was, however, nothing I could do to call further attention to the corruptness with the Department of Labor that I had not already done.

I was to learn in the months to come that with the declination of my cases, OIG officials felt that they could now move against me with impunity. Accordingly, intensive investigations were then launched against me in an effort to get rid of the "Mangieri problem" once and for all.

In the interim, I was concerned with my life on a daily basis within the I.G.'s office. In early July, I was again extended for an additional 120 days, from July 3 to November 2. In response to that unnecessary extension, I was forced to file another informal grievance with Goldstock claiming that such a detail constituted harassment and further discipline. He, of course, disagreed. His reply at the end of the month falsely stated that:

"Your current detail is necessitated by the fact that the Office of Loss Analysis and Prevention is still in the process of being organized. Until we are able to fill positions in OLAP, it is necessary to detail you as well as other employees to that organization to accomplish the work. Consequently, your current detail is in no way an act of harassment. It is a means of ensuring that the work of LAP is accomplished until the organization plan is implemented."

In his memorandum, Goldstock then informed me that my only recourse was to file a formal grievance with Judge Nahum Litt, who, as the Chief Administrative Law Judge, would constitute what is known as the Step 1 level.

The grievance system was fast becoming an exercise in futility, on my part, and delay, on Goldstock's part. I, nevertheless, did so on August 11. In that detailed grievance, I laid out the facts for Judge Litt, commencing with the examination of Goldstock's and Nicholson's travel vouchers, and then mentioning his request for my renewed detail of an additional 120 days. I then wrote:

> "The rationale offered by Mr. Goldstock was that they had been attempting to fill vacancies within the Division to which I had originally been assigned and that my services were still needed. Mr. Goldstock also stated that my original duties were expanded to now include 'additional necessary duties.' ..."

I continued:

> "On June 27, 1980, my detail was approved for an extension of additional 120 days as per Mr. Goldstock's 'justification.'
> "It should be noted that upon analyzing my 'workload' for the life of my details, the following

are also the facts:

"(1) I have analyzed 46 legislative bills or related material in a 16-week period or less than three per week.

"(2) Of the 46 bills that I read, 37 received a 'no comment' response.

"(3) Of the nine bills that I analyzed and wrote up an appropriate response virtually none of these ever reached the Solicitor's Office, as representative of the OIG response.

"(4) During the first five weeks of my second 120-day detail, I have read an additional 12 legislative bills - or again less than three per week.

"(5) Of these 12 bills, 11 received 'no comments.'

"(6) Of the one bill that I analyzed and forwarded to the Solicitor's Office it, too, has been ignored and will not be utilized as an official OIG response.

"(7) There has been no change at all in my duties in my second 120-day detail, although Mr. Goldstock expressly stated that there would be 'additional' duties.

"These facts belie the contention put forth by Mr. Goldstock in his 'justification' to Personnel for the necessity of the continuance of my unique services. It would also contradict his contention in his reply to me of July 31, 1980, that my current detail, 'is in no way an act of harassment.'

"It would appear that the lack of responsible tasks assigned to me, the apathetic approach toward my work products and my 'clean desk' workload over the past five months is totally inconsistent with my experience and is indicative of a continuing pattern of harassment toward me by Mr. Goldstock.

"With the present shortage of Criminal Investigators, and the current policy of actively recruiting and filling existing vacancies — even in my own Field Office — it is inconsistent to state that I am

needed in my present position as a Program Analyst.
There are those individuals who could be effectively
assigned, or detailed, to this Division and be within their career field.

"Mr. Goldstock should be precluded from exercising his abuse of power under the guise of a proper management function. My existing grievances
and other memoranda are all indicative of prohibited personnel practices, which are violative of 5
U.S.C. 2302."

I was not the only one within OIG that reprisals were being
directed against — but I was one of the most vocal and certainly
closest at hand to the front office. Two other agents, William Gamble and John Salvail were also subjected to extreme measures of
retaliation by the Inspector General and her Deputy, as well as another dozen agents throughout the nation. All those other agents were
either threatened with prosecution, or intimidated, because they
dared speak out against the I.G. for failing to carry out her mission.

Gamble, a supervisory investigator assigned to the Organized
Crime and Racketeering Division in Miami, was removed from the
department after speaking with the staff of the TV show *"60 Minutes,"* about the I.G.'s curtailing of labor investigations. The day
that he was to go on camera, his house was placed under surveillance by six FBI agents, reportedly at the instigation of the I.G.'s
office. He was then punitively transferred and subsequently fired,
also on trumped-up charges. He subsequently won a ruling to be
rehired.

What was unique, and undoubtedly similar to my own case,
was Goldstock's comment about Gamble. He had, as testified by
another investigator, "threatened to get (Gamble's) ass."

Salvail, a supervisory investigator in the Boston office was falsely accused of filing inaccurate reports. Although he was threatened
with dismissal, a grievance examiner found in his favor and ordered
him returned to duty, as well.

I, on the other hand, had not yet appeared before a grievance
examiner, and although I was more than ready with ample documentation, I was not confident of the outcome.

I was to learn very shortly the resolution of my grievances.

... 15 ...

On July 23, 1980, my formal hearing finally came before Donald P. Rothschild, who had been appointed as my Hearing Examiner. It was held as originally scheduled. Bridget Mugane was my representative, and Sheila Cronin was the attorney for the Department of Labor. Because Rothschild had been our *third* priority out of the five names that had been submitted to us by the Federal Mediation and Conciliation Service, we were not comfortable with our forced choice. We knew that his role was merely to listen to testimony and then issue his findings and recommendations to an Administrative Law Judge. That judge, designated as the Step 1 level, could then either accept the examiner's recommendations or find his report unacceptable and grant the relief requested. Our concern still lay with Rothschild.

The following grievances, as specified by the Hearing Examiner, were to be considered after testimony was heard and submitted to the ALJ:

"*GRIEVANCE #1:* Whether GRIEVANT'S supervisor David Richard Coffman was guilty of improper conduct after he discovered that Grievant was investigating travel voucher records?

"*GRIEVANCE #2:* Whether removal of GRIEVANT as investigator from the Office of Inspector General (OIG) and removal of his credentials was proper?

"*GRIEVANCE #3:* Whether GRIEVANT is entitled to have retroactive restoration of administratively uncontrollable overtime (AUO)?

"GRIEVANCE #4: Whether GRIEVANT was entitled to administrative travel to Philadelphia in connection with the prosecution of grievances?

"GRIEVANCE #5: Whether GRIEVANT's forced repayment of travel advances at a rate higher that he agreed to was arbitrary, capricious and/or discriminatory?

"GRIEVANCE #6: Whether David Coffman's appraisal of GRIEVANT'S performance should be invalidated?

"GRIEVANCE #7: Whether OIG retention of the appraisal was designed to obstruct GRIEVANT in job competition?

"GRIEVANCE #7: Whether DOL rating panels improperly denied GRIEVANT certification as 'highly qualified' for two positions for which he had applied?"

"Grievances #8 and #9 were filed subsequent to the filing of grievances 1-7. These grievances were considered by the Administrative Law Judge only because they were denied at the informal level.

Both of these two latter grievances dealt with the extension of my 120-day detail, and with my reassignment to a Program Analyst position. They stated that the reasons for the extension and the reassignment were the results of retaliation by my superiors.

The hearing, which comprised four and a half days, July 23, 24, 28, 30 and August 11, produced a 100-page report by the Hearing Examiner on October 29, 1980.

In his "SUMMARY OF RECOMMENDATIONS," issued on October 28, he wrote:

"• There is sufficient testimony to support GRIEVANT'S allegations that he was targeted for unusual and atypical treatment as a DOL employee giving rise to his grievances.

"• That since these grievances were not frivolous, and I found that GRIEVANT was dealt with improperly in GRIEVANCES #1 and #5, I recommend that DOL pay Bridget R. Mugane, attorney for GRIEVANT, reasonable attorney fees."

Under his FINDINGS, of the individual sustained grievances he stated, in part:

"GRIEVANCE #1:

"• The subsequent ruse and investigation technique used by Mr. Coffman was an over-reaction to GRIEVANT'S activities of February 27, 1980.

"• Mr. Coffman's visit to GRIEVANT'S home was unwarranted, unauthorized and improper.

"• Mr. Coffman's seizure of GRIEVANT'S personal property and failure to return it properly was improper.

"GRIEVANCE #5:

"• Mr. Statham ordered Mr. McDonough to seek repayment.

"• Mr. McDonough's repayment terms imposed a hardship on GRIEVANT for family reasons.

"• GRIEVANT made a reasonable counter offer for repayment which was permissible under DOL regulations.

"• Mr. McDonough refused GRIEVANT'S offer and subtracted an amount from GRIEVANT'S paycheck of over double what GRIEVANT had offered.

"• DOL policy for repayment was misrepresented to GRIEVANT.

"• DOL policy was not enforced against other employees.

"• Payroll deductions do not appear to have been enforced against any other employees including those who left DOL employment, except GRIEVANT who was processing grievances against OIG during the time the deductions were enforced.

"• High officials, who under DOL regulations owed the department money were treated differently.

"• Refusal of GRIEVANT'S repayment offer was arbitrary, capricious and discriminatory."

My momentary feeling of elation passed when I noted that the examiner had denied the other five grievances, because his "SUMMARY" also stated:

"There is insufficient evidence to support GRIEVANT'S allegations that the Office of the Inspector General, U.S. Department of Labor engaged in collusive obstruction of GRIEVANT'S investigation of alleged sexual coercion of CETA employees by District of Columbia officials, or retaliation against him for his vigorous investigation of this matter."

"What is this crap?" I said heatedly to Mugane, who was with me when I had read the rest of his "FINDINGS AND RECOMMENDATIONS."

"Just take it easy, Nick," she tried to soothe me. "Let's just go over everybody's testimonies, and analyze them, and then dissect his other findings with regard to the other five grievances."

"And then?"

"Then," she said, "I can prepare what's known as GRIEV-ANT'S COMMENTS to his FINDINGS AND RECOMMEN-DATIONS, to cover any holes in their testimony, or to any other discrepancies."

For the next couple of hours, we both read our individual copies, made our own notes, and then sat down to discuss our comments or feelings on what should have been considered. We both agreed that the testimonies of my witnesses were highly complimentary and supportive of my specific grievances. Countering the derogatory remarks of Goldstock, Statham and Coffman in their testimony as to my incompetence as an investigator, my witnesses refuted them. Barron stated that I was a "very competent investigator," Owens thought I was a "fine investigator," and although Lehrman, in his typical understatement, testified that he considered me an "average investigator," had written otherwise in my evaluation for a supervisory position. At that time, he wrote that I was "very good or outstanding" in 14 categories. Even Stuart Eder, who did not testify, had written that I was "entirely satisfactory" in an evaluation of me the year before.

Although Lehrman had volunteered to help my attorney in an advisory capacity, he still was not fully convinced that the I.G., or her Deputy, had deliberately tried to obstruct my investigations, having never been fully aware of all of their actions. He did not know prior to his testimony, that all of my witness interviews and other evidence were never submitted to the Justice Department by Coffman. Nor, as he subsequently told Mugane, was he aware that immediately prior to my detail to National to be under his control, that Mayor Barry's name came out as one of my targets in my mushrooming investigations. What Lehrman did know, and what upset him the most came out in his testimony:

"The way Braver (a supervisory investigator) was telling me at the time, apparently Mangieri had caused a flap over in the Arlington Office about the sex case. What they (OIG personnel) wanted Braver to do at the time was to do a hatchet job — this is Braver's words — 'a hatchet job on Mangieri' ... ."

When I read that testimony in the Hearing Examiner's report, I couldn't help but say, "Why them no good sonsabitches."

Mugane smiled. "I thought you knew."

"Hell no. That's the first time I heard it."

Although I hadn't heard that particular comment before, I knew it referred to Art Braver, who had been the head of Internal Affairs the year before he retired. I had heard that they held something over his head but I didn't know what it was.

The more Mugane and I compared our notes on what the Hearing Examiner had written about the other grievances, the more worked up I became. "That guy was not only blind," referring to my extensive documentation, "but deaf as well." In frustration, I slammed my hand down on the testimony in front of us. "On top of that," I continued, "he must've know that their side's testimony were all lies."

Mugane tried to calm me down again with her soft-spoken approach.

"I'll bring it all out, Nick," she said confidently. "Just leave it to me."

Although I knew that she was very competent, having read the very extensive *POST-HEARING MEMORANDUM* that she had filed with the Hearing Examiner, I was not satisfied with his *FIND-ING AND RECOMMENDATION* that we had just received.

"He must not have read that MEMORANDUM too carefully," I said still annoyed.

"I know," she had to agree.

On November 12, Mugane submitted her COMMENTS to him regarding those FINDINGS AND RECOMMENDATIONS.

Under her "GENERAL FINDINGS" dealing with "Obstruction and Retaliation," she opened a salvo of rebuttal with:

> "The examiner does not sustain grievant's obstruction and retaliation contentions, yet he finds that grievant was generally 'targeted for unusual and atypical treatment as a DOL employee' ... The examiner presents no alternative motive for this treatment.

(The examiner attributes Coffman's actions after December 1979 to his desire to fire grievant and his displeasure with grievant's work on the investigation ... This begs the question: did Coffman *et al* want to fire grievant because the latter vigorously pursued the

investigations, and/or because of grievant's complaints of obstruction by the OIG?)

> "He ignores the implications of the sequence
> of events outlined in the FINDINGS ... . This
> sequence shows that grievant's problems with his
> employer began shortly after he initiated the sexu-
> al coercion investigation, and that each of his
> employer's actions against him followed a signifi-
> cant development in the investigation, including
> grievant's complaints of obstruction of justice.

(The examiner ... has misdated an important event in the
sequence; the high D.C. official's name emerged in the investigation on June 1, 1979, not June 6, 1979, and thus preceded the
June 5 proposed suspension of grievant).

Mugane then outlined other specific dates, that the Hearing
Examiner had failed to consider that would demonstrate a chronological trail of obstruction. She then wrote:

> "Perhaps most important in proving obstruc-
> tion, the OIG submitted none of grievant's 37 inter-
> views, dated May - November 1979, to Justice when
> the investigation was referred for possible prosecu-
> tion ..."
> "The balance of Mugane's COMMENTS con-
> centrated on GRIEVANCE #2 and GRIEVANCE
> #6A. Under GRIEVANCE #2, my attorney found
> that Rothschild failed to consider that a recent fed-
> eral ruling held that "federal employees have a right
> to remain silent when they are interrogated by their
> superiors in situations that could lead to discipli-
> nary actions ... ."

The Hearing Examiner had found in the department's favor
because I failed to answer why I was investigating Goldstock's travel vouchers and considered it to be "insubordinate."

My attorney also pointed out a procedural defect that Rothschild didn't recognize. He stated in his *FINDINGS* that "policies

and procedures were followed" in my reassignment. However, as Mugane so cogently noted, the regulations at 753 DLS 5-1a were not followed. Those regs state that "when a problem of misconduct is brought to the attention of the appointing officer, he/she shall immediately order an investigation ... (and) have prepared a report."

In my case, on the night of February 27 I was not only barred from my office and placed on administrative leave but was summarily reassigned to the National Office. There was no investigation ordered as the regulations stated and therefore that reassignment was an invalid one.

When Mugane was objecting to Rothschild's improper denial of GRIEVÁNCE #6a, which dealt with bias in Coffman's appraisal, she pointed out what would be a logical outgrowth of Coffman's initial animosity towards me, in her analysis:

> "The examiner finds that Coffman's behavior on February 27, 1980, and March 3, 1980, was variously an overreaction, unwarranted, unauthorized and improper. Yet the examiner fails to find Mr. Coffman's damaging performance appraisal of grievant, written only an month or two later, to be biased. If Mr. Coffman behaved outrageously in late February and early March, out of personal animus for grievant, there is a compelling inference that Mr. Coffman had animus toward Grievant when he made out the highly unfavorable performance appraisal. Indeed, since the Coffman appraisal is at odds with other opinions of grievant's performance, which were favorable (e.g. those of James Owens, Paul Lehrman, Stuart Eder; see Grievant's Post-Hearing Memorandum at 26), the only logical explanation is that Mr. Coffman's animus for grievant still existed, and motivated the appraisal ratings.
>
> "Thus, the Coffman performance appraisal should be removed rather than merely having Grievance 1 Findings attached to it."

To cement any question about an employee's right "to remain silent" when faced with disciplinary proceedings by a supervisor,

Mugane then submitted an *ADDENDUM TO GRIEVANT'S COMMENTS* on November 17. In that Addendum, she cited a specific holding from a recent case that gave a union employee an absolute right to remain silent. That holding stated that:

" ... public employees are entitled like all other persons, to the benefit of the Constitution, including the privilege against self-incrimination ... ."

She then applied the case law to the facts in my own case, and then stated further:

> "Without being informed of his right to immunity, grievant refused to answer certain questions ... , and was removed from his position as an investigator specifically for refusal to answer ... . This was in violation of procedures required by the case law, and thus the Examiner is in error when he finds that appropriate policies and procedures were followed in grievant's reassignment."

We then awaited the DECISION from the Administrative Law Judge to whom it was assigned. Earlier, Chief Judge Nahum Litt had excused himself because of a conflict of interest. Associate Chief Administrative Law Judge Everett E. Thomas was appointed the Step 1 Grievance Official. We both held our breath awaiting his final decision.

"I think we got it all in, Nick," she said cautiously.

"You did a hell of a job, Bridget," I said. "I don't know what else you could possibly have added."

On December 1, we both received our own copies of his DECISION, as did everyone else in the DOL chain. We agreed to meet downtown to review his separate DECISIONS, one on "Formal Grievances 1-7," and the other on "Formal Grievances 8 and 9."

When we both had read our individual copies, looked up at each other and smiled.

"Not bad," I said.

"If you're satisfied, then I am too," she said. "There are some areas that we should have won in, but I think that we've got all your major requests granted."

"I think so, Bridget," and smiled even broader. "I've got no complaints," I added. "What next?"

"Well," she said flipping to page 7 of his first DECISION, that of the Formal Grievances 1 -7, "he agreed with the examiner, in Grievance #1, that your buddy Coffman was guilty of improper conduct toward you. He also agreed with #5 that your repayment was arbitrary and capricious, etc. "

She stopped a moment and stifled a half smile, "He also agreed with the examiner that I should receive reasonable attorney's fees." She continued, "The best part, however, as far as you are concerned, is that the judge did *not* agree with the examiner in Grievance #2 that your removal as an investigator was proper."

"I know," I said confidently.

She read from the "Discussion" section of the DECISION.

> "I do not accept the examiner's finding that the 'GRIEVANT was properly reassigned for insubordination because DOL policies and procedures were followed and reassignment did promote the efficiency of the service.' ..."

"I like his explanation," she said. "The judge didn't buy the examiner's reliance on Lattimore's testimony that from a personnel office standpoint, that the proper forms were filed, and that she saw nothing improper with it."

I interjected.

"I told you that the Personnel Office and the Inspector General's Office were in collusion."

She nodded her head and continued reading, "This is where they shoot the Personnel Officer down." She read further:

> "Therefore, although the proper forms were timely submitted regarding the detail and reassignment of the Grievant, the regulations and a report of the incident before taking any action were not complied with."

Mugane then noted in the *Discussion* section that the judge did not accept the examiner's finding that the "efficiency of the service" was promoted with my reassignment. Nor did the judge accept the examiner's fallacious finding that the OIG's actions "were not disciplinary or adverse." She then reached the section under "Conclusion."

"This is where he pulls it all together," she said:

> "Review of the examiner's findings and recommendations is not a mere rubber stamping of the fact finder's order when the Step I Official is unable to conscientiously conclude that the supporting evidence is substantial or that the decision is in accordance with applicable law. In that instance, the examiner's finding must be set aside.
>
> "In the instant case, the examiner's finding, respecting grievance number 2, that the Grievant's reassignment was proper, is erroneous. After thoroughly reviewing the record as a whole, I conclude that although the proper forms were timely submitted, regulation Interim DLS, Subch. 5-1(a), FPM Ch. 752, which prescribes the procedures to be followed when dealing with misconduct, was not complied with. Additionally, it is found that Grievant's reassignment was disciplinary, regardless of the efficiency of the action. This being the case, agency regulation FPM Ch. 751, Subch. 1-2 prescribes that certain determinations be made before taking any action. Likewise, the evidence shows that this provision was not observed. Therefore, the reassignment was not proper.
>
> "In view of the above, it is concluded that the examiner's findings and recommendation regarding grievance number 2 are not supported by the weight of the evidence and not in accordance with applicable law. They are therefore not acceptable. In light of the findings and conclusions herein, it is accordingly ordered:"

I stepped in again to interrupt her.

"It's about damn time somebody had some common sense," I said unsmilingly. "I was beginning to lose faith in our federal system."

"It's not over yet," she added.

"You're beginning to sound more like Lehrman," I said.

"It's just that I know the system," she said. "In any case," she continued, "this is the part you wanted," and she read the Administrative Law Judge's ORDER:

> "1. Grievant's reassignment to the position of program analyst shall be terminated immediately;
>
> "2. Grievant shall be reinstated as a criminal investigator with the Office of Investigator General; this reinstatement shall be retroactive to February 27, 1980;
>
> "3. Grievant shall be assigned to an office in which he is not supervised by any of the individuals involved in the grievances herein;
>
> "4. Alternatively, the Grievant shall be assigned as a criminal investigator with an office, other than OIG, within the Department of Labor; and
>
> "5. A formal letter of reprimand, detailing the events of February 27, 1980, shall be prepared and placed in grievant's official personnel file."

After she had read item 5 in the ORDER, I asked her: "Why is that left in there?"

"I wouldn't worry about that inclusion," she said. "You have all the reasons that preceded it."

I nodded in agreement.

Mugane then reviewed the ALJ's separate DECISION for Grievances 8 and 9. These both covered my 120-day extension, and my reassignment as a Program Analyst. She commented on the judge's discussion of the propriety and the legality of my reassignment, but also noted that he again found in my favor.

The judge in analyzing Goldstock's *immediate* decision to transfer me out of the Arlington office following my investigation of his travel vouchers, found that his behavior violated agency regulation which stated that:

"Agencies should give consideration to all factors involved when deciding what penalty is appropriate, including not only the gravity of the offense but such other matters as the existence of mitigating circumstances, the frequency of the offense, and whether the action accords with justice in the particular situation."

The judge also stated that, "A review of the record indicates that the above factors were not taken into consideration before reassigning the Grievant. For these reasons I find Goldstock's action in violation of the above regulation."

Mugane particularly liked the judge's comments regarding my "good faith" investigation of Goldstock's vouchers as a result of the informant's "tip." She also found it appropriate that he noted my reluctance to discuss my investigation with Coffman was an accurate appraisal of my viewing of the situation at that time. She also smiled when she read his final comment before his ORDER:

"It is deemed useless to remand this case back to OIG for investigation ... ."

The ORDER, Mugane noted was exactly the same as it was for Grievances 1-7.

She put both DECISIONS down.

"Any questions, Nick," she asked concernedly.

"Yeah, I've got one." I tried to keep a straight face. "When?"

Her serious expression mimicked my own feigned one until she realized what I had said, and then she relaxed.

"As soon as I find out, I'll let you know," she answered.

"The sooner the better," I said. "It's been a long time."

On December 9, I received a call from her.

"I've just submitted a *PETITION FOR FURTHER RULING* to the ALJ," she said, "and you'll be getting a copy soon too."

"Meaning what?" I asked.

"Well," she continued, "we just notified Judge Thomas that we accept his DECISION, and that we do not plan to challenge it or appeal it or in any way to disturb it."

"Good," I answered enthusiastically. "Then?"

"Then," she continued, "I asked that you be assigned or detailed to an office in which none of the individuals involved in the grievances are in the management chain above you, who have the power to remove you.

"Great!"

"There's more," she said.

"Okay."

"I also added that if there were no offices within DOL that have criminal investigator positions, other than the OIG, then you should be detailed outside of the Department of Labor under an IPA agreement."

I had mentioned that possibility to Mugane before, and she had picked up on it. During September, she and Tom Devine of the Government Accountability Project met with Goldstock and his ever-handy sidekick, Shelley Repp, Special Assistant extraordinarc, who a year earlier had participated in derailing my efforts to appear before the Congressional subcommittee.

I reminded her of the episode.

"I remember it well," she said shaking her head slowly, as if trying to erase its memory.

"Was there anything else in your petition?" I asked her.

"Only that you receive all your back pay and benefits, including your administratively uncontrolled overtime."

"Good work," I congratulated her. "I'm glad you're on my side."

"We all agreed that you had a good case. I'm just satisfied that it went as well as it did."

Talking about IPA with Mugane had also brought back unpleasant memories of that incident. The purpose of that September meeting was to facilitate an Intergovernmental Personnel Act (IPA) detail to the Maryland State Prosecutor's Office as a Criminal Investigator because of their apparent need for one in that relatively new office.

Years earlier, when I had worked for the Department of Defense in California, I had effectively used an IPA agreement between the government and the State Capitol in Sacramento to work for one of the investigative committees.

However, as expected, in that meeting Goldstock adamantly refused to allow me to participate in such a detail. Mugane and Devine both sensed that Goldstock would not change his mind, although the hearings were under way. In spite of the fact that there had been no findings or recommendations as yet by Rothschild, the evidence that did come out was damaging to the OIG.

In a letter to the Secretary of Labor the day following the Goldstock meeting, I advised him of Goldstock's inflexible refusal and of his past antics with other investigators. In part, I wrote:

"I was willing to make certain reasonable concessions in my present and in future grievances in order to move on to a more productive field. However, it appears that Mr. Goldstock will preclude any possibilities of agreement or conciliation. Therefore, I am forced to continue my legal battle in order to preserve my rights, my career and my name.

"Mr. Goldstock has not only already cost the Department of Labor several thousand dollars in my recent administrative grievance hearing but also has incurred many more thousands of dollars of DOL monies by his numerous adverse actions against other Office of Inspector General employees — virtually all of which have been reversed by grievance examiners."

In closing out my memorandum to the Secretary, I noted that a detail to the Maryland State Prosecutor's Office, would be "in the best interests of the Department."

There would, however, be no response to my memo, either to me or to my representatives. This was a bureaucratic reaction that although I should have long been used to, I, nevertheless, never was.

In the meantime, GAP, which had also been following my grievance hearing with interest, took another step.

On December 19, Devine sent a second notification to the Merit Systems Protection Board. This one was directed to Mary Eastwood, as the Acting Special Counsel to the MSPB, and officially advised her that they were now representing me as a result of a unanimous decision reached by the GAP Whistleblower Review Panel, which had met on November 20. Enclosed, were a now-expanded notarized affidavit, from myself, that encompassed 17 pages in lieu of the initial 13 pages that were submitted to them in June. Also, GAP submitted its own 15 notarized pages to support its petition for an investigation pursuant to 5 U.S.C. §1206(b)(3), as previously cited.

In its new, harder-hitting letter, GAP opened its request by stating:

"Mr. Mangieri's whistleblowing disclosure

alleges a cover-up by the Inspector General of illegal sexual coercion by top D.C. government officials of CETA employees."

In addition, Devine called Eastwood's attention to GAP's involvement when he added:

"Because Mr. Mangieri has been in the midst of a serious personnel dispute at the Office of the Inspector General, the GAP verification study of his charges was more thorough than usual. As a result of our investigation, we are completely satisfied that he has provided serious evidence of misconduct."

Zeroing in on specific charges, GAP left no doubt as to the reasons for the request of an investigation by the MSPB:

"I. Mismanagement and Abuse of Authority by Marjorie F. Knowles, then Inspector General of the Department of Labor, Ronald Goldstock, then Deputy and now Acting Inspector General, Arnold Juliano, former Agent-in-Charge of the Washington Field Office of the Office of the Inspector General, and Gerald Gotsch, former Assistant Inspector-General-Investigations, through failure to investigate adequately and report on allegations of potential criminal activity, including illegal sexual harassment in the District of Columbia's CETA Program Administration, as well as interference and harassment of good faith efforts by Nicholas Mangieri to pursue the investigation.

"II. Violation of Law by Ms. Knowles and Mr. Goldstock through failure to report evidence of possible criminal violations to the Attorney General."

In a detailed explanation of the first charge, that of the "Management and Abuse of Authority," GAP noted:

"Mr. Mangieri contends that I.G. Knowles mismanaged the DOL/OIG through her inaction in the face of repeated, legitimate complaints that the D.C. government investigation was being improperly obstructed and restricted. The evidence shows that Knowles knew the substance of Mangieri's investigation: leading officials of the D.C. government allegedly had violated federal criminal law in the administration of the CETA program by engaging in sexual harassment of CETA employees. (See newspaper articles, 'Grand Jury...,' 4/4/79, 'City personnel Chief ...' 4/5/79, 'Sex Coercion ...' 4/27/79, Exhibits 5, 6, and 7)."

GAP further noted that:

"Mr. Mangieri gathered evidence on over 30 top D.C. government officials. The investigation consistently produced affidavits and taped statements from complainants, witnesses, and confidential informants. (See Mangieri Affidavit at pages 4 and 5, and Receipt and File Inventory, 12/13/79, Ex. 46). Yet Mangieri was confronted with numerous obstacles in his attempts to pursue the investigation which produced evidence of sexual harassment by 10 top D.C. government officials."

In hammering away at my specific obstacles encountered, GAP commented more in-depth:

"Mangieri was prevented from gaining access to relevant evidence; delayed in presenting Congressional testimony on the investigation until the committee lost interest; forced to fight specious personnel actions; ordered to restrict the scope of the investigation from ten targets to two, against the advice of the assistant U.S. Attorney with whom Mangieri worked; compelled to conduct his investigations one at a time, contrary to standard investigative procedure; required to submit detailed investigative plans, again contrary to normal procedure; excluded from strategy sessions on the case; and eventually removed from the case when he refused to back off. (See Mangieri Affidavit at pages 5 through 15, and related exhibits; for confirmation of the unusual interference, see testimony of Lehrman (Mangieri's supervisor) at Grievance Hearing, 7/24/80, pages 278-280 and 344, Ex. 66 and 67; for identification of officials who carried out this harassment, see infra at 1 and 7)."

GAP also called attention to the confirming remarks of others:

"The interference with Mangieri's investigation apparently continued a pattern established in the I.G.'s office of not fully investigating alleged wrongdoing by high level officials in government. (See Affidavit of Gerald Peterson concerning interference of an audit of Youth Pride, Inc., Ex. 38), Pete Castro, who 'assisted' Mangieri in this investigation, confirmed at Mangieri's personnel grievance hearings that investigations of high-level officials were routinely treated 'differently.' (See again, testimony of Castro, Ex. 64)."

When GAP analyzed the "Violation of Law," in the second charge, it proved to be even more damaging to the I.G.'s office:

"Knowles and Goldstock knew that Mangieri's investigation had revealed abuse of potentially criminal nature within the D.C. CETA administration. The allegations ranged from improper inducement in violation of 18 U.S.C. §665(b) and conspiracy (18 U.S.C. §371). (See Mangieri Affidavit at pages 5 and 6; Investigative Plans, Exs. 27, 29, 32, and 36.)"

GAP noted that:
"Section 4(d) of the Inspector General Act of

1978 requires that:

"Each Inspector General shall report expeditiously to the Attorney General whenever the Inspector General has reasonable grounds to believe there has been a violation of Federal Criminal law."

However, as GAP was quick to point out:

"There is no evidence to suggest that evidence of possible criminal violations uncovered by Mangieri was reported to the Attorney General as required by the I.G. Act. Mangieri personally notified the Attorney General of the existence of serious allegations of criminal activity within the D.C. CETA program administration on November 23, 1979. (See Mangieri Affidavit at pages 13 and 14; letter to Civiletti, 11/28/79, Exs. 39.)"

Further obstruction of justice was evident when GAP wrote:

"Only after Mangieri had been taken off the case did the I.G. send the investigative file in the 'D.C. Government Case' to the Department of Justice. However, the documents sent to Justice were records of interviews conducted in the winter of 1980. The evidence Mr. Mangieri gathered was completely omitted. Not surprisingly, none of the documentation sent to Justice supported Mangieri's allegations of improper sexual harassment."

What was even more indicative of a continuing blatant cover-up — and a conspiracy — in Goldstock's attitude was the following reported incident:

"At an October 23, 1980, meeting between GAP representatives Louis Clark, Thomas Devine and Lindsey Byrne, with the OIG/DOL to discuss Mangieri's allegations, Mr. Ronald Goldstock conceded that it would be a clear violation of his duties

as Acting Inspector General, under the I.G. Act
§4(d), not to turn over to the Justice Department
any evidence indicating or supporting allegations
of criminal activity within the DOL. He pointed
out 4(d) of the I.G. Act and read it out loud."

In the most unequivocal, documented and incriminating part
of the GAP request for investigation was the final section of the
"Violation of Law" by both Knowles and Goldstock:"

"Based on Mr. Mangieri's affidavit and the partial results of a Freedom of Information Act request,
Knowles and Goldstock explicitly disregarded the
substantial work done by Mangieri on the 'D.C.
Government Case.' It is clear that they knew Mangieri's investigative file contained records of interviews tending to substantiate allegations of criminal
activity in the higher reaches of the D.C. government. (Compare DOL/OIG disclosure at Mangieri
Grievance Hearing of interviews sent to Justice,
Exs. 72; with inventory of Mangieri investigative
file and receipt, 12/13/79, Exs. 73, and testimony of Special Agent David Coffman at Grievance
hearing, 7/28/80, Exs. 71, where Coffman
acknowledged that Mangieri had performed at least
34 interviews.)
"The crucial contrast between the documents
Justice received (Exs. 72) and the documents it
didn't (Exs. 73), is the extent to which each set of
documents supports the allegations of improper
sexual harassment in the D.C. Government. Mangieri's investigative file, which was never turned over
to Justice, clearly supports the charges of illegal
activities at all levels of the D.C. Government (See
Exs. 73). The documents that the OIG/DOL
turned over to Justice, purportedly the results of a
'thorough' OIG investigation of the matter, fail to
provide any support for the allegations of improper sexual harassment. The conclusion to be drawn

from this contrast is clear; the OIG knew of the
contents of Mangieri's file and willfully did not turn
over to Justice any material which would support
allegations of criminal activity. ..."

The allegations against the former Inspector General and her
Deputy were more than just words, they were solid accusations —
backed up by evidence and proof — of their malfeasance in office.
However, the exposure of their actions did not deter them. In fact,
it goaded them even more to not only cover up what they had
done, but to openly attack their detractors with any means at their
disposal in order to dispel any doubt about them. Since I was the
most vocal, it was necessary to shut me up as quickly and as effectively as possible. These methods included not only illegal financial background checks on me, discrediting me not only to sources
at the Department of Justice, but to Congressional sources, as well.
In addition, I learned that Knowles had also perjured herself in testimony before Congress to cover up the truth. No stone was left
unturned by either Knowles, Goldstock, or any of their staff – no
matter how it was accomplished.

Although I was unaware of these specific actions at the time of
the grievance hearings and even up to the time of the Administrative Law Judge's entry into the picture, I was made aware of their
general actions throughout the Fall of 1980. I had repeatedly heard
that Goldstock had circulated the word that I was being investigated for criminal activity. When I first heard that rumor, I passed
it off with "He's full of shit. He's trying to get me to back off what
I'm doing." However, as the months wore on, I was advised that
it was more than a rumor, that it was true.

The information came from Tom Devine, and although I still
couldn't believe it, I nevertheless had to put credence into it.

"He's checking into your Alaska background," Devine told
me.

"What about it?" I asked incredulously.

"Apparently they found something that was questionable."

"You mean that I was investigating politicians up there, too,
while I was the Chief of Police in a hick town."

"I don't know, Nick," he replied concerned. "But he thinks
that he has something on you."

"That son of a bitch. They'll stop at nothing to keep me quiet."

"That's Louie's and my view too, Nick," he said, referring to Louis Clark, the Director of GAP. "But we want to be prepared for anything he throws at us about you."

His statement now concerned me. I was musing about what it was that Goldstock could possibly have me investigated for when Devine interrupted me.

"We're having Bridget work up an analysis of your obstruction of justice charges since she's very familiar with the background of this whole affair."

On October 21, she did even more than they had initially requested, she even wrote up a detailed, "Pattern of Retaliation by Labor I.G.: Victims."

In the first part of her explicit "analysis," she broke down into seven major categories the specific examples of how the obstructions were identified. Then under each category she discussed the applicable affidavits, testimonies and other exhibits that previously had been submitted:

"1. Initiation of Sexual Harassment Investigation.

2. OIG Puts on Brakes.

3. Mangieri Pursues Investigation; Barry's Name Emerges; Personnel Actions Taken or Attempted Against Mangieri.

4. Justice and OIG Slow Down and Narrow Investigation in reaction to Congressional Interest.

5. Mangieri Complains of Obstruction; Complaints Not Investigated; Instead, Goldstock Makes Him Write Investigative Plans.

6. Mangieri Goes External; Taken Off Case.

7. I.G. Wraps Up Investigation, Refers it to Justice Which Declines Prosecution."

Under her "Pattern of Retaliation" submission to GAP, she listed nine other investigators throughout the nation who were either known as "whistleblowers" or were union activists. All were at odds with the Knowles/Goldstock regime and were threatened with criminal prosecution.

Special Agents Bill Gamble and John Salvail, both in different Organized Crime Offices, eventually won their appeals for reinstatement.

There also were other targeted agents in various Fraud Offices throughout the country whose threatened prosecutions were eventually denied by the DOJ. However, the other individuals were not in the Washington area, where both Knowles and Goldstock had a personal relationship with the U.S. Attorney.

Even Dick Ross, the former Deputy Director of our original OSI unit eventually was forced out by Knowles, then investigated by the FBI, fruitlessly. He also won reinstatement to the Atlanta office.

There was also a SAC in the Dallas office, and an agent in the New York office, both of whom were threatened with prosecution because of contrived facts drummed up by the OIG officials.

There were two particularly flagrant examples of harassment used by OIG Internal Affairs types. One caused the former SAC of the Los Angeles office to die of a heart attack because of their methods. The other incident involved the former SAC of the Buffalo office. As a result of IA investigators going to the business where the agent's wife worked and implying that he was to be indicted, she had a breakdown.

The investigator in that latter episode was Harold Anderson, who would play a major role in the same type of glaring retaliatory methods used against me.

During that same month, October, when events seemed to be heating up against me — although they had unbeknownst to me occurred long before then — I received an even more disturbing bit of news. Jim Culver, a nearby office acquaintance within OLAP, the office in which I had been detailed, said that he had observed a strange event about noon of October 10. He said he observed that a "coil," a device similar to an antenna, was being taken down from the ceiling about ten feet from my cubicle. What made it even stranger was the fact that this coil was reportedly being taken down by Goldstock and the new head of that office. In addition, Statham, McDonough and another individual were in attendance when it was being done. Although I had no proof I had been 'bugged," the more I thought about it the more I realized it was possible. The content of my phone conversations, and other discussions within my cubicle, magically became known to Goldstock and his subordinates. I didn't put two and two together until Culver confided in me what he had seen that day.

It also was about that time that I received a response from the FBI in reply to my query to DOL about a Freedom of Information-

Privacy Acts (FOIPA) request.

In that reply, I was advised that because my query to the DOL contained an FBI record about me that was "compiled for law enforcement purposes," that it was being denied. When I asked Tom Devine at GAP if he knew what the hell was going on, he said he would try to find out.

At the October 23 meeting, that GAP attended, at which Goldstock was so vocal in doing his *duty*, there also was his Special Assistant Repp, and Sylvia Horowitz of the Department of Labor's Solicitor's Office. During that wide-ranging defensive session of OIG policy with regard to their objective investigations that were "totally non-political," he attacked my character and my ineptness in my investigations even further. He also dropped the comment that he was "cooperating" with the grand jury and couldn't discuss the subject anymore.

Devine in his subsequent detailed "Memorandum for the Record," also reported:

"Finally, we asked if OIG had forwarded to Justice all of Mr. Mangieri's evidence on the sex harassment probe. Mr. Goldstock was certain that everything Mangieri produced had been sent to Justice, both allegations and supporting evidence. Goldstock observed that anything else would be illegal."

Devine, however, *knew* that his answer was false having already obtained information via a FOIA request that showed that none of my affidavits or documentation were submitted to Justice. When Goldstock made that statement to the GAP representatives he knew, or should have known, beyond the shadow of a doubt, that Coffman only submitted an amateurish sanitized version of a "thorough investigation."

Shortly thereafter, I was advised by GAP that I better hire an attorney, "just in case."

"Goddamn it, Tom, I don't have any money."

"I might know somebody," Devine conceded. "Let me talk to him about you. In the meantime, put on your thinking cap, and see what you can come up with."

On December 2, being a member of the Fraternal Order of Police, I did put in a request for legal aid. In it, I covered everything and culminated by saying, "any consideration ... would be greatly appreciated as the financial hardship caused by doing my duty is substantial."

The FOP acknowledged my request and sent me a $1,000 check to be used toward my first bill for consultation fees and preliminary work from John Karr, the attorney that Devine recommended.

Before the year was out, I was to receive even more disconcerting news. However, as disturbing as that disclosure would be, it would pale beside that which would befall me in 1981.

... 16 ...

On December 30, I received a copy of a memorandum from Frank A. Yeager, the Director of Personnel Management, to Ronald Goldstock, advising him that the appointment of Judge Thomas had been improper and therefore the December 1 decision was invalid.

When I first read Yeager's short memo it didn't quite sink in because I wasn't expecting that type of adverse reference to grievances already officially decided. I had to read it again to fully comprehend what he was writing. He basically said that because Thomas was *not* in the organization *nor* in the appropriate chain of command that he could not act as the deciding official.

My hand was shaking with anger as I dialed my attorney.

"What the hell is going on, Bridget?" I said trying to control the rage in my voice.

She was as taken by surprise as I was at the instruction, since she hadn't seen the copy of the letter that I had. She hesitated a moment before she spoke trying to fully understand what I had just told her:

"Exactly what did the Yeager memo say, Nick?" she tried to say calmly.

I read the brief memorandum to her over the phone.

She listened to its contents.

"He's trying to say that the section of the Federal Personnel Manual that deals with appointing grievance officials should not be outside of the agency," she said in disbelief, as she raised her voice also.

"How the hell can he do that?" I asked incredulously. "His personnel officer, Lattimore, told us to use the Administrative Law Judges as the Step 1 level."

"I know, I know," she said quickly. "I've never heard of this being done *after* someone's been told to go this route and *after* someone's won a decision."

"I didn't think so," I said in disgust.

"I'll have to get back to you on this, Nick," she said. "Obviously they're trying to pull a fast one."

"Can they?" I wanted to know.

"I've never heard it done," she tried to reassure me again. "I'll try to get hold of someone today," she said. "If not, it'll have to be after New Year's."

"Goddamn it," I raised my voice again.

"Just try to take it easy until then," she said. "I'll give GAP a call, too, and let them know what's going on."

That exchange of info between us became secondary to the shocking notification that I received from John Karr, the new attorney I had just retained.

On January 7, 1981, Karr wrote advising me that he had just gotten a call from Charles Roistacher, the Assistant U.S. Attorney "in charge of your case."

Before Karr had received that phone call, there had been ominous rumblings from the U.S. Attorney's Office that there was talk of prosecuting me because I had allegedly falsified applications to the DOL federal credit union. When I first heard those reports, I dismissed them with a "bullshit, it's a scare tactic." However, although it was definitely a scare tactic, there was unquestionably no *bullshit* involved because Goldstock, and Knowles before him, had long since laid the groundwork for such a trumped-up charge against me.

Back in June or July, 1979, shortly after my sexual coercion investigation into City Hall and the name of Mayor Barry surfaced, Stuart Eder, the former Acting Chief of Investigations, initiated an investigation of me dating back to my Alaska days in the mid- to late-1970s. It was a wide-ranging investigation that had to be approved by the I.G. at that time, Marjorie Knowles. It was undoubtedly launched with the hope of uncovering something in my background to use against me in order to make my testimony and my evidence less credible.

During the period that this information covered, I had been the Chief of Police in a small town about 40 miles from Anchorage, in what was known as the Matanuska Valley. In my capacity as the chief law enforcement official in that area, I uncovered and investigated corrupt local politicians in a long-standing massive land fraud against the federal government and the state of Alaska. For my exposure of that practice and those participants, I was abruptly ousted from office. I then continued further intensive investigations on my own to prove my allegations. However, because I was fighting a status quo system, and publicity attacking those politicians who had been in the area long before me, it was an uphill — and sometimes dangerous — battle. Not only did my efforts encompass in-depth delving into long-term fraudulent activity and the reopening of closed-out cases that had questionable deaths involved, but included my own extensive litigation. My ongoing civil cases were directed against those city officials who had summarily removed me from duty. The whole process, from my hire as Chief of Police to ultimately leaving the state, was a four-year span. As a result, I went through a messy divorce in which I had obtained custody of my three children, and then was forced to relocate to the East Coast in their best interests. In doing so, I was unable to pursue my final legal remedies against those Alaska officials. Consequently, the condition of my financial indebtedness had been in very poor state. Regrettably, there was absolutely nothing that I could do at the time to resolve my situation.

It was this partial biased information that Eder obtained from Alaska, via Seattle OIG investigators, that was to become what was then referred to as the Alaska packet. Although all the coverage by the Alaska media that should have accompanied it apparently never did because it was highly favorable to me. The overwhelming majority of the fifty newspaper articles that covered the entire episode, especially the Anchorage accounts, accurately portrayed events as they occurred. However, it was the balance of that slanted packet that contained whatever the initial DOL investigator, who was assigned to the task could glean from it, that sought to present me in an unfavorable light. Even Braver who was forwarded the packet to do the "hatchet job" on me in mid-1979, concluded that it had,

"nothing of interest or value relative to Mangieri and his current
employment with the Department of Labor." He then reportedly
gave it to Eder, who claimed that he kept it in his files because it was-
n't "a formal OIG investigation." However, I subsequently learned
from testimony and affidavits that Knowles, and later Goldstock,
would disseminate whatever they considered to be derogatory information about me, especially that which they had obtained from
those same Alaska politicians I had previously investigated. Although
I never knew the full extent to which I was being defamed with
their use of that secret dossier, I learned that the Alaska packet was
specifically being passed around to Department of Justice officials
and to several Congressional sources. One particular source was to
the Senate Government Affairs Committee in December 1979.
Lehrman in an affidavit stated that Goldstock told him that he had
fed that information to the committee when they were discussing
the CETA and Pride charges that I and the former head of the
Audit Division, Gerald Peterson, had disclosed at that time. So
much so, that subsequent to our interview by Senate investigators,
that staff also interviewed Knowles. She reportedly appeared with
six or seven aides and denied every detail of our allegations. Several
days later she also sent a letter to Senator Thomas Eagleton again
denying those same charges that we had previously raised about
the CETA and Pride obstructions. In turn, she brought counter-
charges against us. Also, at about that same time, the DOL Congressional liaison sent a letter to his counterpart at the White House
dismissing our charges as "untrue and to some extent the work of
disgruntled employees." However, because Senate and Department of Justice investigators found Peterson's charges to be credible, DOJ considered prosecuting Knowles and her assistant, Repp,
for lying to Senate investigators about cancellation of the Pride
audit. Unfortunately, they declined to take formal action due to
lack of witnesses.

When I learned that both sets of investigators had found Peterson's information credible, but not my own, I began to realize the
depth to which Knowles and Goldstock had gone to undermine
my character, because of their paranoia. In that same memorandum that was sent to the White House, by Nick Edes, the DOL liaison type, he advised his contact, Frank Moore, that there would
be a report on my case, that had been assigned to Coffman, "with-

in 30 days." Since my Alaska packet had been so freely distributed to any source that had the opportunity to weigh my own credibility, there would appear to be little doubt that DOL had so advised the White House accordingly. I had learned, and would learn even further, that the I.G.'s office would stop at *nothing* to have the blame diverted from themselves.

In spite of the promise that the White House would have a report issued "within 30 days," Coffman did not forward his part of the CETA investigation to the Justice Department until May 2, 1980. Prosecution, of course, was subsequently declined by that agency because of a lack of evidence. Not only was *none* of my evidence forwarded to the Justice Department by Coffman, but his own superficial investigation, with numerous investigators, only produced 17 inconclusive interviews during that five-month period. Cameron Barron, my longtime buddy and one of those assigned to that amateurish probe, would note in a subsequent affidavit that because Coffman had specifically limited the types of witnesses that the investigators could contact that those limitations "were too restrictive to conduct an adequate investigation and that I doubted the legitimacy of the investigation."

In addition to the so-called *Alaska packet* that Art Braver had seen, and scoffed at, there was an even more insidious investigation of me that had been under way since early summer of 1980. That investigation was conducted by Harold Anderson, the same investigator who had previously been used as an effective hatchet man to rid the OIG of individuals whom Goldstock considered to be a threat to him. Two or three months earlier Statham, who had previously testified at my grievance hearing about that packet, stated that those documents were not in any official personnel folder but were "extra-official documents of some kind, kicking around someplace within the agency." He, then provided that packet to Office of Personnel Management investigators who were asked to do a full-field investigation of me. However, in order not to make it appear that a full-field investigation was being requested only for me, Knowles in December 1979, issued a memorandum that all DOL/OIG employees would be subject to the *full field*. Lehrman, who had helped formulate job descriptions when the agency was established, was to testify that because of budget limitations and the $800-$1,000 cost per employee of these investigations the agency had made a policy decision not to require them. Instead the job descriptions only required FBI fingerprint checks. Even the Assistant Director of Personnel was to testify that because, "no requirement existed requiring satisfactory completion of a background investigation as a contingency for continued employment," that the new requirement would be "of no use" for actions against employees who had completed their probationary period. I, as well as the great majority of the other employees, had already done so. A Security Specialist who also was involved in these background checks, also testified that even assuming the security clearance requirement could be imposed *ex post facto,* the appropriate action would have been to impose the more limited "security investigations" instead of full-field investigations. She further stated, "I cannot explain this, other than again it was a specific request by Mrs. Knowles." Also, a few weeks later, in a January 25, 1980, memorandum to Samuel de Genova, the Assistant Director of Personnel, Statham requested that the new OPM investigations cover alcohol and/or drug abuse, conflicts of interest, and, of course, "personal indebtedness or judgments." However, as Linda Furbey, the Security Specialist, was to state in a later affidavit, "This is not a normal occurrence and to the best of my knowledge these specific areas were requested only at the insistence of Marjorie F. Knowles, then Inspector General for the Department of Labor. This is the only occasion I know of where special investigative coverage was specifically requested."

The reason for the close proximity of these events is best described in an analysis given in a future court motion:

> "The principal personnel problem during this period for Mr. Statham concerned Mr. Mangieri. Mr. Statham had terminated Mr Mangieri's detail to the national headquarters just three weeks earlier. Between two weeks and three weeks earlier Ms. Knowles, Mr. Goldstock, Mr. Statham and Mr. Repp had been responding to Senate investigators and Senator Eagleton about Mr. Mangieri's highly publicized political obstruction charges. Another simultaneous DOL/OIG personnel problem concerned Mr. Peterson's highly publicized affidavit and the

Senate investigation of Peterson's charges. Mr.
Mangieri had taken Mr. Peterson's affidavit."

In addition, Goldstock had on February 29, *two days* after I
had inspected his travel vouchers, personally called an OPM official,
Robert Herrman and requested that I be given a "fifteen-day special investigation." Even Statham, in future testimony, was to state
that, to his knowledge, I was the only DOL/OIG employee out of
487 who was selected to be investigated on a fifteen-day expedited basis.

Although I was unaware at the time of all these events and of
the continuing covert actions that were constantly taking place
behind my back, fortunately my gut reactions were usually pretty
good. That *gut reaction* had come into play several months earlier
when I refused to sign a consent form handed to me by Castro
that would release anyone from liability in their investigation of
me. That decision undoubtedly stood me in good stead, but caused
no end of problems for the administration. First, OPM advised me
that they could go no further, without my permission. Second,
which was even more important to me, Goldstock was stymied in
his plans for me.

In a earlier memorandum to Statham on February 12, de Genova informed him that I had a right under the Privacy Act to deny
access to personal records.

In a subsequent affidavit, Goldstock stated that he was convinced OPM would obtain sufficient derogatory information about
me to force me out of DOL/OIG permanently. However, when
their report didn't support his belief, he went a step further. That
step, as Statham subsequently testified, was to order an Internal
Affairs investigation of me because it was decided that the OPM
investigation was incomplete. Anderson, Goldstock's hand-picked
man, who had been detailed into IA, was given the packet on me
in early June 1980. He was specifically instructed by Goldstock to
expand the OPM investigation on the issues of financial irrespon-
sibility and on the probability of false statements appearing on my
SF-171, my federal application. That ludicrous assumption was
based on Statham's observation that two jobs I allegedly had been
fired from in my 30-year history of employment did not appear on
my SF-171. Never mentioned or considered was the fact that in

my early years of employment I held many part-time or temporary jobs in conjunction with each other full-time regular employment. Nor, for that matter, was I ever asked to give an explanation of why a job of a few days or a few weeks never appeared on my application. At that stage of Anderson's inquiry into my extensive personal background, he was directed to find something about me — anything — that they could hang their hat on. Not content to merely have Anderson delve into my personal history to find *something*, Goldstock, at a Fredericksburg, Virginia, manager's conference in early June, announced that I *already* was a criminal. The conclusion had been determined, in advance, and it was left up to Anderson to justify it.

It was not only this background of conspiracy and deceit that preceded the phone call from Roistacher, the Assistant U.S. Attorney, on January 7, 1981, but an even more ominous series of events that had also been set in motion against me earlier.

I was not to learn of the importance of friends or personal connections, especially in the political arena in our nation's capital, until it was too late to stop it.

The U.S. Attorney for the District of Columbia was Charles Ruff. Ruff and Knowles had worked together in the New York prosecutor's office. When Ruff later went to the U.S. Department of Health, Education and Welfare as the Deputy Inspector General, he brought in Knowles as the Associate General Counsel attached to the I.G.'s Office there. Then when Ruff became the U. S. Attorney for D.C., it was reported that he had a formal role in the selection of Knowles as the Department of Labor's first Inspector General. Even Ruff, himself, was to later testify that he was not only a personal friend of Knowles, but admitted he had not only been instrumental in helping Knowles to obtain her job at DOL, but Goldstock's, as well. Further, Ruff testified, that Knowles complained to him about problems she had with me, and other DOL/OIG employees, shortly after she took office in May 1979, and also during 1980. Ruff also stated that Goldstock had first begun to talk to him about me in August 1979, and then continued to complain about my allegations, against him, through 1980 and even up until early 1981.

Ruff also admitted in a future affidavit, that in addition to counselling Knowles on how to respond to my political obstruction charges, and those of others, that he tried to help her expedite investigations of her agents in Boston and Atlanta in the Public Integrity Section of the Department of Justice. He further stated that at his suggestion in August 1980, Goldstock contacted the Chief of the Fraud Division in the U.S. Attorney's Office. That individual, Richard Beizer, testified that he did not understand why Goldstock came personally to make the prosecution, although Goldstock advised him that it was his practice to make personal criminal referrals of DOL/OIG employees. Beizer also testified that Goldstock enthusiastically advocated prosecuting me for violations of the U.S. Code dealing with false statements on loan applications. Goldstock, on the other hand, in the course of an affidavit, disagreed with Beizer. He testified that there, "was no discussion of prosecuting Mangieri at that point. Beizer only agreed to issue subpoenas to several loan institutions, including the DOL Credit Union, to determine if such false statements had been made."

The middle man in all these actions was Harold Anderson. His truthfulness was questioned and the legality of his methods challenged — after the fact.

With this framework of deception being carefully constructed around me, it was no small wonder that of the many thousands of cases that were processed in the Washington U.S. Attorney's Office, normally at the lowest levels *first,* that mine entered and was speedily processed at the highest level.

As Tom Devine of GAP would dryly, but appropriately, comment many months later in one of his perpetual notes to the files, "Mangieri must've had quite a reputation over at DOL."

Karr, in his letter of January 7, continued with the Roistacher message:

"He informed me that he was about to present the case to the grand jury and inquired whether you were interested in the government's plea offer of guilty to one count of 18 USC Sec. 1014 in exchange for the government's dismissal of the other eight "counts."

Section 1014, I knew was "False Statements to a Credit Union," and the other eight "counts" referred to, were eight other applications that I had filed with them since I began employment in 1978.

"Hell no," I said aloud to myself before I continued reading the letter.

"Mr. Roistacher said that if he did not have an answer by a week from today, or Wednesday, January 14, 1981, he would assume that you were not interested in the plea offer and would present the case to the grand jury."

I crumpled the letter in my hand and gritted my teeth before I yelled out, "Goddamn it. Goddamn it," and walked aimlessly around the room for a minute. I took a deep breath, and called Karr.

"Just got your letter, John," I said breathlessly, still trying to catch my breath from working myself up.

"What's your decision?" he said slowly.

"I don't even have to think about it," I said quickly. "It's not only no, it's hell no. I wouldn't even plead guilty to a misdemeanor," I continued. "I know I've done nothing wrong, you know it, and even them sonsabitches know it."

"I'm with you, Nick," he said evenly, "but I just want you to be aware of the consequences."

"What do you mean?" I wanted to know.

"I'm sure they're going to go all out to get you," and he hesitated, "or they wouldn't have gone this far."

"I want to fight the bastards all the way, John."

He took a deep breath as he listened.

"Okay," he said. "If you still want me to represent you, be here early tomorrow morning as we've got a lot of work to do."

"What time?"

"Nine o'clock."

"I'll be there," I said and hung up.

His office suite was located a couple of blocks from the White House, at 15th Street and New York Avenue. When I was ushered into his private office, one of his staff attorneys was with him. They both looked serious, but Karr gave me a quick smile before he motioned to the other man. "I think you know Will, don't you?" I acknowledged that Will McLain and I had met briefly the last time I was in his office, and we all shook hands briefly. With the pleasantries aside, Karr got down to business.

"Before we get down to specifics," he said, "I just want to get into a little background about yourself."

"What in particular?" I asked.

"Well, let's just start with Alaska, for now," he said.

My stomach sank momentarily. *How many times must I repeat this story,* I thought. He must've sensed the uneasiness in my manner, and tried to soothe me.

"Just the highlights, Nick, of what you went through as the Police Chief there and your financial problems there afterward."

I took a deep breath, again, and briefly covered my experiences there: my hire, a corrupt City Manager supported by crooked politicians, my uncovering massive land fraud, the prior violences, threats against me, my termination, my long-term legal battles with them, and, finally, my divorce.

Karr who had been sitting quietly listening to a discourse that I tried to keep down to a minimum, interrupted me, "I want to hear about your finances."

I explained that after I lost my job, I couldn't meet expenses, eventually lost my house, and within a year went through a divorce.

"I think I've got the picture," he said.

McLain stepped in, "Any children?"

"Four," I said, "but one got married before the divorce."

"Who got custody?" Karr asked.

"I did."

"I think I understand about your financial problems," he said.

"What's Alaska got to do with this?" I wanted to know.

"I don't really know," he answered, "but according to the U.S. Attorney's Office, the I.G.'s office at Labor has been probing your background."

"What for?"

"They're saying you didn't list all your bills on your credit union loans."

"Is *that* what this is all about?" I raised my voice as I said it.

"That's about the size of it."

"That's bullshit," I said. "Can they do that?"

"Well," he said, "Let me put it this way, I've never heard of it being done before, especially as I understand you have an automatic payroll deduction on your loan, and I think Tom Devine told me that you had gotten a co-signer for your car before you ever got your first loan."

"Right."

"However," he continued, "they're saying that it's a federal application and that if you omit any bills, it technically falls within the statute of the 'false statements' in 18 USC 1014."

"What a load of crap," I said. "This isn't about omitting any bills, this is about retaliation because I exposed the whole goddamn I.G.'s office."

"Take it easy, Nick." He tried to calm me. "I hear what you're saying, but this is what we're facing."

"What kind of justice is this?"

"This is Washington and this is politics," he said matter-of-factly, "but we'll do our best for you."

I nodded dumbly, not really believing what I was facing.

Karr interrupted my thoughts.

"I'll contact Roistacher again and see what good I can do," he said.

I thanked him, and looked toward McLain, who was taking the whole thing in.

"Is that it?" I asked.

"We'll be in touch, Nick. Just try not to worry."

Easier said than done. My whole life, I had always done my best and sought the truth in everything that I had uncovered. I was raised that way. Now, when I had tried to pursue justice — because that was the oath that I had sworn — it was being turned against me. Sadly, it was not the first time that justice turned the other way when I had tried to do my job. It had happened in Alaska. However, this time it was more than just a case of the system ignoring my investigations, it was a case of the system going after me because I refused to ignore violations of justice that I encountered.

In addition to waiting for the U.S. Attorney's Office to make a final decision about me, and in addition to awaiting word from Karr as to what was transpiring, I also wondered about my unresolved administrative grievances. The last information I had was that Judge Thomas' decision, in my favor, could not stand because he had been improperly delegated that authority.

On January 8, the day following Karr's notification to me about the Roistacher call, there was some movement. I was advised of DOL's next bit of action. In a letter from Goldstock to Mugane, he wrote that the "entire matter" was being referred to Undersecretary Gentry "for a final Step 1 decision." When I asked Mugane what her were feelings on that action and what she proposed to do, her response was as I expected.

"As to the Undersecretary's role in this," she said. "I think we can expect a rubberstamp of Yeager's decision not to honor Judge Thomas' decision."

"Them goddamn sonsabitches," I said.

"I know how you feel, Nick," she said, "but if and *when* it happens," and she stressed the word when, "then our only other recourse is through the federal courts."

I started to ask how much that would cost, but I didn't feel like any more bad news at the moment. She must've sensed my hesitation, and my concern for additional legal expense, because she added, "I think that we can apply for funding to help you in that regard."

"I sure hope so, Bridget," I said dejectedly.

"In the meantime, Nick," she said, "try not to worry about it."

"This is the second time within the past 24 hours that I've heard that," I said.

"I know," she said sympathetically. "I've been in touch with GAP."

The days dragged by slowly, and I finally received a call from Karr.

"I'm sorry, Nick," he said. "I did my best with Roistacher, but I'm afraid that he's going forward with it to the grand jury."

I listened, again, in disbelief at what I had been told.

I sucked in a deep breath and exhaled heavily.

"Goddamn it, John," I said. "How the hell could this happen?"

"I think you know better than I do," was all he could say. "It's up to the grand jury, now."

"Yeah," I said. "And their input is only what Roistacher wants to present."

"Let's just keep our fingers crossed," he said. "We'll keep you posted."

On Monday morning, January 19, before I left for work, I received another call from him.

"Have you seen today's *Washington Star*?" he asked.

"No," I replied, and again had that sinking feeling of what was in store for me.

"When you do, call me back at the office later. I'll be in after nine."

I went out and found the morning edition. I nervously flipped through the pages and there it was on page 3 of "The Capital Report," incongruously right beside a picture of President-Elect George Bush jogging at American University:

AGENT INDICTED AFTER PROBING SEX COERCION
by Kenneth R. Walker

"A U.S. Labor Department investigator who headed a now-defunct inquiry into whether District government officials used a federal jobs program to coerce sexual favors from young women has been indicted by a federal grand jury on charges of making false statements on credit union loan applications.

"The agent, Nicholas J. Mangieri, attached to the Labor Department Inspector General's office, and his attorneys have labeled the criminal probe that led to the indictment as the latest in a series of actions taken in retaliation for Mangieri's complaints of alleged political interference with the sexual harassment inquiry and other investigations.

" 'I've seen a lot of criminal cases,' said one of Mangieri's lawyers, John Karr, 'and this is the most transparent one I've ever seen.'

"Mangieri was notified last week by the U.S. Attorney's Office that he faced indictment for felony charges arising from 1978 loan applications to the Labor Department credit union.

"The agent and his lawyers charge that a number of other so-called 'whistleblowers' in the Labor Department have been subjected to criminal investigation as part of what they describe as a campaign by the Inspector General's office to silence internal dissent.

"Mangieri's troubles first arose 13 months ago when he asked Attorney General Benjamin Civiletti to investigate the possibility that the Labor Department's Inspector General at that time, Marjorie F. Knowles, and her deputy, Ronald Goldstock, conspired to obstruct an investigation into allegations that several District government officials used the federal Comprehensive Employment Training Act program to extort sexual favors from young women.

"That investigation, which began following publication in *The Washington Star* of a series of articles detailing incidents of alleged sexual harassment in the city government, was halted by Labor Department officials over Mangieri's objections.

"Mangieri said in his letter to Civlietti that he perceived 'a subtle coverup' shortly after he began the investigation in the spring of 1979. His assignment was 'quickly changed, 'he claimed, following the receipt of information that a high District government official had 'allegedly sexually harassed' a female employee.

"Mangieri maintained that his investigation had uncovered evidence that one former and two sitting members of the D.C. City Council had allegedly engaged in the practice.

"Mangieri also collected affidavits from other Labor Department investigators alleging that Knowles had ordered a premature halt to an investigation of Youth Pride, Inc., a local self-help organization founded by Mayor Marion Barry and his former wife, Mary Treadwell.

"Mangieri obtained an affidavit from Gerald W. Peterson, a former acting audit chief, swearing that Knowles personally told him to halt an audit of Youth Pride because: 'This is not too smart. Don't you know the mayor's inauguration parade started at Pride?'

"The grand jury is currently investigating allegations of fraud and misappropriation of more than $20 million in federal funds received by Youth Pride. Mayor Barry has not been implicated in any wrongdoing.

"Mangieri said it was after he sent his letter to Civiletti that Labor Department officials referred the loan application allegations to the U.S. Attorney's office.

"The Justice Department later concluded — without interviewing Mangieri — that there were no basis for the allegations of a coverup in the sexual coercion probe.

"However, the Government Accountability Project, a private organization with the Institute for Policy Studies, conducted what it called a 'thorough verification study of Mangieri's coverup charges. 'As a result of our investigation,' the GAP's Whistleblower Review Panel agreed unanimously in a report last November, 'we are completely satisfied that (Mangieri) has provided serious evidence of misconduct.'

"Brigette Mugane, a GAP lawyer who represents Mangieri, said the investigation showed 'very serious improprieties' in the management of the probe. She said the investigation showed that Labor Department officials had barred Mangieri from evidence evaluation sessions with the U.S. Attorney and that 'very little' of the evidence gathered in the sexual harassment probe was turned over to prosecutors, who ultimately decided to close the case due to lack of evidence.

"After his removal from the harassment inquiry, Mangieri initiated an investigation into allegations that Goldstock, as deputy Inspector General at Labor, had filed thousands of dollars worth of unauthorized travel vouchers. In a recent interview, Goldstock — who became acting Inspector General last spring after Knowles suddenly resigned — called Mangieri's allegations 'completely untrue.'

"Mangieri's indictment charges that he failed to include previous debts on nine credit union applications submitted to the Labor Department credit union in 1978. Two of the applications — for $6,000 — were approved after Mangieri obtained a co-signer. The loans have been repaid through routine paycheck deductions.

"GAP attorney Mugane said she is 'absolutely convinced' that her client's legal problems are in retaliation for his whistleblowing activities.

" 'I can also cite six other IG agents who were threatened with or subjected to criminal investigations after, in one way or another, criticizing the management of certain investigations,' Mugane said.

" 'What most alarms me,' Mugane added, 'is the misuse in the IG's office of rather broad police powers — such as its connections to the Justice Department and its ability to lobby prosecutors.'

"Goldstock denied that his office uses its police powers to silence internal dissidents.

"Karr, Mangieri's other attorney, said that in each of Mangieri's loan applications, 'the credit union got computerized credit bureau reports fully outlining Mangieri's very serious financial troubles several years ago, while he was in the midst of a messy divorce.'

" 'He never tried to hide the state of his finances in order to get a loan,' Karr said."

I read it as if I were detached from the whole scene, as though I were reading about someone else. It just didn't quite seem real. In fact, I was more impressed with Walker's coverage of the whole affair, than I was with what the article was all about. Even Karr and Mugane seemed to put everything in its proper perspective. As I put it down, I thought not bad. The immensity of what I was facing, had not yet hit me.

During the upcoming year, there would be another ten, or so, such articles, and all basically in the same vein. As supportive as they would be, I would not have the same strange feelings as I had at that particular moment.

Whether Mugane deliberately sought to cheer me up with her

letter to Goldstock on that same date, or whether it was just a coincidence, didn't matter; it worked. She advised him that the invalidation of Judge Thomas' decision in my grievances was "in violation of well-established legal doctrine," and that if it was implemented, suit would be brought to enforce it. My spirits were lifted temporarily with the thought that a civil case in a U.S. District Court would support our allegations of retaliation against me.

Simultaneously, there was also a memorandum to me, with a copy to my attorney, from the Undersecretary of Labor. As expected, he adopted all of the findings and recommendations of the Hearing Examiner, but denied those of the Administrative Law Judge. This new decision meant only that Grievances #1 and #5 were sustained. Grievance #1 held that Coffman was guilty of improper conduct toward me subsequent to my investigating Goldstock's travel vouchers, while Grievance #5 found that my forced repayment of my travel advances were arbitrary and capricious, and should be "investigated by the DOL General Counsel."

Big fuckin' deal, I said to myself when I read about his agreeing with my repeated position of an unfair repayment schedule that was foisted on me by the I.G. and their subordinates. Those travel advance funds had long since been repaid, by me, with considerable hardship to myself in trying to support my three kids on those greatly reduced paychecks.

Undersecretary Gentry not only denied my reinstatement, but denied payment of attorney's fees to Mugane, that Judge Thomas had previously decreed. A subsequent letter to the Personnel Officer from Mugane, then stated that I wished to appeal to the Secretary of Labor, the final step in the formal grievance procedure. Meanwhile, the *wheels of justice* were grinding inexorably toward me, and I was meeting with both Karr and McLain in discussing defense strategy. GAP, not to be outdone in its own unswerving efforts to help me, sent another letter on January 26 to Mary Eastwood, the Acting Special Counsel of the Merit Systems Protection Board. In that letter, Devine sought not only to expand coverage on those that should be investigated, but sought to rebut Goldstock's outrageous charges against me:

> "On December 19, 1980, I forwarded a whistle-
> blowing disclosure to your office on behalf of Mr.

Nicholas Mangieri, an employee at the Office of
Inspector General ('OIG') of the Department of
Labor. This letter supplements and offers additional
evidence of this first charge, concerning mismanagement and abuse of authority through interference
with the investigation into sexual coercion of CETA
employees by high-level D.C. government officials.

"Initially, Mr. Mangieri wishes to add Mr. Stuart Eder to the list of officials in the mismanagement abuse of authority allegation. At the time of
the indictments in the disclosure, Mr. Eder was Acting Chief of Investigations at OIG. Mr. Mangieri
asked Mr. Eder to halt the initial harassment of the
D.C. government investigation. Instead, Mr. Eder
chose to intensify the obstruction. He opened an
investigation of Mangieri. When Mr. Mangieri's
probe began to focus on Mayor Barry, Eder detailed
Mangieri from the Arlington OIG Office. (See
December 9, 1980, Affidavit of Nicholas Mangieri,
at 4-7, and accompanying exhibits).

"You may also find useful some additional evidence to support Mr. Mangieri's initial disclosure.
In informal discussions, Mr. Goldstock has explained
to GAP representatives that Mangieri was a con-
tinuously disgruntled, incompetent employee who
has been unable to hold a job and lacked sufficient
investigative experience to handle a major probe.
In short, Goldstock has alleged that Mr. Mangieri
cannot be taken seriously due to personal short-
comings. Second, Goldstock has characterized the
alleged D.C. sexual coercion abuses as a figment of
Mr. Mangieri's imagination. Our supplemental information rebuts both responses.

"Initially, we wish to correct the distortions
about Mr. Mangieri's personal background and
competence. While he had held a series of jobs, the
changes were due to promotions and better oppor-
tunities, rather than dismissals. References from
seven employers, ranging from 1972-1976, are

enclosed as Attachment 1. They should be read in
conjunction with Exhibits 2-4 of Mr. Mangieri's
December 9, 1980, affidavit. In general, these former supervisors expressed regret at losing Mr. Mangieri's services.

"Mr. Goldstock has emphasized Mangieri's loss
of an Alaska police chief job as illustrative. If anything, that incident illustrates the current type of
cover-ups and retaliation against Mr. Mangieri,
rather than any incompetence. Mangieri was fired on
petty grounds after he began to aggressively pursue a land fraud scheme. The Alaska judge denied
relief for Mr. Mangieri 'with a heavy heart,' because
Mangieri was a probationary employee with almost
no rights. Several newspaper articles that put the
incident in perspective are enclosed as Attachment
2. Ample additional documentation is available,
upon request. This is the only blemish on Mr. Mangieri's employment record.

"The charge that Mr. Mangieri was too 'green'
to handle the D.C. case competently is insultingly
inaccurate. His police and investigative background
dates back to 1948. In addition, he has taken
advanced training and graduate courses in law
enforcement investigative work. For over two years
he instructed police science courses at the University of Alaska. Summaries of his background are
enclosed as Attachment 3. In short, we would not
be surprised if Mr. Mangieri's experience and training as a field investigator dwarfs Mr. Goldstock's.
Certainly, Mangieri was experienced enough to conduct a criminal investigation.

"The other major rebuttal to Mr. Mangieri's
disclosure is that no significant degree of sexual
harassment exists in the D.C. government. In other
words, Goldstock claims that there was nothing to
cover up. When we submitted Mr. Mangieri's disclosure, we had studied FOIA documents on his
investigation, an affidavit from a D.C. employee,

and received confirmation from three sources who requested anonymity.

"Since December 19, GAP representatives have spoken with three additional witnesses, all whom requested anonymity due to the Special Counsel's inability to guarantee confidentiality. 44 *Fed. Reg.* 75922 (December 21, 1979). In a January 21, 1981, conversation, Mr. Rothberg confirmed your inability to ensure anonymity.* We are attempting to reach two other witnesses, whom we have been informed will provide further verification.

"Two of the sources provided general confirmation of sexual harassment by top officials. Both witnesses explained that its existence is 'common knowledge.'

"A third witness offered a more detailed description of the phenomenon. This witness explained that most of the CETA victims are poor black women who live in low-income housing and are desperate for a job. If they cooperate, they receive gifts such as expensive watches. Particularly attractive women are moved into permanent jobs without undergoing the competitive process of the merit system.

"The witness explained that Mr. Mangieri was on the right track, but due to the OIG coverup (and criminal charges against Mangieri), it will be much more difficult to expose the abuses. Apparently women have been pressured not to cooperate with any new investigations and schooled in stock answers. Some have been promoted from clerical to professional jobs, to 'buy' their silence. However, this witness felt that it is still possible to uncover the truth with thorough digging ... *

* *"Some of these individuals have expressed tentative willingness to speak with the investigator for any §1206(b)(3) investigation you order if that individual can adequately protect their identities."*

The balance of the letter then cited a "Ms. Dollie Marie Honablew" as being "a confirmed example of the unconscionable sexual harassment and abuse that existed in the CETA Program."

Honablew was the individual whom the D.C. Personnel Director, George Harrod, had been initially charged with assaulting two years earlier — and was the case that originally had gotten me involved with my sexual coercion investigations of City Hall.

On the following morning, January 27, the reality of the situation that faced me began to sink in. It was the first of many black days that lay ahead of me, but a faith in a higher power carried me through that difficult time.

There was the inevitable arraignment, where I pled "not guilty" as strongly as I could. However, the machinery of the system was relentless in its operation, and I was escorted through the basement of the federal courthouse to nearby police headquarters. There, I was formally booked, fingerprinted and had mug shots taken. It was a nightmare come true, that only those who have had realistic dreams could understand. Only I knew that this particular nightmare became reality.

The only incongruity that was interjected in this whole serious scene was the comical attitudes of the two officers behind the booking desk.

They had not only heard and read of my situation in the local paper, but when they questioned me as to the facts of my case, couldn't believe the results.

"You mean," one of them said, "if I don't list all of my bills on a loan application this could happen to me too?"

When I agreed with his assessment of the situation, the other officer chimed in.

"Goddamn, they could put all of us in jail then."

In spite of my surroundings, I couldn't help but give a forced smile to their animated reactions. I, however, added in a more serious tone, "if they want to."

Three days later, on January 30, Goldstock issued a memorandum to all OIG personnel, that he was leaving because the "new Administration" had so decided.

I had hoped that with the Republican party in power, things

would be different. I was, however, advised that what had already been initiated would continue.

Although Labor and Justice, with their combined efforts, managed to set in motion a contrived prosecution against me, there would soon be a surge of additional media support in my behalf. I wasn't to learn about Ken Walker's removal from covering cases at the U.S. Attorney's Office, for the *Washington Star,* until the Fall of 1981.

At that time, an analysis of U.S. Attorney Ruff's statement to supposedly unbiased investigators revealed that he sent a letter to the *Star* complaining about Walker, and as a result his assignments were quickly changed. However, the *Federal Times,* a Washington-based periodical covering federal employees and activities, took up the cudgels in my defense for several months. The first very lengthy article came out on February 9, and was titled:

LABOR DEPARTMENT AIDES
ACCUSED OF SABOTAGING PROBES

The article was by Sheila Hershow, who by her continuing objective investigative reporting, was to become knowledgeable of all aspects of the case.

In commenting not only about me, but about Gamble, she outlined an intricate pattern of corruption, cover-up and retaliation by Knowles and her staff:

> "The Government Accountability project has charged that top-ranking officials in the Labor Department's office of the inspector general are waging a war of reprisals against agency investigators who sought to probe allegations of organized crime involvement in labor unions and allegations that prominent District of Columbia officials sexually coerced women hired under a federal jobs program.
>
> "GAP — a support group for whistleblowers sponsored by the Institute for Policy Studies — has asked the Merit Systems Protection Board's special counsel to investigate Labor Department moves to

fire William R. Gamble III and shift Nicholas J.
Mangieri Jr. out of his job as a criminal investigator.

"The public interest group contends that Gamble and Mangieri have been punished for their refusal
to back off politically volatile investigations. 'We
have yet to come across an inspector general's office
so willing to wink at corruption by high- level officials and so extremely zealous at going after petty
offenses by its own investigators.' Thomas Devine,
GAP's associate director, said.

"Gamble and Mangieri are not isolated cases.
A press aide in the Office of Special Counsel said
that OSC has received 'about a dozen complaints
related to the inspector general's office at Labor.'

"OSC launched an on-site investigation last
spring, the aide said, but the probe was halted
'because [the special counsel] faced a crunch in the
budget.' She said that the investigation had been
resumed and should be completed within 'the next
couple of weeks.'

"In a series of interviews with current and former Labor Department employees, *Federal Times*
has heard numerous charges that experienced Labor
investigators were harassed and intimidated, shifted around the country, disciplined on trumped up
charges and subjected to improper surveillance.

" 'I objected violently to the methods used,'
said one Labor investigator. 'I objected to the
gestapo mentality ... It was always overkill. They
were using mail covers on people ...There were character assassination attempts on assistant secretaries.'

"Other Labor investigators said that investigative units assigned to probe labor racketeering had
been gutted and demoralized. Auditors complained
that rampant fraud in the $11 billion Comprehen-
sive Employment Training Act program had been
allowed to flourish while Labor investigators investigated minor offenses by Labor employees.

"Ronald Goldstock, acting inspector general at

labor, acknowledged that his office has been plagued by 'a series' of personnel problems. But he insisted that neither he nor former Labor Inspector General Marjorie Fine Knowles had obstructed investigations of politically sensitive cases. Knowles, who now teaches at the University of Alabama law school, did not return Federal Times phone calls ..."

The Hershow article then went on to describe, in great detail, how Goldstock enacted severe actions against Gamble, as well, and also portrayed him as "a nut." It was a term I thought Knowles and Goldstock had used only against me, but I learned I had no monopoly on that depictment.

The article then accurately reported:

"GAP maintains that the Labor Department's campaign against Gamble was paralleled by a series of fierce reprisals taken against Mangieri, a GS-12 investigator who unearthed 'evidence of sexual harassment by ten top D.C. government officials.'

"'Mangieri was prevented from gaining access to relevant evidence, delayed in presenting congressional testimony on the investigation until the committee lost interest, forced to fight specious personnel actions, ordered to redistrict the scope of the investigation from ten targets to two against the advice of the assistant U.S. attorney with whom Mangieri worked, compelled to conduct his investigations ... contrary to standard investigative procedure ... excluded from strategy sessions on the case, and eventually removed from the case when he refused to back off,' GAP wrote acting special counsel Mary Eastwood.

"In affidavits sent to the Justice Department, Mangieri has charged that Knowles and Goldstock conspired to thwart his probe of allegations that elected and appointed officials in the D.C. government sexually coerced CETA employees. Last February, John C. Keeney, chief of the Justice Depart-

ment's criminal division, wrote Mangieri that the
Public Integrity Section staff had decided there was
no 'adequate basis for further consideration of this
matter.' No one in Justice's Public Integrity Section interviewed Mangieri before reaching this decision.

"Mangieri maintains that Labor Department
officials acted to protect D.C. Mayor Marion Barry
from potentially damaging disclosures. In a sworn
statement, he said that Mayor Barry had interrupted a May 16, 1979, interview Mangieri was conducting with a D.C. Department of Labor employee to ask Mangieri for a copy of his investigative
report.

'I replied it was not DOL/OIG procedure to
show our reports directly to agencies under investigation. I do not know who allowed the mayor to
subject me to this request,' Mangieri wrote.

A month later, he said, another witness accused
Barry of commiting improper actions when he was
a member of the D.C. City Council. Before Mangieri could 'further substantiate this potentially damaging allegation,' he was shifted off the case, the
affidavit says ..."

The story then cited my obtaining an affidavit from Peterson
regarding the shelving of the Youth Pride audit by Knowles. It also
called attention to my subsequent inspection of the Goldstock and
Nicholson travel vouchers, with its resultant severe harassment. It
finally closed the article with my recent indictment and an appropriate remark by my attorney:

"John Karr, Mangieri's lawyer, said that the
Mangieri indictment 'just smells to high heaven.'
He maintains that Mangieri's credit history was
known to the Labor Department as early as 1978.
An experienced investigator told *Federal Times* that
the law Mangieri is accused of violating is seldom
used in prosecutions. 'They don't even prosecute

organized crime figures on this stuff any more,' the investigator said."

In a follow-up "Commentary" article on February 16, in the *Federal Times* again, Hershow incisively took exception to the Reagan administration's plan to replace inspectors general with top cops who are "meaner than junkyard dogs." She noted that junkyard dogs protect trash. "And the last thing that a junkyard needs is a new inspector general who is meaner than Ronald Goldstock."
Her Commentary continued:

> "The Labor Department's office of the inspector general is a case in point. Under former Inspector General Marjorie Fine Knowles and Ronald Goldstock, her hand-picked and recently ousted successor, that office earned a reputation for savagely defending tarnished and possibly rotten officials from scrutiny and potential exposure."

During the course of her reported "three hour interview" with Goldstock whom she noted "didn't see it that way," she covered its content. In the midst of his rantings and ravings, he described himself as "apolitical" and also a "dedicated official who has 'gone through hell' trying to purge his staff of misfits and incompetents."
I wanted to throw up when I read his self-portrayal.
She then continued with his persecution-type comments:
"I think the story here related to a public official attempting to do what's right," she quoted him as saying.
In addition, he blamed his bitter and prolonged personnel battles on a "civil service system that protects 'nuts' ..." and further that it "isn't built to handle lunatics."
Hershow then launched into Goldstock's specific attempts to undermine my investigations, by personally discrediting me. I was, according to his descriptions of me, "a threat to society, a dangerous foul-up, who failed to prove that 26 black officials in the District of Columbia government used a federal jobs program to extort sexual favors from female job applicants."
She reported even further, his barbed defamatory exclamations:
"And that's just for starters. Goldstock also says that Mangieri

was bounced out of several previous jobs, leveled false charges of corruption against an employer who fired him, lied about his employment qualifications, has 'no background in investigations,' and 'has gone across the country ripping off people right and left.'

'He has a lousy background and should not be believed,' Goldstock told this reporter.

As I read, it was hard to contain my anger in the allegations that he was trying to pass off as facts in order to support all the lies that he had previously circulated as truth.

That lying son of a bitch, I said to myself.

The article, however, not only tried to set the record straight but compared my efforts with a more notable individual in the past:

> "The Government Accountability Project — a support group for whistleblowers sponsored by the Institute for Policy Studies — has checked into Goldstock's charges. After months of review, GAP compiled a sheaf of letters of recommendation and other evidence showing that the accusations are, at best, exaggerated, and, at worst, false and scurrilous. But even if Mangieri had precisely the 'lousy background' Goldstock alleges, if he is telling the truth, he should be believed.
>
> "Truth is truth. When A. Ernest Fitzgerald, the famed Air Force whistleblower, exposed a $2 billion overrun on the Lockheed C5A, Air Force officials tried to prove that he was a drunk, a drug addict, an adulterer, a homosexual, a security risk and a crook. He was none of these. But had Fitzgerald been a corrupt, besotted, drug-ravaged, adulterous, bisexual traitor, had he been a lecherous, treacherous villain and mad, to boot, the C5A transport would still have been $2 billion over budget.
>
> "The relevant questions in the Mangieri case are these: Did D.C. government officials bully Comprehensive Employment Training Act workers into trading sexual favors for desperately needed jobs? Was there a Labor Department coverup?"

Hershow in her investigative piece also noted:

> "Mangieri's handling of the sexual coercion
> probe drew high praise from James Owens, the assis-
> tant U.S. Attorney who worked with him. Owens
> still insists that Mangieri is 'an excellent investiga-
> tor.' And he adds that not one of the more than 30
> potential witnesses questioned during the investi-
> gation ever leveled a single complaint about Mang-
> ieri.
>
> "GAP staffers obtained transcripts of some of
> Mangieri's D.C. government interviews. These doc-
> uments — released under the Freedom of Infor-
> mation Act — contain explicit and sometimes har-
> rowing statements from CETA employees who say
> they were victimized. The FOIA file, an affidavit
> from a D.C. government employee, and allegations
> leveled by six confidential sources convinced GAP
> that Mangieri had good reason to believe that at
> least ten high-ranking D.C. officials had commit-
> ted acts of sexual harassment."

Her continued in-depth reporting brought out information
that I had steadfastly maintained, but which the I.G.'s office managed successfully to cover-up:

> "In December 1979, Mangieri was permanently
> removed from the case. He left behind him a list
> of 200 suspects, alleged victims and possible wit-
> nesses. The list was ignored.
>
> "After Mangieri was pulled off the sexual coer-
> cion probe, the Labor Department sent the Justice
> Department a slim file of Spring 1980 interviews
> with D.C. government employees. These employ-
> ees said they had not been sexually harassed. They
> said they didn't know anybody who had been sex-
> ually harassed. They said they had never even heard
> rumors of such goings-on. Completely and con-
> spicuously absent from the submission to Justice

was the damaging and voluminous evidence gathered by Mangieri.

"Goldstock maintains that the alleged widespread sexual coercion of CETA women by D.C. officials did not happen. 'There was nothing there,' he said."

After I read that article, I tried to get Karr to send it to the judge that was assigned to my case, District Court Judge Corcoran, who had been brought out of retirement to preside over it.

"I'm afraid the system doesn't work that way," he said.

System or not, I was looking for all the help I could get.

Concurrent with the criminal action that had been initiated against me, and was hopefully being resolved by John Karr, was my civil action being well-handled by Bridget Mugane.

In a formal letter of appeal, on February 9, to Secretary of Labor Raymond Donovan, with supportive legal memoranda, she attempted to get an expeditious favorable resolution.

In it, she reiterated the Administrative Law Judge's decision to not only reinstate me to my Criminal Investigator position but to grant the award of attorney's fees that had been stipulated by Judge Everette Thomas. Her cover letter cited two major areas:

"1. *Improper Invalidation of grievance decision favorable to Grievant*

"2. *Retaliation against Mr. Mangieri.*"

Under the first area, she stated in part:

"Judge Thomas was deciding official by virtue of designation by Frank Yeager's Directorate of Personnel Management (Department of Labor) in May 1980 (Attachment 1 to the accompanying Legal Memorandum, submitted herewith). On December 30, 1980, after learning of the decisions favorable to the Grievant, Frank Yeager suddenly decided Judge Thomas had been improperly appointed and his decision was thus invalid (Attachment 2).

"It is unconscionable that Mr. Yeager, who was the original deciding official in grievances 6b and 7, and thus can be presumed to know personally who replaced him, and who was personally sent a copy of the grievance examiner's recommendations on October 29, 1980, can be permitted to remove Judge Thomas seven months after the Directorate designated the Judge as deciding official, and only *after* the Judge decided in Mr. Mangieri's favor."

Under the second area, she pointedly referred to events that were occurring against me, which had also been the subject of intense media scrutiny:

"Mr. Mangieri has been very harshly treated by Mr. Goldstock, who removed him from his position as Criminal Investigator and who was later the original deciding official in grievance 2, when he became Acting Inspector General. After Mr. Mangieri filed his grievances against Mr. Goldstock, Mr. Goldstock had Mr. Mangieri exhaustively investigated both by the Inspector General's Internal Affairs Division and the FBI. Mr. Goldstock then instigated criminal prosecution of him for a matter in his private life, unrelated to his work conduct. This prosecution is unprecedented in that no harm or loss occurred as a result of the alleged offense: Department of Justice guidelines preclude prosecution under these circumstances. Mr. Mangieri's case has recently received media publicity because of this retaliation against him via the criminal prosecution and the invalidation of the favorable grievance decision.

Mr. Goldstock has also initiated FBI investigations and attempted to instigate prosecution of numerous other IG investigators on minor administrative matters, in order to obtain their resignations. This is an unconscionable abuse of his authority as a quasi-police authority."

It was a good appeal, and I didn't see how the Secretary could possible deny Judge Thomas' *DECISION,* based on Mugane's excellent legal grounds. However, I was still naive about Washington politics. I still didn't realize that facts meant nothing when a decision had already been reached about a predetermined outcome.

On February 22, 1982, more than a full year after Mugane had submitted her appeal to the Secretary of Labor, he totally ignored the Administrative Law Judge's Decision and supported the Grievance Examiner's minor Findings and Recommendations.

In the interim, there was a continuing flurry of motions to the court by my attorney, and corresponding responses from the U.S. Attorney's Office. It was, as would be characterized in the *Federal Times* many months later, "the longest running show in the courthouse."

... 17 ...

On February 17, Karr filed a MOTION FOR PRELIMINARY RULING AS TO WHETHER DEFENDANT'S SELECTIVE PROSECUTION CLAIM MAY BE TRIED TO A JURY.

It was a strategy that he believed was our best hope because of the demonstrated ongoing retaliation against me from the onset of my investigations.

Officials in the U.S. Attorney's Office naturally opposed it because the contention was there was no selective prosecution involved against me. The supposedly unbiased court agreed with the claim and denied my attorney's MOTION.

While these legal banterings were going on between counsel, the Office of Special Counsel at the Merit Systems Protection Board sent a letter to the Secretary of Labor advising him that they had determined there was "substantial likelihood" there was "abuse of authority or mismanagement" by Knowles as well as the individuals previously cited by GAP. The OSC also mentioned as potential targets "all of the Office of Inspector General in Washington, D.C." They then specifically informed the Secretary that, "the Special Counsel may, under 5 USC 1206 (b)(3), require the head of the agency to conduct an investigation of the matters transmitted and report the findings to Congress, the President, and the Special Counsel within 60 days," or that it could be extended only by written approval.

Meanwhile, under the auspices of the Government Accountability Project, Mugane was attempting to obtain private funding to force the resolution of my formal grievances, which had so far been ignored by the Department of Labor. That resolution basically meant filing a law suit in a federal court to get enforcement of Judge Thomas' *DECISION*. GAP's Louis Clark also wrote a cover letter to that funding source:

"In making your decision, I hope the Fund will also consider the incredible attempt by certain people to destroy utterly a man of principle. It seems that Mr. Mangieri's adversaries will stop at nothing."

Unfortunately, because funding was not available, we were unable to go forward with a civil case. As far as my own ability to handle the expense of such litigation, I could neither cover the legal fees nor the costs.

GAP, in its continuing effort to see justice done, also sent a letter to Secretary Donovan. He was advised that they were representing me. GAP also specified that the five individuals cited — Knowles, Goldstock, Eder, Gotsch and Juliano — had obstructed my investigations and violated the Inspector General Act of 1978 by failing to send the evidence I had gathered to the Department of Justice.

Donovan was told in the letter that GAP had learned "informally" that the new Inspector General might be responsible in conducting an investigation of itself. That individual in an "acting" I.G. capacity, was Frank Yeager, former Personnel Director. "Quite simply," GAP stated, "there is an inherent, institutional conflict-of-interest." In addition, GAP mentioned that although Statham initially was not named as a target, he soon would be included because of his role as a principal in the sexual coercion cover-up. GAP also cited his deep-seated antagonism toward me and included as references to the allegations, various exhibits quoting Statham's testimony about me.

Other private sources also were becoming interested because of the considerable media coverage. One such notable individual was Maurice Marsolais, a six-year employee with the D.C. Department of Employment Services, formerly the D.C. Department of Labor. It was one of the main agencies I initially investigated. My first contact with Marsolais had been two years earlier when he had been one of my informants. Our relationship since that date had strengthened and would last for many years thereafter.

In a lengthy letter to Charles Ruff, the U.S. Attorney, in mid-March, Marsolais gave a supportive — and accusatory — statement in which he said,

> "In 1976, I would say that the majority of employees in my agency were aware that sexual coercion was being practiced rather openly in this agency. It was a favorite topic of conversation, particularly among the agency's female employees.
>
> "In the spring and summer of 1979, we became aware that this situation had attracted the attention of the news media. *The Washington Star* did a series of stories on how D.C. government, and my agency in particular, were mismanaging and misusing CETA funds. A couple of the articles alleged that sexual favors were being extracted from certain female employees in CETA-funded positions in exchange for permanent positions, rapid promotions, free parking and other considerations.
>
> "We next became aware that our agency was under investigation by the U.S. Department of Labor, Office of the Inspector General. This, too, soon became a favorite topic of conversation throughout the agency. Some employees found it embarrassing, but for the most part the investigation seemed to arouse feelings both of relief and anxiety among most agency employees — relief over the fact that widespread illicit practices finally were being exposed, and anxiety as to what might happen to some of the figures involved.
>
> "As suddenly as the investigation had started, it seemed to stop. At the time no one knew why. Within a matter of weeks that agency seemed to return to normal. Employees were heard to make remarks such as, 'We knew the investigation would never be finished because it involved some of the higher-ups,' and 'The guilty have escaped punishment again.'
>
> "There followed a long lull during which time

nothing appeared to be happening. Suddenly, the *Star* came out with a story on December 4, 1979, alleging Mr. Nicholas Mangieri's probe into my agency's affairs had been obstructed by his superiors. Mr. Mangieri then filed an affidavit with the to that effect. That article told the whole story, as far as most employees in my agency were concerned. It was very obvious to us that there had been a cover-up and that there must have been a conspiracy between elected and appointed officials of the District of Columbia government and the U.S. Department of Labor in order to effect the cover-up.

"Nothing more was heard of Mr. Mangieri and his investigation until very recently. The *Washington Star* ran a story January 19, 1981, titled, 'Agent Indicted After Probing Sexual Coercion.' Three later stories, appearing in the *Federal Times* during March, 1981, removed any doubt as to what had happened to Mr. Mangieri and his investigation. In retrospect, it appears that Mr. Mangieri had done his work very well and that he was on the trail of some very big fish.

"I had occasion in mid-November, 1981, to discuss this and other related matters with two agents of the Washington Field Office of the Federal Bureau of Investigation. They seemed to know what I was talking about and the reasons for my concern, but they showed little inclination to do anything about it. In mid-January, 1981, I had occasion to meet with yet another FBI agent. Much of the same material was discussed. There are indications of action on some of the material, but it still appears that there is a reluctance on the part of the FBI to delve into this sexual coercion matter.

"Speaking for myself and a good many fellow employees who have knowledge of this sexual coercion matter from its beginning to the present time, we sincerely hope that the United States Attorney's

Office will discharge its responsibilities in this matter, when the time comes to do so. With the exception of Mr. Nicholas Mangieri who was willing to lay his career on the line rather than surrender his ideals and principles, the record of other federal investigative agencies in this matter is abominable and shameful. Their inertia and lack of interest have led us at times to wonder whose side they were on. A full and prompt disclosure of this entire matter is only the first step toward regaining the public's trust and confidence.

"The *Star* article of January 19, 1981, may have left the impression with the reading public that it was Mr. Mangieri and his reputation which were on trial. Those of us who know the entire story know that it is the District and federal governments which are on trial ..."

Marsolais, of course, would never receive a comment from Ruff, although he elicited it. In his indignation and continuing interest in the entire affair, Marsolais also sent a letter to the local Washington Bureau Chief of *The New York Times*. In that correspondence, with enclosures of newspaper articles from the *Washington Star*, the *Washington Post* and the *Federal Times*, Marsolais appropriately noted:

"Depending on what Secretary of Labor Raymond Donovan does in response to the order of Acting Special Counsel Mary Eastwood, there is a story here that has the potential to topple the Barry Administration. If anything resembling a full disclosure is made as to why Mr. Nicholas Mangieri's investigation became obstructed and sidetracked, we would expect that a Federal Grand Jury might return indictments against several high-ranking and appointed city officials."

Again, for whatever reason, Marsolais was not to receive a response to his professed interest and concern in the matter.

The *Federal Times*, although slightly behind the rapidly moving events as they occurred, reported in its March 16 edition that:

MSPB TELLS DONOVAN TO AIR REPORT OF PROBE SABOTAGE

Marsolais, an individual, I barely knew, attempted to elicit sustained interest in events that, in his opinion, were unjust and worthy of an in-depth investigation.

After the latest *Federal Times* article, Marsolais repeated his story of the apparent FBI indifference to his confirmation of sexual coercion cover-ups. That letter was sent to Mary Eastwood at the Office of Special Counsel.

In that communication, after describing his two meetings with FBI agents he wrote,

> "It is my considered opinion that both the U.S. Attorney's Office and the FBI had extensive knowledge of both the allegations and the cover-up and made a conscious decision not to pursue either."

He continued, in part:

> "I and a small group of colleagues who have followed this matter from the very beginning have a number of grave concerns about the body of administrative law which defines the parameters of administrative privilege and employee rights in federal civil service. If the Nicholas Mangieri situation is in any way typical, then we have to conclude that the scales of justice are very much weighted toward the administrative privilege side, and that a federal agency has carte blanche to crucify an employee, just as the U.S. Department of Labor has attempted with Mr. Mangieri. Were it not for Mr. Mangieri's extraordinary tenacity and sense of purpose, he most certainly would be gone by now — fired, resigned — and the alleged misdeeds of Knowles, Goldstock and associates buried forever.

"The protections afforded employees who want to do an honest job appear inadequate. What incentive is there for conscientious persons to remain in government? How is government to attract young, talented and capable new employees without more assurance that honesty and integrity are valued? It is so difficult and dangerous for an employee to expose wrongdoing in government that it is no wonder so many simply give up and thus become part of an ever-worsening problem ..."

On April 3, Karr with the assistance of his associate, Will McLain, and the sustained, in-depth research afforded him by GAP, filed a MOTION TO DISMISS INDICTMENT* with the court. The basis for that MOTION was that I had been "arbitrarily and discriminatorily selected for prosecution under 18 USC Sec. 1014 in retaliation for his exercise of rights secured by the Constitution of the United States."

The government opposed that MOTION, and the court then scheduled an evidentiary hearing on it to be held on April 21. At that date, my attorney also made an oral motion to continue the hearing on my "selective prosecution" until after the Internal Revenue Service had concluded its investigation of my allegations against the Department of Labor.

The IRS was selected, at that time, as an independent agency, to conduct its own inquiries into the matter. The IRS appointment was requested by Secretary of Labor, Raymond Donovan, who acted in response to the Office of Special Counsel at the Merit Systems Protection Board. As a result of GAP's intervention, it already had been determined that the Department of Labor could not effectively investigate itself.

When I first heard that another agency was to be involved, the Treasury Department, I was optimistic. Others did not share my feelings of enthusiasm, however. "They're just another governmental agency," they said. "It'll just be a whitewash," one said. "I wouldn't get your hopes up, too much," another said.

In spite of those negative remarks, I couldn't allow myself to har-

* *See Appendix A.*

bor similar thoughts. All I could think of was that if they did a good job, they couldn't help but support my allegations of cover-up and retaliation.

In time I learned how naive I was about how government operates.

At the April 21 hearing, my attorney sought a continuance of the trial against me. In honoring the government's opposition to the continuance, the court denied Karr's oral motion and the trial date was set for April 27. Just prior to the commencement of the trial, however, we learned that Castro had improperly obtained credit information in violation of the Fair Credit Reporting Act. Castro, in a previous affidavit, had stated that Michael Treworgy, chief of the Division of Program Investigations Office, requested sometime around May or June 1980, that he obtain credit data about me via a phone check. Although he did as he was instructed, the legality of it troubled him. It was this last-minute discovery that prompted my attorney to file a MOTION TO SUPPRESS EVIDENCE.*

In his MOTION, Karr noted:

"In the course of an investigation by the Internal Revenue Service ... a disclosure was made to IRS investigators that the Office of the Inspector General of the Department of Labor had sought information from EquiFax, Inc. about Mr. Mangieri's credit history."

Karr, in a persuasive argument attempted to have the MOTION considered and acted upon by the court, wrote further:

"Defendant's counsel first learned of this late Thursday night, April 23, 1981, and did not obtain corroborating documentation until late Friday night, April 24, 1981. Under the circumstances, this motion could not have been filed before Monday, April 27, 1981."

As truthful and as logical as that motion would be, it made no difference, at all, to the trial judge. He promptly dismissed it on the morning of the trial, as "untimely." Hershow in a *Federal Times* article would comment on the judge's adamant refusal even more: "He added that he had not even had time to read Karr's nine-page submission."

In that hastily prepared MOTION, my attorney had correctly called attention to the fact that the stated justification for a, "sole source contact" with EquiFax was initiated by Goldstock, himself,

* *See Appendix B.*

ostensibly for the purpose of obtaining financial and personal data
about individuals receiving benefits pursuant to "workmen's compensation" statues. However, as Karr pointed out, I had never been
a part of the workmen's compensation area. Therefore, any release of
credit history about me from EquiFax, referencing that contract, was
done by subterfuge. It was a violation of both the Fair Credit Reporting Act and the Privacy Act. Yet, the judge claimed it was "untimely," and had not even taken the time to read that MOTION, which
couldn't have possibly consumed more that ten minutes of his time.

Attached to that MOTION were three subpoenas. One was to
EquiFax to have them explain exactly what they were requested to provide. The second subpoena was to the Office of Procurement at
DOL, to show what was specifically put down for the "sole source justification" of the EquiFax contract. The third, and final, subpoena was
to have been to Osvaldo Castro. Once on the stand, his part in illegally obtaining credit information would have been divulged.

However, none of this background was permitted to be brought
out in open court, nor for that matter, was anything else of relevance.

The four-day trial proved to be a farce. To begin with, Charles
Roistacher, the assistant U.S. Attorney who had volunteered to
prosecute me over the declinations of others, entered the court
with a supermarket shopping basket. Presumably his theatrics were
to demonstrate to the jury the amount of derogatory information
that Harold Anderson, Goldstock's hand-picked investigator had
uncovered about me.

I subsequently learned that Anderson conducted an investigative odyssey that covered eight states and interviews with 147 people in an attempt to find something in my background that he
could use to discredit me. He even went back to 1950, thirty years
prior, and interviewed former neighbors who knew me and my
family. Among the enlightening things he learned about me was
the fact that as a young man my name was "Martin Roland." It
was a legal name change done in the mid-forties as the result of
my mother's remarriage. It was a name that I entered the military
service with, was first married under, and then served half of my
federal career under. I, then, had it legally changed back to my
birth name, years later. It was this well-known fact that Anderson
would try to attach some sort of significance. He also discovered that
22 years prior, and ten years earlier, I had filed for bankruptcy, both

for legally permissible reasons. Both, unfortunately were necessary. Armed with this meager information, he then visited Alaska and tried to convince a federal grand jury to indict me under whatever trumped-up charges that he could concoct after interviewing my former investigative targets in that state. His efforts, however, were unsuccessful.

I also later learned that his methods of obtaining financial information about my indebtedness also were illegal. With Goldstock, squarely in his corner, Anderson then returned to Washington and ultimately convinced Richard Beizer, the Chief of the Fraud Division in the U.S. Attorney's Office, that I had gone across the country "ripping people off" everywhere I went. To make his presentation to Beizer even more palatable, he even convinced him I was a phony whistleblower in Alaska. That I only reacted publicly *after* I had been ousted by corrupt politicians from my job as Chief of Police there. No one in the U.S. Attorney's Office, especially Roistacher, would check that all of my actions against those politicians occurred before my ouster. No one in the U.S. Attorney's Office, especially Roistacher, would inspect the voluminous newspaper articles about the affair, or listen to the continuing TV coverage of events, at that time.

Beizer, in a future motion, specifically stated that his decision to initiate criminal proceedings against me was not because I was a "phony whistleblower." However, that denial conflicted with his court testimony. He was to admit that my "standard technique" was to allege that I was a whistleblower after I had been "prosecuted" or "gone after for bad debts or judgments, or whatever ..." It was primarily this reason, plus Anderson's picture of indebtedness, that caused him to go forward.

No one checked into Anderson's perjured testimony before the grand jury, or before any other legal body, anymore than they investigated his illegal methods of obtaining credit information. Nor, for that matter, would there be any attempt by any other federal investigative agency to determine whether there had been any form of conspiracy between him and Goldstock to "get me."

The "trial" commenced. Seven witnesses were flown in from Alaska, with four of them being defendants against whom I had previously brought federal actions. However, under Corcoran's ruling, strict limits were placed on the information that could be provided to the jury. Even when Karr attempted to question one of the witnesses about my ouster as Police Chief, Roistacher objected and the judge halted that line of inquiry. In addition, the judge also ruled that the jury was not to be told about my long battle with my superiors at Labor, nor could they be permitted to hear any evidence supporting my allegations of selective prosecution. At each juncture of the trial that Corcoran issued a restrictive ruling, I looked disgustedly at my attorney and shook my head slowly questioning the judge's behavior.

Hershow also had an apt description of him during the trial:

"Corcoran — white-haired, pink-faced, and bearlike — seemed to alternate between boredom and impatience during the proceedings. Sometimes he hunched forward in his robes. Sometimes he leaned far back in his chair placed his hands over his eyes. Sometimes he fiddled with his watchband."

At one point, Karr made a particular comment, "What is crystal clear, is that this statute is probably being applied for the first time to a GS-12 applicant to a credit union. It is not used to prosecute little guys. It is used to prosecute big guys." He then added that I was being tried because my whistleblowing had "riled his superiors."

Corcoran, however, refused to listen to Karr's description and disdainfully answered him, "That is a very interesting theory. The problem is it won't wash."

Throughout that session, which was more like a kangaroo court than a court of law, I was increasingly getting bad vibes.

Although Jim Owens had testified that I was "an excellent investigator — foolishly honest — cursed (because) he could not compromise," and Paul Lehrman testified that I was "completely trustworthy" but "headstrong investigator who stands on his own two feet because he believes he is right," and even Cameron Barron stated that "I consider Nick Mangieri to be a very honest, forthright man" ... none of it would have any effect on the jury. Nor would the testimony of two expert witnesses. The first, a psychiatrist, testified that I was most likely in a state of anxiety when I completed the loan forms and as a result "very probably" were not deliberate falsifications as the prosecution had insisted. The second witness was a director of a Consumer Help Bankruptcy Clinic. He testified that he had one of the most common misconception is the notion that a bankruptcy "is only on your record for seven years."

It was a belief that I had harbored for many years and testified that knowledge accordingly.

However, it was to no avail. After two hours of deliberation, I was found guilty.

"What kind of justice is this, John?" I demanded after the verdict.

... 18 ...

"It's not over yet, Nick," he tried to reassure me. "Remember he's deferring sentencing until after the IRS completes its probe."

On May 15, two weeks after the verdict, Karr filed a MOTION FOR A NEW TRIAL with a SUPPLEMENTAL STATEMENT OF POINTS AND AUTHORITIES IN SUPPORT OF MOTION FOR NEW TRIAL.*

The basis, of course, was not only the court's "refusal to entertain (a) motion to suppress (the) evidence," but that of "erroneous instructions" to the jury. My attorney also noted a "denial of (a) jury poll," which was specifically requested to determine if there were duplicitous charges by the government.

The *Federal Times,* in its continuing coverage and support, came out with a front-page story of the full trial. Although I knew Sheila Hershow was in the audience throughout all of those sessions I was unaware of when it would be reported. On the morning of May 18, as I was walking down Pennsylvania Avenue toward Karr's office, I passed a newsstand and glanced at a new edition of the *Federal Times* in the rack. I was taken by surprise when I saw the picture of myself on the front page with a large caption "JUSTICE OR PERSECUTION?" Just above it was a smaller caption, "Boat-rocker nailed." It wasn't so much that my picture was appearing beside a story in print, but the fact that it was on the stand within a shadow of the White House. It took me several days to get over the shock of what I had seen, and where I had seen it.

The comprehensive three-page article opened by stating:

* *See Appendix C.*

"Nicholas J. Mangieri Jr. — the Labor Department investigator who accused his agency's top cops of quashing a politically explosive sexual coercion probe — has been convicted on nine felony counts for violating a seldom enforced federal law.

"He faces a maximum sentence of 18 years in prison and a $45,000 fine.

"On May 1, after four days of testimony, a jury in the District of Columbia found Mangieri guilty of filing false statements on nine loan applications he submitted to the Department of Labor federal credit union between July 1978 and October 1979. The credit union turned down five of the applications. Mangieri has been repaying the other four loans on schedule.

"Few individuals have ever been indicted under 18 US Code 1014, the charge brought against Mangieri. It is a law that has been used to punish organized crime figures or companies that seek to swindle millions from federal agencies.

"Mangieri's offenses did not cost the government one cent.

"Several U.S. Attorney offices across the country have issued declination guidelines instructing prosecutors not to seek indictments for false credit applications unless the lender suffers substantial losses. Three districts routinely decline cases involving less than $5,000, and two districts set the cutoff point at $10,000.

"Mangieri was indicted, tried and convicted on information gathered by a Labor Department investigator who was assigned to his task after Mangieri publicly accused Marjorie Fine Knowles, then Labor Department inspector general, and Ronald Goldstock, her deputy and successor, of obstructing a sensitive criminal investigation. In an affidavit sent to the Justice Department in November 1979, Mangieri charged that he had been blocked from

probing complaints that ten prominent District of
Columbia government officials — including D.C.
Mayor Marion Barry — used the Comprehensive
Employment Training Act program to extort sexu-
al favors from female job applicants. Barry has denied
committing any improprieties."

In a similar story, a week later, there also was a brief front-page
article about Gamble. Under the heading, "Labor Sleuth vindicated," it reported that "William R. Gamble — an award-winning
crime-fighter — was unjustly fired from his GS-13 job. According
to the reinstatement order, Gamble was transferred, hounded, under
surveillance and sacked in a Labor Department vendetta let by then
Acting Inspector General Ronald Goldstock."

A longer inside article by Hershow also confirmed my continuing allegations of Goldstock's maliciousness. During a three-day
appeals hearing regarding Gamble's reinstatement, the reporter
wrote, "that Gamble had been the victim of a bizarre Labor Department vendetta — was abruptly and punitively transferred, placed
under surveillance by six FBI agents and spied on by a subordinate
who had been wired with a body mike. His telephone conversations were monitored and his mail opened."

As I read the litany of actions perpetrated against Gamble, it
brought back bitter memories of what had been done to me. Yet,
people like Roistacher would believe only what they wanted to
believe. I never learned all that he had been told. In a remark made
to Hershow after the trial, he would not only attempt to justify his
prosecution of me but would totally ignore facts, testimony and
evidence indicating otherwise:

"If I thought the people at Labor were retaliating against this
guy because he was a whistleblower, I would not (have become)
involved in this prosecution ... That's just paranoia. It's nonsense."

In delving further into the Hershow article about Gamble, I
noticed that she also reported on that hearing examiner's observations and conclusions about Goldstock. She noted Goldstock's personal involvement in going after his own investigators, a fact he
always denied in my case. In commenting upon the hearing examiner's analysis of the Gamble decision, she wrote that Goldstock
had "obviously disliked" Gamble had fostered "a climate of dis-

trust, doubt and suspicion" within the office of the inspector general." She also stated that Gamble had reason to believe that Goldstock had obstructed justice when he barred Gamble from pursuing a criminal conspiracy investigation.

In addition, reported testimony, during Gambles' hearing, revealed that one of the agent's in Labor's Manhattan region also stressed Goldstock's vindictiveness. He told the hearing examiner that Goldstock said in his presence, "I'm going to get his (Gamble's) ass," and then "threw his head back and laughed."

All of these elements I had hammered away at in my ongoing accusations against Goldstock and other staff. Yet, my own hearing examiner, Donald Rothschild, was totally oblivious to any proof offered. Judge Everett Thomas, the ALJ, on the other hand, was perceptively aware of OIG retaliation against me. Fortunately, for Bill Gamble so was his hearing official, Stephanie Marks.

Further confirmation of the Department of Labor's dubious reputation appeared in an article about "The Best and Worst Government Agencies" in the May 1981 edition of *The Washingtonian* magazine.

In that particular article, it called attention to the "Most Corrupt Department," as being the Department of Labor. It stated:

> "In an unofficial survey I made of Congressional investigators, the Labor Department won hands-down as the most corrupt of the Cabinet-level departments. For years, New Jersey Senator Harrison "Pete" Williams, former chairman of the Labor and Human Resources Committee, treated the department with velvet gloves and thus maintained the adulation and political support of organized labor.
>
> "The department's Comprehensive Employment and Training Act (CETA) jobs program has been fleeced from one end of the country to the other. Many CETA jobs have gone not to the hard-core unemployed for whom they were intended, but to the political cronies of local politicians or to pay the salaries of sheriffs' deputies and other workers providing day-to-day services that the cities used

to fund themselves.

"'The CETA program is without a doubt the most corrupt expenditure of public funds in the government today,' said a veteran congressional investigator who has been probing the CETA program in preparation for Senate hearings this spring. Reagan, to his credit, has proposed CETA's abolition.

"Moreover, Labor Department files are filled with investigative reports and audits on corruption in labor unions, their pension funds, and their relation to organized crime — problems on which high department officials refused to act in previous administrations, according to congressional investigators.

" 'It is a cesspool of corruption,' says another Senate investigator, 'and CETA and the involvement of criminal elements in the unions is only part of the story.' Utah Senator Orrin Hatch, chairman of the Labor and Human Resources Committee, is expected to hold extensive hearings on the department later this year."

A subsequent editorial in the June 1 edition of the *Federal Times*, titled "ON TRIAL," appropriately commented that, "When the Law is used as an instrument of vengeance democracy is the victim."

In its accusatory tone, the editorial did more than just highlight the retaliations against both Gamble and myself, it cited the fact that there were at least four other whistleblowers in the Labor Department's office of the inspector general (who) were also threatened with criminal prosecution during Goldstock's tenure at Labor."

It also noted, concernedly, that:

"As citizens, we are frightened by the abuse of prosecutorial discretion. It is a potentially lethal threat to our system of government and our freedom as individuals. Our Justice Department becomes an Injustice Department when federal prosecutors ignore well-documented crimes by prominent government officials while invoking rarely enforced laws to punish minor offenses by government dissidents."

It closed out its ominous message with an admonishment to the trial judge in my case:

"U.S. District Court Judge Howard F. Corcoran has set aside the verdict until he determines whether Mangieri was the target of a vindictive and selective prosecution. We hope the judge looks carefully at the conduct of the Labor Department, the Justice Department and, particularly Goldstock, before he reaches his decision.

There is a lot at stake here."

However, in spite of the constant stream of negative publicity that the department would receive, and of the adverse comments about specific individuals, there was little to rejoice about. I was still faced with an uncertain resolution of my case ... and of my future.

The only gleam of hope in a cloud of uncertainty came in early summer with the replacement of the Acting I.G. with a permanent Inspector General. The openly prejudicial Frank Yeager was out, and an unknown Thomas McBride was in. In addition, Senator Hatch was interested in my "allegations of sexual extortion from CETA workers in Washington, D.C." and so informed the new I.G. early in his administration.

In a letter to McBride on July 22, Hatch thanked him and his staff for their apparent cooperation in providing certain materials that Hatch's staff had requested of them earlier. The Hatch committee involvement, that of *Labor and Human Resources,* came as a result of my personally meeting with Frank Silbey of his staff. That contact was an outgrowth of GAP's continued interest and contacts.

With amenities aside, Senator Hatch noted in his detailed letter that certain "specific documents" were missing. He obtained that compilation from information that I had furnished to Silbey, after inspection of the batch of supposedly complete documents that had already been received from Labor. In a list of eleven separate items, he asked for, among many other missing pieces of evidence were: 20 cassette tapes, 30 letters from D.C. Council members to the City Council's secretary name-requesting specific females for hire, ledger sheets containing D.C. officials by name with the names of alleged victims, all hand-written memos, reports of interviews, and investigative notes from April-December 1979, all letters and memos by myself to Knowles, Goldstock and Statham in which I alleged "cover-up," and, one of the first pieces of documentation that I had discovered, "a handwritten memo by Mangieri marked 'IMPORTANT,' to the effect that Mayor Barry had an 'agreement' with U.S. Assistant Secretary of Labor Ernie Green to 'forgive" the District's indebtedness to the U.S. Department of Labor in the amount of $1 million for CETA overpayments."

Hatch then advised McBride, in the letter, that all of those missing items were supposedly taken from me by Coffman, and that, "I consider them of prime importance to the committee's inquiry, and wish them sent as promptly as possible, in their unexpurgated form, to the Senate Labor Committee."

McBride responded three weeks later, with the majority of the items requested. However, still missing from that documentation were the "30 letters from D.C. City Council Members," and the letter from Barry to Green that I had marked "IMPORTANT."

McBride's adroit explanation to the former would be, "Further inquiries have not established the existence of any such letter." To the latter, he would unabashedly claim, "The letter, if it exists, cannot be found."

McBride also noted in his reply that the report that was due from the Internal Revenue Service on my case had not yet been received, although it had been due by August 1.

About a week later, I received a call from Louis Clark.

"We've just had the IRS report delivered to us," he announced in a tone that sounded flat and unemotional.

"Is something the matter?" I wanted to know.

"Tom and I just read it," was his only response. "I think you'll want to read it too."

... 19 ...

When I walked into GAP's offices and saw the somber expressions on Clark's and Devine's faces, I knew there was something wrong.

Before I had a chance to ask either one what the IRS report had said, Clark spoke.

"They didn't find that there was any obstruction of justice in your investigations, nor that there was any retribution against you," he said in a low voice.

"BULLSHIT!"

"I don't understand it either," Devine interrupted, "especially after all that has come out."

His words came out quickly, his eyes darting from me to Clark, who sat motionless watching the both of us.

"Goddamn it," I said. "What kind of a fuckin' whitewash is this?"

They both looked at me silently for a moment, not knowing exactly how to respond to my reaction. Although both had been minutely involved in my whole case, both had different aspects of it. Clark, was the Director and was responsible for the overall picture, while Devine as the Associate Director handled the day-to-day activities of legal research and actions.

Devine's expression still registered disbelief as the three of us sat looking at each other. Finally Clark, who apparently had been mulling over the situation, spoke slowly in his low voice.

"There are three parts of this report," he said tapping three bound volumes of documents on his desk. "One contains the Summary, another Exhibits and the third Affidavits."

"Why don't you take this *Summary* over there," he said gesturing to a nearby desk. "Read it and give me your comments."

Clark could tell from the look on my face that I was fed up with what had just transpired, and he added in a more patient tone.

"It's important, Nick," he said. "We're going to have to know exactly how to respond to it."

Devine, whose disappointment must have been as great as my own, had already composed himself and was ready to go back to work on it.

"I'll be nearby too, Nick," he said, "looking it over more carefully. If you need me for anything, just holler."

I nodded knowingly, also took a deep breath, and then sat heavily at the desk with the *Summary* in my hand. I avoided reading it for a moment, and then wearily glanced down at the "Introduction" section to the Summary.

It began with:

> "The investigation developed no direct evidence to support MANGIERI'S allegation that Management officials in the Office of Inspector General, Department of Labor, were involved in a criminal conspiracy to obstruct justice by interfering with MANGIERI's efforts to conduct an investigation of sexual harassment of CETA employees by officials of the District of Columbia Government. In addition, no evidence was developed to indicate there was any effort on the part of management to impede MANGIERI's progress during the course of his investigation, or to cover-up any evidence he had developed."

I read it again because I still couldn't believe their findings when they wrote,

"The investigation developed no direct evidence ..."

How the hell could they find no evidence? I said to myself. *What the hell were they doing all this time?*

The "they" I referred to were Steve Marica and Tom Lock, both of an Internal Security Division within the Internal Revenue Service. I met with them at the onset of the investigation. At the time, I was unaware there were five other members of their investigative team. It was apparent to me, however, that Marica was heading up the investigation. I also was unaware that this Internal Security Division was acting under the control of the *Inspector General's Office* of the U.S. Treasury Department. Had I known that another political I.G. was involved, I might not have been as optimistic about the end result as I was at the time they were assigned.

It was this IRS team that was assigned the task of investigating my allegations of cover-up and retaliation. Throughout the investigation I received favorable feedback from people I knew who had been interviewed. It was their feeling that the investigators had been given sufficient information to confirm my allegations. However, what they would do with that information, or how they would interpret what they had, was a different matter.

The balance of that introductory section revealed the same type of denial syndrome about the Youth Pride audit as it did about my CETA investigation. They expressed negative views, in spite of reliable testimony and evidence to the contrary:

> "The investigation examined all of the incidents referred to in MANGIERI's allegations, including KNOWLES' decision concerning Youth Pride, and developed no evidence to link the actions by MANGIERI's superiors to any direct or implied instructions by KNOWLES that she did not want the CETA investigation pursued."

Although the investigators managed somehow to correctly deduce that there had been a series of reprisals against me, their short-sighted conclusions were inaccurate:

> "The investigation did, however, indicate that some of the actions taken against MANGIERI were of questionable validity, and in some instances, the results of personality clashes between MANGIERI

and some of his superiors. Nonetheless, these
actions could not be proven to be an attempt to
impede MANGIERI, and there was no evidence
developed to indicate any connection between these
actions and the CETA investigation."

By the time I reached the last paragraph at the end of that section, I knew the rest of the report would be the "whitewash" I
had been warned about.

"The investigation into the alleged acts of retribution for MANGIERI's whistleblowing activity
disclosed no evidence that any action taken against
him was connected in any way to his involvement
with the CETA investigation."

I knew then that I would have to analyze every word in every
paragraph of the 20-page summary to refute their findings. I asked
for and received a legal pad and in the next two hours hastily scribbled out thirty-seven pages of analytical comment about each item
I knew to be inaccurate or taken out of context. My written
remarks to Clark and Devine contradicted the comments given by
two other officials involved in the administrative end of the report.
The first of those officials was the Inspector General of the IRS
Paul Krause. In his "Dear Tom" cover letter of August 13 to the
new Labor Department Inspector General Thomas McBride, he
noted that the investigation was "extraordinarily thorough" and
supported the IRS team's findings of total denial.

In Roistacher's final motion in my case several months later,
he gloatingly stated that it was as "comprehensive an investigation
as could be imagined."

It is doubtful that one could characterize omissions of fact,
incomplete interviews, limited investigations or misinterpretations,
as "thorough" or "comprehensive." However, that is exactly what
happened. Whether it was done intentionally or negligently was
unknown, but the bottom line is that *it was done* and relied upon
as gospel from that point forward.

When I submitted my own factual analysis, both Clark and
Devine read it over carefully and said they would add their own

comments and get back to me.

On September 15, Devine gave me a detailed 21-page, 10,000-word digest of the report he was submitting to "the files" for future reference. In that very *thorough* and *comprehensive* analysis, Devine read and dissected every section of the 276-page report and referenced it by page number. He then wrote the investigators' findings, followed by his own analytical comments based upon his extensive knowledge of the case file.

His concluding comments were that their "conclusions are significant, but they are made without weighing or referring to the evidence. The findings are extremely sympathetic in tone to OIG management, but fail to first weigh the conflicting evidence that is in the report, let alone follow the relevant leads that should have been pursued ..."

Of the approximate 100 segments that Devine selected to read and comment upon, the majority indicated a failure to take certain facts or actions into consideration. In doing so, the findings and conclusions were based on partial or inaccurate information. The balance of Devine's very methodical observation noted that there were glaring omissions by the investigative team, either in failing to pursue a specific line of questioning or failing to interview certain key personnel.

In this latter category, in which there were more blatant weaknesses, Devine noticed in the *methodology* that was described in the investigation, that:

"IRS failed to interview Frank Silbey and apparently didn't get his files — inexcusable in light of Silbey's intensive ongoing effort."

Devine also commented upon the fact that IRS "didn't have follow-up interviews." A common procedure that would certainly be necessary to determine who had initially lied or had given conflicting accounts of a situation to the investigators.

Devine also observed that IRS did not interview Don Hehir, my supervisor at OLAP, where I had been detailed as an analyst for over a year. In Devine's comments, he wrote, "Hehir's opinion might show whether Goldstock-Eder-Repp party line on Mangieri (that I was unsupervisorable) was BS." Nor did IRS interview any of Harold Anderson's investigative team who participated with him in his illegal credit search. Neither did the IRS interview or take affidavits from anyone at the Credit Union. In Devine's word, that was "inexcusable," since there were "lots of questions to ask," especially on a questionable, if not an illegal system wherein DOL merely had to call in its account number for credit information on individuals.

In addition to these, and many other interview oversights, the IRS team neglected to state that Coffman had confiscated certain incriminating documents from my office. These included the Peterson Affidavit on the Pride cover-up, that I had obtained, and the 1/20/80 Letter to the Editor at the *Washington Post*. Further, the IRS failed to mention the grievance decision of ALJ Judge Thomas, who found retaliation in the loss of my credentials and in illegal personnel practices. As Devine noted, "key omission."

He also extensively covered Anderson's lack of documentation that he was required to keep in his investigative efforts, and questioned the many obvious gaps in Anderson's testimony, that IRS didn't pursue. In addition, Devine noted numerous discrepancies between Anderson's, Beizer's and Goldstock's statements, yet no indication of further IRS clarifications as to why they had disagreed with each other.   Also, Devine called specific attention to the affidavits and conflicting statements of conversations between U.S. Attorney Ruff and that of Harold Greene. He was the former Director of Court Operations who was later to become a Superior Court judge.   Their conversations concerned me. As Devine noted, "Greene's testimony devastates Ruff's claim of not speaking with Greene. Two, or perhaps three conversations at most nine months previously, Ruff claiming he had followed up on Greene's concerns and Ruff threatening disciplinary action (against Owens). Summary in front does not mention Greene's affidavit or any of the inconsistencies."

In a particularly damaging analysis of Roistacher's statement to the IRS agents, Devine notes from the IRS report, that *the Roistacher interview is summarized*. However, Devine pointedly asks, "Why no affidavit?" Devine also notes from the IRS report that Roistacher "says Beizer referred the case to him in September or October, with Anderson" and that he, "had no discussion with Ruff." However, as Devine cogently states, "Again inconsistent with Greene affidavit. Ruff was lying to Greene about speaking with Roistacher or Roistacher is lying to the IRS. Why no questions to Roistacher about the call from Greene? Why didn't Roistacher speak with Mangieri and get his side before prosecuting? The IRS asked Beizer about that, who passed the buck to Roistacher. The IRS then fails to bring the subject up with Roistacher."

The balance of Devine's analytical digest was in the same vein and specifically called attention to the IRS investigative team's failure to conduct the "thorough and comprehensive" report that was alleged — and subsequently passed on to Judge Corcoran for his consideration of selective prosecution against me.

As impressed as I was with Devine's product, it was not the only effort that GAP was making in my behalf. About that same time, another legal intern was researching a "violation of the Fair Credit Reporting Act by the U.S. Department of Labor and Credit Bureau, Inc. in procuring credit reports on employees for use in criminal prosecution." The particular issue that was researched and submitted in a 4000-word legal brief to GAP by that intern, Mimi Cowan, on 9/9/81, was whether the two entities cited above, "wilfully failed to comply with 15 USC 1681 b 'Permissible uses of Consumer Reports' ..." and whether the releases of consumer reports, "in the course of a criminal investigation is a wilful noncompliance and subject to civil sanctions imposed by 15 USC 1681d ..."

Her well-documented conclusion showed that the actions of both entities "have been shown to be in clear violation of the Fair Credit Reporting Act."

Mugane, my standby attorney, also was doing her best to contribute information. In a letter to both Karr and McLain in late September, she specifically addressed two issues that the attorneys might find helpful in my upcoming selective prosecution hearing and appeal for ruling on exclusion of evidence. In her first topic, that of "evidence of illegal release of information by Credit Union," she asked a rhetorical question:

"If the basis for the referral was misrepresentations to the Credit Union, what information did Goldstock have then and how was it obtained?

Tom Devine says Goldstock told other IG employees as early as June 1980 that he was going to get Mangieri for crimes; how could Goldstock know there were criminal offenses prior to the subpoenas?

The answer would appear to be that Credit Union records or

information was illegally obtained prior to subpoenas."

In her second topic, "selective prosecution," she again offered precise questions about Goldstock and Knowles in their contrived attempts to have OPM proceed with expedited security clearances against me and no other employees.

The following week, Devine again was busily attempting to compile as much evidence as he could on my behalf. He sent a letter to Frank Silbey on October 8 thanking him for his offer to obtain additional documentation that I needed, and couldn't obtain. In that letter, Devine requested assistance in several areas that developed from the IRS report, but were not presented or summarized by them. Among those were:

* The DOL/OIG Internal Affairs investigative final report, along with all notes and documentation ("to see whether Anderson gathered anything that he did not have the legal option to obtain.")

* Subpoenas that were issued by Beizer ("the details on the subpoenas may help to reveal whether Anderson illegally knew more than he now admits when he met with Beizer on August 20.")

* Documentation presented to the U.S. Attorney in Alaska by Anderson in July 1980 in his unsuccessful attempt to have me prosecuted there first ("their records or version of Anderson's referral again may document whether he illegally obtained evidence before getting subpoenas for it.")

In addition to those three areas, there were two related requests regarding possible illegal release of credit information by both the DOL Federal Credit Union and the Credit Bureau, without my specific written request. The final bit of information we wanted dealt with a 2/28/80 memo from Coffman to Statham recommending my dismissal. Devine adds, "This memo is cited in the IRS report but not included as an exhibit. Since Coffman prepared it two days after ransacking Mangieri's files (which were packed with whistleblowing disclosures and evidence), it may reveal how aware and threatened the agency was by his disclosures."

If Devine's requests were ever followed through by Silbey, I never knew.

In the ensuing two weeks, Devine was still occupied with analyzing issues and facts and compiling them for my upcoming evidentiary hearing on November 3 before Judge Corcoran.

On October 23, he submitted a voluminous memorandum to Karr and McLain that was in excess of 10,000 words again. It dealt with "issues" for the hearing and covered every conceivable detail indicating an ongoing retaliation and every aspect concerning Anderson's illegal actions.

At the hearing, which ran for two days, Karr requested dismissal of the May conviction. He advised the court that I had been prosecuted by the government under a rarely-enforced law and that there had been threats of similar reprisals against other OIG agents who had run afoul of the same officials I had accused of covering up my investigations. Karr called several witnesses to confirm my allegations and introduced new evidence that had not been allowed at the trial. Roistacher in turn, questioned the relevancy of the testimony, as it was obviously detrimental to his case. He also strenuously objected to the inclusion of new evidence that would further jeopardize his contentions.

Karr contended that top Department officials were "out to get" me because I had uncovered a sex scandal involving CETA funds. Roistacher objected to that claim and attempted to show that I was merely an employee who couldn't get along with his supervisors. To bolster his assertions, he called those same witnesses who were part of the OIG hierarchy.

Karr then tried to show that information about my finances were obtained illegally by an investigator who allegedly had discovered "gaps" in the general background check performed by OPM.

Although DOL initially claimed there was an unexplained "two-year gap" in my 30-year employment background, GAP had shown that it was actually only a *three-month* "gap."

Roistacher, who had objected to Karr raising the issue of the illegality of that financial check, put Anderson on the stand. In perjured testimony, he insisted that he had conducted the inquiry properly. His continued blatant testimony was not only contra to what GAP had already strongly indicated otherwise, but also refuted Castro's sworn prior affidavit that his credit searches were improper. In addition, the in-depth analysis of numerous inconsistencies in the IRS report dealing with various actions and time periods also pointed out that Anderson had to have lied through-

out the various stages of his IA inquiry of me. Those lies were
then carried through to Beizer, to Roistacher and to the IRS investigators. To cover his tracks, he undoubtedly perjured himself
before the grand jury, as he had done before the court in the evidentiary hearing.

As a subsequent *Federal Times* article was to report on that
two-day session:

"The testimony became so involved and detailed that Corcoran
abruptly arose from his chair and walked out, indicating he would
sort it all out later."

At the termination of the hearing, Karr was instructed to present his written arguments to the judge by November 23, after
which Roistacher had a week to respond.

As we were leaving the courtroom, Devine who had been hud-
dling with Karr and McLain, pulled me aside.

"Hang in there, Nick," he smiled. " We'll give him a strong
motion."

... 20 ...

On January 12, 1982, Karr filed the motion that the judge had requested in late November. It was, DEFENDANT'S PROPOSED FINDINGS OF FACT AND CONCLUSIONS OF LAW ON MOTION TO DISMISS FOR SELECTIVE PROSECUTION,* and it was lengthy — 30 pages under the "Proposed Findings of Fact," with an additional eight pages under "Proposed Conclusions of Law." There also was an Appendix that contained a three-page letter dated July 30, 1981, from the Office of the Special Counsel to Frank Yeager, who was the Acting Deputy Inspector General at the time.

Although the MOTION was due about three weeks earlier, my attorney had filed an "enlargement of time" with the court because the transcripts of the November 3 and 4 evidentiary hearings were not received in time.

I was amazed at the detailed content of that MOTION. It was "strong" as Devine had promised. He and his staff must have labored long and hard to put together what I considered a superb legal brief. It contained every known fact, plus their relationships with the OPM interviews, the IRS affidavits and exhibits and the transcripts from court testimony. After reviewing it, I believed the judge couldn't possibly rule against me; the evidence was overwhelming.

I would find out, in due time, how wrong I was — again.

The letter in the Appendix to the MOTION was to Yeager from Alex Kozinski, the Special Counsel, and commented at some

---

* *See Appendix D and Appendix E.*

length on a prior Yeager memo to OIG employees that had been characterized as a "gag memo" because it prohibited them from discussing agency matters with individuals "on or off duty." In his letter, Kozinski chastised Yeager because his memorandum "appears to impinge upon significant employee rights under the Civil Service Reform Act ... the right to free speech ... and the right to communicate with members of Congress ..." Kozinski further noted that since, "the matter falls within our jurisdiction and is of great concern to this office, I have therefore directed my staff to initiate an investigation ..." He gave him ten days, however, to voluntarily retract that memo before a formal OSC investigation would be initiated.

It was that April 22 memorandum, prior to my trial date of April 27, that not only prevented, but forbade OIG employees from cooperating with my attorneys. It also was the specific reason why information damaging to the prosecution was not discovered. That derogatory information dealt with the illegal methods used to obtain my credit background. The inability to present it would be used against my defense by the court. It was the judge's ruling that the last-minute information uncovered by my attorney *could have* been ascertained *before* the trial date. The judge would not accept my attorney's valid explanation as to why he could not possibly do so.

In the government's opposition to my MOTION, Roistacher decided that "the decision to prosecute him was without malice." Also, in spite of all testimony and evidence to the contrary, Roistacher maintained that Statham and Anderson were honorable men. In addition, he held that the IRS had "fully explored" my claims of "cover-up," "obstruction," and "retaliatory prosecution" and that they, too, had found my claim "meritless." He further noted that the court "fully supports the administrative findings of Mr. Rothschild," who had found nothing substantial during my grievance hearing.

Judge Thomas' favorable decision, however, would never be referred to, because it would certainly have clouded the government's position.

In a weak brief that covered only seven pages of "Findings of Fact," Roistacher cited self-serving statements by those same "honorable men," previously mentioned, and their stop-gap activities to justify their contrived actions. He also used an additional three pages of "Q" and "A" of Beizer's testimony in court. Apparently, this transcript inclusion was done for the purpose of authenticating his "Findings."

Of course, none of the inconsistencies in the Beizer-Goldstock-Anderson affidavits would be mentioned if, in fact, they were ever even considered.

In an even weaker two-page "Conclusions of Law," Roistacher closed out his reply by stating I not only failed to mention race and religion as reasons for the selective prosecution, but I also left out another element. I did not claim an "exercise of a constitutional right" had anything to do with the indictment.

Apparently, Roistacher decided to ignore the First Amendment violations that my attorney very extensively, and appropriately, cited.

Because of the selective prosecution, the judge, in a February 3 order, denied our motion to dismiss. He concluded that, "Defendant has not persuaded the court that his case was referred to the U. S. Attorney in an attempt to curtail his alleged 'whistle-blowing' activities."

When I saw that *order*, I was speechless for the moment and could only shake my head wearily.

When I finally regained my senses, I said, "How the hell could he *not* be persuaded. The overwhelming weight of documentation would make anybody see it."

Both Clark and Devine were with me when I read the judge's *order*.

"It doesn't look good, Nick," Clark volunteered.

I just dumbly nodded my head in agreement, realizing only a miracle would change the situation.

Devine, who had been standing by silently, quietly added, "It's not over yet, Nick. We still have some other motions to file."

"Like what?" I wanted to know.

"Karr's your attorney," he said, "and it's his final decision as to what will be done, but we'll be in touch with him later."

Within the week, another motion was prepared and filed with the court on February 10, a MOTION TO RECONSIDER ORDER DENYING MOTION TO DISMISS.*

In the opening of that motion, it was noted that the court "mistakenly accepted an erroneous factual characterization by the gov-

* *See Appendix F.*

ernment and ignored significant evidence to conclude that there
was no improper motivation by the United States Attorney."

It also stated that the court relied on the findings of the IRS
investigation. However, that reliance was contra to the extensive
discussion on that issue during the evidentiary hearings. The judge
had agreed to exclude the IRS findings and weigh the evidence at
hand. That agreement, however, was never honored.

The MOTION further noted that the IRS findings could not
represent final conclusions because the Office of Special Counsel,
as the requesting authority, had not yet evaluated the report. It
also was pointed out that there were other incidents, not summarized in the IRS report, that should have examined the immediate
cause of Anderson's investigation of me. Among these were the
discovery by Coffman of my letter to the *Washington Post,* my Youth
Pride obstruction information, and even my FBI referrals of Goldstock. Although he was ostensibly "exonerated" by them, it was
because he claimed the use of *one* government-paid consultant on
a private venture in which he was engaged, whereas *two* consultants had reportedly been involved. This inaccurate information
was allegedly relayed to the FBI in the course of their investigation of him and in an interview with him.

The MOTION then discussed Beizer's reactions to Goldstock's
opinion of me, rather than drawing his own conclusions from independent investigation. It correctly identified the prosecution against
me as a "direct attack" on my First Amendment rights and asked the
court to reconsider and grant the motion to dismiss.

However, it — as others before it — proved to be an exercise
in futility.

On February 11, with virtually all of my immediate remedies
exhausted, I was ordered to appear before Judge Howard Corcoran for sentencing. My sister, brother-in-law, and Tom Devine all
sat together. Scattered throughout the courtroom were other friends
and supporters, but I was too engrossed to notice who was there.
I did see Sheila Hershow from the *Federal Times* continuing her
coverage of what she also considered a farcical trial.

I knew, or so I was told, that I faced a maximum sentence of 18
years, based on the nine "counts," of two-year sentences each, and
a possible $45,000 fine. However, I also *knew* that I had done no
wrong and that the only reason I had been prosecuted was because

I tried to do my job. I felt that I could not in good conscience apologize to the judge and throw myself on the mercy of the court. I also felt strongly that I would not only be betraying myself, and all that I believed in, but I would be letting down all others who had followed my activities and the actions of my superiors.

Before I walked into that courtroom Tom Devine asked what I would say to the judge when I was given the opportunity to address the court before sentencing. I didn't even have to think about what words I would use. I told him in no uncertain terms that I would attack those that unjustly persecuted me and would condemn the proceedings against me.

"You can't, Nick," he insisted worriedly. "You can't do that in front of this judge."

"Why not?" I wanted to know. "He's already decided what he's going to give me."

"You can't take that chance, Nick," he still insisted. "He could throw the book at you."

I could see the concerned expressions on both my sister's face and that of my brother-in-law's, as they overheard our animated conversation.

"Don't do it, Nick," my sister pleaded. "It's not worth it. You've got to think about your future and that of your kids."

We were called into the courtroom, and I sat beside my counsel, John Karr, for the last time.

When I was asked to stand and address the court before sentencing, I looked at my sister, brother-in-law and Tom Devine, who all were wondering what I was going to do.

I took a deep breath, hesitated, and then heard myself utter words in that hushed courtroom that I didn't expect myself to say.

I heard myself tell the judge that the omissions on my loan applications were "stupid errors of judgement." I then added as an afterthought, because I still felt that I had to, "I always try to do my best."

I glanced over at my sister and the others, who looked relieved at my watered-down statement. Devine was slowly nodding his head in approval with a weak smile on his face.

I then turned back to the judge.

His sentence came quickly in that still quiet courtroom. "Two years on probation."

I sat down, not relieved nor concerned, just numb. At that point, I wasn't thinking about tomorrow, nor even what the government managed to accomplish against me. All that would come later.

Roistacher was asked what his comments were. He advised the court that he agreed with the judge's sentence and would not "ask for incarceration." However, he did recommend that I be directed to seek, "some kind of psychiatric treatment," because he claimed that, "every time he gets into an argument with a supervisor" he claims he is being persecuted as a whistleblower.

Momentarily, I felt the blood rush to my face listening to his inane description of my actions, but I let it pass because there was nothing I could do.

I even heard Roistacher recommend that I be required to perform some kind of community service during my probation.

The judge waived aside both of Roistacher's recommendations and quickly ruled them out. Instead, he directed that I keep repaying the balance of my $1,400 debt to the credit union.

It was an obligation that I had been continually meeting, via payroll deductions, ever since the loans commenced, so his order added nothing to my "sentence."

As we rose to leave the courtroom, Karr patted me on the arm to tell me how sorry he was. My sister and brother-in-law, looking more relieved than they were before we entered the courtroom, rushed over to console me. I saw Hershow talking to Devine for his views on that session.

As the *Federal Times* would later report his comments:

"We're thankful that Judge Corcoran had the sense of decency not to send a courageous whistleblower to prison — Mr. Roistacher's suggestions of psychiatric treatment was representative of the government's position that those who challenge the system are crazy."

Even Marsolais, the D.C. Department of Labor employee who had been an expressed ardent supporter through his prolific letter-writing campaign, would make the same type of comment.

In a future "Letters to the Editor," section in the *Federal Times,* he poetically compared my efforts to the novel, *"Catch 22"*:

"There are shades of 'Catch 22' in this whole chronicle of the government frantic efforts to do in the messenger who insisted on bringing home the bad news — and who then exposed the government's efforts to hide the bad news."

In that very descriptive analogy, Marsolais put his finger on the pulse of what I had personally observed, and experienced in the preceding three years:

"When government employees 'go along with the game,' as the overwhelming majority seem to do, we soon find ourselves in a morass similar to that depicted in ' j,' in which norms become very fuzzy, and we find it very difficult to distinguish between good and bad, up and down, right and wrong."

In spite of his continuing vocal support, and that of others, and in spite of ongoing efforts by the printed media and even a radio commentary on my case by Public Broadcasting, nothing would change. I still had been convicted in a court of law, and that specter would haunt me for many years to come in a variety of ways, of which I was unaware at the sentencing session.

Karr, on February 17, filed a *motion to withdraw* as my counsel, and to substitute new counsel. The court approved the motion, and a new younger attorney, Lynne Bernabei, took his place. She was associated with GAP and would prove to be very thorough and effective. Unfortunately, she faced formidable odds and her able professionalism could not overcome the impediments that were thrown at us by the trial judge.

The first of these stumbling blocks was painfully apparent when her MOTION FOR NEW TRIAL,* filed on February 19, was quickly denied by the judge, after the government opposed it. In that forceful MOTION, Bernabei requested a new trial, "based on newly discovered evidence which indicates the chief prosecution witness, Department of Labor investigator Harold Anderson, perjured himself at trial and during the post-trial hearing on selective prosecution."

That new evidence was an affidavit from my ex-wife, and an interview with a bank official in California, as well as an analysis of "44 investigative interviews" conducted by Anderson, which would have contradicted his sworn testimonies in court and before the IRS investigators.

With the failure of that cogent MOTION, with its supportive MEMORANDUM OF POINTS AND AUTHORITIES ..., as well as its attached AFFIDAVITS, all doors were being shut, one by

* *See Appendix G.*

one, as to any resolution of all that had befallen me.

The only hope that remained was at the appellate level. Accordingly, Bernabei with the continuing assistance of the Government Accountability Project, and additional financial backing of a grant from the Fund for Constitutional Government, filed an appeal with the United States Court of Appeals for the District of Columbia Circuit on June 10, 1982.

In that impressive 10,000-word appellate brief, she raised every legal issue that had been presented at the trial court — but had been consistently denied by the judge: the refusal to consider, or hear, evidence presented prior to trial; the refusal to dismiss based on selective prosecution; the abuse of discretion in denying a new trial based on newly discovered evidence; the deliberate withholding of materials from the defense attorney; and even questionable jury instructions.

On June 15, Bernabei supplemented the appellate record to include all of the exhibits and affidavits attached to the Internal Revenue Service Report. We hoped these attachments would, if correctly viewed and interpreted, favorably impress the appellate court. However, that was not to be the case. On September 16, Bernabei gave effective oral arguments before the court, arguments, that audience members said were presented in a hard-hitting, knowledgeable style that seemed to impress the three judges sitting on the bench.

On November 23, the results of her massive efforts were known. The court handed down a decision that nobody, including myself, was really expecting.

It rejected all of Bernabei's very lucid arguments and affirmed the judgment of the district court. Their decision was based primarily on the belief that all of the testimony and the evidence offered by the government and its witnesses was accurate. It also held that the particular motions being appealed by my appellate attorney could not be considered because they were not filed in a timely manner in the trial court.

My reaction as I read the decision in GAP's offices was strangely subdued. Although I fully believed that the district court's verdict would be overturned, and that I would be completely vindicated, I cannot say the decision was unexpected.

The appellate court's holding was merely a culmination of all the actions by the government to stop me from exposing the truth — in a city where that becomes the greatest crime.

As I was preparing to leave GAP to return home, Tom Devine made a final parting comment. Our association had come to an end and I also had just retired from the federal government with 23 years of service.

"I don't know how closely you've read their 'Conclusion,'" he said, "but they *did* have some unanswered questions, and they *did* make some suggestions for future cases."

I nodded as I hesitatingly took my own copy.

"One last thing though," he continued. "I wouldn't put too much stock in what they said about the U.S. Attorney's Office — we all know otherwise."

On the long Metro ride to suburban Maryland late that afternoon, I slowly extracted the copy from my briefcase, looked at it carefully for a few moments, turned it over several times, and finally decided to read the "Conclusion" again:

"None of the appellant's contentions rise to the level of reversible error. Yet we take the liberty of commenting that the case has many disturbing aspects that compelled close scrutiny. We believe, for instance, that the administration of justice might be improved if our district courts employed the District of Columbia courts' particularized instruction on unanimity when a single count contains several distinct acts, any one of which will support a guilty verdict. We also believe that district courts should ordinarily permit defense counsel to file motions to suppress evidence even if they have reason to deny them for untimeliness. Finally, although we continue to wonder at the extensive agency resources devoted to the investigation of one controversial employee's background, we find reassuring the independent stance of the U.S. Attorney's office in reviewing a client agency's referral of a troublesome employee for prosecution. Its awareness of the potential dangers in such a case, and its indisputable vigilance made both the district court's and our task easier as we sorted out the tangle of allegations underlying the selective prosecution claim."

As I replaced it in my briefcase and looked out the window at the beauty of the setting sun, I was suddenly at peace with myself. I knew that I had done the best I could possibly do. *There's a higher power out there*, I thought. *He'll take care of the situation.*

... Appendix A ...

**UNITED STATES DISTRICT COURT
FOR THE DISTRICT OF COLUMBIA**

UNITED STATES OF AMERICA
          v.   Criminal No. 81-19
NICHOLAS J. MANGIERI, JR.

Defendant

**STATEMENT OF POINTS AND AUTHORITIES
IN SUPPORT OF MOTION TO DISMISS INDICTMENT**

Nicholas J. Mangieri, Jr., the defendant in this case, is employed as an investigator with the Office of the Inspector General of the United States Department of Labor. He is charged in a 9-count indictment with violations of 18 U. S. C. Sec. 1014. The indictment alleges that while an employee with the Department of Labor, he misstated information on nine separate applications for loans from the Department's Federal Credit Union.[1]

---

[1] The applications were made between July, 1978, and October, 1979. Seven of trhe nine were rejected by the Credit Union because of Mr. Mangieri's poor credit history; two of the loans were made, one of the purchase of a car and the other to pay utility bills. Both of the loans were granted on the strength of two co-signors, and the automobile, of course, was used to collateralize the lager loan.

In the spring of 1978, Mr. Mangieri applied to the Office of Special Investigations of the Department of Labor for a position as investigator. A background check was done then by Mr. Paul Lehrman, a supervisor in the Office of Inspector General. Mr. Lehrman interviewed Mr. Mangieri and also inquired into his activities in Alaska, where Mr. Mangieri had been living and working since the spring of 1974. Mr. Mangieri was hired on July 3, 1978. In October, 1978, the Office was absorbed into the newly-created Office of the Inspector General.

On April 3, 1979, a grand jury of the Superior Court of the District of Columbia indicted George E. Harrod, the personnel director of the District of Columbia government; Mr. Harrod was charged with having assaulted a young woman employee who had been employed under the provisions of a federal CETA program. A newspaper article which reported the indictment also described the employee's additional charges that Mr. Harrod had sexually exploited her as a condition of her employment (a copy of the article is attached hereto as Exhibit A); those allegations prompted Mr. Mangieri to undertake an investigation of the CETA program in the District of Columbia.

As Mr. Mangieri's investigation progressed, he collected statements and affidavits from other CETA employees working for the District of Columbia government which suggested widespread abuses in the CETA program by high-ranking District of Columbia officials. On May 16, 1979, Mr. Mangieri conducted an interview with a CETA employee in the District Building; the interview was interrupted by the Mayor of the District of Columbia who demanded that he be provided with a copy of Mr. Mangieri's summary of the interview. Soon thereafter, Mr. Mangieri learned that a second comprehensive investigation of his past had been undertaken by the Inspector General of the Labor Department. That investigation included the dispatching of a Labor Department investigator to California and Alaska. The investigation into Mr. Mangieri's background included detailed examination of Mr. Mangieri's previous employments; financial obligations he had incurred during a bitter political fight following his dismissal as police chief of Palmer, Alaska; and details of a domestic dispute that culminated in a contested divorce and custody case.[2]

At approximately the same time that Mr. Mangieri began his

investigation of apparent abuses of CETA employees by high-ranking officials of the District of Columbia government, a corresponding investigation of the federally-funded District of Columbia organization called Youth Pride was undertaken by the Department of Labor. That investigation was conducted by Paul Lehrman, the supervisory inspector, and the Chief of the Audit Division of the Office of the Inspector General for the Department of Labor, Mr. Gerald W. Peterson. On June 15, 1979, Mr. Peterson was summoned to the office of the then Inspector General, Marjorie Fine Knowles, and for plainly political reasons (see Affidavit of Gerald W. Peterson, attached hereto as Exhibit B), instructed to abandon that investigation.[3]

For some years preceding the events just described, the Department of Labor had been subjected to criticism for alleged susceptibility to political pressure in organized crime investigations. Those criticisms climaxed in a Senate investigation conducted in 1977 and 1978 by Senator Sam Nunn. On completion of the Senate inquiry in April, 1978, the Assistant Secretary of Labor who had been in charge of the Department's organized crime investigations was fired, and a reorganization of the Department's criminal investigative staff was conducted. The Department of Labor committed itself to a revitalization of its attack against organized crime, and that effort proceeded smoothly until the involved personnel merged into the Department's Office of Inspector General following the effective date of the Inspector General's Act in October, 1979. Following the appointment of Ms. Marjorie Fine Knowles as Inspector General, Rocco DeMarco and his assistant, Richard Ross, were summarily removed from their positions, although they had been responsible for organizing the new investigative staff to pursue the labor racketeering and CETA fraud problems which had been iden-

---

[2] Mr. Mangieri obtained custody of his children from an Alaskan court, following which he moved to Maryland.

[3] In the spring of 1980, Ms. Knowles resigned her position under fire for her instruction to Messrs. Lehrman and Peterson to abandon the Youth Pride investigation.

tified in the Senate hearings. Ms. Knowles then appointed as her deputy Mr. Ronald Goldstock, who assumed direction of the organized crime program. Throughout 1980, the organized crime and CETA fraud investigations were abruptly side-tracked by transfers, disciplinary actions and threatened criminal prosecutions against the handful of aggressive agents who had been energetically pursuing those investigations. Mr. Goldstock took over as Acting Inspector General following Ms. Knowles' resignation.

The Knowles-Goldstock purge was directed at two categories of Departmental employee: "whistle-blowers" and union activists. A common thread was the threat of criminal prosecution. Mr. William R. Gamble, a special agent in charge of the Department's Los Angeles strike force, was threatened in August, 1980, with a federal prosecution for misuse of the franking privilege in an amount alleged to be $116, and for having recorded two telephone conversations with Mr. Goldstock. Also in August, 1980, Mr. Gamble was scheduled to be interviewed by CBS' Sixty Minutes program about the Department's derelictions in investigating labor union corruption. Despite an unblemished 10-year record of success as a Department of Labor investigator, and despite the recommendation of a hearing examiner to reinstate him as the special agent in charge of the Los Angeles strike force, Mr. Gamble was fired in December, 1980. His termination is presently on appeal.

Mr. Richard Ross, the former Deputy Director of the Office of Special Investigations, and the acting deputy Inspector General until Ms. Knowles was appointed, and a critic of Ms. Knowles, was threatened with federal criminal prosecution for alleged travel voucher misuse. He was fired from the Department, appealed, and in March, 1981, was ordered reinstated by the Office of Personnel Management.

Mr. John Salvail, a union activist and the special agent in charge of the Boston organized crime division, was threatened with federal prosecution and fired in connection with alleged fabrication of a report of a kidnapping plot. Although Ms. Knowles and Mr. Goldstock referred the matter to the Department of Justice, Mr. Salvail was not prosecuted. He won reinstatement to his position of employment by a decision of the Merit Systems Protection Board.

Neil Broadbent, the special agent in charge of the Buffalo Inspector General's office, was threatened with prosecution for alleged false entries regarding his overtime hours. Because of the mental breakdown of his wife as a result of the ensuing investigation, Mr. Broadbent resigned and is now employed by another federal agency.

Sam Littleton, the special agent in charge of the Dallas Inspector General's office, refused to hire an unqualified person pre-selected by Mr. Goldstock (who had by then succeeded Ms. Knowles as Acting Inspector General), and was threatened with prosecution for alleged pay-offs. Mr. Littleton had also refused to change a performance evaluation ordered by Mr. Goldstock's deputy. Mr. Littleton was removed from his position as a special agent in charge but has not yet been prosecuted for any crime.

It was against that back-drop of punitive actions against vocal employees that Mr. Mangieri was told to abandon the investigation of CETA violations by high- ranking officials of the District of Columbia government. When he protested, he was stripped of his responsibilities and transferred to another assignment. He invoked the Department's grievance procedure, and following a lengthy hearing, the hearing examiner recommended that he be reinstated to his position. That recommendation was rejected by the Inspector General. On February 20, 1981, the Office of Special Counsel, Office of Personnel Management, sent a directive to the new Secretary of Labor (a copy of which is attached hereto as Exhibit C), in which the Secretary is ordered to respond to what Special counsel has found to be a prima facie case of abusive and unlawful treatment of Mr. Mangieri. So far as we know, Mr. Mangieri is, to date, the only one of the handful of aggressive investigators who has actually been criminally prosecuted.

Following disclosures by Mr. Mangieri to congressional investigators and the press, yet another investigation of Mr. Mangieri's background was undertaken under the direction of Mr. Goldstock. Most of the ground covered in the 1979 investigation was recovered, including forays into California, Alaska, Nevada and Alaska; however, most of the information turned up in 1980 was the same as that which appeared during the background checks in 1978 and 1979. The only new material which emerged were the nine applications Mr. Mangieri had made for loans to the Department of Labor Federal Credit Union from July, 1978, to October, 1979. (Since the two loans actually granted were made on the strength of the two additional co-signors and collateralization of the car, and since those loans have been routinely repaid by a check-off from Mr. Mangieri's bi-weekly government paycheck, we do not suppose that those applications emerged because of any irregularity in the loans themselves.)

Mr. Mangieri listed a variety of debts on each of the applications filed with the Credit Union. The Credit Union obtained an independent credit check through the Credit Bureau, Inc., and thus was adequately apprised of Mr. Mangieri's financial condition at the time he sought the loans. Indeed, the Credit Union has never loaned money to Mr. Mangieri on the strength of his own credit. Therefore, it follows perforce that the Credit Union would not have loaned any money to him if he had listed any additional debts. Both his previous financial, political and family troubles have been known to the Labor Department from the time he was employed there. It was only after his public complaints that the Inspector General was covering up CETA fraud for political reasons that he, like the other agents described above, was threatened with criminal prosecution and in Mr. Mangieri's case, actually prosecuted.

The brief but sorry history of the Knowles-Goldstock regime (which ended with Mr. Goldstock's removal shortly after President Reagan's inauguration), was punctuated with reprisals and retaliations against dedicated investigators who sought only to honor their oath of office and to pursue real crime. The facts recited above convincingly support our position that this is a selective, retaliatory prosecution designed solely to punish Mr. Mangieri. There can be no doubt that the Knowles-Goldstock regime wanted to be rid of Mr. Mangieri (see portion of Lehrman testimony in grievance hearing attached hereto as Exhibit D). When they failed to accomplish that end by other means, Mr. Mangieri became the first victim of their recurring threat to achieve it by another, more sinister method — criminal prosecution.

Mr. Mangieri is prepared to prove the foregoing allegations at an evidentiary hearing. If he does, the instant indictment should clearly be dismissed. Almost one hundred years ago, the Supreme Court held that equal protection principles are offended when penal laws are administered "with an evil eye and an unequal hand, so as practically to make unjust and illegal discrimination between persons in similar circumstances ..." *Yick Wo v. Hopkins,* 118 U. S.

356, 373-374(1886). In the years since the Court's decision in *Yick Wo,* it has become firmly settled that a defendant may not be singled out for criminal prosecution on the basis of such impermissible considerations as race, religion, or the desire to deter or punish the exercise of constitutional rights. See, e.g., *Oyler v. Boles,* 368 U. S. 448(1962); *Two Guys v. McGinley,* 366 U. S. 582(1961); *Edelman v. California,* 344 U. S. 357(1953); *Snowden v. Hughes,* 321 U. S. 1(1943); *Ah Sin v. Wittman,* 198 U. S. 500(1905); *United States v. Oaks,* 508 F.2d 1403 (9th Cir. 1974); *United States v. Ahmad,* 347 F. Supp. 912 (M.D. Pa. 1972), *aff'd sub nom., United States v. Berrigan,* 482 F.2d 171 (3rd Cir. 1973); *United States v. Falk,* 479 F.2d 616 (7th Cir. 1973) *(en banc); United States v. Crowthers,* 456 F.2d 1074 (4th Cir. 1972); *United States v. Steele,* 461 F.2d 1148 (9th Cir. 1972); *Moss v. Hornig,* 314 F.2d 89 (2d Cir. 1963). The rationale of the cases is not difficult to discern; as the court explained it in *United States v. Berrios,* 501 F .2d 1207 (2d Cir. 1974):

> Nothing can corrode respect for a rule of law more than the knowledge that the government looks beyond the law itself to arbitrary considerations, such as race, religion, or control over the defendant's exercise of his constitutional rights, as the basis for determining in its applicability. Selective prosecution then can become a weapon used to discipline political foe and the dissident. The prosecutor's objective is then diverted from the public interest to the punishment of those harboring beliefs with which the administration may disagree. [Id. at 1209 (citations omitted).]

That is a prosecutorial purpose which should not be countenanced by this Court. The instant motions should accordingly be granted.

John W. Karr
Karr and Lyons
625 Washington Building
Washington, D. C. 20005
Attorney for Defendant

... Appendix B ...

**UNITED STATES DISTRICT COURT
FOR THE DISTRICT OF COLUMBIA**

UNITED STATES OF AMERICA

v.   Criminal No. 81-19

NICHOLAS J. MANGIERI, JR.

Defendant

**STATEMENT OF POINTS AND AUTHORITIES IN
SUPPORT OF MOTION TO SUPPRESS EVIDENCE**

Defendant Nicholas J. Mangieri, Jr., is moving the Court for an order to suppress all evidence based upon or obtained as a result of information about Mr. Mangieri secured by the government from Equifax, Inc. (hereafter, "Equifax") in violation of various federal statutes and regulations.

Equifax (formerly Retail Credit Company) is

... one of the nation's largest consumer reporting agencies. Directly or through its subsidiaries, among other things, it supplies financial and credit reports for use in evaluating the financial reputation and payment history of individuals who seek credit; sells personnel selection reports used to evaluate applicants for employment; supplies insurance companies with information used to determine the desirability of applicants as risks for insurance; and prepares information used to assess claims made against insurers.[1]

In mid-1980, the Office of the Inspector General of the Department of Labor (hereinafter, "Department") decided that "[d]ata bases exist within the private sector that would be most helpful in combating fraudulent [workmen's] compensation claims. In order to test our idea we wish to perform a feasibility study and we believe that Equifax Corporation is a unique organization for [that purpose] . . ."[2] Sometime thereafter, the Department apparently let a sole source contract to Equifax to supply the Department's Office of Inspector General with financial and personal data about persons receiving benefits pursuant to workmen's compensation statutes.

Despite the fact that the Department had contracted with Equifax solely to provide information about potential violators of workmen's compensation laws, at some point during a departmental investigation of Mr. Mangieri (who obviously was not suspected of having violated any workmen's compensation statute), departmental officials asked Equifax to transmit to the Department information concerning Mr. Mangieri's credit history. The information supplied by Equifax in response to that departmental inquiry apparently became the basis for the present accusation that Mr. Mangieri submitted falsified loan applications to the Department's credit union in violation of 18 U.S.C. Sec. 1014. For the reasons next stated, we contend that all information about Mr. Mangieri's financial history received by the government from Equifax was unlawfully obtained and should accordingly be excluded as evidence in this prosecution.

To begin with, the Department has never, so far was we can determine, complied with the mandatory publication requirements of the Privacy Act, 5 U.S.C. Sec. 552a(e)(4), with respect to the

---

[1] The above-quoted description of Equifax's activities appears in an opinion of the Federal Trade Commission accompanying an order to cease and desist issued by the Commission in In the Matter of Equifax Inc., F.T.C. Docket No. 8954 (December 15, 1980), pp.4-5.

[2] Undated memorandum from Ronald Goldstock, Acting Inspector General, Department of Labor, to James V. Mason, Office of Procurement, Department of Labor (attached hereto as Exhibit A). Defendant believes that this memorandum, which concerned "sole source justification" for the Equifax contract, was prepared in either May or June, 1980.

records system created by its contract with Equifax.

To be sure, the Department did apparently attempt to comply with the requirement of Sec. 552a(e)(4)(D) that "routine uses" of the records systems (including, we gather, the Equifax records system) of the Office of Inspector General be published annually in the *Federal Register.* See 44 F.R. 61680 (October 26, 1979); 45 F.R. 56214 (August 22, 1980); 46 F.R. 12350 (February 13, 1981). However, nothing in any of those Federal Register publications even remotely purports to identify the name and location of the Equifax record system, as required by Sec. 552a(e)(4)(A); the categories of individuals on whom records are maintained in the Equifax records system, as required by Sec. 552a(e)(4)(B); the categories of records maintained in the Equifax records system, as required by Sec. 552a(e)(4)(C); the policies and practices of the Department regarding storage, retrievability, access controls, retention, and disposal of Equifax records, as required by Sec. 552a(e)(4)(E); or the categories of sources or records in the Equifax system, as required by Sec. 552a(e)(4)(I).[3]

The violations of the Fair Credit Reporting Act, 15 U.S.C. Secs. 1681, et seq., are considerably more egregious. Sec. 1681b defines the permissible purposes of credit reports as follows:

A consumer reporting agency may furnish a consumer report under the following circumstances and no other:

(1) In response to the order of a court having jurisdiction to issue such an order.

(2) In accordance with the written instructions of the consumer to whom it relates.

(3) To a person which it has reason to believe —

(A) intends to use the information in connection with a credit transaction involving the consumer on whom the information is to be furnished and involving the extension of credit to, or review or collection of an

---

[3] The contract between the Department and Equifax also appears to violate Sec. 552a(e)(1) of the Privacy Act, in that it seems most unlikely that the records system is truly "necessary" to accomplish the purposes of workmen's compensation statutes. Surely fraudulent workmen's compensation claims can be detected by methods less intrusive than monitoring the credit records of some 70,000,000 citizens. (See Exhibit A, attached hereto).

account of, the consumer; or

(B) intends to use the information for employment purposes; or

(C) intends to use the information in connection with the underwriting of insurance involving the consumer; or

(D) intends to use the information in connection with a determination of the consumer's eligibility for a license or other benefit granted by a governmental instrumentality required by law to consider an applicant's financial responsibility or status; or

(E) otherwise has a legitimate business need of the information in connection with a business transaction involving the consumer.

It is plain on the face of the statutory language just quoted that the Fair Credit Reporting Act did not authorize the contract between Equifax and the Department, and it follows that any credit histories — including Mr. Mangieri's — obtained by the Department pursuant to that contract were acquired in violation of the Act.[4]

Finally, it seems clear that the Department violated its own arrangement with Equifax by seeking and obtaining Mr. Mangieri's credit history, since even by the Department's light the only "routine use" of the Equifax records system is to gather information about possible violators of the workmen's compensation laws — violations which Mr. Mangieri has never been and could not be suspected of having committed.

It is a "well-settled rule that an agency's failure to follow its own regulations is fatal to the deviant action." *Union of Concerned Scientists v. Atomic Energy Commission,* 163 U.S. App. D.C. 64, 77, 499 F .2d 1069, 1082 (1974). *See also, Morton v. Ruiz,* 415

---

[4] The government may argue that even if the contract between Equifax and the Department is illegal, resort to the Equifax records system was lawful in this particular instance under the "employment purposes" provision of Sec. 1681b(B). While we would dispute that construction of Sec. 1681 (b)(B), we would also note that Mr. Mangieri never received the notifications required by Sec. 1681k when credit reports are furnished for employment purposes. Accordingly, the Act was violated in any event.

U.S. 199 (1974) (requiring Bureau of Indian Affairs to follow its internal manual regarding benefits); *Yellin v. United States,* 374 U.S. 109 (1962) (reversing contempt of Congress conviction where committee had not complied with its rules); *Vitarelli v. Seaton,* 359 U.S. 535 (1959) (reversing dismissal of government employee where agency's procedural requirement not adhered to); *Service v. Dulles,* 354 U.S. 363 (1957) (reversing dismissal of government employee where regulations adopted by head of agency were not followed); *United States ex rel. Accardi v. Shaughnessy,* 347 U.S. 260 (1953) (habeas corpus release required where agency's procedural regulations were violated); *Bridges v. Wixon,* 326 U.S. 120 (1945) (petitioner could not be deported because evidence admitted in violation of agency rule that all statements must be in writing).[5] As the Court stated the principle in *United States v. Nixon,* 418 U.S. 683, 696 (1974), "[s]o long as [a] regulation remains in force the Executive Branch is bound by it, and indeed the United states as the sovereign composed of the three branches is bound to respect and to enforce it."

Moreover, it is particularly important that an agency scrupulously observe its own rules, regulations or procedures where such rule, regulations or procedures are required by statute. Thus, in *Miller v. United States,* 357 U.S. 301(1958), the Court considered the question whether evidence obtained in violation of a District of Columbia "no-knock" statue required suppression of the evidence seized. The Court expressly limited its discussion to sanctions required for violation of the statute, and did not consider the question whether the facts gave rise to a constitutional violation. *Id.,* at 305. The Court concluded that the petitioner had not received the statutorily required notice of authority and purpose, *id.,* at 313, and held that the seized evidence must therefore be suppressed.

---

[5] It is irrelevant that an agency's rules, regulations or procedures may be more restrictive than Constitutional requirements, since "it is incumbent upon agencies to follow their own procedures ... even when the internal procedures are possibly more rigorous than otherwise would be required." Morton v. Ruiz, supra, ("It is of no significance that the procedures or instructions are more generous than the Constitution requires.").

In concluding that suppression was the required remedy for the statutory violation, the Court observed:

> We are duly mindful of the reliance that society must place for achieving law and order upon the enforcing agencies of the criminal law. But insistence on observance by law officers of traditional fair procedural requirements it, from the long point of view, best calculated to contribute to that end. However much in a particular case insistence upon such rules may appear as a technicality that inures to the benefit of a guilty person, the history of the criminal law proves that tolerance of shortcut methods in law enforcement impairs its enduring effectiveness. [*Id.*, at 313]

Similarly, in *Lee v. Florida*, 392 U.S. 378 (1968) (holding that evidence obtained in violation of a federal statute must be suppressed in a state criminal prosecution), the Court commented that "the decision we reach today * * * is buttressed ... by the 'imperative of judicial integrity.' Under our Constitution no court, state or federal, may serve as an accomplice in the willful transgression of the Laws of the United States ... '" *Id.*, at 385-386 (citation and footnote omitted).[6]

Our position, in short, is that courts should not become partners with executive branch agencies in unlawful invasions of privacy,[7] and that such illegal actions should "find no sanction in the judgments of the courts." *Weeks v. United States,* 232 U.S. 383, 392 (1914). In the present prosecution, the government's case is built

---

[6] More recently, in <u>United States</u> v. <u>Caceres</u>, 440 U.S. 741 (1979), the Court noted, in considering the questions whether evidence obtained in violation of an agency's rules must be suppressed in a criminal prosecution, that "[a] court's duty to enforce an agency regulation is most evident when compliance with the regulation is mandated by the Constitution of federal law." <u>Id.</u> at 440.
Although the Court in <u>Caceres</u> did not find that exclusion of evidence was the appropriate sanction for violation of a regulation which was not required by the Constitution or by federal law, it specifically observed that its decision was not governed by <u>Miller</u> v. <u>United States, supra</u> "[s]ince no statutes were violated ..." 440 IU.S. at 755, n. 21. In the instant case, of course, Mr. Mangieri is asserting a violation of federal law, and <u>Caceres</u> is thus inapposite here.

[7] The Privacy Act and the Fair Credit Reporting Act are meant, no less than the Fourth Amendment, to preserve a sense of individual security and autonomy.

upon evidence obtained in violation of the Privacy Act, the Fair Credit Reporting act, and the Department of Labor's own rules, and the only remedy for those violations is suppression of all information and evidence unlawfully obtained, as well as the fruits of that information. *Wong Sun v. United States,* 371 U.S. 471 (1963); *United States v. Scios,* 191 U.S. App. D.C. 254, 590 F .2d 956 (1978) *(en banc).*

John W. Karr
Karr and Lyons
625 Washington Building
Washington, D. C. 20005
Attorney for Defendant

... Appendix C ...

UNITED STATES DISTRICT COURT
FOR THE DISTRICT OF COLUMBIA

UNITED STATES OF AMERICA
v.   Criminal No. 81-19
NICHOLAS J. MANGIERI, JR.

Defendant

SUPPLEMENTAL STATEMENT OF POINTS AND AUTHORITIES IN SUPPORT OF MOTION FOR NEW TRIAL

Defendant Nicholas J. Mangieri, Jr., asserts that a new trial should be granted in this cause of the following reasons:

I. *Refusal to Entertain Motion to Suppress Evidence*
On April 27, 1981, the day that trial was scheduled to begin in this case, defendant's counsel attempted to file a motion to suppress evidence[1] and requested that it be heard[2] and decided before

---

[1] The motion, with its supporting memorandum and exhibits, is attached hereto as Exhibit A.

[2] Defendant was prepared to go forward with his factual presentation immediately. See copies of the subpoenas attached hereto as Exhibits B, C and D. The subpoenas duces tecum directed to the general manager of Equifax, Inc., and to a Department of Labor procurement official are self-explanatory. (Defendant has since obtained a copy of the contract between the Department of Labor and Equifax, Inc.; a copy is attached hereto as Exhibit E.) The issuance of a subpoena ad testificandum to Osvaldo Castro, an employee of the Office of Inspector General of the Department of Labor, was based upon defendant's information and belief that Mr. Castro was the person who actually initiated (at the direction of his superiors) the inquiry to Equifax, Inc. about Mr. Mangieri's credit history.

a jury was impanelled. The Court refused to permit the motion to be filed on the ground that it was untimely. However, as the motion recites, defendant's counsel first learned of the facts underlying the motion on Thursday night, April 23, 1981, when the information was volunteered to defense counsel by an informant within the Department of Labor, and counsel did not obtain corroborating documentation until Friday night, April 24, 1981. Moreover, the facts which gave rise to the suppression motion involve matters which neither defendant nor his counsel could have otherwise discovered throughout the exercise of due diligence.[3] Plainly, then, the motion to suppress simply could not have been prepared and filed prior to Monday morning, April 27, 1981, given that defendant was not aware of the grounds for the motion until then, and it was consequently an abuse of discretion for the Court to refuse to permit the motion to be filed on that date. The motion to suppress clearly raises substantial questions about the legality of the methods by which evidence against this defendant was obtained,[4] and it is beyond peradventure that convictions based upon such tainted evidence should not be permitted to stand.

II. *Erroneous Instructions*

Defendant first contends that the Court's instruction to the jury that "it is your duty" to convict the defendant upon the finding of certain facts beyond a reasonable doubt[5] was merely anoth-

---

[3] Indeed, in light of a memorandum dated April 22, 1981, from the Department of Labor's Acting Deputy Inspector General to all national and field office employees (a copy of which is attached hereto as Exhibit F), it is remarkable that defendant was ever able to learn of the matter. The April 22 memorandum is . plainly meant to discourage employees of the Inspector General's Office from cooperating with counsel or other employees of the Office.

[4] After trial, defendant learned for the first time that Department of Labor agents also requested and on October 7, 1980, received Mr. Mangieri's file from the Credit Bureau in Langley Park, Maryland. Absent a court order authorizing it, this action was unlawful for the same reasons set forth in the motion to suppress evidence obtained from Equifax, Inc.

[5] The "duty to convict" language was employed by the Court both in its principal charge to the jury and in its later reinstruction concerning the elements of the crime charged.

er form of the instruction condemned in *United States v. Hayward,* 136 U.S. App. D.C. 300, 420, F.2d 142 (1969) (sixth amendment right to trial by jury violated by instruction that jury "must" convict defendant if certain facts were found beyond reasonable doubt). Second, defendant asserts that the mistake of law instruction,[6] as given by the Court, was too narrow, and that defendant's proposed jury instructions Nos. 2 and 3 should have been given in the language requested by him.

III.   *Denial of Jury Poll in Form Requested by Defendant*

After the jury returned its verdicts, defendant requested that the jurors not only be individually polled with respect to their general verdict on each count of the indictment, but that each juror also be individually asked to state specifically which of the various loan application misstatements and omissions, alleged in each count of the indictment, were found to have been proven beyond a reasonable doubt. The denial of that request was, defendant contends, erroneous. In *United States v. O'Neill,* 463 F. Supp. 1200 (E.D. Pa. 1979), the court considered a defendant's claim that an indictment for violations of 18 U.S.C. Sec. 1014 was duplicitous where the counts of the indictment charges two false statements as the basis for single charges. The government disputed that claim, and further argued (as it did in the instant case), that if the defendant made any one of the false statements charge in each count, the defendant was guilty of a Sec. 1014 violation. The court rejected the defendant's contention that the indictment was duplicitous, but then commented:

> A trial on this indictment, however, will present some of the same problems as a trial on a duplicitous indictment. In particular, without proper instructions to the jury, it would be possible for some members of the jury to vote to convict on a

---

[6] This instruction was, of course, crucial to defendant's theory of the case with respect to the alleged misstatements about previous bankruptcies.

count on the basis of a belief in the falsity of one
of the representations charged and the other members of the jury to vote to convict on the basis of the
other. I will therefore charge the jury that, in order
to convict O'Neill on any count charging two or
more misrepresentations, the jury must be unanimous as to at least one of the allege misrepresentations before it can convict on the count. Further,
in order to insure that, in the event of post- verdict
motions or appeal, the sufficiency of the evidence as
to any count on which O'Neill may be convicted
can be tested in light of the misrepresentation which
the jury found, I would be prepared to entertain a
motion — if defendant is so minded — to submit
to the jury a verdict form which would allow the
jury to indicated, as to any count, which misrepre
sentation or misrepresentations, if any, it unanimously finds O'Neill to have committed. [*Id.*, at
1205 (citations omitted).]

In the present case, defendant preferred not to waive his constitutional right to a general verdict, see *United States v. Spock*, 416 F .2d
165 (1st Cir. 1969), and accordingly did not ask for a special verdict. His request of a "special poll," however, would have effectively
prevented the evils identified by the *O'Neill* court without forcing
defendant to forego his right to a general verdict, and his request
for such a poll should have been granted.

IV. *Insufficiency of the Evidence*
Finally, defendant contends that when the evidence, particularly the unrebutted expert psychiatric testimony of Harold Kauf-
man, M.D., and the unrebutted testimony of bankruptcy expert
Richard Wills, Esq., is considered in its totality, it is clear that the
evidence was insufficient to establish beyond a reasonable doubt
that he knowingly submitted falsified loan applications to the Department of Labor credit union with the specific intent to influence
the action of the credit union.

V. *Conclusion*

For all of the foregoing reasons, the interests of justice require that this motion be granted and that a new trial be had in this cause.

John W. Karr
625 Washington Building
Washington, D. C. 20005
Attorney for Defendant

... Appendix D ...

DEFENDANT'S PROPOSED FINDINGS OF FACT AND CONCLUSIONS OF LAW ON MOTION TO DISMISS FOR SELECTIVE PROSECUTION

Proposed Conclusions of Law

1. Mr. Mangieri seeks dismissal of the indictment against him on the ground that he has been selectively prosecuted in violation of the equal protection guarantees, incorporated within the Fifth Amendment of the United States Constitution. *Yick Wo v. Hopkins,* 347 U.S. 497 (1954); *Two Guys From Harrison-Allentown, Inc. v. McGinley,* 366 U.S. 582 (1961). To establish illegal selective prosecution, a defendant must establish "intentional, purposeful discrimination." *Teague v. Alexander,* No 79-2951 (D.C. Cir. August 24, 1981); *United States v. Diggs,* 198 U.S. App. D.C. 255, 613 F .2d 988, 1003 (1979); *Washington v. United States,* 130 U.S. App. D.C. 374, 401 F .2d 915 (1968), and that the selection to prosecute him was based on an unjustifiable standard such as exercise of First Amendment rights. *United States v. Wilson,* 639 F .2d 500 (9th Cir. 1981); *United States v. Scott,* 521 F .2d 1188, 1195 (9th Cir. 1975); *United States v. Steele,* 461 F .2d 1148, 1151 (9th Cir. 1972); *Attorney General v. The Irish People, Inc.,* 502 F. Supp. 63 (D.D.C. 1980).

2. Mr. Mangieri has demonstrated that other federal employees similarly situated to himself have not been prosecuted for false credit applications. See generally, *United States v. Choate,* 609 F .2d 21 (9th Cir. 1980); *United States v. Berrios,* 501 F .2d 1207 (ed Cir. 1974). Joseph McGowan, president of the Department of Labor ("DOL") Federal Credit Union stated in his affidavit that the Credit Union had developed a standard procedure to deal with false statements made on loan applications. He stated further that in the 14 years he had been with the Credit Union, he knew of

absolutely no other individual who had been criminally prosecuted for false statements, and he emphasized that the Credit Union had not participated in the decision to prosecute defendant. Ms. Lina Gray, manager of the Department of Labor Credit Union, said she knew of no person other than Mr. Mangieri who had been prosecuted for any matter having to do with the Credit Union. She said she did not approve of criminal prosecutions for false credit applications unless the Credit Union initiated the actions. Because criminal prosecution of Mr. Mangieri is in direct violation of DOL Federal Credit policy it is inherently suspect. See *United States v. Falk*, 479 F .2d 616 (7th cir. 1973) (*en banc*). Moreover Assistant United States Attorney Richard Beizer testified that he knew of only one section 1014 prosecution other than that of defendant which had been pursued during his tenure at the United States Attorney Office. Mr Beizer testified that, contrary to normal procedure, in Mr. Mangieri's case he did not consider administrative sanctions prior to prosecution. United States Attorney Charles Ruff said that since he had been head of the office, only two section 1014 prosecutions had been brought.

3. Mr. Lehrman testified that as early as May, 1979, he was told that upper-level managers of the I.G. Office wanted Mr. Eder and others to do a "hatchet job" on Mr. Mangieri. The three investigations of Mr. Mangieri conducted by the Department of Labor were part of a single investigative design intended to silence Mr. Mangieri from dissenting from policies of the IG Office publicly and internally. These three DOL investigations formed the basis for the United States Attorney's subsequent grand jury investigation and indictment of defendant. In May, 1981, the clear intent of the third remaining DOL investigation was to find evidence to charge Mr. Mangieri with a criminal offense. Because this last DOL investigation, carried out by trained criminal investigators with orders to find violations of the criminal law, was a criminal investigation and formed the basis for the indictment in this case, actions of DOL employees and officials can be imputed to the United States Attorney's Office. See *United States v. Bourque*, 541 F .2d 290, 293 (1st Cir 1976) ("personal vindictiveness on the part of a prosecutor *or* the responsible member of the administrative agency recommending prosecution would also sustain a charge of discrimination")(emphasis supplied).

4. Information about the exercise of the government's prose-cutorial discretion almost always lies within the sole knowledge and possession of the government. *See generally,* Note, *Defense Access to Evidence of Discriminatory Prosecution,* 1974 ILL. L. F. 648. Most courts, therefore, shift the burden of proof to the govern-ment to prove a prosecution was not discriminatory once defen-dant initially shows "reasonable doubt" regarding the legitimacy of the prosecution, *United States v. Falk, supra* at 620-21, or demon-strates that the record "strongly suggests invidious discrimination and selective application of a regulation to inhibit the expression of an unpopular viewpoint, *"United States v. Crowthers,* 456 F .2d 1071, 1078 (4th Cir. 1972), or points to evidence which creates a strong inference of discriminatory prosecution, *United States v. Steele, supra* at 1148; or presents a *prima facie* case of selective prosecution, *United States v. Scott, supra* at 1195. *See generally Attorney General v. The Irish People, Inc., supra* at 65-66. In the instant case, Mr. Mangieri has met his burden of establishing a *prime facie* case that he was singled out for criminal prosecution in retaliation for having engaged in protected First Amendment activities, and of demonstrating that his criminal prosecution was an attempt to silence him and others who dissented publicly and inter-nally from policies and practices of DOL management. Specifical-ly, Mr. Mangieri has shown that:

(A) DOL's multiple investigations of Mr. Mangieri led eventually to his indictment, were initiated to stop him from continuing his investigation into alle-gations of sexual harassment and assault of CETA employees by District of Columbia government officials. Particularly, DOL officials wished to pre-vent Mr. Mangieri from carrying out a thorough investigation which might implicate high District of Columbia officials, and from speaking to the newspapers about his investigation and attempted obstruction by DOL/OIG management of the investigation.

(B) At the same time a DOL auditor charged that the scheduled audit of Youth Pride had been can-celled or postponed for political reasons.

(C) In addition, DOL management in at least 11

other instances retaliated against investigators who disagreed with the policies and practices of the OIG.

(D) DOL's first investigation of Mr. Mangieri, from June to July, 1979, was

initiated after the local press carried articles about his investigation into sexual coercion. The press clearance policy then in effect at OIG, since rescinded, was virtually identical to a later policy which was determined by the Office of Special Counsel to be a unconstitutional abridgment of the First Amendment rights of OIG employees (see the July 30, 1981, letter from Special Counsel to the Acting DOL IG, attached hereto as an appendix).

(E) DOL management believed that Mr. Mangieri was responsible for leaks to the press and commenced the so-called "Alaska investigation:" to collect information against him in retaliation.

(F) Messrs. Eder and Braver spoke to investigators in Seattle, Washington, about obtaining information on Mr. Mangieri from Palmer, Alaska, where he was formally police chief. The Seattle agents sent a package of documents to Mr. Braver in Washington. According to Mr. Statham's testimony at the hearing on Mr. Mangieri's dismissal motion and other affidavits of DOL employees submitted to the IRS, this "Alaska packet" was widely distributed through the DOL and maintained outside Mr. Mangieri's official personnel file.

(G) The "Alaska packet" contained information about Mr. Mangieri's financial problems and "whistleblowing" activities in Alaska.

(H) On June 5, 1979, Messrs. Eder and Juliano tried, but failed, to suspend Mr. Mangieri administratively for his protected First Amendment activities of speaking to the press about his investigation and pursuing his investigation vigorously despite management instructions not to do so.

(I) DOL, retaliating against Mr. Mangieri because of his charges to IG Marjorie Knowles and to the press that his CETA investigation was being frustrated, transferred Mr. Mangieri to Arlington, Virginia.

(J) The second DOL investigation of Mr. Mangieri was ordered by IG Marjorie Knowles on December 27, 1979, when she requested OPM to do full field background investigations on all employees in her office. The purpose of these checks was to discover information to prosecute or retaliate against those DOL criminal investigators who dissented publicly or internally from Ms. Knowles' policies and practices. Ms. Knowles wished to retaliate against Mr. Mangieri because of December, 1979, newspaper articles which exposed the obstruction of his investigation and the Youth Pride audit for political reasons.

(K) OPM told Ms. Knowles that the field investigations could not be used to take personnel actions against any DOL employee who had passed the probationary period.

(L) The OPM security checks ordered for all DOL Inspector General office employees on December 27, 1979, including Mr. Mangieri, focused on unusual factors. Linda Furbey, security specialist with the DOL Inspector General office said these checks, unlike all other security checks were extensively concerned with individuals' financial problems. Ms. Furbey never evaluated the final OPM report on Mr. Mangieri because it went directly to Messrs. Statham and Goldstock. Mr. Mangieri's OPM check was the only one reviewed personally by Mr. Statham rather than by a member of his staff.

(M) DOL's special handling of Mr. Mangieri's background check was in retaliation for his lawful review of travel vouchers of DOL managers Goldstock and Nicholson on February 27, 1980. After Mr. Mangieri conducted, based on credible information supplied to him, an examination of Mr. Goldstock's travel vouchers, Mr. Mangieri was held, searched, and interrogated by Mr. Coffman of the Philadelphia IG office. Mr. Coffman also seized

Mr. Mangieri's personal documents and kept them, including a letter Mr. Mangieri had drafted to the editors of *The Washington Post* in response to Labor Secretary Marshall's claim that the Pride investigation had not been obstructed for political reasons. (N) DOL thereafter ordered a "fifteen-day special" check by OPM of Mr. Mangieri. Mr. Mangieri was the only one of the 487 DOL employees on whom a security check wa completed whose records at the Federal Credit Union were checked. (O) On March 3, 1980, Mr. Coffman, after reading through Mr. Mangieri's private papers, recommended an internal administrative (IA) investigation of Mr. Mangieri, explicitly because Mr. Mangieri had given information to *The Washington Post* about political obstruction of his investigation. Mr. Statham made the same recommendation, based on Mr. Mangieri's communications with   the press.
(P) The OPM investigation was not completed until late April, 1980. Therefore, as with the prior two investigations of Mr. Mangieri, the decision to conduct the third, IA investigation was made to retaliate against him for the exercise of his First Amendment rights during May, 1980, and before, and, from the beginning was intended to construct criminal charges against Mr. Mangieri.
(Q) The IA investigation opened on June 2, 1980, was of extraordinary scope and expense. Mr. Anderson made trips to New York, California, Nevada and Alaska. Mr. Goldstock approved the IA investigation against Mr. Mangieri, in part because Mr. Mangieri was assisting a *Washington Post* reporter who was scrutinizing Mr. Goldstock's personal use of government auditors for a course Mr. Goldstock had taught at Cornell University prior to coming to the IG's office. Thus Mr. Goldstock ordered the IA investigation because of Mr. Mangieri's constitutionally and statutorily protected "whistleblow-

ing" activity. Mr. Goldstock himself said that the IA investigation was necessary to follow up on possible violations of the criminal law uncovered by OPM. (R) Mr. Anderson's referral of his investigative materials on Mr. Mangieri to the Alaska's Untied States Attorney's Office and to the FBI in Alaska on July 18 and July 20, 1980, respectively, suggests that the IA investigation was intended to uncover evidence of Mr. Mangieri's purported criminal conduct. It also indicates that at least one United States Attorney's Office declined to prosecute Mr. Mangieri on the same evidence which supported the indictment here.

(S) The Alaska, OPM, and IA investigations of Mr. Mangieri were initiated and carried out in order to stop him from speaking out about his sexual coercion investigation and what he believed to be obstruction of his investigation, and to prevent him from speaking to the press, in violation of the First Amendment.

(T) By the spring of 1980, these investigations were intended to uncover information to prosecute Mr. Mangieri criminally as punishment for exercising his First Amendment rights.

5. In conducting all three investigations of defendant, DOL resorted to illegal methods of investigation and in so doing violated Mr. Mangieri's rights under the Fair Credit Reporting Act, 15 U.S.C., Sec. 1681, et seq., the Right to Financial Privacy Act, 12 U.S.C. Sec. 3401, et seq., the Privacy Act, 5 U.S.C. Sec. 552(a), et seq. and rights guaranteed by the First, Fourth, and Fifth Amendments to the United States Constitution, and DOL regulations. These illegal methods of investigation include the following:

(A) Violations of the Fair Credit Reporting Act:

(1) OPM credit checks of Mr. Mangieri through Credit Bureau, Inc., with knowledge that Mr. Mangieri had refused consent for release of financial data;

(2) Mr. Castro's telephone call(s) to Credit Bureau, Inc., at Mr. Anderson's direction, during the summer of 1980, for the explicit purpose of furthering a criminal investigation;

(3) the illegal,ongoing contract between DOL and Credit Bureau, Inc., whereby DOL obtains credit information unrelated to employment purposes.

(B) Violations of the Right to Financial Privacy Act:

(1) Mr. Anderson interviewed Lina Gray of the DOL Federal Credit Union during the summer, 1980, even though he knew he was not entitled to any information other than the name of any accounts Mr. Mangieri held with them;

(2) Mr. Anderson used the same illegal method to gather credit information on Mr. Mangieri from other employees of financial institutions in Alaska and California.

(C) Violations of the Privacy Act:

(1) DOL maintained records on Mr. Mangieri's First Amendment activities, including the "Alaska packet" which included information on Mr. Mangieri's whistleblowing in Palmer, Alaska, and the personal papers seized by Mr. Coffman on February 27, 1980, which include Mr. Mangieri's letters to the editor of The Washington Post, all in violation of 5 U.S.C., Sec. 552a(e)(7).

(2) IG management level employees disseminated possibly harmful information about Mr. Mangieri throughout the IG's office, apparently by means of documents contained in the "Alaska packet." These documents were passed around as a "secret dossier" on Mr. Mangieri of which he was unaware, and whose accuracy he could not challenge.

(3) DOL failed to comply with the mandatory publication requirements of 5 U.S.C., Sec. 552a(e)(4) regarding records maintained through DOL's contract with Credit Bureau, Inc., or its parent company, Equifax.

(D) Constitutional violations:

(1) On February 27, 1980, Mr. Coffman violated Mr. Mangieri's Fourth and Fifth Amendment rights by subjecting him to custodial interrogation without informing him of his right to remain silent or to consult an attorney, by forcing him to remain in an office at the Department, and by seizing and then searching his personal papers.

(2) DOL, through its multiple investigations of Mr. Mangieri violated his First Amendment rights to freedom of
speech, to petition the government for redress of grievances, and to express himself within the bounds of the
law about his work and investigations.
(E) Violation of DOL regulations:
(1) Mr. Anderson carried out the IA investigation in
explicit violation of DOL's investigation guideline.
Although he maintained notes of some witness interviews,
for others which could have revealed violations of the Fair
Credit Reporting Act and the Right to Financial Privacy
Act, he did not. DOL/OIG policies required all investigators to keep full and comprehensive notes of every investigative interview and encounter.

6. In addition, the record permits an inference that much of the
information eventually received by the grand jury which indicted Mr.
Mangieri was collected illegally by DOL investigators prior to the
issuance of valid grand jury subpoenas for the information.

7. The widespread and deliberate use of illegal investigative
methods detailed in paragraphs 5 and 6 above tainted DOL's entire
investigation and the ensuing criminal prosecution of Mr. Mangieri.
See *Miller v. United States*, 357 U.S. 301 (1958); *United States v.
Pappas*, 613 F .2d 324 (1st Cir. 1979); *United States v. Sito-Soto*, 598
F .2d 545 (9th Cir. 1979). That DOL officials were willing to,
and in fact did resort to such illegal investigatory tactics further
supports the conclusion that their purpose was, at all costs, to silence
Mr. Mangieri and other investigators who were internally dissenting from OIG policies and practices.

8. The decision to prosecute Mr. Mangieri was made at the
highest level of the United States Attorney's Office, and only after
concerned questioning by the then head of Superior Court Operations, Henry Greene, now judge of the District of Columbia Superior Court, and the refusal of Mr. Ruff from any participation in
the decision. In other circumstances a simple prosecution under 18
U.S.C., Sec. 1014 surely would not have attracted so much prosecutorial attention. See *United States v. Falk, supra* at 622. Moreover,further evidence of retaliatory motive is found in Assistant
United States Attorney Beizer's testimony that he, as chief of the
Fraud Section, decided to prosecute Mr. Mangieri in part because

he was a "phony whistleblower."

9. Mr. Anderson's testimony at the hearing on the motion to dismiss was often inconsistent with his prior sworn testimony or affidavits to the IRS, and with the sworn testimony of other witnesses. Among the inconsistencies are the change in the date he contacted Lina Gray of the DOL Federal Credit Union. Mr. Anderson's testimony varies from Ms. Gray's affidavit. Another inconsistency between Mr. Anderson's testimony at the hearing, his testimony before the grand jury, and the affidavit of Lina Gray is his behavior upon meeting Ms. Gray. Did Mr. Anderson ask Ms. Gray for information beyond whether or not Mr. Mangieri maintained an account at the Credit Union? If he asked nothing further, what was Mr. Anderson's purpose for speaking to her, since he already knew that the Credit Union had given defendant a car loan? Ms. Gray says he pressed her for more information.

10. Other inconsistencies include the date of the first telephone check with Credit Bureau, Inc. on Mr. Mangieri, and the loan information Mr. Anderson gave to Mr. Beizer in referring the case to him. Did Mr. Anderson tell Mr. Beizer that defendant had one or two loans? Mr. Anderson's testimony and Mr. Beizer's affidavit differ. The number and seriousness of the inconsistencies in Anderson's testimony signal possible misrepresentations and suggest an attempt to cover up a truly selective prosecution carried out by illegal methods.

11. For all the reasons set forth above, Mr. Mangieri has demonstrated a *prima facie* case of selective prosecution based on the impermissible ground of his exercise of First Amendment rights; further, the government has failed to rebut Mr. Mangieri's showing that this was an improper, illegal, and unconstitutional prosecution, in violation of the Fifth Amendment to the Constitution of the United States. The instant indictment must therefore be dismissed. *United States v. Crowthers, supra.*

Respectfully submitted,

———————————————

John W. Karr
625 Washington Building
Washington D.C. 20005
Attorney for the Defendant

... Appendix E ...

OFFICE OF THE SPECIAL COUNSEL
1717 H Street, NW
Washington, D.C. 20419

July 30, 1981

The Honorable Frank Yeager
Acting Deputy Inspector General
U.S. Department of Labor
Washington, D.C. 20210

Dear Mr. Yeager:

I have received your letter of July 17, 1981, concerning your April 22, 1981, memorandum cautioning employees of your office not to discuss "substantive agency matters with unauthorized individuals."

As I noted in my June 30 letter, in the interest of preserving the integrity and efficiency of the Government, it is essential that we protect the free speech rights of federal employees as guaranteed by the First Amendment of the Constitution and the whistleblower protection provisions of the Civil Service Reform Act. We interpret these guarantees as placing a dual responsibility on agencies: (1) not to punish employees for past exercise of these protected rights; *and* (2) not to deter the future exercise of such rights by adopting overboard or vague prohibitions which fail to precisely differentiate between protected and unprotected speech. Despite your argument to the contrary, we continue to believe that your April 22, 1981, memorandum is inconsistent with the second of these responsibilities.

Your letter raises three arguments in support of your position. First, you attempt to distinguish *Tygrett v. Barry*, 627 F .2d 1279 (D.C. Cir. 1980), and *Pickering v. Board of Educ.*, 391 U.S. 563 (1968), on ground that they "involved situations where an actual adverse action had been taken against a public employee." You contract your situation because it "does not involve the Government's imposition of sanctions against any particular employee but instead merely involved the OIG's issuance of a policy statement." This is a distinction without a difference since under principles well established by the Supreme Court, a governmental directive which has the effect of chilling First Amendment rights is as offensive œ and as unlawful œ as an attempt to punish the exercise of such rights post facto. *Nebraska Press Ass'n v. Stuart*, 427 U.S. 539, 556-61 (1976); *New York Times Co. v United States*, 403 U.S. 713, 7'14 (1971); *Organization for a Better Austin v. Keefe*, 402 U.S. 415, 419 (1971); *Carroll v. Princess Anne*, 393 U.S. 175, 181 (1968); *Bantam Books, Inc. v. Sullivan*, 372 U.S. 58, 70 (1963); *Near v. Minnesota ex rel. Olson*, 283 U.S. 697, 716 (1931).

Second, your letter suggests that the memorandum is designed merely to protect "OIG's legitimate interest in ensuring the confidentiality of its internal operations." However, the language of the memorandum is much too broad for that purpose. By its terms, the memorandum cautions OIG employees not to discuss "substantive agency matters with unauthorized individuals." the prohibition is breathtaking in its scope, potentially deterring any whistleblowing activity on the part of OIG employees.* The problem lies in the definition of the term   "substantive agency matters." While it doubtless includes confidential information, the disclosure of which may be prohibited, the term also would include information as to every other aspect of the agency's operations, much of which is freely disclosable. Indeed, the substance of any whistleblowing allegations by a federal employee necessarily involves information which can comfortably be classified as "substantive agency matters."

Your third contention appears to be that the April 22 memorandum is inoffensive since it "does not contain any threats of adverse action against employees." Surely, however, you did not go to the trouble of writing and distributing the memorandum in the expectation that it would be ignored by your employees. Even absent the fear of punishment, most employees will do their best to comply with the agency's policy directives. In any case, such directives from managements always carry with them the implicit threat of punishment. Indeed, your letter suggests that you may resort to discipline against some employees violating the directive, but would leave the First Amendment concern to be resolved at that time. This approach unfairly — and unlawfully — places upon employees the burden of guessing what is, in fact, punishable and what is not. Employees, fearful of potential discipline, will err on the side of caution and refrain from speaking even where it is lawful and desirable for them to do so. That is the very essence of an unlawful prior restraint on free speech, *Bantam Books, Inc. v. Sullivan*, 372 U.S. 58, 70 (1963), and a most effective way of discouraging whistleblowing activities by employees.

In light of this analysis, I was surprised by your conclusion that "we see no need to amend our policy statement at this time." Hopefully, my letter will clarify these issues and cause you to retract or amend the April 22 policy memorandum.

Since your memorandum appears to impinge upon significant employee rights under the Civil Service Reform Act (*e.g.*, the right to free speech guaranteed by 5 U.S.C. §§ 2301(b)(2), 2302(b)(11) and the right to communicate with members of Congress guaranteed by 5 U.S.C. § 7211, the matter falls within our jurisdiction and is of great concern to this office. I have therefore directed my staff to initiate an investigation pursuant to 5 U.S.C. §1206(e)(1)(D). However, in light of the possibility that you may voluntarily retract or amend the April 22 memorandum, commencement of the investigation will be delayed for ten days to give you an opportunity to inform us of any action you may have taken.

Sincerely,

Alex Kozinski
Special Counsel

... Appendix F ...

**UNITED STATES DISTRICT COURT
FOR THE DISTRICT OF COLUMBIA**

United States of America
                    v.   Criminal No. 81-91
Nicholas J. Mangieri, Jr.

MOTION TO RECONSIDER ORDER
DENYING MOTION TO DISMISS

Defendant Nicholas Mangieri, pursuant to Rule 47, Fed. R. Crim. P., and through undesigned counsel, moved this Court to reconsider its February 3, 1982 order (February 3 order) denying his motion to dismiss on grounds of selective prosecution. The order erroneously relied on a report prepared by the Internal Revenue Service (I.R.S.) to conclude that there was not retaliation against MR. Mangieri for his "whistleblowing" activities at the Department of Labor (D.O.L.) Office of Inspector General (O.I.G.). Further, the order mistakenly accepted an erroneous factual characterization by the government and ignored significant evidence to conclude that there was no improper motivation for the prosecution by the United States Attorney.

I. THE I.R.S. REPORT AND RETALIATION AT D.O.L.

In the February 3 order, the court concluded that "defendant has not persuaded the Court that his case ws referred to the U.S. Attorney in an attempt to curtail his alleged 'whistleblowing activities.' " (February 3 order, p. 3). The only support for this conclusion came from the finding of an I.R.S. investigation into possible retaliation against Mr. Mangieri. A the court explained, "The IRS, after an exhaustive investigation, found no evidence of retaliation or reprisal by D.O.L. against the defendant for his alleged 'whistleblowing activities.' " (*Id.*, at 3, n. 1.)

Initially, it was error for the court to permit introduction into the record of any findings by the I.R.S. There was extensive discussion on this issue at the November 3 and 4 evidentiary hearing. (Tr. 282-90, 459-61). The court unequivocally excluded the I.R.S. findings and agreed to weight the evidence, rather than permit an administrative agency to substitute of the court's fact-finding function. (Tr. 461).

There is ample evidence in the record for the court to make its own findings of fact on whether Mr. Mangieri suffered retaliation for constitutionally protected speech. (Defendant's Proposed Findings of Fact and Conclusions of Law, pp. 1-30)

Second, the I.R.S. findings do not represent final conclusions, even within the administrative process. The Special Counsel of the Merit Systems Protection board ordered the I.R.S. report pursuant to 5 U.S.C. §1206 (b)(3) after finding a substantial likelihood that Mr. Mangieri's charges evidenced O.I.G. obstruction of his investigation into sexual coercion; and personal harassment of himself. Under 4 U.S.C. § 1206 (b)(6) the Special Counsel also must evaluate the completed report to determine if it is comprehensive and if the findings are reasonable. The Special Counsel has not yet evaluated the I.R.S. report.

Third, I.R.S. findings which did not sup[port Mr. Mangieri's whistleblowing charges decisively support his allegation of selective prosecution. For example, the I.R.S. did not consider the unconstitutionality of the press gag order D.O.L. O.I.G. used to justify a June 1979 proposed suspension of Mr. Mangieri. As part of the "investigation" into this adverse action, O.I.G. obtained the Alaska packet of Mr. Mangieri's finances.

Similarly, the I.R.S. report concludes that then Deputy Inspector General and later Acting Inspector General Ronald Goldstock initiated personal involvement into the O.I.G. actions against Mr. Mangieri because Mr. Mangieri investigated Mr. Goldstock's travel vouchers. (I.R.S., p. 36). In direct response to Mr. Mangieri's travel voucher investigation, his O.I.G. supervisor David Coffman searched Mr. Mangieri's office and seized all of his personal papers. (Defendant's Proposed Findings of Fact and Conclusions of Law, pp. 15-17).

The I.R.S. report does not present any of the seized documents, which included a detailed letter to the editor of the *Washington Post,* with attachments. In that letter, Mr. Mangieri only briefly mentioned his investigation into sexual coercion. Instead, he concentrated on O.I.G. political obstruction of a proposed audit survey of Youth Pride, Inc. as well as travel abuses and misuse of government-aid consultants for personal business by Mr. Goldstock. (Tr. 111, 112-15; Defendant's Exhibit 34). Mr. Coffman and Mr. Statham wanted to investigate Mr. Mangieri immediately for this disclosure to the press, but Mr. Goldstock decided a "fifteen day special" O.P.M. investigation he had personally arranged would serve the same purpose. (Defendant's Proposed Findings of Fact and Conclusions of Law, pp. 17-18).

The letter to the editor unquestionably rep[resented speech protected by the First Amendment. The I.R.S. failed to include the letter in the investigative report, however. As a result, the evidence was not considered as a contributing factor to O.I.G.'s investigations and prosecutive referral.

Fourth, the I.R.S. conclusions do not even address the immediate case of Mr. Anderson's criminal investigation. Mr. Mangieri had referred the evidence of travel and consultant abuses to the Federal Bureau of Investigation (F.B.I.). On April 30, 1980, the F.B.I. exonerated Mr. Goldstock for, *inter alia,* personal use of *one* government-paid consultant. (The April 30. F.B.I. report is attached as Exhibit 1). Mr. Mangieri knew, however, that two consultants had been involved in the questionable project, suggesting that Mr. Goldstock may have provided false information to the F.B.I. He shared this discovery with a *Washington Post* reporter, who during may 1980 asked O.I.G. management about the discrepancy. Id., p.20).

Mr. Goldstock was aware of this new whistleblowing activity since he testified to that effect at Mr. Mangieri's grievance hearing in July 1980. (The testimony is attached as Exhibit 2.) The disclosure to the *Post* was the last straw. Almost immediately Mr. Goldstock began to prepare Mr. Anderson for an internal affairs investigation which ws officially opened in early June. This final whistleblowing disclosure also represented protected speech under the First Amendment, and O.I.G. counterattacked with a retaliatory criminal investigation of Mr. Mangieri. The I.R.S. report completely ignores the issue, however, which is critical to Mr. Mangieri's allegations of selective prosecution.

Finally, if the court is going to defer to outside findings the I.R.S. conclusions are not the only findings of fact on O.I.G. retaliation against Mr. Mangieri. After an extensive grievance hearing, on December 1, 1980 Administrative Law Judge Everette E. Thomas held that O.I.G. illegally removed Mr. Mangieri's investigative credentials in retaliation for his investigation of Mr. Goldstock. (the relevant decisions are enclosed as Exhibit 3.) Since the grievance hearing covered both Mr. Coffman's seizure of the letter to the *Washington Post,* the conclusions of the Administrative Law Judge are more accurate than the I.R.S. report to consider O.I.G. reprisals against these key instances of constitutionally protected speech.*

In *United States v. Ness,* 652 F .2d 890 (9th Cir. 1981), the court explained the standard for a successful defense of selective prosecution: "[A] defendant must show evidence of impermissible motive at some crucial stage in the procedures leading to the initiation of the prosecution." "Crucial" stages leading to prosecution comprise agency investigations in addition to the ultimate decision by the Department of Justice to prosecute. *United States v. Erne,* 576 F .2d 212, 216 (9th Cir. 1978); *United States v. Ojala,* 544 F .2d 940, 943 (8th Cir. 1976).

In this case, the prosecution has relied entirely on the I.R.S. report to justify all relevant O.I.G. actions against Mr. Mangieri. Since the I.R.S. report directly or indirectly ignored the two most crucial instances of retaliation for protected speech, Mr. Mangieri's defense remains unrefuted.

---

*Significantly, the same Department of Labor official who selected Mr. Thomas as the Presiding Official later refused to honor Mr. Thomas'l decision on grounds that Mr. Thomas had been selected improperly. (The relevant brief is enclosed as Exhibit 4.)

II. MOTIVES OF THE DEPARTMENT OF JUSTICE OF THE GRAND JURY INVESTIGATION

The court accepted Assistant United States Attorney Richard Beizer's claim that he did not intend to use the U.S. Attorney's Office to retaliate against Mr. Mangieri. In drawing that conclusion, the court apparently accepted the government characterization that Mr. Beizer did not brand Mr. Mangieri as a "phony whistle-blower." (Government's Proposed Findings of Fact and Conclusions of Law, p. 11). The passage cited by the prosecution did not touch upon *Mr. Beizer's* conclusions, however. Rather, the prosecution referred to testimony where Mr. Beizer attempted to interpret *Mr. Goldstock's* opinion of Mr. Mangieri. (Tr. 456).

Mr. Beizer testified that in *his own* mind he concluded that Mr. Mangieri had a "standard technique" of alleging whistleblower retaliation in response to prosecution or attempts to collect bad debts. Mr. Beizer testified that "at that point" he decided to pursue the criminal case against Mr. Mangieri. (Tr. 448). This testimony is consistent with Mr. Beizer's observations in an affidavit to the I.R.S.;

Thus, it was apparent to me that Mangieri was a man who went around the country piling up bad debts and that he sought to evade financial responsibility by claiming actions against him were the product of his investigations into corruption. I felt Mangieri would commit his crimes until someone attempted to stop him, and then in response, he would allege 'obstruction' or 'cover-up' of a major investigation he was conducted and claim the prosecution of him was retribution ... Based on all of the above, I decided to open a Grand Jury investigation into Mangieri's activities.

(Defendant's Exhibit 3). The distinction is semantic at best between this conclusion and the characterization of Mr. Mangieri as a "phony whistleblower."

Mr. Beizer made no attempt to verify the accuracy of any of Mr. Mangieri's whistleblowing charges. He was wrong empirically that Mr. Mangieri had rationalized previous debt collections and prosecutions as whistleblowing retaliation. In fact, Mr. Mangieri had never faced criminal prosecution before Mr. Beizer opened the Grand Jury investigation. O.I.G. had not even initiated the O.P.M. investigation when Mr. Mangieri alleged a cover-up of the sexual coercion probe. Mr. Mangieri did not content that Mr. Beizer was vindictive. Rather, for whatever reason the U.S. Attorney's Office became an unintentional pawn of the O.I.G. retaliation. As a result, the prosecution must be dismissed. *United States v. Bourque,* 541 F .2d 290, 293 (1st Cir. 1976); *United States v. Steele,* 461 F .2d 1148, 1152 (9th Cir. 1972).

CONCLUSION

In *United States v. Steele, supra,* the court succinctly stated the philosophy behind the selective prosecution defense:

An enforcement procedure that focuses upon the vocal offender is inherently suspect since it is vulnerable to the charge that those chosen for prosecution are being punished for their expression of ideas, a constitutionally protected right. That is precisely the setting for the Government's extra-ordinary campaign against Mr. Mangieri. D.O.L. O.I.G. directly or indirectly investigated Mr. Mangieri on three occasions from June 1979-August 1980. The investigations covered literally hundreds of witnesses and nearly all of Mr. Mangieri's acquaintances back to the early 1950's.

In each instance, the investigations were undertaken as reprisals or counterattacks against constitutionally protected conduct. It is a tribute to Mr. Mangieri's integrity that it took such a massive effort to uncover wrongdoing. This prosecution represents a direct attack on the First Amendment. This Court dismissed Mr. Mangieri's selective prosecution claim by erroneously accepting and attempting to apply the I.R.S. report to issues raised at trial but not considered in the I.R.S. investigation. Further, the court permitted the government to grossly distort the Assistant U.S. Attorney's position after the significance of his testimony became clear. For these reasons, the Court should reconsider the February 3 order and grant Mr. Mangieri's motion to dismiss.

Respectfully submitted,

John W. Karr
625 Washington Building
Washington, D.C. 20005
202/737-3544
Dated: February 10, 1982

... Appendix G ...

**UNITED STATES DISTRICT COURT
FOR THE DISTRICT OF COLUMBIA**

UNITED STATES OF AMERICA
                                    v.   Criminal No. 81-19
NICHOLAS J. MANGIERI

                                    Defendant

MOTION FOR A NEW TRIAL

Defendant Nicholas Mangieri, pursuant to Rule 33, Fed. R. Crim. P., and though undersigned counsel, moves this court for a new trial based on newly discovered evidence which indicates the chief prosecution witness, Department of Labor investigator Harold Anderson, perjured himself at trial and during the post-trial hearing on selective prosecution.

The newly discovered evidence is contained in an affidavit of Shirley Caillouette, Mr. Mangieri's ex-wife, and an interview with ms. Elizabeth Kuchinski, vice-president of the Bank of California, Sacramento, California.

Evidence gathered by defense counsel indicates that Mr. Anderson perjured himself in sworn testimony at trial, at the hearing on selective prosecution, and in his sworn affidavit to the IRS, during its investigation into Mr. Mangieri's charges that his protected whistleblowing disclosures revealed mismanagement and abuse by high officials of the Inspector General's Office of the Department of Labor.

In support of his motion, Mr. Mangieri submits an affidavit of Shirley Caillouette, an affidavit of counsel indicating the substance of an affidavit of Elizabeth Kuchinski which will follow, and 44 investigative interviews conducted by Mr. Anderson, many of which contradict Mr. Anderson's sworn testimony.

This newly discovered evidence indicates not only perjury by the prosecution's chief witness but also that Mr. Anderson during his investigation employed largely illegal methods of gathering evidence. Mr. Anderson's use of such methods violated the Right to Financial Privacy Act, the Fair Credit Reporting Act, and the Privacy Act, and requires this court to suppress all evidence gathered in violation of these federal statutes.

Only by granting Mr. Mangieri a new trial can this court uphold Mr. Mangieri's due process right to a fair trial, free of tainted evidence and knowing or negligent government misconduct.

Respectfully submitted,

Lynne Bernabei
1901 Q Street, NW
Washington, D.C. 20009
(202) 234-9382
Attorney for Defendant

DATED: February 19, 1982

... Index ...

Order Form

POSTAL ORDERS:
Integrity Publishing, Inc.
Nick Mangieri,
P.O. Box 369, Lightfoot, VA 93090

FAX ORDERS:
(757) 565-0827

PAYMENT:
by check or money order

AMOUNT:
Book. $19.50

SHIPPING:

Book rate: $2.00 for the first book and
$1.00 for each additional book. (surface mail) . . . ._____
Priority Mail: $3.00 per book . . . . ._____

SALES TAX:

Add 4.5% for books shipped to Virginia addresses . ._____

Total   _____